HEROES AND VILLIANS

ALSO BY DAVID HAJDU

Lush Life: A Biography of Billy Strayhorn

*Positively 4th Street: The Lives and Times of Joan Baez,
Bob Dylan, Mimi Baez Fariña and Richard Fariña*

*The Ten-Cent Plague: The Great Comic-Book Scare and
How It Changed America*

HEROES AND VILLAINS

Essays on Music, Movies, Comics, and Culture

DAVID HAJDU

DA CAPO PRESS
A Member of the
Perseus Books Group

First Da Capo Press edition 2009
Published by Da Capo Press
A Member of the Perseus Books Group
http://www.dacapopress.com

Da Capo Press books are available at special discounts for bulk purchases in the U.S. by corporations, institutions, and other organizations. For more information, please contact the Special Markets Department at the Perseus Books Group, 11 Cambridge Center, Cambridge, MA 02142, or call (800) 255-1514 or (617) 252-5298, or e-mail special.markets@perseusbooks.com.

Editorial production by The Book Factory.
Design and composition in Caslon by Cynthia Young.

Library of Congress Cataloging-in-Publication Data

Hajdu, David.
   Heroes and villains : essays on music, movies, comics, and culture /
   David Hajdu. — 1st ed.
      p. cm.
   Includes index.
   ISBN 978-0-306-81833-2
   1. Music—History and criticism.   2. Musicians.   I. Title.
ML60.H178 2009
781.64—dc22

                                          2009026583

1 2 3 4 5 6 7 8 9 10

To Leon

Contents

Foreword

by David Yaffe

Miles Davis, who was as discriminating in his praise as he was in his playing, provided a terse comment for the cover of the album *Everybody Digs Bill Evans*, which was released by Riverside Records in 1958. "I've sure learned a lot from Bill Evans," he wrote. "He plays the piano the way it should be played." Dare I conjure up Davis's spirit to apply a comparable hymn of praise to the essays included in this volume? David Hajdu plays culture writing the way it should be played.

This is not to say that there is only one way to write great essays on culture—just as Miles Davis would surely have said that Bill Evans hardly represented the only way the piano should be played. But the essays in this book do contain something definitive, distinctive, and very rare about how, exactly, one should write about the arts. This book offers a broad range: a reconsideration of standards from Tin Pan Alley to hip hop; a revisionist look at the land where blues began, thrived, and mutated; aging pop icons; technology; weirdos; and more. Hajdu approaches these topics from the standpoint of a provocateur, but he is also supplicant to music, or the muse in general. His novelist's gaze can be merciless in the groves of music—think Balzac in a jazz club—but his appreciation for beauty can be boundless. He is, needless to say, a tough room, but tough in the sense of tough love.

I first came across the writing of David Hajdu when I was an undergraduate and happened upon *Lush Life*, his biography of Duke Ellington's then-under-appreciated collaborator Billy Strayhorn. I knew every chord and every word of the title song of Hajdu's book up and down. (My attempt to imitate Johnny Hartman's version was a sure-fire room clearer.) But I had never dared think about how Strayhorn, as a nineteen-year-old in Pittsburgh, 1937, could write, in the opening line of "Lush Life," "I used to visit all the very gay places" and mean it with all its contemporary ramifications. But of course! Cary Grant did the same thing that year in *Bringing Up Baby!* Why didn't I think of that? But then Hajdu showed me how, in prose that was so entertaining, it didn't even feel like the academic scholarship I was also taking in. Yet it was just as startling, bold, and complex as any arguments I had seen from the scholars I was reading, even if it felt more like reading a novel.

The essays in this collection—on subjects as diverse as Mos Def, Paul McCartney, Billy Eckstine, Starbucks, Joni Mitchell, Bobby Darin, and Elmer Fudd—are, in the tradition of Edmund Wilson's *Classics and Commercials,* all instances of cultural criticism. That is to say, they do the kind of work that academics do, they just do it implicitly, aphoristically, and for a broad intelligent audience. Before Hajdu came along, there was little writing on pop music and jazz in the pages of *The New Republic* (at least since the Otis Furgeson years) and *The New York Review of Books,* and as I was reading those publications in the midst of college procrastination (important things do happen in these moments), it didn't even occur to me that there was a place in these venues for topics that had consumed my misspent youth. The reason, perhaps, that such publications spent little time on these topics was not because they were of no cultural relevance, but because so much of the writing on pop and jazz is too figural and self-referential. How, in short, does writing on pop and jazz—not to mention comics and gadgets—fit into the literary world? There's not necessarily a plot in the work of the work of the creative figures in this book—at least not the musical ones—but there is a story about them.

The stories are vast in this book, and the stories about the stories are even vaster. In his definitive profile of Wynton Marsalis, he shows how one stolen moment at the Village Vanguard could demonstrate both his brilliance and his moment of crisis, which is also, in turn, jazz's moment in crisis. In the scene, Marsalis is in the middle of playing a glorious solo on the standard ballad "I Don't Stand a Ghost of a Chance With You," when an interruption from a cell phone threatens to ruin the magic:

> The cell phone offender scooted into the hall as the chatter in the room grew louder. Still frozen at the microphone, Marsalis replayed the silly cell-phone melody note for note. Then he repeated it, and began improvising variations on the tune. The audience slowly came back to him. In a few minutes he resolved the improvisation, which had changed keys once or twice and throttled down to a ballad tempo, and ended up exactly where he had left off: "with . . . you . . ." The ovation was tremendous.

This is jazz writing at its finest. We are viscerally there, nursing our drink minimum in Manhattan's most illustrious cellar, taking in a moment of spontaneity and virtuosity. (When I taught the essay in a graduate seminar, a student said, "I wish I could have been there," and I explained that such moments occur frequently in New York jazz clubs but are seldom reported.) Here we see a fall and a rise, but with a question that's harder to resolve than an impeccably crafted solo. Marsalis won the moment, but there will be more cell phones, fewer record labels, and smaller audiences for the next young lions. Or not—Hajdu will be ready at the next cultural moment, whatever it is.

It is fitting that Hajdu would be so dead on when reporting in depth on Marsalis's—and jazz's—midlife crisis. Many of these pieces deal with subjects that began as youthful obsessions that matured into considered, elegant thought. Maturation is not usually appreciated by pop audiences, even by those who are getting on in years themselves. But Hajdu is no nostalgist. He can wear the hat of the professional fan, or he can be the intrepid anthropologist. The culture of music can be seductive up close, but Hajdu tends to cast a colder eye, or at least let the temperature drop a little. He is attuned to the irony about what happens when rock and roll stars stay in one place or veer into ambitious directions. On Elvis Costello, he is gentle; on Joni Mitchell, a little tougher; and on Sting, he is absolutely devastating. Hajdu begins the Sting essay with a portrait of the survivors of the first generation of rock and roll. Before he even contemplates the mixture of pretension and shamelessness that makes Sting's career so frustrating and ripe for critical ribbing, he pulls back the lens on what happens when rockers never evolve:

> Rock and rollers, as they age, sometimes find themselves outgrowing a music they cannot outlive. Rock, a style invented for teenagers—or more precisely, one adapted from an older style made originally for adults, the blues—endures as a bluntly, rudely cogent expression of adolescent anxiety, rage, and sexual fantasy. *Long live rock and roll! The beat of the drums, loud and bold!* Over the decades since Berry wrote that pithy, hard-driving couplet, Berry has sustained a career into old age by serving as a nostalgist.

This paragraph continues to deliver splendors, which you must turn the pages to attain. But even in this beginning of a beginning, it is already apparent that what will follow will be thorough and brimming with a finely tuned irony. The joke is that septuagenarian icons like Little Richard, Jerry Lee Lewis, and Berry are still singing songs about adolescence as very old men performing, usually, for rather old consumers, ignoring what could be deeper art about the indignities of age, if only they could summon their inner *King Lears*. But then the payoff is coming: Sting, coming upon fifty, and an uncommonly skilled musician among his pop peers, looks further back—all the way to the seventeenth-century lutenist John Dowland, but it is ridiculous, a shameless audition for knighthood. Keeping up the teenage anthems in one's seventies is poignant; egotistical rock stars with delusions of grandeur can make royal asses out of themselves, and Hajdu calls them like he sees them in prose that is as merciless as it is meticulously crafted.

If there is a grand theme that unifies all the essays in this book, perhaps it is the collision between youthful exuberance and maturity. I should know. When I was ten years old, while other kids were playing *Dungeons & Dragons* or reading *Lord of the Rings*, I was supplementing a subscription to *Rolling Stone* with as many dusty old issues as I was allowed to bring home. I thought at the time that there would be nothing finer than to write for the magazine, interview rock stars, get free records, and find an ink-stained way into the rock and roll fantasy. Then I learned about jazz, and realized most of the world wasn't paying attention anymore. By the time I was a college sophomore, when I was listening to an increasing diet of classical music, I thought it was time to put away childish things. I was filling my head with great books, and found myself at a crossroads one day at the campus post office. One postcard came from *Rolling Stone,* and said something like, "Hey, dude. Roll up your buds and renew your subscription." Another came from *The New Republic,* and began, "Dear Intelligent American." *I want to be addressed as an intelligent American!* I thought, and flipped my subscriptions. Almost immediately after, I became a critic, and I found myself, like so many others that came before me, negotiating high and low, and learning through experience that only certain publications truly allowed one to be smart in public. Eventually, as David Hajdu became music critic for *The New Republic,* I realized: He's a little ahead of the rest of us. It turned out that it was possible to draw upon subjects of my youthful ardor while also being an Intelligent American—or intelligent human, for that matter. The proof is right here. The essays in this book are for intelligent readers everywhere, but they also swing, rock, and draw funny pictures. All of it is played the way it should be played.

David Yaffe is the author of *Fascinating Rhythm: Reading Jazz in American Writing* (Princeton, 2006). He is at work on *The Many Roads of Bob Dylan* (Yale, forthcoming) and *Reckless Daughter: A Portrait of Joni Mitchell* (FSG, forthcoming).

PART I

B's World

Billy Eckstine
The Man Who Was Too Hot

On the morning of August 27, 1986, five federal agents broke into a pastel-green bungalow on the grounds of the Las Vegas Country Club and hunted the premises, hoping to find a quarter of a million dollars worth of removable contents. The U.S. Treasury Department had ordered a raid to settle a tax debt that the resident, William Clarence Eckstine, had failed to satisfy, despite more than a dozen liens on his property over the preceding eight years. When the agents left, they had 110 items for the government to sell at public auction—nearly all of them artifacts of Eckstine's sensational, ground-breaking, and ultimately tragic life as a pop singer.

The IRS agents took three of the gold records awarded to Eckstine three decades earlier, when he was the most popular male vocalist in the country, more successful than Frank Sinatra or Bing Crosby, with twelve top-ten hits on the charts between 1949 and 1952. (One of those records happened to be titled *Everything I Have Is Yours*.) The agents took dozens of musical instruments, reminders of Eckstine's days as the leader of a legendary jazz orchestra—a radical young group that virtually invented a new style called bebop, which changed the course of American music. The Billy Eckstine Orchestra had a roster never matched in the history of jazz, with Miles Davis, Dizzy Gillespie, Charlie Parker, Dexter Gordon, Fats Navarro, Sonny Stitt, Kenny Dorham, Gene Ammons, Art Blakey, Frank Wess, and a second singer, Sarah Vaughan.

What else filled the crates the IRS labeled as "memorabilia"? There might have been a movie poster or a lobby card from Billy Eckstine's days in Hollywood, where he became the first performer ever signed—for an unprecedented million dollars, when that represented incomprehensible wealth—to make both films and records for a major studio, MGM. There might have been a few samples of the fashions he designed and marketed, setting an original standard for hipster style that sparked crazes for the "Mr. B collar" and the "Mr. B wraparound coat." If Eckstine kept his correspondence, letters alone could have filled a van; his fan clubs once had some 100,000 members organized in groups whose names said much about their numbers' enthusiasm, such as Girls Who Give In When Billy Gives Out and The Vibrato's Vibrators. At one time, a thousand Eckstine fans mailed requests for photographs every week.

Meanwhile, less tangible effects of Billy Eckstine's life and work were everywhere in 1986. Nearly half a century after Eckstine started in music, his influence on American music and American pop culture was pervasive, and it remains so two decades later. The once jarring, *outré* style of music he pioneered, bebop, grew on others with time and became jazz's dominant style; ever since, it has been the common language of jazz. When Miles Davis wrote his autobiography, he began with the moment that had inspired him most: seeing the Billy Eckstine Orchestra perform. He described hearing the Eckstine band as "the greatest feeling I ever had in my life—with my clothes on." He went on, "Man, that shit was so terrible it was scary. I mean, Dizzy Gillespie, Charlie 'Yardbird' Parker, Buddy Anderson, Gene Ammons, Lucky Thompson, and Art Blakey all together in one band, and not to mention B: Billy Eckstine himself. It was a motherfucker. Man, that shit was all up in my body." If Miles Davis represented the birth of the cool, Billy Eckstine was its conception.

As a singer, moreover, Eckstine simply redefined what it meant to be black and a celebrity in America. Gorgeous and smart, fiercely gifted, and defiant in his projection of black masculinity in the era of segregation, Eckstine strode coolly across the old line dividing the worlds of white and black singers. On one side, the likes of Rudy Vallee, Bing Crosby, and Frank Sinatra had become pop idols and movie stars as surrogate lovers, crooning love songs to young women; on the other, African Americans such as Louis Armstrong and Fats Waller sang "cute" as funny, sexless novelty figures, unthreatening to womanhood of any color. Eckstine, physically magnificent as he sang in his rich, mellow baritone voice, gushed sex appeal. He introduced an overtly carnal, black masculinity to American popular culture.

"He was just a knockout," says Tony Bennett. "He was just so handsome, everybody was envious of him."

"The interesting thing and the important thing about Eckstine was that he was such an influence beyond music," said Dan Morgenstern, director of the Institute for Jazz Studies at Rutgers University. "He was about *style*."

"He stood out like a sore thumb, because there weren't a lot of masculine-type singers, and the girls loved him," says Dr. Billy Taylor, the pianist and broadcaster. "Boy, he'd just knock 'em on their knees."

Billy Eckstine defied the rules, changed them, and became a new kind of role model for generations of black singers, from Sam Cooke and Marvin Gaye to Diddy and Kanye West, and actors, from Harry Belafonte and Sidney Poitier to Will Smith and Jamie Foxx. For them and their peers, expressing a savvy, daring, masculine black intelligence in music or film—or venturing into both fields while, say, exploiting one's sense of style by designing a fashion line—is to play the game by the rules Billy Eckstine laid down. The paradigm Eckstine established, B's world, is the world we live in.

"I packed up and left Jamaica when I saw what Billy Eckstine made possible," Harry Belafonte told me. "He opened the door for me and a thousand others who came after us."

Why, then, isn't Eckstine better known today? How could his star have fallen that far from such heights? What forces—within him or in the world he challenged—provided Eckstine with so much, only to reclaim it in the end?

*　*　*

An internal tension underlay Billy Eckstine's public image—one that had to do with class as well as race, at least in the beginning. Like two of the great white heart-throbs of twentieth-century film, Humphrey Bogart and Cary Grant, Eckstine embodied two realms of social strata at once. Bogart, a Yalie blueblood (related distantly to the English crown family), made his name playing New York toughs; Grant, a Cockney waif who grew up in Dickensian poverty, created a persona synonymous with aristocratic *savoir faire*. Eckstine was much like both of them. Raised in relative comfort in a predominantly white, middle-class district of Pittsburgh called Highland Park, Billy (whose father was a chauffeur) was drawn to the street, where he cultivated a bad-boy reputation and, initially, rejected the arts as effete. "I thought guys in music were a little on the lavender side," Eckstine later recalled to an interviewer.

"He was like the black sheep," remembered Linton Garner, the Pittsburgh-born trumpeter and pianist (and older brother of jazz composer and pianist Erroll Garner), who was close to Eckstine in their youth. "He wanted to be his own man. We used to hang out down around what we called the Hill, and he was with the pot smokers. The girls liked him, and girls down in the Hill district were pretty fast girls." By adulthood, when Eckstine started emceeing and singing in Pittsburgh nightclubs, he had learned to contain his unsavory side, upending racist presumptions by projecting an almost parodic air of sophistication.

Pittsburgh was an efficient incubator of jazz talent. According to the late drummer Kenny Clarke, the cooperative, multicultural nature of jazz has something in common with work life in the Pittsburgh steel mills. As he explained to Dr. Nathan Davis, the musician and jazz historian, the "mentality of Pittsburghers" is ideally suited to jazz: "Even though there was racial discrimination, they got along," Davis said, "because they all had to go down in the steel mills, and down there, everybody watched everybody's back, because if you were an asshole, you might end up in the fire." Pittsburgh contributed a disproportionate share of important musicians to jazz during the early decades of the last century: among them, Art Blakey, Ray Brown, Buddy De Franco, Roy Eldridge, Earl Hines, Lena Horne, Amad Jamal, Billy Strayhorn, and Mary Lou Williams, in addition to Eckstine, Clark, and the Garner brothers.

While still a youngster in Pittsburgh, Eckstine found himself fronting his first big band, hired by the musical director primarily for his athletic good looks. Eckstine was always a stunning man: tall and olive-skinned, with crystalline hazel eyes and a jaunty, pencil-thin mustache. His appearance served as a social lubricant for most of his life, easing his way personally and professionally—perhaps too well; according to the pianist with whom Eckstine would work most closely, Bobby Tucker, his good looks imparted in him a sense of privilege that veered into one of entitlement. As Linton Garner, who was playing trumpet in the band, recalled, "It was just because he had the personality. It wasn't because of his musical ability. Billy had the looks and everything, and he just sort of waved a stick, and it looked good. He had all the moves." The job proved to be an enlightening apprenticeship: The group specialized in recreations of Duke Ellington music, advanced orchestral jazz that Eckstine needed to learn well enough to convince the audience that his presence as conductor wasn't entirely ornamental.

Eckstine was also starting to develop an original vocal style. While no recordings of his work at this stage exist, Eckstine, Garner said, was beginning to sound as he would for the rest of his life—that is, like no one else. "Maybe the most important thing was that I never modeled myself on other singers," Eckstine once told a columnist. "I was inspired by instrumentalists, by real musicians. There wasn't any singer I tried to pattern myself after."

From early on, Billy Eckstine's voice was instantly recognizable and irresistible to imitators, like Louis Armstrong's: a primary sound. It was a deep, rich, strong baritone, vigorous and sure, yet warmly sensuous. Bing Crosby, the most popular singer of Eckstine's day (and, as such, an inevitable influence on anyone singing then, if only as a point of departure) had a style that was elementally romantic and swinging, like Eckstine's, but not so muscular. Paul Robeson sang with much of Eckstine's force, but his approach was more cerebral, his passions tempered. Eckstine communicated carnal authority and a sensitivity to the delicacies of its application; he put whatever he learned on "the Hill" in Pittsburgh to creative use.

If Eckstine sounded like any instrumentalist, he was Ben Webster, the tenor saxophonist renowned in jazz circles for his dark, earthy tone, his lyrical melodic sense, and his signet feature: a sumptuous and dramatic vibrato. Eckstine's vibrato was so wide and so emphatic that it verged on excess—surely, part of its appeal. Hearing him turn one note into a chain of long, voluptuous warbles, you wonder: How far from the realm of the ordinary will that fellow go? He seemed unfettered by conventions, a man without limits—beneath his elegant veneer, perhaps a bad boy, too.

Pittsburgher Earl "Fatha" Hines was a thirty-four-year-old jazz veteran, esteemed for his piano work on Louis Armstrong's historic "Hot Five" sessions from the 1920s, when he asked Eckstine, then twenty-five, to sing in his big band. This was in 1939, the swing era, though some adventurous young musicians were beginning to experiment with an edgy, demanding musical style called rebop or modern jazz, eventually named bebop or simply bop. Eckstine had an ear for it—and an eye for the aura of sophisticated cool that association with the music conferred. For all of Hines's brilliance and importance as an innovator a decade earlier, his big band was relatively conventional, until Eckstine and his allies persuaded the pianist to hire a couple of players in the new school, the alto saxophonist Charlie Parker and the trumpeter Dizzy Gillespie. The orchestra steadily expanded its ranks of like-minded spirits until it was composed largely of bop-oriented musicians, including an unknown singer (doing double duty as a second pianist) named Sarah Vaughan, whom Eckstine brought in and mentored. Although most of the arrangements the group performed on the bandstand were fairly traditional, its members used their time on the bus and backstage jamming, conspirators plotting the coming musical revolution.

Eckstine was the chief agitator—de facto band contractor, headlining singer, and also instrumentalist now. Determined to become a "real musician," he decided to take up the trumpet under the tutelage of his bandmates, only to confront the tyranny of their example. "Dizzy Gillespie does so well playing that instrument that in order to beat him you have to be able to make a hot dog come out of the end of your horn," Eckstine explained in an interview. "So I've taken up the valve trombone, which is easier to play and adds a little color to the band." And which no one else was playing in Hines's troupe.

Lee Young, the jazz drummer and record producer (and younger brother of the late tenor saxophonist Lester Young), was playing in the Lionel Hampton big band while Eckstine was with Hines, and they met in a hotel in Oakland under Asian ownership, one of the nicer places in the area hospitable to African Americans. Young was resting in his room after the night's gig when he heard a ruckus in the hall—it was Eckstine, reveling. "Billy had gotten a little high that night," Young recalled, "and he came out in the hall and started shooting [a pistol] at the roof of the hotel. I just thought that was so funny. That was the first time we met. Billy's shooting, and this little Chinese guy is running around, calling for the police."

Encouraged by Gillespie, Eckstine left Hines in the spring of 1944 to start a big band of his own, and he took with him the bebop heart of his boss's organization: Gillespie, Parker, Vaughan, arrangers Budd Johnson and Gerry Valentine, saxophonist Wardell Gray, trumpeters Freddie Webster and Shorty McConnell, bassist Oscar Pettiford, and drummer Shadow Wilson. Jazz has never had a bloodier uprising. Earl Hines refilled the chairs of his big band and carried on in proficient inconsequence, while Billy Eckstine assumed leadership of the first orchestra devoted to a new type of jazz.

The Billy Eckstine Orchestra was a startling, fearless, intelligent, sexy group—the Clash or NWA of its time. To a generation of jazz enthusiasts and musicians accustomed to the infectious dance beats and buoyant riff tunes of the swing bands, the angular rhythms and vertiginous instrumental solos of Gillespie, Parker, Dexter Gordon, and others under Eckstine were a musical catharsis. "I never heard nobody play that," Art Blakey told an interviewer. "The only big band I ever liked was Billy Eckstine, 'cause everybody in that band could play. Now, that is a jazz orchestra! I've heard a lot of big bands, and they sound good, perfect, but . . . too perfect. Jazz is not clinical. Jazz is born by somebody goofin'. So if you feel that band hasn't got that looseness, they're not creating. In that band, it was a pleasure; it was like working in a small combo."

There is some film footage of the group, shot in 1946 for the Negro-circuit movie short *Rhythm in a Riff.* Eckstine looks virilely debonair, swaying on the bandstand so languidly that he's almost out of time, while the orchestra rages behind him. The high musical standard drops only when Eckstine solos on the valve trombone, teetering off pitch. More than fifty years after the footage was shot, the music sounds utterly contemporary, like the jazz being played in a good club tonight.

That is to say, it was unfamiliar and challenging to the public and the critics of its own time. Dance audiences would stand still on the floor, confounded. "We tried to educate people," the late Sarah Vaughan told an author. "We used to play dances, and there were just a very few who understood who would be in a corner . . . while the rest just stood staring at us." The idea of sitting down and listening to a jazz orchestra as one would to a symphonic one was not unprecedented, but it was still a novelty and largely reserved for special events in formal settings legitimized by white society, such as Ellington's annual concert at Carnegie Hall.

Eckstine found the cultural terrain too rocky for trailblazing, as he told various interviewers over the years: "We were doing new things. People were used to dancing, and they couldn't dance to it. They just stared at us—some with distaste. . . .We knew we had a great band. But it was a little too new for people. . . . It was . . . new usages of chords in harmonic structures that had never been done before. And for that, we would get a lot of heat from different critics because they didn't know what the hell we were doing. But the younger people loved us and the musicians were just agog with that band. . . . Most of the jazz critics roasted us. They said the band was out of tune because we were playing flatted fifths and flatted ninths, and it was strange to their ears."

A *Variety* critic wrote in 1946:

> Billy Eckstine, slim fellow from Harlem, has a band that jumps in the most aggravating way. The rhythms are over-stylized and jerky and the melodic instruments are very reluctant to play a tune that is recognizable. The band stays away from riffs but what it uses is no better.

Eckstine struggled to keep the band together and often lost to the occupational hazards of alcohol and drugs. "Billy was a musician's bandleader," recalls Martin "Van" Kelly, Jr., who played saxophone in Eckstine's orchestra. "A lot of bandleaders back then were not that way. Other bandleaders would not have tolerated what he tolerated. In other words, he believed in giving guys a break. Even after I joined the band, there were nights when there'd be no one in the reed section except me and Gene Ammons. Many of the musicians he had in the band, he never knew whether they were going to show up, and sometimes when they did show up, they weren't in a position to play adequately. There were so many outstanding names in the band, but, you see, these guys weren't dependable. Half the time, they were high."

As a bandleader, Eckstine soon realized that his most bankable asset was his star singer, Billy Eckstine. He was the group's primary draw, especially among the audience most important to nightclubs and record companies: young women. "When he came out," Kelly remembers, "the girls were screaming and everything." Although the couple of dozen recordings the orchestra made were too unorthodox to be best-sellers, the New York disk jockey Symphony Sid made Eckstine's ascension official by granting him a nickname—Mr. B. Friends would call him simply B.

"His persona was one of utter confidence and lots of charm," explained the singer and pianist Bobby Short, who saw the Eckstine Orchestra on several occasions. "Don't forget, he was also a fashion figure. Billy was given to wearing zoot suits and large hats. He was a package."

Linton Garner said emphatically, "Don't take this lightly, and don't think that I'm dreaming when I say *Billy Eckstine was the man.* His name became so big that people told him, 'Billy, you don't need the band.' He loved the band. But, you know, the money people control everything, and they were looking at the figures, and they said, 'We'd get the same results from Billy's popularity without the expense of a big band.'"

The main money person in Eckstine's organization was his manager, Milt Ebbins (brother of Eckstine's road manager Bernie Ebbins), and Eckstine held him in such esteem that he called Ebbins "my right tonsil." Ebbins saw the band as an encumbrance to Eckstine's larger potential as a solo star in the mode of Crosby and Sinatra, and the left tonsil assented.

"It was a fantastic band, but it was not a commercial band," Ebbins says matter of factly, "It was strictly a cult band, and we found it very difficult to book. At that time, everybody was putting bop down, stepping all over it. I said, 'Billy, drop it. Let's try a single. Let's try a single and see if we can do it.'"

How did Eckstine feel about disbanding the group he took such pride in leading? "Billy was no fool," says Ebbins. "He understood immediately where we were going."

The Billy Eckstine Orchestra played one of its last engagements at Boston's Circle Lounge, a spacious nightclub with a runway projecting about fifteen feet from the stage into the dining area. Eckstine strolled out during a number, as Linton Garner watched from the piano. "There was a couple of white girls with their boyfriends," Garner recalled, "and this one girl kept saying, 'Sing it, Chocolate, sing it!' And when the number was over, Billy went over to the table, and told the guys, 'You should teach these girls some manners.' And this one guy got up and took a swing at B, and B flattened him. Oh, he could fight, and he wouldn't take any lip from anybody, black or white. And the whole band came off the stage, and Art Blakey had a chair in his hand. They finally quieted everything down, and they canceled us that night. They said they didn't want any trouble."

Every moment is an ending and a beginning, if you want to get Zen about it. But few qualify as a cultural flash point, the close of an era and the opening of another. Billy Eckstine sparked just such a moment in the spring of 1950.

It had been several years in the making. In the late 1940s, MGM launched its own record company (the first movie studio to do so) and sought out Eckstine. "MGM came to us," recalls Milt Ebbins. "They went looking for an artist who was hot, and Billy was hot. It was a ten-year deal—a million dollar deal. Big time." Exploiting his strengths as an attractive, romantic figure—much the same leading-man material MGM had been packaging for years, but black—the label had Eckstine record the kind of love songs and sentimental ballads that had helped make Rudy Vallee, Crosby, and Sinatra idols in the past. Ebbins helped choose the material, largely dispensing with jazz and blues in favor of valentines such as "Everything I Have Is Yours," "Temptation," and "I've Never Been in Love Before," lushly arranged by studio pros for strings instead of a bebop band.

The new approach suited the singer's vocal style and played to his aspiration to transcend racial stereotypes. "He didn't want to be a bebop singer or a jazz singer—just a singer," said the pianist and arranger Bobby Tucker, who joined Eckstine as his musical director in 1947 and would remain with him for the rest of the singer's life. "He didn't want a label."

As a "major" record company rather than a "race" outfit like National, which had recorded Eckstine and his own orchestra, MGM afforded Eckstine access to the white world, where he was a revelation—especially to young women. One after another, Eckstine's releases for MGM topped the record charts. "Up until then—Fats Waller made no money," Tucker pointed out. "Louie Armstrong eventually made money, but later. The big money was in records—not 'race records,' [but] records across the board. With Billy at MGM Records, as soon as the record comes out. . . . " Tucker arched the palm of his hand upward, like a jet taking off. "This was the first time it was that a black man could sing ballads and white girls could listen. Not before it—everything was blues."

Now in the club of black performers welcome in "mixed" venues catering mainly to whites, Billy Eckstine opened on April 20, 1949, with Duke Ellington and His Orchestra at New York's Paramount Theater, the site of Frank Sinatra's celebrated rise to bobbysoxer glory. Ellington was the featured act, Eckstine an added attraction; long before the end of the three-week run, however, their status unofficially reversed.

One night, Ellington, who took special pride in his stylish presentation and his allure to women, caught sight of Eckstine and immediately sent his valet home to get an extra trunk of clothes. "Billy and Ellington had a clothes war going on," recalls Kay Davis, the Ellington Orchestra vocalist. "They each had these fabulous wardrobes—mostly very light-colored suits, like pale pistachio green and peach with matching shoes and everything, and Duke would come out, and the band would all grin and everything, and then here comes Billy in something equally sensational. Every show they would change, and all week long it was a fashion show of two very beautiful black men groomed to the nines. I think it was a challenge (to Duke). He knew he was good-looking and together. He was going to show Billy a thing or two!"

Before long, though, Davis says, Ellington accepted that "Billy Eckstine was the star" of that show. "The girls were in there falling away. They screamed and carried on."

Although that had happened before at the Paramount, this was a hormonal display of a different color. "We had 90 percent white women—90 percent—and they were throwing their panties onto the stage," recalls Milt Ebbins. "It was unbelievable. There was no color line with those kids. They loved him. Girls threw their panties, their keys, and everything. I'm not kidding you—it was pandemonium."

In the spring of 1950, the most accurate barometer of popular interests was not the television of the time, but the mass-market picture magazines, *Life* and *Look*. Both responded to the developments at the Paramount by planning major features on the Eckstine phenomenon. *Life* (the bigger of the two) acted first and sent photographer Martha Holmes to capture the new singing sensation and his fans in action. She spent about a week with Eckstine, on stage and off. She joined him, Ebbins, and their entourage for dinner and went with them to the movies. "We went to Sardi's, and people like Milton Berle would drop in on the table—everybody bowed and scraped," remembers Holmes.

One evening, she captured a moment. "It happened, and it was candid, and I got it," says Holmes.

In the photograph, we see Eckstine meticulously groomed in a white shirt with a high, loping Mr. B. collar and a tailored, plaid jacket. His hair glistens softly, and his eyebrows have been tweezed and brushed. His physical beauty has an almost unnatural perfection. He is standing tall and rigid, surrounded by fans, all of whom are lovely, young, white women. Something had occurred an instant before the shot was taken, but we don't know what. We've been given witness to the response, an *effect*—one woman is buckled over in laughter, others are giggling, and one in the foreground, in the center of the image, has collapsed onto Eckstine's chest. She is grinning with her eyes closed. He peers down at her and roars. It's a shared moment of a kind of ecstasy, the nature of which we are left to imagine.

It was nearly kept from publication, when, as Holmes recalls, a distraught (white, female) editor at *Life* protested because the picture shows a white woman touching a black man. The decision was left to Henry Luce, the Time Inc. publisher, who said, simply, "Run it." Someone nonetheless intervened to soften the image's impact with a caption pronouncing, "Billy is rushed by admirers. Most profess to have a maternal feeling for him." (When asked if she thinks the feelings she witnessed on the scene were maternal, Holmes laughed—"No, no!")

The photograph appeared in the April 24, 1950, issue of *Life*. For years afterward, many people would mistakenly remember it as a cover picture. In fact, after Eckstine's death in the 1990s, so many obituaries referred to the imagined *Life* cover that the magazine issued a press release to correct the record.

What people were recalling was the photograph's impact—on the whole of our popular culture, as well as on Eckstine's life and work. "That picture was my favorite—favorite, because it told just what the world should be like," remarks Holmes. Indeed, for black men struggling in the performing arts at the time, such as Harry Belafonte, that image of Eckstine seemed to represent new cause for hope, a breakthrough in acceptance and opportunity. "When that photo hit, in this national publication, it was as if a barrier had been broken," Belafonte says. For Eckstine, however, having that image in every barber shop and doctor's office in the America of 1950 was a barrier dropped and locked in place. As much as the moment was a beginning for his peers or an inspiration for his successors, it was the beginning of Billy Eckstine's end.

"He ran into a lot of bigotry because *Life* magazine did a double-page of him in the middle of a whole bunch of white girls just swoonin' all over him," recalls Tony Bennett, who got to know Eckstine in the 1950s and became one of his closest friends. "There was a big circle, like a beehive, around him, and in those days, it was so ahead of its time. You know, now it would be a normal thing. It was such a complete shock that that one photo hurt his career. It changed everything—before that, he had a tremendous following, and everybody was running after him, and he was so handsome and had great style and all that. The girls would just swoon all over him, and it just offended the white community." Helen Merrill, then a young woman with dreams of becoming a singer, kept a glossy picture of Eckstine hidden in her bedroom. "I had it under the pillow," she recalls, "because I didn't want my father to see it."

Dr. Billy Taylor, the pianist and broadcaster, discussed the subject with Eckstine himself late in the singer's life. "We talked about what a hard time he had," says Taylor. "When he played the Paramount, that should have been his really big break. Many [white] people who were hearing him were hearing him for the first time, because they never heard him in the white theaters. And so now, they were saying, 'Gee, oh, man, this guy can sing—wow!' The girls loved him, everything was great. But the coverage and that picture just slammed the door for him. I mean, there are a lot of things that would have happened to him and had been happening to him prior to that that were not open to him anymore."

Lured to MGM by a million dollars in promises, Billy Eckstine had gauzy visions of a future in movies, music, and business. He moved with his stunning first wife, June, from New York to a plush, eleven-room estate in Encino (complete with a private four-hole golf course), a three-iron drive away from the homes of Clark Cable and Mary Astor.

"You know, I don't especially like working in cabarets," he mused to an interviewer in 1951. "The clubs are close and smoky, and my throat becomes irritated. That bothers me! If I can get to the point where I can make a movie now and then, do a couple of theater dates a year, and recordings, then I'd have time to do what I want. I want to go into the cattle business and stay out in the air for the rest of my life."

For a time, the studio tried to pacify him with standard talk about development problems. "The producers said, 'We're looking for a vehicle for you, we're looking for a vehicle for you,'" remembered Bobby Tucker. "It was going on and on and on."

When MGM producer Joe Pasternak finally offered Eckstine a part he considered right for him, the role was a nightclub singer named Billy Eckstine. The movie was *Skirts Ahoy*, a WAVES recruitment film disguised as a proto-feminist musical (produced at the request of the secretary of the navy, who saw the swimming star Esther Williams as a good role model for women in the military). Eckstine had no lines, and he was called upon to appear in one scene extraneous to the plot, so it could be deleted from prints of the film distributed in the South. (Pasternak made a specialty of "stunt" appearances by ostensible exotics such as Xavier Cugat.)

"There was a scene where I was watching him sing in a nightclub," recalls Williams. "Barry Sullivan and I were sitting in the nightclub, and I couldn't figure out why Billy never looked at me. Billy told me at one point, when we were shooting, it was because he was instructed by the unit manager of the company not to look at me. It would look as if he was on the make for the leading lady, the white woman. I couldn't believe it.

"I said [to Eckstine], 'Listen, I'm the leading lady of the movie—I expect to be looked at.' And he said, 'Well that's how far racism is going.' We were in the midst of a lot of racism at that time."

A profile of Eckstine published in *Sepia* magazine in the year of *Skirts Ahoy*'s release raved in bold type, "This is only the beginning of long contract with the studio." The film would be the only one he made for MGM.

"In those days, he didn't have a dog's chance of being in the movies, *because*," says Lee Young, who performed in *Skirts Ahoy* and was a regular on the set of

MGM musicals as rehearsal percussionist for the choreographers Marge and Gower Champion. "To be very frank with you, he was too good-looking. They didn't have the kind of roles for blacks to be lovers. They didn't go for that. They only had the kind of roles where you were laughing and giggling. They wouldn't accept a handsome black guy."

Lena Horne and Dorothy Dandridge had a comparable quandary as gorgeous, talented women at MGM in the same years. "They did the same thing to Billy they did to me," says Horne. "They wouldn't give him a decent role. They would put us in one scene they could cut out in the south. He should have been a leading man. But they were afraid to use him. I wish I could find the boys who made those decisions. I'd cut off their balls."

Eckstine left Hollywood and looked back only to aim his spit. "I had a chance in the old days to do some 'Uncle Tom' crap in the movies," he groused to a reporter in the 1970s. By then, he had been divorced twice and was living alone in Las Vegas. "They wanted me to play a red cap and carry Betty Grable's things and maybe sing a song. I would refuse, and they'd label me. They'd say, 'He must think he's white.' I could have used the bread a lot of times, believe me.

"I've got five sons and two daughters. Suppose they're watching the late show and I come shuffling out of a barn carrying Dan Daley's bags. They'd say, 'Man, Dad's been all talk.' I've never been given a chance to act."

* * *

By 1955, when Eckstine was forty-one, the black magazine *Tan* was asking in a headline, "What Happened to Billy Eckstine?" The writer optimistically left the question open, but the answer was already evident. Disowned by a white-controlled entertainment industry at once obsessed with and fearful of black male sexuality, Eckstine became an untouchable. He watched as unthreatening lessors such as Perry Como and Andy Williams got contracts at the top record labels and their own prime-time network television shows. He played Vegas, the nightclubs he long ago admitted to hating, and he hardened. Always a proud and defiant man, he grew bitter over his missed chances and lashed out, damaging what was left of them. He would insult deejays for ignoring him and decline interviews with journalists who had written about other singers. After seeing him performing many times and reviewing him in the 1980s, favorably, I interviewed him once, by telephone, on the subject of Pittsburgher Billy Strayhorn; Eckstine began the session with a lecture on the irrelevance of our conversation. "What did you people ever do for me?" he growled, although he did share some invaluable memories of working with Strayhorn in their youth.

"He was bitter because he had everything it took to have stardom," says the singer and educator Jon Hendricks. "He could be mean. But I think what he did was take out the frustrations of his career on whomever he met."

From time to time, old friends such as Sarah Vaughan and Quincy Jones would set up opportunities for Eckstine to record, and he would excel with little apparent effort. Vaughan is understood to have bankrolled their fine album of duets of Irving Berlin songs, recorded in 1957, and her nurturing presence inspired him to sing as warmly as ever, though the album fizzled in the marketplace. Under Jones (and his arranger Billy Byers) a few years later, Eckstine nearly returned to jazz with a handful of gently swinging albums such as *Billy Eckstine Now Singing in 12 Great Movies* (in which he murmured the love themes to "The High and the Mighty" and "Three Coins in a Fountain"). But he would come no closer to singing or acting on screen until his last years, when he qualified for cameo roles as a fiery old man in films such as Richard Pryor's *Jo Jo Dancer, Your Life Is Calling*.

Eckstine wasted most of his time and energy straining to project some dignity as he sang in ever-shrinking rooms and recorded increasingly insipid and inappropriate material, such as "Love the One You're With." "The powers that be never permitted him to fulfill his potential," Quincy Jones says. "He could have been a sex symbol. If he were a white man, nothing would have stopped him. He would have reached the top. As things were, he never got to make movies or have his own TV show. It's a tragedy. He was always fighting the system, and B was a fighter. But that was too much for any one man." In 1968, Eckstine was doing dinner theater with Betty Grable and Joey Adams.

"I'm satisfied with what I've been able to do," Eckstine claimed in a late interview, quickly qualifying the statement. "I'm not satisfied at the breadth of my career. I'm constantly on the road. You take the white stars. Once they get the breaks, they come off the road and make their money sitting on their behinds. I think I've contributed enough to music that I could collect the fruits, not the dregs."

As his possessions were being prepared to be auctioned, an anonymous longtime friend (rumored to be Sammy Davis Jr.) interceded, bought everything at a price satisfactory to the IRS, and returned it all to Eckstine. He didn't enjoy his things much longer, anyway. After a devastating stroke in 1992, Eckstine moved back to Pittsburgh and lived under the care of one of his sisters until his death at the age of seventy-eight on March 8, 1993.

On one of the last days he was able to speak, Tony Bennett called him. "He was magnificent," Bennett says. "I can't believe how under-appreciated. He was a great romantic, he was a gentleman, and he loved life. There wasn't an ounce of

Uncle Tom in him at all. He was the beginning of a whole new 'This is who I am, and if you don't like it, you can fuck it . . . '

"We had a lot of great moments, especially in the early pioneering days of Las Vegas, and right when he was dying, toward the end of his life, I was on the phone with him and reminiscing. We had so much fun swingin' through Vegas in those early days—with a lot of gals, you know—a lot of beautiful nights. I told him, B—remember when Frank Sinatra and Dean Martin used to tell their press agents, 'Sneak up and find out what Tony Bennett and Billy Eckstine are doing, and put in the paper that we're doing that'?

"He could barely talk, and he said, 'Don't forget, T—it's just you and me. It's just you and me, T. Now it's just you.'"

PART II

Whose Standards?

Mos Def and the American Songbook

The view of Tin Pan Alley from Harlem was so bad during the first decades of the twentieth century, a great time for white songwriters, that the African American lyricist Andy Razaf wrote a mordant work of verse on the subject, a "prayer for the Alley." Published in the 1930s in *New York Amsterdam News*, the black daily, the piece lamented the Midtown center of popular music as "lacking in soul," a place "where something original frightens the ear" and pandering technicians produce "dull similarities, year after year." Razaf, who died in 1973, never lived to see the glorious songs that he wrote with Fats Waller revived on Broadway in *Ain't Misbehavin'* in the 1980s. Nor, of course, did he get to see that show's breakout star, Nell Carter, parlay her stage success into a career on television sitcoms, beginning with the now-forgotten *You Take the Kids*. Nor, accordingly, could Razaf have foreseen that a talented kid from Brooklyn named Dante Smith would play Carter's son on that series, would later go into music under the professional name of Mos Def, and would, in January 2007, lead off the season of Lincoln Center's American Songbook series with a concert of defiantly black, genre-smashing music that challenged the standard definition of that songbook. Mos Def enacted Andy Razaf's revenge.

Launched eleven years earlier under the stewardship of Jonathan Schwartz, the onetime rock deejay whose evangelical devotion to pre-rock music is the badge of the convert, the American Songbook series began as an effort to confer the legitimacy of institutionalization upon Tin Pan Alley—or, more precisely, upon the canon of popular songs and theater music created by the iconic tune-smiths Jerome Kern, Irving Berlin, George and Ira Gershwin, Cole Porter, Harold Arlen, Richard Rodgers and his partners Lorenz Hart and Oscar Ham-merstein, and their acolytes, including Jonathan's father, Arthur Schwartz—the dead white men of American song. Their music, though immeasurably rich and hardy, was, in 1998, no longer popular, in the sense of having favor with the young-music-consuming masses of the day; rock and soul and their cousins and offspring had long supplanted it on the sales charts. The music of Tin Pan Alley had become an object of connoisseurship. Hence it qualified for protection under the auspices of Lincoln Center, which was in an expansive mode and had already accepted jazz as a constituent, alongside symphonic music, ballet, and opera.

The proposition that vintage pop tunes constitute a body of work worthy of ongoing appreciation, reconsideration, and preservation—that the songs belong in a book—was not new in the late 1990s; nor was the idea as old as Tin Pan Alley songs themselves. I remember one of the early American Songbook con-certs, a tribute to Rodgers staged at Alice Tully Hall in 1999, at which Schwartz toasted the proceedings by remarking that songs of the past need to be per-formed "live" to stay alive. While that is true, it was not live performances but recordings that first established popular songs that were no longer popular as a repertoire; indeed, our conception of this music as a songbook is largely a sec-ondary effect, a happy accident of a development in recording technology during the 1950s.

The current era of popular music has something in common with the first half of the last century in that the dominant form of recorded music is and was the single (today through Web-based file-sharing and downloading; then through 78-rpm acetate records). In pursuit of new hits, the singers of the 78 age, like their counterparts in pop today, sang new songs as a rule; there seemed no point in recording material that the public had heard and had decided to buy or not to buy years earlier. Popular music, then as now, was thought to derive its value from its freshness, like ideas and fruit. With the advent of the long-play-ing album, which rose in popularity during the 1950s, record producers and singers found themselves needing to fill twelve or so tracks on each disk, and there simply were not enough good new songs in supply to meet the LP's demands. Billy May, the swing-band arranger who worked often with Frank Sinatra, among others, recalled how Sinatra was early to suggest filling albums with songs he happened to like, regardless of their age.

Among the tunes that Sinatra, Ella Fitzgerald, Peggy Lee, Nat King Cole, and their peers gained the license to record were vintage theater songs that might have seemed too sophisticated, too character-oriented, or too situational to have been recorded with hit-making in mind. Thus, record buyers of the '50s found LPs full of well-wrought but already old tunes from long-gone shows and films—such as Gershwin's "Embraceable You," from *Strike Up the Band* (1930); Kern's "Smoke Gets in Your Eyes," from *Roberta* (1933); and Rodgers and Hart's "My Funny Valentine," from *Babes in Arms* (1937). With men such as Sinatra now singing greater numbers of theater songs originally written for women, and with women such as Fitzgerald singing more tunes composed for men, both the songs and their singers seemed to deepen and to expand in emotional range.

A common repertoire of durable, adaptable songs written throughout the first half of the twentieth century, the songs we have since come to know as standards, began to coalesce. Fitzgerald, working closely with Norman Granz at Verve Records, helped give form to this repertoire through her duly revered series of LPs devoted to the canonical songwriters Kern, Berlin, Porter, and the rest—with Ellington included, in his case as both composer and band leader—each titled as the composer's Songbook. A recording format called the album got us thinking of the old music on those recordings in new terms, as pieces in a portfolio of treasurable mementos.

That a different sort of music for the young audience—rock 'n' roll—was emerging simultaneously would ensure that the great American songbook would be frozen stylistically in the past that it salvaged. In the best sense of honoring a worthy legacy, then, the songbook has always been a book of the dead. Such is the body of Tin Pan Alley works that Jonathan Schwartz set out to preserve when he organized the early programs of Lincoln Center's American Songbook series. Under new management, the series has sought in recent years to break free of the standard definition of the popular songbook as the book that defines popular standards. The series has largely abandoned its charter missions of canonization and conservation, and this has been a wondrous thing to behold, something close to a miracle at Lincoln Center.

Over the past few seasons, the American Songbook series has focused mainly (though not exclusively) on interesting, venturesome composers of the present day, such as the singer-songwriters Sufjan Stevens, Nellie McKay, and Stephin Merritt, the last of whom performed with his pop-rock band The Magnetic Fields, and Fred Hersch, the jazz pianist and composer, who premiered a cycle of art songs concerned with the subject of photography. The aesthetic of the series has changed from one in which a song's value was measured by its universality, its accessibility, and its durability to one that prizes singularity, surprise, and timeliness. This is a clubby, downtown approach, rare even in the clubs downtown, and it is wonderfully unnerving to find it in a major New York performing-arts institution.

Mos Def led off the spring 2007 American Songbook season with a concert that took the series as far from the antiquarian preservationism of Jonathan Schwartz as Mos Def has taken himself from *You Take the Kids*. When Mos Def first began acting, playing variations on the Dickensian cliché of the devilishly cute little street tough on various series and made-for-TV movies (working then under the stage name Dante Beze), he was already experimenting with music at home, making up his own words to records by 1980s rappers such as Big Daddy Kane, Rakim, and De La Soul. "They happened together," he later said of the dual interests he has sustained throughout his career. "I started rhyming when I was nine years old, and I caught the [acting] bug in [elementary] school, so there's no separation to the genesis of all this." As an actor, he grew up on camera in both senses of the phrase, maturing to handle better and better roles in films, including *Bamboozled*, *Monster's Ball*, and *The Italian Job*, as well as on Broadway, in *Topdog/Underdog*. As a musician, too, he demonstrated a drive to set new challenges and meet higher standards with each of the four CDs he recorded since 1998.

The first, the collaboration *Mos Def & Talib Kweli are Black Star*, was most striking for its cynical take on the violence and posturing in hip-hop culture, though its beats and aural textures were typical for the day. His debut solo album, *Black on Both Sides*, released the following year, built on Mos Def's now-established strength as a lyricist with a compelling bravura rooted not in material conquest but in racial pride. Then, in 2004, came *The New Danger*, Mos Def's breakthrough as a musical artist. Picking up where the black-rock movement of the 1980s left off, he constructed a hybrid of hard rock, funk, and hip-hop—power chords, dance beats, and rap. Here and there between rhymes, he did a bit of singing—crowing, more like, in a scratchy tenor, but in tune or close enough, and with a palpable exhilaration in the making of unusual music. A follow-up in this vein, *True Magic*, was released in December 2006, though Mos Def was already working on a greater breakthrough, experimenting in low-profile performances with ideas that took full form at Lincoln Center in January.

That concert was held in the Allen Room, a nightclubbish theater in the cheesy mall complex that houses Jazz at Lincoln Center. The space has a stunning view of Central Park South through a floor-to-ceiling glass wall behind the stage, and the scenery served well as a diversion as the show opened with a quartet (piano, electric bass, drums, and alto sax) repeating a one-chord funk pattern for several minutes. Just as the trees and the traffic lights began to lose their interest, the sound of a New Orleans–style brass band blurted from the back of the room, and Mos Def marched the band down the aisles toward the stage. A gimmicky way to enter, probably old stuff already at the turn of the last century, it always thrills. Mos Def took the center of the stage, dressed in perfectly weathered jeans, sneakers, and a hoodie, flanked by the eight players of the brass band standing in an arc, and he began to sing—well, with fervor, to what took shape as a variation on Nina Simone's version of "I Put a Spell on You."

Then things got interesting. After singing a couple of verses, Mos Def switched to rapping over "I Put a Spell on You," improvising twists on the song's original lyrics interspersed with lines of his own. The piece set the scheme for the evening, an amalgam of jazz, pop, funk, and hip-hop, with bits of rock—essentially, the history of black music in America in one night. Only Duke Ellington and Billy Strayhorn tried something more outlandish with their number "The History of Jazz in Three Minutes," and that was meant as a novelty. Mos Def was not joking here. He is charming and good at clowning between songs—at one point, he looked behind the stage and said, "I feel like Al Pacino in *The Devil's Advocate!*"—but in his music, he tends to be serious to the brink of solemnity.

"This is the American Songbook series," he reminded the audience. "So I have to do some American songs. I know some American songs." The drummer and bassist laid a funk pattern out for him, and Mos Def started to croon "America" ("My Country, 'Tis of Thee"), singing through the line "Land where my fathers died," which he repeated several times, emphatically. He rapped a bit and drifted into "The Star-Spangled Banner," picking up the anthem with the couplet "And the rockets' red glare/The bombs bursting in air," and he repeated that—and repeated it louder each time as the brass band countered the phrase with a terse, dissonant riff. With a bit too heavy a hand, perhaps, Mos Def made a musical collage of images heavily loaded, in every way, to take on America of the past and the present.

Rapping, then singing, talk-singing, and sing-talking to the accompaniment of jazz instruments, Mos Def would seem to be inventing a new music with familiar materials. In fact, he is building on a tradition of mixing up spoken language, verse, and melody that dates back to ragtime and runs through the history of jazz. (Nearly every style of music has incorporated speech in some way at one time or another.) As early as 1908, Scott Joplin composed what might qualify as the first proto-rap song, "Pine Apple Rag." In the swing era, Louis Armstrong, Don Redman, Cab Calloway, and Slim Gaillard all made specialties of recitative in tempo. In fact, Gaillard, late in his life, was recruited by a Canadian hip-hop group, Dream Warriors, to rap on a straight-ahead hip-hop record, *Very Easy to Assemble But Hard to Take Apart.*

If the existence of Canadian hip-hop with Slim Gaillard at the microphone teaches us anything it is that oddball combinations of musical, cultural, and historical elements are easier to assemble than one might think. The importance of Mos Def and His Big Band lies not in its uniqueness, but in how fine and true it sounds. The music, for all its surprise, has heart and the resonance of inevitability. It is mash-up music of a high order, the sound of the current era of recording—the iPod age—as live art. If it does not quite fit in our understanding of a songbook, so be it. Mos Def is now an exemplar of something else: the great American playlist.

Rodgers and Hart

E arly in Richard Rodgers's career as a musical-theater composer, his rapid ascension on Broadway earned him an invitation to one of Elsa Maxwell's masquerade balls. He was expected to wear a cheekily imaginative costume, and Rodgers came up with something appropriate. Looking exactly as he always would, conservatively attired in a dark business suit and tie, Rodgers went as Zeppo Marx—the Jazz Age image of normalcy. A New York newspaper would later describe Rodgers as a person "like anybody else." Indeed, despite the extravagant success of his music during most of the past century, he would always seem a figure of indeterminate identity, a man whose image is most striking for its extraordinary ordinariness.

June 28, 2002, marked the hundredth anniversary of Rodgers's birth to a doctor and an amateur pianist in Jewish Harlem. It was the latest in a string of centennials of composers and other musicians whose work contributed substantially to twentieth-century American culture, including Duke Ellington (1999), Aaron Copland (2000), and Louis Armstrong (2001). Like those peers of his in jazz and concert music (and hybrids thereof, in Ellington's case), our most celebrated composer of music for the theater got the full centennial treatment: new productions of his shows in New York and Los Angeles (including a much-praised restaging of *Oklahoma!* by the English National Theater, brought to Broadway); tribute CDs; a PBS documentary; a gossipy biography by Meryle Secrest (author of books on Leonard Bernstein and Stephen Sondheim), researched with the cooperation of Rodgers's estate; and, to promote it all, a Web site designed with an online gift shop offering "Rodgers Centennial merchandise."

The world would scarcely seem in need of a Richard Rodgers revival. The 1965 film version of *The Sound of Music* is not only one of the best-selling videos ever released, but also an ongoing box-office phenomenon as the backdrop for a kitchy sort of group karaoke; meanwhile, the other most-famous Rodgers and Hammerstein musicals (*Oklahoma!, South Pacific, Carousel,* and *The King and I*) are running in perpetual rotation at numerous high school and summer theaters across the country. What we could always use is help in reconciling Rodgers—the composer "with the soul of a banker"—with the emotional depth and complexity of his best work, which is by no means his most popular. Secrest's biography is of welcome use, then, for its portrayal of Rodgers as a man with dark, hidden passions, as well as one with a gift for producing unshakable melodies. His benign façade, that appearance as the Zeppo of American music, may have been a disguise after all.

Besides composing "My Funny Valentine" (with Lorenz Hart, his first important partner), "I Have Dreamed" (with Oscar Hammerstein II, his second), and dozens of other standards of American popular song (including a few written with lyricists such as Sondheim and Sheldon Harnick), Rodgers apparently drank too much, suffered bouts of depression so serious that he required hospitalization on occasion, and had a shadowy sex life (with the chorus girls in his shows, among others). That is, Rodgers was a lot like Hart—far more so than anyone, especially the former, would ever acknowledge. (Secrest leaves this parallel implicit.) A lyricist of exquisite sensitivity and wit, Lorenz Hart was also a notorious drunk, emotionally tortured, and a sexual enigma; the collaborators submitted to kindred demons. No wonder Rodgers found Hart discomforting, "a permanent source of irritation," while they worked together to write bittersweet and wry popular masterpieces.

If Rodgers has had an uncertain place in the public consciousness, one reason is that he was never an artist in the romantic American mold, no rebel outcast following his vision to buck the status quo. Composing on demand, he would meet the dramatic needs of a show like manufacturing specs, and the results were geared for mass consumption. "This isn't a question of sitting on the top of a hill and waiting for inspiration to strike," he told an interviewer in the 1950s. "It's work. . . . It's my job." He liked to collaborate and preferred to have a full set of lyrics ready to be set to music—a completed purchase order. Rodgers was a creative person who worked cooperatively and with exceptional powers of empathy and who did so with the fixated discipline of a piece worker.

Ever since Rodgers broke away from Hart in the early 1940s to write *Oklahoma!* with Hammerstein, it has been a truism of the American musical theater that there were essentially two Richard Rodgerses: the Rodgers "and Hart" and the Rodgers "and Hammerstein." The point bears emphasis more than half a century later, if only to remind the generations overexposed to the Hammerstein musicals that the Hart era existed and as something other than Rodgers's apprenticeship; it was nothing of the sort but, rather, the period of Rodgers's most mature songwriting. (Compounding the matter, Hammerstein got favored treatment in the publicity surrounding the Rodgers centennial, which was supervised by the Rodgers and Hammerstein Organization.) Anyone tempted to dismiss Richard Rodgers's work as theme-park Americana, children's music, or camp is likely thinking of the Rodgers of Rodgers and Hammerstein.

Hart, who was seven years older than Rodgers, prodded and inspired his junior partner nearly as much as he vexed him from the first years of their professional relationship, when they were laboring for a Theater Guild inconsequence of the 1920s called *The Garrick Gaieties*. As Secrest points out, Hart "insisted they write something of value for this frivolous undertaking." Their contributions included an early "jazz opera" (*The Joy Spreader*, long forgotten) and the song "Manhattan" (or "I'll Take Manhattan"), a hummable little paean to amorous delusion that has endured for more than eighty years, through countless transformations in New York's physical and social landscape. In more than five hundred songs written primarily for stage musicals and films, Rodgers and Hart brought the value of art to the realm of frivolity. Their legacy as collaborators is a body of (mostly) sophisticated, musically resourceful, emotionally probative, multidimensional songs written for otherwise artless and duly forgotten musicals: mournfully lyrical ballads such as "Blue Room" from *The Girl Friend*, "This Funny World" from *Betsy*, and "A Ship Without a Sail" from *Heads Up!*; and swinging provocations such as "You Took Advantage of Me" from *Present Arms* and "A Lady Must Live" from *America's Sweetheart*, the last of which concluded, in 1931, "With my John and my Max, I can reach a climax/That's proof positive that a lady must live." Hammerstein was already prominent as coauthor with Jerome Kern of *Showboat*, which was revered as the first American musical with the formal integrity and grandeur of operetta. Yet Rodgers preferred Hart during most of their years of association and took pride in the venturesome modernity of the work they did together—particularly their mordant vernacular masterpiece, *Pal Joey*. Hammerstein "had always been part of a romantic, florid kind of theatre, more operetta than musical comedy, which was quite different from Larry's and mine," Rodgers wrote in his memoirs.

The notion that Rodgers's move from Hart to Hammerstein was evolutionary, an act of progression, is pervasive but wrong. In his lucid and thorough biography of Lorenz Hart, Frederick Nolan recounts an anecdote that the lyricist Alan Jay Lerner used to tell. He and his partner Frederick Loewe were stuck in the dark with Hart during a wartime air-raid drill a short while after Rodgers had teamed up with Hammerstein. Hart clicked through the channels on a radio, and Lerner could see his cigar glowing redder and redder as every station played a different song from *Oklahoma!*. "They knew what they had witnessed was the sight of a man made all too painfully aware of his own obsolescence," Nolan writes. Well . . . *Oklahoma!* may have been an epiphany for Lerner and Loewe, who proceeded to devote their careers to writing Rodgers and Hammerstein emulations such as *Camelot* and *My Fair Lady*; but whatever pain Hart was suffering then, as ever, had sources even more insidious than "Oh, What a Beautiful Mornin'." (He died soon after, in 1943.) For all its triumphs as an integration of theater music, character, and dance, *Oklahoma!* was a show with vastly different aesthetic intentions than Hart's signature work with Rodgers—affirming and sentimental, provincial and bright, rather than defiant, sexy, urban, and bleak. Just the right thing for a homefront audience several years into a vast war, Secrest points out, *Oklahoma!* spoke to "the need to believe in a brighter future." Hart's world was a place that makes fun of the things you strive for, laughs at the dreams you're alive for. How could Hart have felt obsolete if life is a pointless joke?

Lorenz Hart and Oscar Hammerstein had little in common, except Richard Rodgers, and he was different with each of them. Rodgers publicly held Hart in contempt, berating him for his unconventional work habits and "morals." (According to Secrest, he once told Diahann Carroll, when they were rehearsing *No Strings*, "You just can't imagine how wonderful it feels to have written this score and not have to search all over the globe for that drunken little fag.") Still, he seemed wholly attuned to Hart's melancholy sensibility in their songs; the melodies ache as deeply as the lyrics. In fact, the music came first for most of the great Rodgers and Hart songs (despite Rodgers's preference for working the other way around). Performed as an instrumental, "My Funny Valentine" is no less poignant; nor, for that matter, is "Little Girl Blue," "It Never Entered My Mind," "Nobody's Heart," or "Spring Is Here." There are so many pieces of wracking beauty in the Rodgers and Hart catalog and they ring with such veracity that ultimately one wonders whose sensibility was whose. As Secrest shows us repeatedly, Rodgers kept his darker self concealed, releasing it only in the wrenching music he made with the partner he resented.

Working exclusively with Hammerstein from 1943 until the lyricist's death in 1960, Rodgers achieved what Secrest calls "a new unanimity of tone." Rodgers and Hammerstein, who had known each other since boyhood, proved compatible: assimilated New York Jews, buttoned-down, family men, gifted, and compulsively disciplined. Gone was the personal conflict Rodgers had with Hart, along with a certain tension in the music. That loveless spring passed. June was bustin' out all over. The grays and muted hues began to disappear from Rodgers's musical palette, and the light tones brightened. Although his emotional life remained troubled, Rodgers no longer had a collaborator eager to give those troubles voice. Jerome Kern, Rodgers's youthful idol, called his new music "condescending."

Sensitive to charges of excessive sentimentality in his music with Hammerstein, Rodgers told an interviewer, "What's wrong with 'sweetness and light'? . . . I love satire but couldn't write it." He had evidently forgotten what he once could do; with Hart he had written one of the most piercing satires of romance ever set to notes, "I Wish I Were in Love Again" ("When love congeals it soon reveals the faint aroma of performing seals/the double-crossing of a pair of heels . . ."), as well as a serial murderer's lament, "To Keep My Love Alive" (rhyming "mattress side" with "patricide")—and, for *Pal Joey*, a scathing parody of the sort of mush he would make a specialty with Hammerstein, "Flower Garden of My Heart."

Rodgers and Hammerstein's career ballooned in accord with the rest of mainstream America during the postwar years. In the early 1950s, Secrest reminds us, they had four shows (*Oklahoma!*, *South Pacific*, *The King and I*, and *Me and Juliet*) running on Broadway at once, and New York Mayor Robert F. Wagner made a proclamation for Rodgers and Hammerstein Week. Ed Sullivan devoted two consecutive hour-long programs to their music (with some Rodgers and Hart included). In 1954, a ninety-minute tribute to Rodgers and Hammerstein aired simultaneously on all four television networks of the era (ABC, CBS, NBC, and Dumont)—a national event, accorded the same kind of attention as the McCarthy hearings and the World Series. Meanwhile, young people were beginning to reject what they saw as inflated artifice in the musical theater Rodgers and Hammerstein represented (and the generation which that theater represented), and they were turning to the simple, intimate, and earthy sounds of rock-and-roll and folk music. In 1956, Ed Sullivan's star attraction was Elvis, who did not sing "Some Enchanted Evening."

Richard Rodgers kept working. While he talked about Kern as a primary musical influence, his real role model was Lew Fields, a one-time vaudeville comedian who took up producing and built a theatrical empire in the first decades of the twentieth century, when Rodgers was knocking on doors, Fields's among them. (Rodgers and Hart astutely chose Fields's son Herbert to write the books to several of their early shows.) Unlike Hart, who called himself an artist and rationalized his erratic behavior as the product of a creative temperament, Rodgers saw honor and opportunity in business, and he flourished within its structure; even when he was composing, he always went to an office, where he worked from nine to five. Rodgers, once established with Hammerstein, built a theatrical and music publishing operation to surpass Fields's, producing not only his own shows (on Broadway and in touring companies around the world), but musicals by others (including Irving Berlin's *Annie Get Your Gun*) and straight dramas (such as Norman Krazna's *John Loves Mary*). By 1953, Rodgers was chairman of the board of a conglomerate (based in a ten-room complex on Madison Avenue) with gross revenues of between $15 and 20 million.

During the rock era, popular musicians took to condemning business as corrupting—the Beatles gave away assets on principle when they formed their own company—and Richard Rodgers, the organization man of American musical theater, fell further into disfavor with young people who knew anything about him. Not only did he write the music on all those original-cast albums their mothers played around the house; *he was a suit, man.* Some of his colleagues in the Tin Pan Alley tradition were rediscovered from time to time; Harold Arlen came into vogue briefly (thanks to Barbara Streisand), as did Hoagy Carmichael (through Maria Muldaur), Kurt Weill (by way of Lou Reed), and others for varying periods. Not Rodgers. He was too tainted by the monolithic conformity of his success. Only recently in the hip-hop world have pop musicians again taken up moguldom with social impunity, founding their own companies, producing other artists, and diversifying beyond entertainment businesses for the same benefits (profit, freedom, power, esteem) that Lew Fields and Richard Rodgers sought.

He kept right on working until the last weeks before he died in December 1979. Rodgers had a new musical open in May of that year: *I Remember Mama*, a misguided affair cowritten by two dissimilar lyricists, Martin Charnin (of *Annie*) and Raymond Jessel (brought in when Charnin was fired) and starring Liv Ullmann (who could not sing a note), which closed after 108 performances. It was the only Richard Rodgers show I saw during his lifetime, so I am inclined to view it with proprietary lenience. I've always thought of it as a *joli-laid* work undervalued by critics expecting a Richard Rodgers musical. He was ravaged by cancer and no longer the Richard Rodgers anyone knew; the music he somehow mustered is simple, repetitive, and almost unbearably fragile. In its best moments (the ballads "You Could Not Please Me More" and "Ev'ry Day"), Rodgers's final music had an unmannered delicacy all too rare in his big, famous shows.

Rodgers was dispirited by the course popular music had taken in his last years. He didn't care much for rock and told a friend that his kind of musical theater was "over." He had begun writing in the days of the Charleston, and *I Remember Mama* closed with Michael Jackson's "Don't Stop Till You Get Enough" on the radio. Rodgers's work endures decades after his death, of course, still split on the planes of his major partnerships. The beloved Hammerstein musicals will no doubt be running somewhere forever; being works of nostalgia from the beginning, they can never go out of date. As for the Rodgers and Hart songs, jazz musicians and singers have been rediscovering them for decades.

In the first week of September 2001, I met an old colleague, the magazine writer Kristin White, at the Oak Room in the Algonquin Hotel. We were both there to see Eric Comstock, the jazz-cabaret singer and pianist. We had cocktails in the hotel lobby after the show, and Comstock joined us. Five days later, Kristin was on the flight out of Boston taken down in a field in Pennsylvania. When I heard the news, I put on Comstock's most recent CD and listened to it through track number eleven, an obscure tune from *Lido Lady* that no one had bothered recording before, called "What's the Use?" It's a funny, plaintive song about futility and confusion, written in 1926 by Rodgers and Hart.

Sammy Davis, Jr.
Two Lives

Somewhere in the netherworld of Hollywood's unborn, the place where failed TV pilots go, there is an unsold dramatic series called *Poor Devil*. It was to have starred Sammy Davis, Jr. as a dutiful minion of Lucifer struggling each week to lure another unwitting earthly soul to his or her eternal doom. For some reason, it didn't sell, although the casting was inspired. Sammy always had a way of tempting people to devilish thinking, and, decades after he died of throat cancer at sixty-four, he is still doing so.

Part African American, part Latino, a converted Jew, diminutive, funny-looking, blind in one eye, and wildly theatrical in manner and attire, Davis has long been a multipurpose target of enmity. "When I move into a neighborhood," he used to joke, "people start running four ways at the same time." Even his famous buddies—Frank Sinatra, Dean Martin, and the rest of the Rat Pack—ridiculed Davis mercilessly under the cover of macho shtick. "Hurry up, Sam, the watermelon's getting warm," Sinatra would bark, and Martin would hoist Davis up and announce, "I'd like to thank the NAACP for this award." Desperate for acceptance, Sammy only diminished himself with his indiscriminate sycophancy, fawning over Richard Nixon and falling off Johnny Carson's couch in convulsive laughter at middling patter. Today our collective image of Davis is largely inseparable from Billy Crystal's blackface impersonation of the aging entertainer as a pandering show-biz phony, a glitzy minstrel act. We don't remember Davis for who he was or what he did when he mattered most as much as for the wicked joke he let himself become.

Two biographies published in 2003, Will Haygood's *In Black and White* and Gary Fishgall's *Gonna Do Great Things* (both of which are subtitled "The Life of Sammy Davis, Jr."), do their subject a great service by casting light on his early glory as a singer, dancer, actor, musician, and impressionist, regarded in his prime as "the world's greatest entertainer." Haygood, a staff writer for the *Washington Post* who is the author of a poignant family history, *The Haygoods of Columbus*) and a lively, piercing biography of 1960s political gadfly Adam Clayton Powell Jr. (*King of the Cats*), does even more by portraying Davis's Herculean achievements and epic decline in intimate detail while also putting them in historical and social context. *In Black and White* is nearly as ambitious as its subject was. Fishgall, a Hollywood biographer who has written about Burt Lancaster, Gregory Peck, and James Stewart, lays out the facts of Davis's life in a breezy fashion. Of the two books, Fishgall's provides the greater wealth of raw information, particularly on Davis's recordings and television work; however, it leaves the reader to make sense of it all. As a biographer, Fishgall presents his findings in black and white; Haygood aims to do great things.

Both books follow the broad contours of the story Davis told in his two memoirs: *Yes I Can*, the critically acclaimed best-selling epic of youthful vainglory published in 1965, when Sammy was forty years old, and its 1989 follow-up, *Why Me?*, which had none of its predecessor's charm or success. (Both books were ghostwritten by Burt Boyar, a former gossip columnist and press agent, and Boyar's wife, Jane, from tape-recorded interviews with their subject.) Sammy was born into show business, the son of an African American vaudeville hoofer, Sam Davis, and a Cuban American chorus girl, Elvera Sanchez, who met while performing in a touring revue staged by the "Chitlin Circuit" impresario Will Mastin. (Davis avoids the issue of his mother's ethnicity in *Yes I Can*, which was published three years after the Cuban missile crisis; for much of his life he claimed to be partly of Puerto Rican extraction. Haygood, who tracked down Davis's mother and interviewed her shortly before her death in 1996, is illuminating on this count.)

Sammy began performing in Mastin's troupe at age four, and through the compound benefits of his genetic inheritance, the nurturing of his father and

Mastin (his mother having left to dance elsewhere) and the laxity of the child labor laws—particularly for Negro children—he developed with stunning precocity. At age eight, he starred in his first movie, a demeaning all-black musical short called *Rufus Jones for President*, wherein imagined African American lawmakers shoot craps and eat fried chicken in the Senate chambers, but which Sammy almost redeems with a wonderfully arch rendition of "I'll Be Glad When You're Dead, You Rascal You." By the time the boy was ten, his savvy boss had reformulated the act as Will Mastin's Gang Featuring Little Sammy. Davis grew up without a day of education apart from his round-the-clock schooling in showmanship.

In academic circles, it has been the rage for some time to view human behavior as performance and see identity as a social "construct." One wonders what the theorists of this school would make of Sammy Davis, Jr., who was essentially custom-bred solely to perform—in conditions close to laboratory isolation from the society that shapes the rest of us. When he reached adulthood, Davis was already a show-business veteran and a master of virtually every art of popular entertainment: a virtuoso tap dancer, a powerful singer, a musician adept at no fewer than six instruments (piano, vibraphone, guitar, bass, trumpet, drums) and, perhaps most significantly, an impressionist of unnerving skill. He could mimic anyone he heard. "I just decide, 'I think I'll do Bing Crosby,'" he once explained, "and I can do him." As a theorist might theorize, the young Sammy Davis, Jr. had little sense of his own identity, a plight compounded significantly by being black in a white-dominated world. He could do everything as anyone except himself.

In Haygood's *In Black and White*, the author cites one of Davis's 1950s girl-friends, the singer and actress Peggy King, as saying she believed that "Sammy simply wanted to be someone else." Drawing upon the substantial evidence of his interviews, Haygood concludes that the person Davis wanted to be was a white man. We hear it over and over: From another of his lovers, Helen Gallagher: "He did so want to be white." From the producer Hugh Benson: "He wanted to be white. His close friends were white. Deep down in his heart, he wanted to be white." From the director Richard Donner: "I think he would have given anything to be white." From Sammy himself to Alex Haley in his 1966 *Playboy* interview: "You'd just like to look like everybody else so that people wouldn't automatically start hating you a block away. White cat sees you walking down the street, maybe from across the street, and he never saw you before in his life, and he's not even close enough to distinguish anything about you except that you're not his color—and just for that, right there, snap, bop, bap, he HATES you! That's the injustice of it, that's what makes you cry out inside, sometimes, 'Damn, I wish I wasn't black!'"

Davis's comment doesn't really address white identity; it is a call for equal treatment, and it is predicated on a healthy sense of self-worth. Sammy may not have always known who he was, but he knew full well what he could do, and he was convinced that his talent made him no one's inferior. Haygood quotes him, in reference to the racism he faced during his brief stint in the army: "While I was performing they suddenly forgot what I was and there were times when even I could forget it. . . . It was as though my talent was giving me a pass which excluded me from their prejudice." Fishgall likewise cites him as saying: "My talent was the weapon, the power, the way for me to fight . . . the only way I might hope to affect a man's thinking. . . . I lived 24 hours a day for that hour or two at night when I could stand on that stage, facing the audience, knowing I was dancing down the barriers between us." I wonder: Did Davis really want to be white or merely to gain the social acceptance that he saw whiteness conferring in his youth? After all, he was reared on the stage, trained to work for applause. Public approval was the only validation he knew.

If Sammy wanted to be white, why did he convert to Judaism at age thirty-one? Shouldn't he have become an Episcopalian? While Fishgall portrays Davis's pursuit of the Jewish faith as Sammy always did—as a purely spiritual matter that began with the 1954 auto accident that cost Davis his left eye— Haygood is more cynical, even sarcastic about it: "He became a Jew. He was a Jew. A Negro in Jew's clothing. It was tender, and it was strange. . . . Actually, it was just Sammy being Sammy—shrewd, opportunistic, heart-touched, and childlike." Perhaps; just as significantly, though, Davis's choice of Judaism rather than any of the Christian denominations of the white mainstream seems a claim to exceptionalism rather than a submission to conformity. In embracing the faith of an ethnic minority with a legacy of transcending subjugation and persecution, Sammy sought to retain his otherness without accepting subordination—a coded blackness in the tradition of the early twentieth-century Church of God (the "Black Hebrews"), which appropriated Judaica as a way to elevate Negro pride. "These are a swinging bunch of people," Davis said of his adopted tribe. "I mean I've heard of persecution, but what they went through is ridiculous. There wasn't anybody who didn't take a shot at 'em. The whole world kept saying, 'You can't do this' and 'You can't do that,' but they didn't listen!" No, Davis might have added, they said, "Yes we can."

As the civil rights movement gained momentum and Davis matured, he grew more comfortable asserting his black identity. He performed on behalf of the NAACP and marched with the Rev. Martin Luther King, Jr., who came to value Davis as a stalwart ally. Haygood quotes Gallagher (who is white) on meeting her old beau for the first time in several years in the late 1960s: "I got backstage. . . . Everybody's black. He says, 'This is my soul brother, this is my soul sister.' I said . . . 'I knew you when you were white.'"

Gallagher must not have owned a radio, because Davis had conducted his struggle with race consciousness in public—through the music he made in the 1960s. Neither Fishgall nor Haygood delves fully into Davis's extraordinary recording career, although "Gonna Do Great Things" (whose title comes from a line in one of Davis's records, *Once in a Lifetime*) provides some details on much of Davis's most notable music. Like all jazz-pop vocalists of his era, Davis sang a mix of theater songs, popular standards, and hit tunes of the day. Everybody recorded "The Way You Look Tonight" and "My Funny Valentine," as Davis did without distinction. Important singers develop their own signature songs, however, and Sammy Davis, Jr.'s are unique in the popular canon for their absorption with the entwined themes of alienation, discontent, and pride rather than conventional romance.

In "I've Gotta Be Me," Davis pleads, "What else can I be, but what I am?" In "Stranger in Town": "Everywhere, everyone I see / Seems to wonder who I can be / But I swear no one seems to care." In "What Kind of Fool Am I?": "Why can't I cast away this mask of play and live my life?" In "Night Song": "Life is going by and I stand and wonder / Who the hell am I? In "At the Crossroads": "This way or that way, which way should I go / Toward the left or the right / The day or the night / The dark or the light / Only my heart can know." As much as any singer at Motown in the same period, Davis put the black experience on the pop charts.

Davis was obsessed with proving his worth through performance. In 1965, the year he turned forty and broke free from his long-standing contract with Mastin, he starred in a Broadway hit, *Golden Boy*, the Charles Strouse-Lee Adams musical drama adapted from Clifford Odets's play. In Davis's hours off, he promoted *Yes, I Can*, which was published the same year, and played the lead in a feature film, *A Man Called Adam*, which he also produced. He made two television specials and, Fishgall tells us, eight guest appearances on the *Tonight Show* (in addition to hosting the program once); he popped up regularly on TV shows such as *Hullabaloo*, and he did a hotel concert in San Juan, Puerto Rico, a benefit in St. Louis, and a nightclub gig in Atlantic City, among other performances around the country. And, oh—the same year, he released no fewer than five LPs. (One discography lists eight Davis albums issued in 1965.) Still, he never danced down the barrier between his ego and his insecurity. As Fishgall quotes him on the subject of his fellow Rat Packers' racist taunts, "Yeah, the jokes were offensive. But, man, look at the company I was keeping. I had to put up with it."

Both biographies have much to commend them: Haygood's breadth, vivid portraiture, and novelistic scenes; Fishgall's no-nonsense detail and readability.

(To pick nits, I might point out that Haygood makes a few minor errors: Jule Styne was not a lyricist; Jackie Wilson's "Lonely Teardrops" was not one of Motown's first hits but a Brunswick release composed by Berry Gordy before he founded Motown; and the veteran actor who did a soft-shoe in "Broadway Answers Selma" was not "the old cowboy movie star Dan Duryea" but the one-time song-and-dance man Dan Dailey.) Still, neither book really succeeds at cutting through Davis's burnished razzmatazz to illuminate the inner Sammy. Nor did either of Davis's chatty, anecdotal memoirs, for that matter.

His grave marker—a small, tasteful marble block at Forest Lawn in Glendale—is engraved "'The Entertainer' He Did It All." Indeed, what Sammy Davis, Jr. did may be all he was, and that was quite enough.

Anita O'Day

Anita O'Day, the unblushing archetype of the jazz-singing bad girl, died of a heroin overdose in 1966, or so reported at least one newspaper after she was found unconscious on the floor of a restroom in a Los Angeles office building, a hypodermic needle dangling from one of her arms. The first doctor to see her detected no heartbeat and mistook her for dead—much as several times before and after that day, jazz listeners and critics gave up on O'Day and thought her finished, only to watch her revive, unaccountably. In April of 2006, at the age of eighty-six, she released a new album, *Indestructible!*, which is also the title of a documentary film about O'Day. She defied her assessors one last time that Thanksgiving Day, when she finally did die, for real, of complications from pneumonia.

Most of the encomia published about O'Day immediately after her death portrayed her as she had been depicted since the first of her four drug busts, nearly sixty years earlier—as a jazz cliché, a hedonistic misfit who endured self-inflicted torture for her art. The *New York Times*, in the headline of its obituary, referred to O'Day as the "Hard-Living Star of the Big Band Era and Beyond," and the *Los Angeles Times*, likewise, called her the "Renowned Singer Billed as the 'Jezebel of Jazz.'" Online, the chat among devotees of jazz and cabaret singing tended toward a contrary extreme, striving to extricate O'Day's legacy as an artist from her popular image on the ground that her work should stand on its own strengths, untainted by her personal weaknesses and adventures.

O'Day took both points of view about herself in various stages of her long life. She came up with that billing, the "Jezebel of Jazz," herself. (O'Day started singing professionally in her native Chicago in 1939, a few months after the release of the Bette Davis movie *Jezebel*, and in her pert manner and clipped speech O'Day always had a hint of Davis.) She was candid about her drug use (outside the courtroom) and blunt about her thirst for kicks. "Three-quarters of the time, I was higher than a kite," she noted in her memoir, co-written with George Eells and titled *High Times Hard Times*. "All my life I've wanted to be where the action is. My ambition? Be street smart. Brazen it out. Never look back. [I] gloried in shocking people."

But when her book was published and the resulting publicity centered on her drug use, her abuse of alcohol, and her sexual exploits, O'Day recoiled. In 1981 she walked off the set of the *Today* show when she was asked how long she had done heroin, and she resented the new faces in her audience—the "different breed of cat" she perceived as "there to stare at the woman who'd done all the things they never dared to do." O'Day suffered what she called a mini-break-down and retreated to the three-room mobile home she kept in a trailer park on the outskirts of Palm Springs.

A few years later, I interviewed her briefly in her dressing room before she performed at Rainbow and Stars, the nightclub that used to be atop Rockefeller Center, and she was drunk and quick to say so. "I'm smashed," she said, by way of an introduction. "It helps me swing." With that comment—and, more elo-quently, with the enchanting, mercurial music she made later that evening—O'Day showed the error in defining her by either her substance abuse or her singing alone. The two were not inextricable; they were one.

Although O'Day performed and recorded proficiently when she was straight—in her early days, as a singer with the Gene Krupa big band, as well as in her final decades, after she kicked her sixteen-year heroin habit—O'Day did her greatest, most enduring, and most influential work while she was stoned out of her mind. More to the point, the music was not merely made possible by drugs; it was music of the drug experience, an expression of what it meant for its singer to be high. It remains potent, music of euphoria and aban-don, and the fact that it derives its potency not simply from human gifts but from the submission of those gifts to narcotics is the treachery, the exhilarating and harrowing glory, of Anita O'Day's music.

The high points of her career, in every sense, were the albums that O'Day recorded between 1954 and 1961 for Verve Records, many of them made under the direct supervision of the label's founder, Norman Granz. In the early 1990s, Granz remembered his sessions with O'Day as extraordinarily efficient, almost effortless—that is, from the time she entered the studio to the time she left, a short while later. "All the work [had to be] done in advance," Granz recalled. "I'm talking about the set-ups, the run-throughs, everything but her part," because O'Day refused to rehearse or record more than one take, as a rule. "It had to be spontaneous for her," Granz said, "regardless of what that involved for the rest of us."

Indeed, O'Day spoke from time to time of her fondness for winging recording sessions and live performances. She preferred to work with musicians who were new to her, doing arrangements she had not heard before. The pleasure that O'Day sought from music was purely experiential—kinetic, fleeting, druggy. She thought of music as something she would rather not think about, but simply feel and do. When singing with unfamiliar musicians, she once explained to an interviewer, "the whole timing is a little off balance, and it keeps you on your toes. When you get your own group going, it gets too relaxed. The way I do it, each tune is a horse race."

Most of O'Day's output for Verve can be downloaded through iTunes or the Web site of PolyGram/Universal, and the spontaneity of her singing for the label is still thrilling to hear some fifty years after the recording sessions. She blurts out phrases, dispenses with the composers' melodies, drops lines at whim, breaks words into odd-shaped bits, and slips off the charts altogether into riffs of scattershot notes and guttural quasi-notes. Her strength was not a commitment to the material, but a devotion to the moment. This approach gave her music a disarming off-handedness—genuine casualness, rather than the affected nonchalance of, say, Mel Torme. Among the best evidence: "Honeysuckle Rose," from the 1955 album *This Is Anita*, the watershed of O'Day's tenure at Verve; "Don't Be That Way," from its fine 1956 follow-up, *Pick Yourself Up with Anita O'Day*; and "Tea for Two," recorded live with a jazz combo in 1958 for *Anita O'Day at Mister Kelly's*.

O'Day's casualness could also drift into indifference, undermine the song, clash with its arrangement, or throw off the musicians in the band. Ill-suited to the meticulously elliptical melodies of Jerome Kern and the unorthodox, rangy tunes of Duke Ellington, she faked her way through demanding numbers such as "I'm Old Fashioned" and "Do Nothin' Till You Hear From Me." As she explained in interviews, melodic precision never interested her because it calls for discipline and a regard for convention. "It gets a little dumb singing melody every night," O'Day said. Nor was she particularly concerned with lyrical content. On the whole, O'Day employed words for their sounds rather than their meaning, as if they were scat syllables that also happened to be in the dictionary. She seemed deaf to lyrical subtext—and often to the text itself, sometimes ignoring even the basic sense of a song. If she wanted to swing it, she simply did not care if "Ten Cents a Dance" was supposed to be a melancholy lament.

O'Day used her voice like a jazz instrument, and it sounded like one. She had a dry, chilly tone, a sister to the sound of Miles Davis's trumpet. Like Davis, she articulated in short bursts with little or no vibrato. (When O'Day was a child, a surgeon accidentally sliced off part of her uvula during a tonsillectomy, limiting her ability to employ vibrato, even if she wanted to. On several occasions when I saw her perform, she appeared to rattle her head slightly to produce a vibrato-like effect.) Chris Connor and June Christy, both of whom followed O'Day in and out of the Stan Kenton Orchestra, emulated O'Day, as have countless lessers who have wanted to imitate that cool-jazz vibe. O'Day, for all the good work she left the world, is also to blame for Sade.

Reared as a singer in Gene Krupa's hard-driving dance band, O'Day had impeccable time. Whatever the tempo, she swung. Her scat singing had dazzling rhythmic vigor and complexity. (Will Friedwald, the author of the fine book *Jazz Singing*, has described O'Day's bravura scatting as "rhythmic exhibitionism.") Her first husband was a drummer, as was her longtime best friend John Poole, who served as the only constant in her bands for decades and who, at O'Day's insistence, first turned her on to heroin. "Rhythm is my thing," O'Day said matter-of-factly in my only interview with her. Her breath control was inadequate to sustain notes, she explained, so she compensated by accentuating time. Besides, she said, inimitably, "sustained notes are boring."

Boredom was the one thing that was intolerable to O'Day. Her music was the manifesto of her devotion to kicks at all cost. Ecstatic, indulgent, risky, excessive, and volatile, it was drug music, improvised in a state of simulated euphoria and imagined immunity. To make such music was an act of fearlessness, though not of bravery. O'Day, pickled by dope, knew no fear; but it was Ella Fitzgerald, lucid as she willed impossible scat lines into being, who was brave.

O'Day has long been an artist more difficult to accept than she is to appreciate because of the primacy of dope in her aesthetic. We like our junkies tragic, preferably taken before their time, like O'Day's long-gone contemporaries Charlie Parker and Billie Holiday (or, in rock 'n' roll, Janis Joplin and Kurt Cobain); and in their music we want to find the evidence of mad genius run wild (Parker) or gothic decay (Holiday). We know that heroin is an evil, soul-killing venom, and that is pretty much all we want to know about it. We want to hear only about heroin's inevitable betrayal, not about its seduction. We most certainly do not want to think that music as spirited and delightful as Anita O'Day's work in her prime could be good because of its debt to heroin.

"I've sometimes thought there's a Good Anita and a Bad Anita fighting for dominance," O'Day ruminated in her memoir, adding that the latter, "who wants to shock, mock and put everything down," was "definitely in control" during the early 1950s. She had plenty of practice. O'Day first earned her reputation as a bad girl while she was an actual girl, quitting high school and leaving home at age fourteen to make her living as a dance partner for hire in the Depression-era dance-a-thon events (as in *They Shoot Horses, Don't They?*, speaking of heroin). Recalling the work years later, O'Day described it as "the endurance business." As such, it clearly trained her well. She changed her surname from Colton to O'Day—"pig Latin [for] dough, which is what I hoped to make"—and started singing at the dance-a-thons for extra income. By the time she was nineteen, she was singing in Chicago's Off-Beat Club, where Gene Krupa heard her and signed her in 1941.

She was attractive—"Anita O'Day could stand and let the customers be happy just looking, but for good measure she swings the hottest songs," wrote a critic for the *Chicago Tribune* before O'Day joined Krupa—but declined to serve as a "trinket to decorate the bandstand," insisting on wearing a band jacket "just like the guys" in the orchestra. It was a radical step at the time, and one that prompted early rumors that O'Day was a lesbian. "She was a wild chick, all right," Krupa later said, "but how she can sing!"

Her best-known recording for Krupa was "Let Me Off Uptown," a duet with Roy Eldridge, the brilliant trumpeter and occasional singer. The record was scandalous in its day for the saucy interplay between Eldridge and O'Day, a black man and a white woman, not to mention the fact that O'Day asked, in the lyrics, to be dropped off alone in the section of town where "it's rhythm that you feel" and "it's pleasure you're about." Rhythm and pleasure, race and sex: all O'Day needed was drugs to cement her name as a hepcat girl gone wild, and she took care of that with her first bust, for possession of marijuana, in 1947.

"I tried everything—I was curious. I went my own way," O'Day told me, not long before she abruptly snapped that the interview was over because she was bored. She had nothing to say that she hadn't told someone else before, and she couldn't stand to repeat herself. "This is corny," she said. She chastised me for failing to come up with questions she had never heard. She finished her drink and said, "I think this stuff is keeping me alive."

Bobby Darin
Roman Candle

B obby Darin, the changeling prince of American popular music, has been an object of fascination, suspicion, adulation, and ridicule since the height of his popularity, in the early 1960s. His hit records in myriad styles—including, among others, the early rockers "Splish Splash" and "Queen of the Hop," the swinging standards "Mack the Knife" and "Beyond the Sea," and the folk ballad "If I Were a Carpenter"—endure all over the radio dial, and much of his recording catalog still sells on CD. Since his death from heart disease at age thirty-seven, Darin has been the subject of several books; most notable is an examination of the singer's life and work by David Evanier, a former senior editor of *The Paris Review* and the author of a good biography of the Mafia's favorite tenor, Jimmy Roselli. Like *Bobby Darin: A Life*, by Michael Seth Starr, Evanier's *Roman Candle: The Life of Bobby Darin* was published in time to ride the coat-tails of *Beyond the Sea*, a film about the entertainer directed by and starring the lifelong Darin fan Kevin Spacey, which opened in December 2004.

Evanier's portrait, true to its title, is one of a bright talent that soared quickly and erupted in a flash of glory. The facts of Darin's life certainly tempt cliché and hyperbole. Born Walden Robert Cassotto, to an impoverished single mother and a father who skipped away without ever learning of the pregnancy, Darin was raised in the tenements and housing projects of Harlem and New York's Lower East Side by his maternal grandmother, a would-be singer turned morphine addict whose husband, a two-bit hood called Big Sam Curly, died in prison while serving time for petty larceny. Darin grew up thinking that his mother was his sister. (Late in his life, when he was considering a run for political office, she decided to tell him the truth before reporters looked up his birth records.) Having been stricken with rheumatic fever as a child, he suffered from a weak heart that precluded horseplay, alienated him from his peers on the street, drew him inward, and threatened to cut short his life. His family doctor expected him to live no more than sixteen years—perhaps twenty-one, with luck.

Endowed with a high I.Q. as well as a knack for music, Darin was admitted to the elite Bronx High School of Science, where he joined a swing combo as the drummer (using a borrowed kit). He entered Hunter College on a scholarship but quit after one term, impatient to move on to the next thing—thereupon setting the pattern for his career. In 1958, when Darin was twenty-two, "Splish Splash," which he had written in thirty-five minutes, became a Top 10 hit and made him a star of the young music for young people: rock-and-roll. The next year he shook off rock to sing Tin Pan Alley numbers with a swing band and had a far bigger hit with "Mack the Knife." Quickly established as a major attraction on the jet-set nightclub circuit, he soon shifted styles again and wrote a couple of country-and-western hits ("Things" and "You're the Reason I'm Living," both of which became country standards); then he decided to record some folk music. He signed a multi-picture deal to act on screen and got an Oscar nomination for his performance as a cocksure World War II pilot in *Captain Newman, M.D.* (1964). After recording one album of Broadway hits, one geared for children (the songs from *Dr. Dolittle*), and a few others, Darin decided to abandon traditional show business altogether. He gave away most of his possessions and moved into a trailer in Big Sur, where he spent his time chopping wood and reading at the public library. He stopped wearing his toupee, grew a moustache and long sideburns, and started writing and singing bleak protest songs under the Dylanesque name of Bob Darin. By the early 1970s he had given that up to make money again, and he was back in a tux and under a toup, snapping his fingers to "Mack the Knife" in his own TV variety series. On December 20, 1973, he died after unsuccessful open-heart surgery.

Evanier makes a commendable effort to explicate this made-for-movie-treatment life story, although he falls short in his analysis of the music that ultimately raises Darin above gossip fodder, and he fails to come fully to terms with Darin's absorption with the counterculture of the late 1960s and early 1970s. Frustrated and enraged by his childhood poverty, confounded by a vague sense of wrongness at home, Darin set out to use his intelligence and creative talent to prove his worth to himself and the world. "Bobby was the unloved orphan, at least in his own mind, dispossessed and homeless," Evanier writes. "There was always a fierce cynical calculation in Bobby's moves. . . . " Without doubt, the careering in Darin's mode of careerism often seemed conspicuously tactical if not desperate—the quixotic strategy of a man so determined to prove he was somebody that he tried to become everybody.

Too bookish and fragile for the projects, too rough around the edges for the New York intelligentsia to whom the Bronx High School of Science introduced him, Darin felt lost in his youth and carried a quality of lonesomeness to the end of his life. "I didn't belong, at school or anywhere else," he told the jazz writer Gene Lees. You can see it in the glossy pictures taken for his record jackets and movie posters: there's a distance in his eyes, and when he smiles, his brow scrunches in a quizzical way, as if his face were surprised to be called on to look happy. You can't miss it in the video clips of him performing, especially in the last footage of Darin in concert, taped for television in 1972 and issued in a CD-DVD packaged titled *Aces Back to Back*. He would often sing with his eyes closed or nearly so, even on up-tempo numbers, and he had a habit of gazing off to the side when he spoke, like a schoolboy whose mind is elsewhere. Above all you can hear it in his music, especially in ballads such as "Black Coffee," "The Gal That Got Away," and the high point of *Aces Back to Back*, "Alone Again (Naturally)," an insipid, bubble-gummy tune that Darin transforms into a wrenching capitulation to despair.

Evanier, echoing a theme of previous books about Darin, portrays the singer's outsize ambition as a side-effect of his illness. He quotes Harriet Wasser, Darin's onetime publicist:

> He was consumed with his mortality . . . He was going to show that if he was not going to live long, he was going to give everything he had. Because he wanted people to remember him.

As Darin once explained to Connie Francis, his girlfriend and female counterpart in teen idoldom, he wanted "to establish myself as a legend by the time I'm twenty-five." In the same vein he told the *New York Post* in 1959, "I want to do everything that anybody's ever done, but better." The following year he told *Life* magazine, "I want to make it faster than anyone has ever made it before . . . I want to be in the upper echelon of show business to such an extent it's ridiculous."

Bobby Darin's ambition was more frightful than ridiculous. Still, when seen as a strategy for combat with the Grim Reaper, it begins to make sense; in fact, it takes on a dark poignancy.

Although Evanier gives due attention to Darin's preoccupation with death, he does not do justice to the artist's extraordinary treatment of the subject in several of his best-known songs. In his one-page analysis of "Mack the Knife," Evanier points out that the Brecht-Weill composition was originally titled "Moritat" ("Murder Ballad") and traditionally performed as a dirge. He calls Darin's radical upending of the piece "joyous," "celebratory," and "warm-hearted." But how could someone with a life-threatening heart ailment find such joy and cause for celebration in death? Rather, I think, Darin seems to be mocking death with the extravagant zeal of his "Mack the Knife"; the record is a masterstroke of satire, a punitive swipe at the singer's ever-present antagonist. He does the same thing in "Clementine," a hard-swinging twist on the old American lament to a young woman who falls from a bridge and drowns, and in "Artificial Flowers," an even harder-swinging take on the story of an orphaned child who freezes to death in her tenement room. The three records are as unnerving as they are exhilarating.

Children of the rock era have always been quick to ridicule Darin for his frequent metamorphoses. Neil Young told an interviewer in *Rolling Stone*, "I used to be pissed off at Bobby Darin because he changed styles so much." (Young went on to say that he later came to see Darin as "a fucking genius.") At the same time, no music has been more susceptible to mutation than rock, and many of its most revered figures have long histories of reinvention. Bob Dylan, the Beatles, David Bowie, Madonna, and even Neil Young all changed styles—and appearances and, in some instances, attitudes—repeatedly without alienating many fans for long. It seems to me that Darin's sin was not really that he took up different sorts of music but that he played to different audiences—moreover, to different generations. In his switch from rock-and-roll to swing he left the Boomers for their parents, an unforgivable transgression in a culture where age is the dominant class system. When Darin attempted to return to the rock generation with his folk-protest work, he was no longer welcome.

Evanier is rough on Darin's venture into gritty, topical music. "He not only removed the tuxedo, he removed the essence of his voice—his whole soul—in the folk period," he writes.

> When Bobby muted his voice, put on his leather cowboy hat, moustache, and sideburns and sang mournfully of dusty roads and buried bodies of convicts in the Arkansas dirt, he did a reasonable impersonation of Dylan, Dave Van Ronk, Arlo and Woody Guthrie, and Pete Seeger. But why? An artist's obligation is to probe his own soul, not to impersonate the soul of others.

Actually, Darin sounds much less like Dylan, Van Ronk, and those others on his folk-oriented records than he sounds like Frank Sinatra, Tony Bennett, and Johnny Mercer on his swing albums. (Evanier himself mistakes Mercer's voice for Darin's and attributes to the latter a line that the former sings on their album of duets, *Two of a Kind*.) His singing on "If I Were a Carpenter," "In Memoriam" (an homage to his friend and idol Robert F. Kennedy, whose assassination devastated him), "Song for a Dollar" (a scathing critique of his own nightclub years), and other tunes of their ilk is intimate, unaffected, and deeply emotive. Darin sounds very much as if he is probing his soul musically, perhaps for the first time. "Years ago I had the choice between ethnic and plastic, and I chose plastic," he explained late in his life. "And twelve or thirteen years later, it dawned on me that I'd chosen the wrong one." According to Walter Raim, an old friend of Darin's who arranged and conducted his first folk albums, "Bobby saw in folk music a sophistication of some kind, a higher calling. He had in his mind that he was doing something more important than singing Las Vegas standards. He was attracted to the realness, the down-to-earth thing." It is startling to read this and to think of Darin as a paragon of authenticity.

Ultimately, "If I Were a Carpenter" is surely Darin's truest moment as an artist. His theme, for once, is the illusory nature of his own identity. Would you still love me, he asks, if I were not what I seem, if I were someone much simpler? Evanier is scarcely the only Darin fan inclined to answer no.

Susannah McCorkle

I cannot say I had the pleasure of hearing Susannah McCorkle sing. I heard her perform many times—at least a dozen, perhaps twenty times from the spring of 1981, when my late friend Roy Hemming, a pedigreed cabaret hound, first brought me to see her at Michael's Pub, to the autumn of 2000, when she had her final run at the Oak Room in the Algonquin. I went to three of her last ten shows. On all those occasions, I rarely drew from McCorkle mere pleasure, but derived many other things of value—illumination, wonderment, flashes of horror, and stimulation to self-reflection and doubt. I admired her deeply and cheered the bravery of her work, though all I ever wrote about her were a few sentences in 1991.

On one of those last nights at the Algonquin, I brought as my guest the singer Jane Monheit, who, at the age of twenty-two, was a rising sensation in jazz. I was working on a magazine piece about Monheit, and I wanted to see how the green, young singer would respond to this veteran who embodied cloudy grays. (Monheit remarked, in the idiom of her generation, that

McCorkle was "awesome.") When I filed the story, I included a note about McCorkle to my editor:

> *McCorkle might be a great subject some day. Right now, she's in a weird lull. The room's half empty most nights. She's an acquired taste and hard to take sometimes. I think a lot of her own fans sort of take her for granted these days. But I think she's going to be one of those people who everybody rediscovers late in life.*

I pictured McCorkle aging into a figure like Blossom Dearie, an odd bird revered after a long career as an endangered species.

About six months after that, McCorkle rendered moot my theory and all other theories about her future by jumping out of the window of her sixteenth-floor apartment on Manhattan's Upper West Side. In the months to follow, the awful story of her death brought more attention to McCorkle than she had ever enjoyed in life. Encomia to McCorkle and her music appeared in *Time, Entertainment Weekly*, and *The New Yorker*, and the writer Linda Dahl, author of two books on women in jazz—*Morning Glory: A Biography of Mary Lou Williams* and *Stormy Weather: The Music and Lives of a Century of Jazzwomen*—began work on a biography. That book, called *Haunted Heart*, after the ballad by Arthur Schwartz and Howard Dietz that McCorkle recorded on her final album, was published by the University of Michigan Press in 2006. Subtitled "The Secret Life and Tragic Death of a Great American Songbird," it is an intimate and blunt book, full of details about McCorkle's spicy romances, along with material on the creative work that makes her worthy of attention years after her death.

McCorkle, who would have turned sixty in the year the book was published, was a child of the rock era who sang the music of another generation—the Tin Pan Alley hits and theater songs of the first half of the twentieth century. The status of this material as a canon, the "Great American Songbook," was not yet solidified when McCorkle started singing, in the early 1970s. For some years, she made a specialty of tunes composed in the 1920s and 1930s, many of them sung originally by Billie Holiday, her first idol and vocal model, or by quasi-proto-feminists such as Mae West, Bessie Smith, Ethel Waters, and Mildred Bailey.

In Dahl's telling, McCorkle's choice of musical direction was a radical one that defied the hippie culture of the young singer's native Berkeley. But the history is more complicated. The Bay Area scene was infused with kitschy nostalgia for the 1920s and the early 1930s. While McCorkle was still in school, Janis Joplin was growling songs by Bessie Smith and Big Mama Thornton and releasing them on albums with cover art by Robert Crumb that captured the

Haight-Ashbury sensibility by appropriating the 1920s. Mama Cass made "Dream a Little Dream of Me" a hit in 1968. The Grateful Dead, a mutated jug band, would jam all night to old numbers like "Ain't Nobody's Business." For a Berkeley girl to turn to the early swing of the 1920s and 1930s was less a rejection of the music of her peers than a distillation of an element in its essence—a claim not to exceptionalism, but to purity.

When Paul McCartney manufactured his own vo-de-oh-do ditties for the Beatles, John Lennon mocked them as "granny music." He nailed both their ridiculousness and their power. What made songs such as "When I'm Sixty-Four" and "Honey Pie" palatable, even appealing, to baby boomers was the fact that they skipped over a full generation. They were granny music, not mommy-and-daddy music. So it was with McCorkle's early repertoire: she would do an old Rodgers and Hart tune such as "Manhattan," from 1925, but not Rodgers and Hammerstein's "My Favorite Things," from her parents' record collection. She was not close to her mother or her father, and she would not trust a song under thirty, at least not until she had been performing for a few years and matured as an artist.

She began singing professionally at twenty-five, while living in Rome. A drifting expatriate, McCorkle had gone to Europe to write fiction and ended up falling under the sway of a group of continentals infatuated with vintage swing and the free, fun pre-war America that it evoked. She moved on to London, where other Americans such as the writer and cornet player Richard Sudhalter and the English pianist Keith Ingham were part of a cliquish swing revival. It was a parochial movement, rigid, zealous, almost a cult—and thus ideal for McCorkle at the time. She had attended fourteen schools before college, tugged around with her mother and two sisters as her father, who suffered from acute depression, bounced from job to job. Rootless and insecure, McCorkle no doubt found comfort in the impassioned surety of the swing revivalists.

As Dahl points out, McCorkle learned her craft by mimicking Billie Holiday. So did countless other singers inspired by Holiday; original voices frequently begin as imitations. My wife, who is a singer, admits to an early debt to Doris Day, who, she adds, started by imitating Ella Fitzgerald, who, she notes, began by emulating Connee Boswell. (No anxieties of influence here, just a lot of keen apprenticeships.) All of them found their own styles quickly, and so did McCorkle, who studied early jazz singers so assiduously that she probably knew who Boswell was copying. By the time I first saw McCorkle, just a few years after she had moved from London to build a career in Manhattan, the only traces of Holiday remained in the way she hung under a note—sometimes too far under—and let her vibrato crumble at the end of a phrase for dramatic effect. She developed a singular approach, working from both her strengths and her weaknesses.

A good (though not great) writer of prose fiction and nonfiction, McCorkle wrote short stories and worked on drafts of novels until her last days. One story written in her twenties, "Ramona by the Sea," was awarded an O. Henry Prize and anthologized after its initial publication in *Mademoiselle*. As a singer she remained a storyteller, attentive not only to the meanings of individual words, phrases, and lines of lyrics, but also to the narrative contours of the song. At this McCorkle had few equals other than Mabel Mercer, Frank Sinatra, and Sylvia Syms. Her skill at finding the shape of a song—or molding a flat song into a form of her devising—is especially striking in "The Waters of March," the chant-like tune by Antonio Carlos Jobim that she made one of her signatures. (A former linguistics student and onetime translator, McCorkle was fluent in Portuguese and understood the fragility of Jobim's songs.) Through the careful modulation of tone and the astute use of dynamics, she carries us with the spring waters from the death of winter to the new season's promise of rebirth. On her collection of Cole Porter tunes, *Easy to Love*, she even builds "Let's Do It," the listiest song on the composer's long list of list-songs, to a slyly referential climax.

McCorkle's most extraordinary gift as an artist was her command of the dark colors in the emotional spectrum. "I definitely became a singer in order to sing sad songs," Dahl quotes her as saying. She sought out music of heartbreak and loss, and she found it in varied quarters—in the blues of Bessie Smith and Mildred Bailey, naturally, and also in little-known theater songs from the teary scenes in forgotten shows, such as "This Funny World," a paean to futility from Rodgers and Hart's *Betsy*, a Broadway fizzle staged in 1926. McCorkle was uniquely adept at unearthing the melancholy parts of well-known songs—songs within the songs. Her masterpiece of internal excavation was surely her version of the hoary Irving Berlin anthem "There's No Business Like Show Business." She slowed the tempo nearly to a halt and clung to a few bittersweet phrases that most singers gloss over ("they smile when they are low," "brokenhearted, but you go on"), transforming a show-stopper into a piece that stops the heart. In the absence of sorrowful lyrics, McCorkle was content to upend whole songs through interpretation, as she did with Harold Arlen and Yip Harburg's tune for the Tin Man in *The Wizard of Oz*, "If I Only Had a Heart."

That is to say, she sought herself in the material. Ingham, her onetime mentor and second husband, groaned about this to Dahl. "By 1982 or so, every song had to relate to something totally in her own life somehow, everything had to be from a point of view that she agreed with or was about her, and she wouldn't sing many, many songs because she objected to them," he said, belittling McCorkle for being an artist rather than a professional. She was a tortured soul; Dahl reports that, in clinical terms, she suffered from bipolar II disorder. As an artist first and a psychiatric patient second, McCorkle gave voice to her torment in her music. After reading Dahl's book, I downloaded eight of McCorkle's CDs onto my iPod and listened to them closely for the first time in several years. I found the music more beautiful and sadder than I recalled. It is precious work of profound melancholy and hopeful—sometimes desperate—yearning entwined with a stark fatalism.

As several musicians mentioned to Dahl, McCorkle was self-centered and ambitious. Hel-*lo*! She was in *show business*. Her self-absorption was more conspicuous and out of place in her prose writing. McCorkle published several essays on her musical influences and interests, such as Ethel Waters, Mae West, and Irving Berlin, in American Heritage, and they are all a bit too much about Susannah McCorkle. In the piece ostensibly about Berlin, the word "I" appears twenty-four times in the first twenty sentences. The fiction of hers that I have seen, much the same, seems limited by its author's experience and not fully imagined; it reads like journal entries.

Speaking of which, I know McCorkle was a copious correspondent and journal-keeper. She wrote to me half a dozen times, and I scarcely knew her. Her journals, along with a vast archive of other materials—comprising nearly all her unpublished writings, her music, her business and personal records, even the contents of the hard drive on her computer—are in repository at the New York Public Library, a donation of McCorkle's estate. According to the librarian in charge of the archive, Dahl had access to much, but not all, of this material. (Many of the electronic files were damaged and unreadable until the library had them recovered.) Dahl's book renders McCorkle artfully, but incompletely. As one still hungry for more information to help unravel the enigma that Susannah McCorkle remains, I look forward to a second biography of her, drawing more fully on the archival materials. An additional book on McCorkle might also help salvage her from her dubious status as the singer who committed suicide.

When McCorkle died, I was in London with my wife. She and I had divvied up the sections of the *International Herald Tribune* to read over breakfast, and I heard Karen gasp when she saw a sizable photograph of McCorkle in the paper. "Good for Susannah!" she said. As soon as she realized that the photo was an illustration not for a profile of McCorkle, but for her obituary, Karen started to quake. McCorkle's death was a tragedy for many people—her admirers, of course, and also for a great many more who never heard her music and came to know her only as the suicide girl. Today, most of McCorkle's CDs are out of print, and her longtime label, Concord, is doing little to preserve her legacy. There should be a second book about McCorkle, and then others, if only to keep us thinking about her and returning to the dark well of her music.

PART III

Blues and the Abstract Truth

A Hundred Years of Blues

In the lexicon of upholstery, no other material has the cheeky pizzazz of Naugahyde Zodiac Glitter Vinyl. You know the stuff, if you are familiar with the 1970s; it's a gleaming polymer blanket filled with neon-colored sparkles. When I was an undergraduate at NYU some time ago, I knew a high-spirited young woman in Greenwich Village who owned a handbag made of it, and I think of her and what that handbag expressed, multiplied exponentially, every time I walk into Linda's Lounge, a small blues bar on West 51st Street on the South Side of Chicago. The place is covered floor to ceiling with Naugahyde Zodiac Glitter Vinyl in cherry red—the bar, the walls, the shelves, the drawers of the cabinets, everything. Linda's Lounge has a coating of festive glitz, an almost literal insulation from the bleakness outside, where empty lots between buckling clapboard buildings serve as both garbage dumps and playgrounds.

Like half a million other music fans from around the world, I came to Chicago in May 2003 for the city's twentieth annual Blues Festival, and I dropped by Linda's after the scheduled events on Saturday night. (I had come to know Linda's and Linda herself earlier in the year, while doing a writer-in-residency at the University of Chicago, located nearby in Hyde Park.) There were fewer than a dozen people in the club when I walked in, a bit after ten o'clock—a tiny, quiet old fellow in a brown suit and a rakish, diamond-crown fedora; an ebullient middle-aged man in a black, double-breasted sport jacket with no lapels; and two youngish women, one in a ruffled pink dress, the other in a one-piece black-lace pants outfit configured with an almond skin-tone lining to give the impression that she was practically naked; and several others. I recognized a few of them, either from my previous nights at Linda's or from the snapshots of the same ensemble during their many previous nights at Linda's, which were Scotch-taped neatly onto a long mirror across from the bar. To the right of the bar, a quartet played a set of soft jazz and soul ballads, while one couple slow-danced. I was the only white person there, until around eleven o'clock.

Then, carloads of people, none of them African American, began emptying into Linda's, and the place changed. The band, apparently anticipating the onslaught, dropped the soul-jazz in favor of blues warhorses like "Sweet Home Chicago" and brought on a vocalist, L-Roy Perryman, a brassy showman in a blue jumpsuit who bellowed and strutted through the crowd. The bartender discreetly removed the basket of free hard-boiled eggs from the bar. One of the new customers pulled out a 35-mm camera with a telephoto lens and followed Perryman around. In the midst of singing "The Thrill Is Gone," Perryman turned on his heels and mugged into the lens. The quiet old fellow snapped down the brim of his hat and strode out. The couple that had been dancing followed him. By midnight, Linda's was packed tight. I counted thirty-seven white faces—the pair of women in the pink-and-black lace were the only African Americans left at the bar. The decibel level seemed to have doubled. L-Roy Perryman boomed into the microphone, "Are you having a good time?"

"Yeah!" the crowd replied in ragged unison.

"Isn't this a party?" Perryman prodded them on. "I say, isn't this a party?"

"Yeah!" the crowd responded, hooting and applauding.

The woman in the pink turned to her friend in the lace, and she muttered, "Yeah," oozing sarcasm. "For who?"

* * *

In 1903, a theatrical revue called *An English Daisy* opened in Boston. Although it would never reach Broadway, the show is noteworthy for marking the professional debut of composer Jerome Kern, the father of the American musical. In the same year, Claude Debussy started work on *La Mer*, an experiment in orchestral music that brought Impressionism to the symphony. That year, too, the *New York Herald* published a series of articles about a bouncy new style of popular song being produced in a row of storefronts on West 28th Street between Sixth and Seventh Avenues, which the author, the songwriter Monroe Rosenfeld, named "Tin Pan Alley." Bing Crosby, whose intimate, conversational way of singing would make him the first major pop star of the age of electronically produced music, was born in 1903, as well. At some point in that year, also, the African American bandleader and composer W. C. Handy was waiting in a rail station in Tutwiler, Mississippi, and he heard a black musician playing a guitar with the blade of a knife—"the weirdest music I had ever heard," Handy later wrote, thereupon documenting the earliest known performance of the blues.

In 2003, then, there were no fewer than five centennials of events that, while varying in prominence when they occurred, turned out to be touchstones in the history of twentieth-century music: one in musical theater, one in formal music, two in popular song, and one in folk music. As far as I know, three of the anniversaries came and went largely unnoticed, with only Bing Crosby's birthday and the emergence of the blues commemorated prominently. In honor of Crosby, there was an academic conference at Gonzaga University (his alma mater), and there were a few CD reissues. To celebrate the blues, there was a mammoth, year-long hundredth birthday party, launched with a Congressional resolution, proclaiming the period of February 1, 2003, to January 31, 2004, as "The Year of the Blues." The act conferred institutional legitimacy upon the anniversary and supplied it with a slogan that proved handy (no pun intended) to innumerable concert promoters, record companies, film and television producers, and T-shirt manufacturers. More than thirty blues CDs were released, many of them reissues packaged as centennial commemoratives, and dozens of blues festivals were staged around the country under "Year of the Blues" banners.

The motive force behind the "Year of the Blues" was Paul Allen, the middle-aged co-founder of Microsoft, and his Experience Music Project, the multimedia shrine to rock 'n' roll and postwar popular culture that he built in Seattle in June 2000. Part museum, part research center, part video arcade, the EMP houses a collection of memorabilia such as the Martin 00–17 acoustic guitar that Bob Dylan played as a young Greenwich Village folkie; it maintains an archive of documents of interest to pop-culture scholars and critics (for whom the EMP has hosted annual conferences on popular music); and it entertains some 40,000 to 60,000 tourists per month with interactive kiosks devoted to subjects such as the twelve-bar blues and Jimi Hendrix's lyrics—all in a flashy building designed by Frank Gehry. Working under Allen, Robert Santelli, the EMP's executive director, helped set up the Blues Music Foundation (not to be confused with the decades-old Blues Foundation, which oversees the annual blues awards, the Handys) and he used it to persuade Congress to make its proclamation on the blues. (Santelli is a former rock critic and author of several books, among them a reference work on the blues, a listener's guide to Sixties rock, and a book about rock drummers.) Allen and Santelli, through EMP and the Blues Music Foundation, organized and supervised the whole "Year of the Blues," a music project which, like the EMP, was essentially an elaborate, expertly coordinated effort by aging baby boomers to enshrine the enthusiasms of their youth.

Boomers hardly invented the blues, of course; being at least one hundred years old, the music predates the postwar generation by no less than half a century. The blues took form in the cotton-rich delta surrounding the Tutwiler station not long before W. C. Handy discovered it there. It had been invented by sharecroppers and the itinerant black musicians who entertained them on Saturday nights, an art form pieced together with local materials—the anguish and fury of a subjugated people, coded in lyrics about romantic suffering and defiance, set to three chords (tonic, dominant, and subdominant) transformed with syncopated rhythms and "blue" tonalities adapted from African music, and performed on inexpensive, portable instruments, usually guitars. (Drums were long banned on most Southern plantations.) What W. C. Handy likely heard as "weird" was the blues' unapologetic rawness—the moan of a singer unconcerned with formal notions of sound purity and intonation, the extra-musical scream of guitar strings scraped with a knife blade, the quality of a wound exposed.

David "Honeyboy" Edwards has lived the whole history of the blues. The great-grandson of slaves and son of sharecroppers, Edwards started singing and playing guitar on the Delta plantation where he lived in 1929, at the age of fourteen. He was a protégé of Big Joe Williams and friends with Sonny Boy Williamson and Tommy Johnson. Among blues aficionados, it is a badge of high seriousness to know something about Robert Johnson (no relation to Tommy), the iconic master of Delta blues who is said to have sold his soul to the devil in exchange for his guitar style. Honeyboy Edwards was at Robert Johnson's side on the last night of his life.

Edwards, who is still as smoothly charming as his perennial nickname suggests, performs forty to fifty shows per year, and he says he would do more if the work were there. When he's not traveling, he rests up and entertains friends in his apartment. It is a cozy place, a few rooms in a square brick building about thirty feet from the elevated lanes of Interstate 90 in South Chicago. To get to it, you walk into an alley, through a gate topped with barbed wire, and up three flights of pine-board steps. I came to see him under the wing of a mutual friend on a Saturday afternoon in the spring of 2003, and he was not expecting me, but he was impeccably dressed in pressed black pants, a blue checked shirt, and suspenders. He was on his bed, watching a rerun of *The Addams Family*. There was a suitcase atop a bureau on the left side of his bed, ready to go, and a Bible on a flaking radiator to the right. If you were sitting up on his mattress, as he was, you would look ahead and see a wall covered with newspaper and magazine clips, record covers, snapshots, and other memorabilia of his seven decades in the blues—quite a thing to ponder before you go to sleep.

"I'll tell you how the blues started," Edwards said, his hands folded neatly on his lap. "It came from our side of the world. The blues started from slavery, by people working in slavery. They start to holler songs, and they holler all day to make the day pass by quick. That's how the blues started, and it's been the blues ever since."

Edwards spoke quickly and confidently, pausing only now and then to make sure I was following him. "The young musicians don't have their own style," he said, shaking his head. "No, they just play whatever they learned and get up there, playing fast. They're not thinking about it. They got no feeling to it, no sir. They just pick up the guitar, and they run off. They're mostly clowning. They're not playing no music. They ain't got no feeling to it in there. Instead, they look like they're just trying to put on a show. The young musician, out there dressed up and going on and on—and doing nothing.

"I'll tell you, some guys can make so many chords it don't sound good. They're making too many to put into one place—you know what I mean? You take another guy with one chord—only one chord. He just hold one chord, and everybody looking at him all day. One chord can kill a man dead. One chord and hold it there, you can kill a man dead.

"The blues is the tallest mountain," Edwards said, and he crossed his arms and grinned.

I mentioned that I didn't recall hearing that phrase before. "I just made it up," he barked, clearly offended. "What do you think I been trying to tell you? That's the blues!"

An astute critic of his art, Honeyboy Edwards provides a cogent analysis of the shift within the blues over the years—from an early modernism, giving primacy to personal expression, to a mandarin absorption with craft. The blues, once an intimate, veracious, and mercurial way of telling idiosyncratic stories about men and women and everything that unites and divides them, has grown progressively orthodox, self-referential, and fixated on instrumental technique. In other words, the blues has become more like its miscegenational spawn: pop music of the classic-rock era.

I asked James Cotton, the revered elder of blues harmonica long associated with Muddy Waters, how the music has changed since he started playing sixty years ago. "The first thing is," he said with a chuckle, "it's changed from black to white—it's changed from black to white. People listened to the Rolling Stones playing the music, and they wanted to know where it come from." Indeed, the Stones, Led Zeppelin, Cream, and other blues-oriented rock bands of the '60s opened the ears of young white people to the blues; but in an aural equivalent of the Heisenberg principle, the listeners altered the music. A powerful bloc of ticket buyers and record collectors, they sought the blues that reminded them most of classic rock.

"When I came to Chicago in the '70s, blues was considered a music of older people, of Southern people, of people who came from poverty—not upscale, not hip, not fresh—already old and a little stale," recalls Bruce Iglauer, the founder of Alligator Records, one of the leading independent blues labels. "Then white people discovered it, and there began to be good gigs for blues musicians working for white people. Black blues artists were beginning to see that there was a good future performing for white audiences who got turned on to blues through rock 'n' roll. There was the economic reality of 'Hey, some white people are going to pay some money to hear us,' and it's going to be a more secure existence, because the black clubs, if they had a bad night, the likelihood of not getting paid was pretty great."

Because the sound of the electric guitar dominated rock, young whites gravitated toward guitar-heavy blues, and veteran bluesmen known for their guitar work—chief among them, B. B. King—found a new audience. (King's peers who were primarily vocalists, such as Bobby "Blue" Bland, would never achieve the same kind of crossover success.) "Suddenly," says Iglauer, "the flashy guitar solo became much more the centerpiece of the musical event than the words or the singing."

Bob Koester, a firebrand who has run the jazz and blues label Delmark Records for fifty years, assesses the rise of guitar worship more bluntly. "A lot of white blues fans," he says, "remind me of the idiot who goes to the opera house to listen to the orchestra."

Even listening has come to seem less and less the point in recent years, as the House of Blues chain (run by "Blues Brother" Dan Aykroyd) and tourist-oriented nightclubs such as B.L.U.E.S. in North Chicago have repackaged the blues as an entertainment experience. Artful, idealized evocations of gritty authenticity, they have made the blues into a theme-park ride—a simulation that feels a little dangerous but doesn't really take you anywhere. At the same time, the rise of blues festivals across the country has further commodified the blues as a feel-good music geared largely to whites. There were no fewer than 280 such events in 2003, in locations from Anchorage to Fort Lauderdale. Chartered to conjure an atmosphere of casual fun in the name of boosting tourism and civic pride, the festivals use live blues as background music for families and young singles checking out the concessions and each other.

"I think that what happened to the blues," says Tom Mazzolini, director of the San Francisco Blues Festival, the longest-running event of its kind in the country, "is that it became a kind of a boogie thing. A good time—'Let's have a party!' I really feel that the blues has gotten away from what this music is supposed to be about. Once upon a time, it was a way of culture, a way of life. I think that a lot of people who go to blues events don't think, 'What is this music about?' I think a lot of events are just perpetuating a lot of beer drinking."

From a financial point of view, Mazzolini says, festivals are essential to the blues' survival. Record labels and musicians cater to the festival audience, which they need to stay in business. "I'm all for that," he says, but he worries about the spiritual toll on the music. "Every community in America wants to have a blues festival. You know what it is? It's a generic festival. It's the same names going from town to town. Where's the uniqueness? Where's the magic?"

To their municipal sponsors, moreover, blues festivals serve as a civic gesture toward black culture—but an abstracted black culture of the past, only distantly connected to the contemporary world of hip hop and its less-than-boosterish view of urban life. "The blues has become a good civic device," notes Koester, who struggled for decades to give African American artists broader exposure. "I mean, white politicians who used to try to 'keep the niggers in the alley' now invite them to perform in the city's annual blues festival."

I spent two days at this year's Chicago Blues Festival and had a few beers myself. There was some exquisite music—Otis Rush, as fierce as ever—as well as too many interchangeable bands noodling predictably. Within two hours on one afternoon, I heard "Sweet Home Chicago" three times. I stopped some people at random to ask them about their interest in the blues, until one fellow stumped me with better questions than my own. He was a casually dressed African American man who said he was thirty-two and named Thomas. "Do you want to talk to me because this is a blues festival and I'm black?" he asked firmly. "Because that would be presumptuous."

I showed him my credentials and told him I was trying to get a feeling for the crowd.

"I can't help you there," he said. "But do you mind if I ask you something? What the fuck does it matter if I'm black or if these other people are white, green, or purple? We all came out for this music. What more do you need to know?"

* * *

When W. C. Handy was walking through Tutwiler station, American popular music had not yet pulled out of the nineteenth century. The songs of the day, published in sheet music for womenfolk to play in parlor musicales, tended toward sing-along novelties and Victorian laments such as "Oh Promise Me." They had their moments and passed as all fashions do—much like innumerable other musical styles popular at one time or another during the twentieth century: ragtime, the Charleston, boogie-woogie, the rumba, calypso, doo-wop, disco. . . . Yet the blues endure. The music's historic masters—Robert Johnson, Bessie Smith, Charley Patton, Blind Lemon Jefferson, and their progeny—have achieved iconic status, with their music preserved, fetishized, and repackaged in increasingly elaborate boxed sets. Their music is a canon, like the classical repertoire, interpreted and imitated by generation after generation of admirers, black and white, male and female.

"The music is so universal," says Susan Tedeschi, a Grammy-nominated blues guitarist and singer who is in her mid-thirties, white, and female. "It talks about the relationship between a man and a woman. That's what Son House used to say: 'Blues is about a man and a woman—everything else is monkey junk.' He's got a point. You're talking about everyday-life stuff that people can relate to because it's funny or it's raunchy or it's sad or it's uplifting and exciting. It makes sense that all kinds of people are into it."

To at least one rising musician, though, the essence of the blues is not its universality but its specificity as an expression of African American discontent. Chris Thomas King is wholly capable of replicating the style of the Delta blues; the Coen brothers chose him to portray Tommy Johnson in *O Brother, Where Art Thou?* His blues pedigree is unimpeachable: Literally raised in a juke joint (Tabby's Blues Box in Baton Rouge, which was run by his bluesman father), King, who was thirty-nine in 2003, was the last blues musician to be discovered and recorded by a folklorist from the Smithsonian. However, the music he makes today draws upon and recombines a range of musical resources, including rap as well as the blues of his antecedents. He released his most recent album, *Dirty South Hip-Hop Blues*, on his aptly named label, 21st Century Blues.

As King sees the musical tradition of his heritage, the blues is a philosophy more than a form. "What a lot of people have been calling blues for the last ten, fifteen years is not what the blues is, and it doesn't represent my culture," King says. "If you really knew what the blues were, you would not be trying to preserve that. The essence of the blues is, people didn't sing in the cotton fields because they were happy. You know what I'm saying?

"When my dad opened his place," King explains, "he opened it in a part of town that was decaying. Everybody started moving out. But the blues didn't leave. The blues never left the hood. People don't really know how to make the connection from Muddy Waters to Master P, but it's all the blues."

How can hip hop also be the blues? "Because it comes from a disaffected people," he says. "It comes from people who don't really have a voice, don't really have an outlet. When people say it's the devil's music, that's the first sign that there's some blues in it—nwa or 'Cop Killer,' you know, things that mainstream black Americans are ashamed of. Back in the '30s, if you were a white kid, you couldn't bring some poster of Robert Johnson home and put it on your wall and say, 'Hey, Mom, Dad, this guy's cool—listen to this.' That's about the equivalent of bringing 'Cop Killer' home and putting a poster of Ice-T on your wall.

"I'm talking about honest music. It's not music that's eager to please or find acceptance. Does it sound like Muddy Waters? No. Does it sound like Blind Willie Johnson? No. Is it the blues? Yes."

If King is right, then perhaps the legend of Robert Johnson is wrong. The devil took only his body. His blues soul lives on in an unknown kid at the next crossroads, inventing a new sound to scare the hell out of the rest of us.

Alan Lomax

The Grammy Awards, which endure as one of American popular culture's more shameless celebrations of artifice, infantilism, and evanescence, will occasionally make a grand gesture in the name of authenticity, adult-hood, or posterity by honoring an esteemed old-timer who hasn't sold any records since anyone can remember. In 1997, Pete Seeger, then seventy-seven, won this semi-annual Compensation and Distraction Award for what was then his most recent CD, titled *Pete*—a collection of plaintive moral and political parables much like the dozens and dozens of albums that he had been recording for more than fifty years. I was in the press horde at the Grammys that year, and I spent some time with Seeger backstage at Madison Square Garden as he waited for his allocated time on stage. For nearly an hour, he stood straight-backed, looking disarmingly natty in a tuxedo, greeting well-wishers and watch-ing the event on a closed-circuit TV monitor. There were performances by Eric Clapton, Sheryl Crow, and the Smashing Pumpkins. After hearing them all, Seeger said, "I wonder what the music experts of the 1930s would have thought if you had told them that the greatest influence on the popular music of this century would be some unknown black prisoners and field workers."

Six decades earlier, American popular music was certainly different from the earthy, rough-edged, blues-based sounds of rock-era artists such as Clapton and his contemporaries. In the age of Tin Pan Alley, most popular music was jazzy and sounded urban, and it endeavored to project an aura of sophistication. It was music created by professionals to reflect and to exploit the social aspirations of a people striving to recover from (or at least to forget) the Depression. Being jazz-oriented, much of the music of the time was to a large degree black music, or a white imitation thereof—more specifically, a citified black music drawn from the urban experience of African Americans who had moved north in the Great Migration. Many of the artists whose songs made the Hit Parade in 1937—the vocalists Bing Crosby and Connee Boswell, the songwriters Cole Porter and Johnny Mercer—may have come from working-class immigrant stock (Crosby) and may have been Midwesterners (Boswell, Porter) or Southerners (Mercer), but owing to the lithe swing of the tunes, the singers' nonchalant crooning, and the sleek orchestral arrangements, everyone sounded like an urbane Manhattanite.

The contemporaneous music of Negroes laboring in prison or incarcerated in fieldwork—the blues of artists such as Leadbelly (Huddie Ledbetter, who had been an inmate at Angola Penitentiary in Louisiana) and Muddy Waters (McKinley Morganfield, who had been a farm laborer in Mississippi)—was not wholly unknown in the 1930s. It had innumerable practitioners and admirers within the culture of poor, rural, Southern blacks. Owing to its provenance, however, this music was largely unheard or unrecognized within the white musical establishment of the time. By the end of the 1950s, the blues would emerge as a permeating influence on American popular music. One generation after another, American young people raised in prosperity would turn to rock 'n' roll and its various incarnations (folk-rock, country-rock, punk, grunge, alt-rock, and the rest), all elementally indebted to the blues and to its aesthetic of raw, unaffected veracity. In the rock era, singers and songwriters (most artists now taking on both roles, as blues musicians always tended to do) may be from England (Clapton) or a middle-class neighborhood in Missouri (Crow), but they all seem to want to sound like old black prisoners and fieldworkers.

American popular music not only changed styles, it jumped traditions, abandoning the formal and the schooled for the informal and the vernacular. It became more like nonliterate music—like folk music. How or through whom? A creditable school of thought attributes much of this transformation to the folklorist, author, performer, and entrepreneur Alan Lomax, the man who "discovered" and first recorded Leadbelly and Muddy Waters. Seeger, writing in 1958, said that "[Lomax] is more responsible than any other single individual for the whole revival of interest in American folk music." Brian Eno, the English art-rock composer, has gone further, writing (in 1993, in a blurb for Lomax's book *The Land Where the Blues Began*) that "without Lomax, it's possible that there would have been no blues explosion, no R&B movement, no Beatles and no Stones and no Velvet Underground." *Newsweek* has instructed its readers that "if not for Lomax, few people would have heard 'Tom Dooley' or 'Goodnight Irene,' and Bob Zimmerman might be singing 'Feelings' at Holiday Inns around Hibbing, Minnesota."

Lomax, who was otherwise disposed against popular opinion, would surely have agreed. He was a fearsome advocate of artists in whom he believed, and he himself needed no other champion. He wrote and edited nine major books (three with his father and mentor, the early-twentieth-century folklorist John A. Lomax) during his eighty-seven years, and most of them are essentially about Alan Lomax. *The Land Where the Blues Began* begins where everything seemed to begin for Lomax—with Lomax. The opening paragraph alone contains thirteen references to the author, who aligns himself with his subjects as a noble, homespun victim of bias and elitism. ("Even after being snubbed, lectured, arrested, and once or twice shot at, I still persist in plunging straight for the bottom where the songs live.") His songbooks have aggrandizing accounts of Lomax's Homeric song searches, followed by lyrics and music inevitably "arranged and adapted" by Lomax (with his father, in many cases). And in 2003, a year after his death, a new Lomax miscellany, *Alan Lomax: Selected Writings, 1934–1997*, edited and well annotated by the respected folk-music historian Ronald D. Cohen, fits neatly in the literature of Alan Lomax vainglory.

In an autobiographical section of the book, "Saga of a Folksong Hunter," Lomax muses that future scholars may see the twentieth century as "the age of the golden ear, when, for a time, a passionate aural curiosity overshadowed the ability to create music." In other words, those who merely composed and performed music were less important than appreciative listeners such as Lomax. If so, then what was the reason for such passionate curiosity? Prospectors, after a few big strikes, used to suffer the same delusion: that the gold was in them rather than in the stones.

Lomax was born into folklore. He was only eighteen when he made his first field recordings of rural folksingers, accompanying his father, a folksong scholar then sixty-five years old, in the summer of 1933. The first piece of Lomax's in this volume is his account of that trip, "Sinful Songs of the Southern Negro." It is a boyish narrative, infused with the thrill of discovery, blithely arrogant, ignorant of the strain of exoticism tainting its enthusiasms, adolescent in its obsession with the salacious—and demeaning to its subjects, many of whom considered themselves above the bawdy material that Lomax prodded them to sing. They expressed their offense to him, but futilely. "We is all 'ligious men an' don' sing anything but sperchils, except maybe a few hollers now an' den when we got 'bout forty rods o' de devil in us," one singer told Lomax, who pressed to hear those "hollers" another time. Undaunted, Lomax soon located a more promising subject, Henry Truvillion, but found him "most disappointing" in his reticence to sing the unsavory tunes Lomax wanted. "We thought that if we could carry Henry off some Saturday night to a place where he could sit and talk out of sight of his wife or her callers, we should be able to get a marvelous store of songs and stories from him. This spring we intend to do just that."

Over the years, Lomax would always see folklore as "pure adventure" and something heroic. As he said at the Midcentury International Folklore Conference at Indiana University in 1950, in an address transcribed in *Selected Writings*, folklorists "rescue materials from oblivion" and "are making a better present and preparing for some sort of juster future for all people." By 1937, when Lomax was scarcely twenty-one, he was serving as director of the Archive of American Folk-Song at the Library of Congress. American culture was rising in prominence, elevating with it an interest in our native identity. As Lomax remarks in an interview edited into an article for this book, "The developing concern about what our own American culture was actually like, about who we were as people, peaked at this time. And the search for American folk roots was part of this."

Lomax saw the music of the rural underclass as the unfiltered essence of the American ideal—"an expression of its democratic, interracial, international character . . . a function of its inchoate and turbulent many-sided development," he wrote in 1941. Already a zealous archeologist of America's living folk culture, Lomax became its omnipresent spokesman and promoter, hosting radio programs, staging concerts, publishing songbooks, and producing records. Under Lomax, the Library of Congress amassed an archive of some twenty thousand pieces of American folk music, and the books of songs that Lomax collected (with his father and on his own) became fixtures on parlor spinets, in grade-school music classes, and in summer camps everywhere. Lomax remains best known and most esteemed for his work assembling and disseminating American folk music, which occupied him from the late 1930s until the 1950s (when he moved to London, expanding his research into the folk music of other societies).

Lomax was so close to the roots of our musical culture that he saw nothing higher. "Of all . . . creations, which culture is the most valuable?" Lomax asked. "And by this I do not mean culture with a capital 'C'—that body of art which critics have selected out of the literate traditions of Western Europe—but rather the total accumulation of man's fantasy and wisdom . . . that still persist in full vitality in the folk and primitive places of our planet." More bluntly, he stated outright elsewhere that "folklore has a staying power unrivaled by even the greatest of cultivated art." However spirited his talk about "democratic and equalitarian beliefs," Lomax had no interest in challenging the idea of a hierarchy within the arts; he wanted only to alter the rankings, with his own preferences at the top.

Lomax's patronage was exclusionary. He reveled in his position as the Maecenas of rural America—"The role of the folklorist is that of the advocate of the folk," he said, and he defended his constituency with fervor. Seeing a kind of Rousseauian purity in the ascetic lives of the impoverished country folk whom he encountered in his field research, Lomax (who grew up in Texas, where his father was teaching college) characterized their lore as intrinsically virtuous, as an expression of "the beautiful and the good." "In folklore . . . you get a general ethical tone," he observed, "a kind of rudimentary humanistic approach to life . . . a very deep sense of values." Even in the South, where the folk culture of rural whites was steeped in racism, Lomax argued, "Jim Crow prejudice has been inoperative in folklore."

By extension, Lomax tended to demonize what he perceived as forces in opposition to those of his favored rural South: the North, the city, technology, business, "sophistication"—and jazz, being a sophisticated music associated with Northern cities. Lomax did write a biography of Jelly Roll Morton, who considered himself the inventor of jazz, but he dismissed most jazz as a corruption of folk music. In his preface to the 1993 edition of that book, moreover, Lomax added a bizarre rant against Harlem and its reputation as a black cultural center—"New York's Harlem, which so often has taken all the credit for black cultural innovations. . . . [And] where the carriers of the great tradition were few, where big bands with horn sections were replacing the lacy counterpoint of New Orleans." Why did his sympathies for the disenfranchised preclude the urban underclass? In Lomax's account, the Mason-Dixon Line is a moral and aesthetic barrier, and folk poetry could never come from the city street.

Wheeling his sound-recording gear around Negro quarters of the segregated South, Lomax never realized how far he was from familiar ground. His writings show that his understanding of black culture was critically flawed, and that his attitudes toward African Americans were discomforting, no matter how pure he may have held his motives to be. His descriptions of his hosts and their environments are shaded with an air of superior bemusement ("A billowing Negro matron in a beautiful red turban and her husband, a toothless cotton-headed old fellow with a mouthful of snuff"), and his manner of re-creating dialogue is straight out of an Uncle Remus story: "I'll sing dat song right easy foh you, ef you want me!" and "Dat's a sho'-God song!"

Lomax seemed to think that he was extending compliments when he was oozing noble-savage condescension, praising Leadbelly's musical skill as "natural" and describing black faith as a "primitive" Christianity. In his songbook *American Ballads*, Lomax wrote that "modern education prove[d] disastrous to the Negro's folk singing, destroying much of the quaint, innate beauty of the songs." When a Negro inmate at Tennessee State Prison expressed a hope that the recording he made would help him gain his freedom, Lomax said he found the prisoner's dream "pathetic beyond tears."

His conception of the African American musical tradition was no more enlightened. In preparing the words and the music that he collected for publication in songbooks, Lomax was frustrated to find the verses to some songs he recorded Negroes singing to be "jumbled" and "disconnected." Storylines changed in the middle of songs, characters appeared and disappeared without explanation, the point of view shifted. The songs were not linear narratives, adhering to familiar story patterns. They were more like mixed-up puzzle pieces or collages of imagery that played off one another in unexpected ways. Lomax's response was to edit and to re-organize the lyrics, taking one verse from one singer's version of a song and one from another's, fashioning a composite that was conventionally lucid, all in the name of "coherence." In the process, he stripped off a layer of the songs' black identity—their way of provoking feeling through juxtaposition and mystery, an African American tradition—and replaced it with a sleek white gloss.

Lomax made some contributions of great merit; he was hardly all bad. He took blues seriously at a time when few whites in the cultural establishment gave it much thought. Through his field research and his advocacy of the music, exposure and opportunity came to blues and folk artists (such as Leadbelly, Muddy Waters, Sun House, and Aunt Molly Jackson) who had enjoyed limited regional recognition or none at all. Would they have surfaced without Lomax? Perhaps. Isn't the blues something that cannot be denied? Absolutely. But so is the historical record. However things might have gone hypothetically, the way they happened was that Lomax introduced the world at large to several of the most original and influential blues and folk musicians in American history.

Through his Library of Congress recordings and his songbooks, Lomax imparted institutional legitimacy upon a minority music and helped to bring it to a broader public. One could argue that the formal documentation of any folk materials kills them: by definition, a folk song is supposed to be orally transmitted and unfixed—there should be no "correct," official version. If so, one could counter, the traduction—no, the violence—that Lomax committed was justifiable. Not long ago James Taylor gave a nationally televised concert from a theater in New York, and he sang a powerful traditional tune called "Wasn't That a

Mighty Flood," mentioning on the air that he had learned it from a performance by the veteran blues singer Eric von Schmidt. I asked von Schmidt where he had learned it, and he said he discovered it in the late 1940s, when he and a friend had driven from his native Connecticut to the Library of Congress in a pilgrimage to hear the Lomax recordings. There they found the song, sung a cappella "as a prison kind of spiritual" by a singer whom von Schmidt recalls as Sin-Killer Griffin.

As an early proponent of ethnomusicology, moreover, Lomax was forward-minded in his interest in the relationship between music, gender, and sexual mores. (Although Lomax was engaged in aspects of musicology and ethnomusicology, at points deeply, he kept his distance from academia, declining numerous offers of university posts.) Ultimately, though, Lomax's self-interest and sense of proprietorship poisoned his legacy. While he thought of the last century as his era ("the age of the golden ear"), he was really a nineteenth-century figure—a domestic colonialist who mistook "discovery" for creation and advocacy for ownership.

The details of Lomax's association with Leadbelly are a case study in exploitative paternalism. Lomax first encountered Huddie Ledbetter in 1933, during one of his song-collecting ventures with his father. As the younger Lomax recalled in *Selected Writings*, "Leadbelly called himself 'de king of de twelve-string guitar players ob de world.' He wasn't modest, but he was right. From him we got our richest store of folk songs, over a hundred new songs that Leadbelly had heard since his childhood in Morningsport, Louisiana, and had varied to fit his own singing and playing style." Leadbelly, incarcerated at the time, "begged us to help him get out of prison," Lomax wrote. In their benevolence, the Lomaxes assented. When the newly freed musician heard that his benefactors were heading to New York, he "begged to accompany us," Lomax continued.

Working with his father and later on his own, Alan Lomax oversaw Leadbelly's career, setting up concerts, nightclub engagements, and recording sessions. Lomax also had that rich store of Leadbelly's songs published, with his own name (and in many cases his father's name, too) listed as a co-composer on more than three dozen of the works, ensuring that Lomax (and his heirs) would earn as much in royalties as the musician who brought him the songs. These swindled compositions included "Rock Island Line" and "Goodnight, Irene," the latter of which, in its recording by the Weavers in 1950, was the number-one hit single on the pop-music charts for thirteen weeks and sold 2 million copies. Lomax liked this classic show-business grift of "cutting in" on song royalties, an old favorite of powerful business managers (such as Irving Mills, who put his name on the credits of dozens of early Duke Ellington works) and singers (including Elvis Presley, acting under the direction of his overseer Colonel Tom Parker). He liked it so much that his name appears next to those of Leadbelly, Memphis Slim, Vera Hall, and others on the copyrights of nearly one hundred compositions, including "Tom Dooley" and "This Train."

Lomax endures as an influence of multiple dimensions. The earthy, unadorned music that he loved pervades our society. (How would American industry sell its cars, its snacks, and its drinks without the electric guitar music in its commercials?) Yet variations on the Lomax model of cultural imperialism continue—indeed, they have gone global, with American record producers and music promoters (and musicians such as Paul Simon, David Byrne, and Ry Cooder) scouring the world for worthy musical discoveries whose "authenticity" might also happen to benefit their own careers. Alan Lomax deserves recognition, even gratitude; but so does my paperboy, and that doesn't make him the author of the stuff.

Dinah Washington
Queen

Heartbreak has always been central to country music. In 1953, the Grand Ole Opry star Hank Snow had a hit record called "It Don't Hurt Anymore," a folksy paean to a broken heart that began with a lyric that abstracted the theme idiomatically: "It don't hurt anymore/All my teardrops are dried. . . ." Snow moaned the words to the accompaniment of a mewling fiddle, fixing our attention on the singer's past suffering. The following year, Dinah Washington, a jazz vocalist who had come up through gospel music and the blues, remade the song. Her first variation was grammatical, a switch of the opening pronoun to the first-person singular. Washington's recording begins with her voice, a cappella, blaring like a civil defense alarm: "IIIIIIIIIII!" After a beat, she continued the opening phrase ("don't hurt anymore . . ."), and a full jazz orchestra kicked in with a hard-driving rhythmic pattern. The singing continued in this crushing mode: Washington hurled out the words as she stormed through the song. Despite the lyrics, she sounded impervious to pain of any sort, and supremely capable of inflicting it.

Recorded a few weeks before Dinah Washington's thirtieth birthday, in 1954, "I Don't Hurt Anymore" typifies the work of a singer who, through the force of her personality, shifted nearly everything she sang into the first-person singular, whether or not she changed the words. Her music is fiery, uncompromising, and devoid of self-pity. Washington, who made dozens of albums before she died from an overdose of prescription drugs in December 1963, was a rarity among singers, male or female, in the popular music of her era: an unflinching, even merciless figure who was also sensual and musically sophisticated. There were steely women singing before her—Bessie Smith in the blues, Sophie Tucker in the music hall, Mildred Bailey in jazz, Ethel Merman on Broadway, Maybelle Carter in country. Yet Washington was unique in her day and an influence on countless singers to follow for her refusal to play her power for laughs (as Smith, Tucker, and Merman did) or (like Bailey and Carter) to downplay her considerable sex appeal.

So popular during her lifetime that she was known initially as the Queen of the Blues and later as the Queen of the Juke Boxes, Dinah Washington is not well remembered today. Her recordings, while still in circulation on CD, no longer appear on the best-seller charts, as do reissues of the music of her idol Billie Holiday and her contemporary Ella Fitzgerald. Nor has her voice been appropriated to add a gloss of cool to the marketing of luxury cars or banking services, as the music of many deceased African American jazz artists has been. Her face is probably unrecognizable to all but her old fans, pop music scholars, and collectors. A 2003 biography of Washington by Nadine Cohodas, the author of a good social history of the Chicago blues impresarios Leonard and Philip Chess, has added considerably to the thin literature on Washington.

The single previous life of the singer, James Haskins's *Queen of the Blues* (published in 1987 and now out of print), was short (202 undersized pages of text) and low on biographical and musical detail. Cohodas, drawing upon Haskins's papers and fresh interviews with Washington's childhood friends, business associates, fellow musicians (including her one-time lover, the jazz arranger and conductor Quincy Jones), and other sources, provides much new information about the singer's vast creative output, which once made Washington an inescapable presence on American radio, as well as about her volatile personal life, which made her nearly as prominent on the gossip pages. (Among other things, she had at least seven, perhaps eight, husbands.)

Born Ruth Jones in Tuscaloosa, Alabama, in 1924 to struggling parents—a lumberyard worker and a homemaker with some musical talent—the future Dinah Washington moved north with her family during the Great Migration and grew up in Chicago when the city was a hothouse of jazz, blues, and gospel music, all three of which had also been transplanted from the South not long before then. The Jones household was a devoutly Baptist one where "everything was geared to the church and old-fashioned strictness," Washington would later recall. Encouraged by her mother, a church pianist who gave her some music lessons, Washington started her career at fifteen, performing gospel songs in recitals—initially as the vocalist in a mother-daughter duo, soon afterward as a member of the Sallie Martin Singers, a touring group based in Chicago. The teenager was already too free-spirited for the gospel world, however. "Ruth could sing, but I don't think she liked the [gospel] robe. She was in the group but not of it," a minister's daughter told Cohodas. A high school friend of Washington's whom Cohodas interviewed remembered her as "already stormy" and "wild . . . boy crazy." Washington would never be at a loss for men, nor would she be satisfied with any of the ones she attracted.

The sacred and the secular have always been inextricable in African American popular music—that is, in American popular music, just as black and white are. Dinah Washington's debt to the gospel music of her apprenticeship is explicit in her earliest secular recordings and it remains in her last, although she never made an album of worship music. Her singing has the ringing power and the free-flowing emotion of gospel. In some songs, such as her version of Irving Berlin's "Blue Skies," her phrases seem to sway back and forth in time, and they build steadily in intensity, the way Baptist preaching does. Cohodas makes frequent mention of Washington's use of devices common in gospel singing, such as her habit of peppering phrases with interjections such as "Lord!" and emphatic moans or hums. (Cohodas calls them "tics," and that is what they eventually became.) Indeed, Washington often sounds in the midst of a call-and-response exchange with herself. Above all, what she derived from gospel—and carried to an extreme in her secular music—was a sense of certainty. There is no doubt in Dinah Washington's singing; it is music that *believes*, no matter what the songs are saying, and it expresses its conviction with an almost evangelical zeal.

Washington, like many others who have successfully survived the shark pool of the entertainment industry, was buoyed by an outsize ambition. She married the first of her husbands when she was seventeen, because, she told an interviewer, he "said he'd help me get into show business. I figured this was my opportunity." Although his assistance proved evanescent, Washington advanced so quickly in the ranks of secular music anyway that she was singing and recording with the popular vibraharpist and big-band leader Lionel Hampton before her nineteenth birthday. (She had by then dropped her first husband and her original name, adopting Dinah Washington, which at least three of her mentors, including Lionel Hampton, would later claim to have given her.) As *Variety* described her New York première with Hampton at the Apollo Theater in Harlem, "Her fortissimo is socko in a blues speciality that stamps the comely femme as a comer."

Because we now tend to think of the blues and jazz of the swing era nostalgically and associate the music with older listeners, it is difficult to imagine someone like Dinah Washington, whose portrait has even been on a U.S. postage stamp (depicted with graying hair, which she never lived to have), as she was when she first attracted national attention: a hypersexual eighteen-year-old. The fact is, Washington represented the norm for what was then a music made primarily by and for young people. Hampton was playing dance music derided in its time as juvenile and vulgar. Indeed, like Washington, most of the singers (and many of the instrumentalists) in big bands during World War II were teenagers speaking to their peers when they made their first records: Ella Fitzgerald was seventeen; Doris Day, sixteen; Billie Holiday, eighteen; Mel Tormé, nineteen. (The heart of Hampton's theme song, "Flying Home," was an exhilarating tenor saxophone solo by the late Illinois Jacquet, who was nineteen when he recorded it.) They were the Britney Spearses and Justin Timberlakes of the World War II generation—kids trading in sexual fantasy. Unlike most of her contemporaries both white and black, however, the young Dinah Washington dispensed with the niceties of romantic allusion and announced her sexuality in vivid terms. Six decades before Britney Spears was cooing "Oops! I Did It Again," Washington was crowing "I Know How to Do It" in one of her first recordings:

> I may be old-fashioned
> I may be dumb
> I may be a square
> And I may be a bum
> But I know how to do it

Her earthy, assertive style of singing was ideally suited to the blues, which had been a forum for black women to express their authority on matters carnal and otherwise since Bessie Smith, the "Empress of the Blues," in the Twenties. In fact, the image of the big, bad black woman belting out the blues was already a cliché by the mid-1940s, when Dinah Washington made her name singing a wry sort of jazz-blues—blues material sung and played with a swing feeling and a wink. Before her first recording session in December 1943, her producer, the white Englishman Leonard Feather, handed Washington one of several songs he had written for her: a near parody of a Bessie Smith–style tune called "Evil Gal Blues":

I'm an evil gal
Don't you bother with me
I'm an evil gal
Don't you bother with me
I'll empty your pockets
And fill you with misery

Cohodas quotes a remark Washington made to Feather, in a comment he would later recount with pride, "Shit, you really think you know me, don't you?" Of course, as Washington implied with the question, "Evil Gal Blues" speaks more of then-prevalent white perceptions of black defiance than it does of her personality.

Cohodas casts light on Washington's reputation for toughness. We see her at work playing rough in order to maintain her personal and artistic standards and to protect other African American artists from racial prejudice. She would hush up a musician who overplayed or scold a member of the audience who disrupted her show. After she was successful, she became "the boss in the studio" and once halted a recording session when she saw that the entire orchestra was white. She resumed the next day, when black musicians were included. During one performance in Las Vegas, the hotel pit boss lowered Washington's volume to satisfy a high roller from the South who didn't like her singing; Washington left the stage, walked through the casino, and told the boss, loudly enough for her audience to hear, "Motherfucker, I'm going to turn that [sound] back where it belongs, and if you touch it, I am going to break your fuckin' ass."

A friend of hers who witnessed the scene explained to Cohodas, "As long as you treated her with respect, she loved you. If you were going to make her a secondary citizen, you had a tigress on your hands."

* * *

In the caste system of musical categorization, the genre of popular standards—that is, the pre-rock music of Tin Pan Alley and Broadway—was historically seen as something a step or two above the blues, in large part because the former carried associations with white people, the metropolitan Northeast, and professionalism, the latter with African Americans, the rural South, and the folk arts. That the blues is a subtly complex and sophisticated music with its own aesthetic concerns—dissidence, idiosyncrasy, an active disregard for whiteness (in musical terms and otherwise)—took some time to sink in, even within some circles of black society. "I hate blues. You can't do anything with them," Billy Eckstine told an interviewer in 1947, after he had abandoned the gut-bucket blues that gave him his first hits and began specializing in romantic ballads.

For black singers of Dinah Washington's generation, to work in the blues idiom and then to take up the pop repertoire, as both Eckstine and Washington did, was thought of as aiming higher. Washington began recording Tin Pan Alley songs such as "Embraceable You" and "I've Got You Under My Skin" after she signed with Mercury in 1946, and, at the time that the black middle class was rising, she was soon doing standards almost exclusively. Chicago's black newspaper *The Defender* reported that Dinah Washington "has moved up the ladder to become a 'pop' singer." (Today, by contrast, the blues is held in such esteem that if a young master of the idiom such as Keb' Mo' started crooning Sinatra songs, he would be considered a sellout.)

What Washington did was challenge the entire notion of a hierarchy in musical form by ignoring it. In her hands, gospel, the blues, Tin Pan Alley, and country and western music are all of a piece. She treated everything she sang as the rawest of materials, equal opportunities to impart her ebullient fury. When a British journalist asked her what kind of singer she considered herself, Washington said, according to Cohodas,

> I don't think of myself as anything except a singer. I like to sing, and I'll sing ballads, church songs, blues, anything. I'll sing [the Hebrew song] "Eli, Eli" if you hang around. To me the important things are soul and conviction. . . . The Negro has been downtrodden in America for a long time, as you know. Maybe when you're singing a certain song you think of things that happened to you years ago. . . . Spirituals, blues, ballads, it doesn't matter.

In Dinah Washington's music, the traditional roles of the singer and the song are inverted: Washington provides the meaning, and the words and the music add the shading. When she sings Bob Russell and Carl Sigman's "Crazy He Calls Me," which might seem to call for a touch of wistful self-deprecation, Washington tosses off the words with her usual assurance, sounding wholly in command of her senses. We think: why, that fellow in the song must be the crazy one to talk to her like that. When she sings Jimmy Van Heusen and Johnny Mercer's "I Thought About You," a few lines of it recall a doomed love affair, but with an air of satisfaction, rather than regret. I thought about you, she seems to be saying, and I thought, "Good riddance!" Self-confidence, rapture, wrath: these are what Dinah Washington came to share with us, and they were extraordinary to find on the same radio as the sweet murmurings of Doris Day and Teresa Brewer.

She had a strict policy of recording only one take of a song, thereupon terrorizing the producers, the conductors, and the musicians playing in the sizable orchestras that frequently accompanied her in an era when records were made "live" in the studio, without overdubbing to patch flubbed notes. As one of her producers, Clyde Otis, warned the arranger Belford Hendricks, "Work out all the kinks in the orchestration. . . . If she's gonna give you one take, that's what you're gonna get." At least once, Washington left a recording session before others were satisfied; as Cohodas describes the scene, she headed toward the door and said, "It's not going to get any better. You fix it."

As a result of her refusal to give more than one take, her work lacks the refinement that we tend to associate with the music of café society, but it has the fire, the tension, and the surprise often lacking there. It is also impressively short on vocal errors, although Washington sometimes avoided making them by simplifying the melodies.

Cohodas's *Queen*, for all its value in treating an underappreciated subject seriously, would have benefited from an injection of Washington's vigor. It is a placid book weakened by slack prose. ("Recording companies provided for such payments, but the amount depended on the cost to make the record and the number sold.") The author's grasp of the history of American popular music seems shaky at times, as when she is mystified by Washington's having recorded such novelty tunes as "One Arabian Night" in 1954. ("Perhaps someone at the label knew the writer and wanted to do a favor or take care of a debt.") In truth, novelty songs (many of which drew upon the music of distant cultures as exotica) were a craze in 1954, when the "Hit Parade" was filled with ephemera like Frank Weir's "Happy Wanderer" and the Gaylords' "Little Shoemaker." The ubiquity of this silliness was the plague that rock 'n' roll promised to cure.

Ravaged by hard living, diet pills, and alcohol, Dinah Washington's voice grew stiff and dry in her late thirties. She began to overuse her signature gesture, her way of abruptly clipping off the last word of a phrase, the vocal equivalent of a boxer's jab, and took up parlando, talking her way through some lyrics instead of singing. Although she was not yet forty, she sounded at least half again as old. One of the last songs she recorded was "Stranger on Earth," the lament of an embittered outcast:

> *Some fools don't know what's right from wrong*
> *But somehow those folks belong,*
> *Me, I travel all I'm worth*
> *But I still remain a stranger on this earth*

Washington called it "the story of my life," and she sang it in full, strong voice, tapping what was left of her old reserve. It became the story of an alien who refused to be alienated. Whatever the singer had suffered in the past, it didn't hurt anymore.

Ray Charles

In March 1962, Atco Records issued a harbinger of the 2004 winter movie season: the album *Bobby Darin Sings Ray Charles*, in which one of two popular singers famous for crossing multiple genre lines paid homage to the other. Hollywood delivered Jamie Foxx as Charles in Taylor Hackford's screen biography *Ray* (which was called *Unchain My Heart* prior to its release), followed by Kevin Spacey in a self-directed Darin bio called *Beyond the Sea* (which should have been titled *Bobby*). In the former, we see Charles, early in his career, imitating both Nat "King" Cole and the suave blues singer Charles Brown. "I can mimic anybody I hear," he explains in the film. Of course, Ray Charles found a genuinely distinctive and profoundly influential voice of his own, and he employed it to monumental effect for decades, as the absence of a record called *Ray Charles Sings Bobby Darin* reminds us. When Darin took up rock 'n' roll, abandoned it for swing, and then dropped that for folk and country, he subordinated himself to each type of music; he shrank to fit every style he tried. Charles, by contrast, drew from all those genres and others, subsuming them into his own musical personality; he grew with every genre he absorbed.

The muscular and sensual music of Ray Charles was in the air again, in part because of the new movie and all the talk about Foxx's uncanny performance, and also because Charles's last album, *Genius Loves Company*, a collection of duets with contemporary pop stars and other big-name singers released not long after Charles's death from liver disease that June, proved to have enough of the intended crossover appeal to become a bigger hit than Charles had had in many years. Suddenly nostalgic for Charles, I bought a small pile of CD re-issues of his early albums on Atlantic, which I had only on vinyl LP. (Some of his best output, recorded for ABC Records between 1960 and 1973, is not available on CD; Charles retained ownership of the masters and always focused on touring and making new recordings, rather than on his past work.) "He's really popular lately," the thirtyish man at the checkout counter said as he rang up my sale. Noticing that one of the CDs in the stack was titled *The Genius of Ray Charles*, he asked earnestly, "Is that true? Was he really a genius?"

If the Atlantic marketing people were the first to say so, no one except Charles himself ever came forth to argue otherwise. Frank Sinatra called Ray Charles "the only true genius in our business" and demonstrated his admiration by emulating Charles on the gutsier recordings he started making in the mid-1960s. If not for Charles, we would surely not have "That's Life" and its ilk. (Whatever the merits of that music, it is striking for Charles's effect on the generally impenetrable Sinatra.) Nor would we have the countless rock artists, from Mick Jagger to Bruce Springsteen, who have aimed to convey an earthy authenticity by singing in a raw, volatile growl. Nor, arguably, would we have the very art of soul music, which Ray Charles virtually invented by combining traditional gospel music with postwar rhythm and blues.

Charles, who had been raised in merciless poverty in the rural South, would always take pride in his status as "raw-ass country." He was far too humble about his musical achievements and uncomfortable with his longtime sobriquet. As he told David Ritz, the co-author of his memoir, *Brother Ray: Ray Charles' Own Story*, which appeared in 1978, "I never came up with that 'genius' tag. Someone else did. I don't like the genius business. It's not me. Erroll Garner was a genius. Art Tatum. Oscar Peterson. Charlie Parker. Artie Shaw. Dizzy [Gillespie] was the genius. . . . I learned it all from others."

Before he went blind at the age of seven (from an undiagnosed disease that he later believed was glaucoma), Charles had had a bit of musical coaching from a boogie-woogie piano player who ran an all-purpose shop near his saltbox house in the backwoods of northern Florida. His sole formal training came at the state-run St. Augustine School for the Deaf and the Blind, where he learned to read and to write music in Braille and to play classical studies on the piano and the clarinet. Upon the death of his mother when he was fifteen, Charles quit school and started pursuing work as a jazz pianist. After a few years of apprenticeship, he headed for the city by bus, making Seattle his destination of choice because it was the farthest city from his hometown in the continental United States.

All the pianists Charles said he admired most—Garner, Tatum, and Peterson—had an orchestral approach to the keyboard. Their conceptions are epic, layered with ornament and intensely dynamic. That's not the way Charles played (at least not on record, nor in his known performances); to the contrary, he was a forceful but disciplined pianist who tended to limit himself to laying down a rhythmic foundation for his own vocals. His contrapuntal work was mainly chordal, and the obbligato lines that he would play were imaginative but sparse, like those of Nat Cole or Hank Jones. Even on instrumentals, such as "Doodlin'" and "Deed I Do" on his non-vocal jazz albums, Charles played with the discretion of a sympathetic accompanist.

It's his singing that was orchestral. The proof of Charles's genius lies not in the breadth of his influence but in the depth of his music, and he was a singer of almost otherworldly originality and emotive power. His phrasing was naturalistic and seemingly spontaneous, yet the lyrics invariably swung to a pulse. Verses exploded with surprise: he might stop dead and then whisper a few words or break into a whoop. Apparently lost in ecstasy, he would burst into a giddy falsetto or interject a conspiratorial aside: "Looky here. . . ." Although the gravelly texture of his voice is immediately recognizable and has been widely imitated, he could conjure a considerable range of timbres, and he used them commandingly, often playfully. On his familiar rendition of "America the Beautiful," from 1972, he begins the second chorus like a choirboy, crooning in a sweet tenor, and then appears to change characters: now a preacher, he hurls out the words in fiery bursts.

Charles's vocal intonation was so complex and nuanced that he could make a world out of a note. He rarely sang any note dead on pitch, but preferred to work in shades of microtones around the center. Often he would sing near the top end of notes—almost sharp but not quite, to conjure a sense of yearning or, when he pushed the effect, a feeling of teetering on the emotional brink. At other times he would hang toward the bottom of a note to evoke melancholy or to set the listener up for a subtly uplifting glissando at the end of a phrase.

One of the secrets of Charles's potency as a singer is the extraordinary sensitivity under the powerhouse surface of his presentation. A brawny, square-jawed man from the backcountry with a rough-hewn voice, Charles was also a person of delicate temperament, prone to crying jags. He generally drank milk because his stomach was too sensitive to tolerate tap water. "I know that men ain't supposed to cry, but I think that's wrong," he said in his book. "Crying's always been a way for me to get things out which are buried deep, deep down. When I sing, I often cry. Crying is feeling, and feeling is only human. Oh yes, I cry." When, in 1979, the state of Georgia proclaimed his recording of Hoagy Carmichael's "Georgia on My Mind" the official state song, Charles stood in the chamber of the state legislature and bawled. "I felt kind of stupid standing there crying," Charles later recalled, "but I couldn't help it."

The same unfettered emotionality permeates his music, not only ballads such as "What'll I Do," "You Don't Know Me," and "Born to Lose," but also many up-tempo numbers such as "Just for a Thrill" and "Let the Good Times Roll," which have something—a gentleness at their heart—that prevents their essential bravura from seeming overly aggressive. Country singers such as George Jones and Italian American crooners such as Frank Sinatra and Tony Bennett share this counter-balancing combination of conspicuous tenderness and conspicuous toughness, though few, perhaps none, to the extremes of Ray Charles.

The tension between elements in opposition also informs Charles's lasting creation as a composer and arranger: the union of sacred music and carnal sensibility that came to be known as soul music. An interpretive artist by inclination, Charles became a songwriter (of sorts) by necessity when, in the early 1950s, he began recording in earnest and had trouble finding material that suited his impulses. (Bob Dylan, about a decade later, took up songwriting for a similar reason: as he once observed, no one else was creating the kind of songs he wanted to sing.) Charles, who recalled the fervor of gospel music from his youth, sought a musical vehicle with the capacity to express the roiling passions of adulthood and decided to adapt the former to the latter purpose. (Thomas A. Dorsey, the father of gospel music, composed bawdy secular songs as well as hymns, but his two sets of works are largely unrelated, musically and lyrically.) Charles took gospel pieces, presumably in the public domain, and modified the lyrics: "This Little Light of Mine" became "This Little Girl of Mine"; "Talkin' 'Bout Jesus" became "Talkin' 'Bout You"; "You Better Leave That Liar Alone" became "You Better Leave That Woman Alone," and so forth. Even "What'd I Say" and "Hit the Road, Jack," while not derived from specific sacred tunes, drew expressly upon the call-and-response tradition of the gospel style.

Charles's method offended traditionalists, including the blues singer Big Bill Broonzy, who groused that "he's mixing the blues with spirituals. I know that's wrong. . . . He should be singing in church." Some radio stations banned "What'd I Say" for the sexual suggestion in Charles's groans, but the music rang true because it was utterly true to its singer, who was far more interested in matters of the flesh than in matters of the spirit. It carried no ethical compromise for Charles. "If Mama gave me religion, the religion said, 'Believe in yourself,'" he told David Ritz. "Jesus was Jewish, and if he couldn't convince his own people he was the messiah, why should I be convinced?" The musical amalgam that Charles created had the passion of gospel, but no piety—indeed, no reverence for anything but the earthliest sort of love. In this regard, it was an inspiration to generations of soul singers profoundly concerned with the body, from Marvin Gaye to Prince (who has conflated the divine with the hardcore throughout his career).

In the 1950s, few African American men dared to present the overtly sexual package that Charles offered to black and white men and women. Billy Eckstine, the boyishly handsome singer and bandleader who had outdrawn Sinatra at the Paramount and outsold him on records for a time, was nearly banished from show business in 1950 after a photograph in *Life* magazine showed him surrounded by worshipful fans—all of them young, white females. (Prior to Charles and Eckstine, most African American singers who appealed to white audiences survived by playing "cute," like Louis Armstrong and Fats Waller, or exuded the sex appeal of a Sunday-school teacher, like Nat Cole; either way, they appeared unthreatening to women of any color.) Charles prevailed, no doubt, because of his blindness; his Ray-Bans shielded him. Had he had the same chiseled good looks, swayed his body in time with the same intensity, sung the same licentious songs, and made eye contact with the white women in his audiences, his obituaries might have been published fifty years sooner.

Oddly, though, the dark-glass barrier between Charles's eyes and ours always made the experience of seeing him uncommonly intimate. We are accustomed to watching performers' eyes for innumerable signals. How can we tell what the person is thinking and feeling when the window to the soul is closed? We turn to the body. I saw Charles in concert half a dozen times, once from the distance of a few feet at the Blue Note in New York. My memories are of his shoulders, bobbing from side to side; his hands and arms, locked in place as he blocked chords on the piano; and his right leg, kicking out from under the piano in time. Rarely does one attend so closely to the body of someone other than a lover, apart from when watching dance performances, during which one can also see the dancers' eyes.

Charles ended up having two careers: one prior to his arrest in Boston in 1964 for heroin possession, and one beginning the following year, when he voluntarily detoxed in a Los Angeles hospital. To acknowledge the higher level of innovation and greater vitality in the first period is neither to endorse hard drugs nor to deny the occasional spikes of glory in Charles's last four decades. His commercials for both Coke and Pepsi ("Uh huh") were delightful; his uncharacteristically lugubrious reading of "America the Beautiful" at the Republican Convention in 1984 was less so. His recording of *Porgy and Bess* with Cleo Laine in 1976 had enough fine moments—particularly Charles's singing on "Summertime"—to excuse the project's mimicry of the landmark Louis Armstrong-Ella

Fitzgerald version. Five of the six country albums that he made in the 1980s are embarrassments, though the one of duets with George Jones, Merle Haggard, Johnny Cash, Willie Nelson, and others is spirited and shows Charles in far stronger form than *Genius Loves Company*.

As for the latter album, Charles's whispered good-bye from behind the shadows of some friends (and some lessers), it has a couple of lovely, poignant tracks: "Sinner's Prayer," a salty blues Charles used to do fifty years earlier, which he and B. B. King pull off with old-rascal wile; and "It Was a Very Good Year," Ervin Drake's bittersweet lament to aging, done with Willie Nelson, who sounds more than ever as if he were singing to himself in his car. Last works are often just occasions for mourning, beyond the scope of criticism, and in this instance I say so be it. Ray Charles made two hundred fifty other recordings, and they are much more than relics.

PART IV

Growing Up

Elvis Costello at Fifty

W hy don't we let rock stars grow up? The pop music domain is like a confederation of Never-Never Land and the Island of Lost Boys, where nobody can ever grow old, and nasty behavior is the social code. It is some fifty years now since rock 'n' roll began to emerge as a musical style and a cultural phenomenon, originally of a piece with the adolescent rebellion against postwar conservatism that the rebelled-upon used to call juvenile delinquency. The music's surviving originators—Chuck Berry, Little Richard, and Jerry Lee Lewis, old men now—continue to make their livings singing the same raucous, primal tunes about high school, fast cars, and sex to aging fans who may not have experienced some of those things in a while. No matter that Berry would rather be performing Tin Pan Alley standards such as "I'm Through With Love," nor that Little Richard, an ordained Seventh-Day Adventist minister, prefers to sing gospel music. (Jerry Lee Lewis is congenitally delinquent, but that's another issue.) Rock 'n' roll is here to stay put.

Disposed to more expansive conceptions of rock's potential, venturesome musicians of succeeding eras—such as Bob Dylan, the Beatles, Marvin Gaye, Pete Townshend, and their heirs—have stretched and re-shaped rock 'n' roll innumerable times, and many others, including Paul McCartney, Joe Jackson, and Stewart Copeland (the former drummer for the Police and no relation to Aaron Copland, though he refers to the composer as his "honorary uncle"), have dropped the genre—temporarily, as a rule—to experiment with classical forms such as the symphony and the oratorio and the opera. Still, we tend to prefer our rockers young and angry. We look cynically upon overt demonstrations of creative ambition as over-reaching, especially when popular artists dare to cross the chalklines of category and genre. We dismiss as pretentious their efforts in musical styles positioned above rock on the artistic hierarchy, which is unfair regardless of the fact that McCartney's *Liverpool Oratorio*, for example, is terminally overwrought. (A few of McCartney's less grandiose concert pieces, among them a tuneful piano study called "A Leaf," have a genial charm.) Many of us of the postwar generation submit to a kind of philistine elitism, rejecting the privilege of an artist successful in an informal discipline to attempt a formal art, because we see the latter as bourgeois and the interest in it as a betrayal of the anti-establishment ethic to which rock 'n' roll still lays claim, decades after it became the music of the establishment. By the same token, we are quick to embrace the latest young group of rough-hewn bad boys (Pantera, Turbonegro) and to exalt them for their puerility and their crudity.

I suspect that thoughts of this sort have occasionally struck Elvis Costello, whose brave, mercurial career achieved a denouement in 2003 with the release of *North*, his twenty-fourth album, a collection of somber art songs in the vein of Kurt Weill and Bertolt Brecht. Asked about the title, Costello explained: "That's where I'm headed." Clearly he sees the project as a mark of his creative progress; he has noted that he wrote all the songs at the piano, like the composers in our mental image of the great masters, rather than on the guitar, historically the instrument of vernacular musicians. He also wrote the album's orchestrations for twenty-eight strings and nine horns (using a pencil on music paper, not a computer), and he conducted the orchestra himself. "I don't think the New York Philharmonic is going to call me up," he joked to *Rolling Stone*. Then again, Costello did not call Lorin Maazel. Twenty-six years after he borrowed Huey Lewis's backup band to make his first album for a start-up punk-rock label called Stiff Records, Costello could assume the podium to lead a sizable orchestra on a recording for Deutsche Grammophon. To misquote the title of his famous second album, this year's is a luxury model.

The route that Costello has followed to northerly artistic territory has been serpentine, with pins all over the musical map. Raised in Birkenhead, across the

Mersey River from Liverpool, he started in his teens as a pub-band singer and songwriter indebted to the Beatles and their influences—that is, to all of pop music history. His debut LP, *My Aim Is True*, which appeared in 1977, was an international hit of the punk/New Wave years, and permanently cemented his public image as a volatile nerd, somewhat obscuring the discipline and the sophistication already evident in songs such as "Alison" and "Watching the Detectives." Following a series of infectious, aggressively clever albums made with his deft little band, the Attractions, Costello took a hard turn westward and released an album of his favorite country tunes called *Almost Blue*, performed demurely, with reverence, in 1981. Costello's audience started looking for the exits.

In the 1980s, Costello reached his maturity as a pop songwriter, producing a fine collection of buoyant tunes about betrayal, duplicity, and related hazards of his romantic paradigm in *Imperial Bedroom* (1982), as well as a couple of near-equals in *King of America* (1986) and *Spike* (1989), the latter a wildly eclectic pastiche of things from several albums that Costello had abandoned. "By the time I got to my fifth album, by the early eighties, I wasn't listening to pop music—I was listening to all jazz," Costello told the music journalist Fred Schruers. "You can hear [that] the shape of songs starts to change." Though he was still writing in the pop milieu and would have a hit from time to time (such as *Spike*'s "Veronica," co-written with McCartney), the growing subtlety of his lyrics (which relied less on gimmickry and shock value, and more on narrative detail) and the complexity of his music (which broke away from traditional popular-song forms and broadened harmonically to accommodate a diversity of guest musicians, including jazz bassist Ray Brown and the Dirty Dozen Jazz Band) were making Costello an increasingly specialized taste.

What had happened was that he was asking to be taken seriously, much to the puzzlement of fans who had always mistaken him for a musically gifted novelty act. Stage-named like a cartoon character and decked out like one in oversized horn-rims and pompadour, Costello allowed himself to be packaged as punk's delegate to the house of Spike Jones and Ray Stevens, and when he started crooning "Almost Blue" (a ballad highlight of *Imperial Bedroom*, not on the earlier album of the same title), his audience heard the second act of *Pagliacci*. What was so rattling about Costello's change was that he was not being ironic. Ever since McCartney started putting music-hall numbers such as "When I'm Sixty-Four" on Beatles albums, listeners have been primed to accept pre-rock styles only if they are used ironically—a generous misreading of the sentimental Paulie's likely intentions, I suspect.

Costello, who turned forty in 1994, spent most of the 1990s trying to figure out how to be a grown-up musician. For starters, he grew a beard, which in time became enormous. (My son Jake has a theory that the self-seriousness of each of the Beatles' music was directly proportionate to the mass of his facial hair, and the evidence is persuasive.) Costello turned to styles and forms of music that are traditionally deemed more serious than rock, pop, or country: jazz and formal composition. He sang with the Jazz Passengers and the Mingus Big Band (adding lyrics to several Mingus compositions as well); and he accepted two commissions to compose orchestral scores, one in 1991 for the BBC television drama *G.B.H.*, the second, four years later, for the BBC mini-series *Jake's Progress*. Both were written in collaboration with the prolific British screen composer Richard Harvey, who helped to translate Costello's melodies into musical notation.

Frustrated by his musical illiteracy, Costello set out to learn how to read and write the music that he could always hear and play on the guitar. "I realized it was really self-defeating to maintain this mental block that I had about musical notation," he explained to the journalist Christopher Porter.

> I wasn't able to communicate very accurately to [the orchestra]. I had done some film music where I had composed the themes, but they'd always had to be orchestrated by other people. . . . I was very frustrated that some ideas were getting bent out of shape, so I enlisted some help . . . and I got through this mental block [about notation]. . . . It's a very foolish one to describe, but I got through it, and within six months I was writing four-part string parts. And now I just wrote [a] two-hundred-page orchestral score with a pencil. So, I learned really fast. I've always been able to hear harmony really clearly, so it wasn't a question of I didn't understand the music. I understood very well what I was doing. I just had no need to write it down [before].

As Costello must have known, there is more to music theory than a gifted musician could intuit with the keenest ear for harmony (there are counterpoint and form, for instance), and composing orchestral music is as much a matter of learning notation as writing a novel is a matter of learning the alphabet. It is a marvel that the string-quartet settings that he composed in 1993 for *The Juliet Letters*, an album of songs featuring the Brodsky Quartet, are so lovely—simple and largely imitative, but gently appealing. Lyrically, the record was a nostalgic homage to epistolary expression, and it was the same thing musically; Costello had become enchanted with the act of putting pen to paper while the rest of world was lost in computers.

Costello gave his curiosity free rein over the musical landscape. Before he was finished with the 1990s, he had made a burnished album of ballads co-written with Burt Bacharach, the grand old lion of refined commercial pop; he had written songs with or for Aimee Mann, Johnny Cash, Roger McGuinn, Bonnie Raitt, and Paul McCartney (with whom he had started writing in the 1980s); he had composed an entire album of new tunes for the folkish British provocateur Wendy James; and he had performed with the uncategorizable American guitarist Bill Frisell—in addition to all his other work in pop, jazz, and formal music. A Google search of "Elvis Costello" and "eclectic" generates more than ten thousand hits, most of them involving his work in the last decade. Little of this genre-roving has sat particularly well with the pop audience, which prefers its explorers to cross borders of place rather than time. Costello's breach of rock protocol is his pursuit of musical styles associated with the past or with older people, such as country, classical music, Tin Pan Alley, folk-rock, and the rest, instead of contemporary music of places such as Africa, Cuba, or the Middle East, which are seen as cool.

Costello (like Paul McCartney and Jerry Garcia) is the son of a big-band musician, and his childhood of singing standards in parlor musicales (as both McCartney and Garcia did with their fathers) has informed his own music (as it has or did in the cases of McCartney and Garcia). Costello's father, Ross Mac-Manus, a bebop trumpeter who became fairly well known in Britain as a vocalist for a Glenn Miller–style pop ensemble called the Joe Loss Orchestra, had used the pseudonym Day Costello—taking his grandmother's surname—when he did some moonlighting from his duties for Loss. (Ross MacManus even had a minor hit under the Day Costello name, a rendition of McCartney's wholly unironic ballad "The Long and Winding Road," in 1970.) His son Declan's first words were supposedly "skin, mommy"—an entreaty to hear his favorite record at the time, Frank Sinatra's exultant rendition of Cole Porter's "I've Got You Under My Skin." In taking up rock 'n' roll under a stage name, he became the Elvis of the Costellos; and, in 2003, approaching fifty—Ross MacManus's age when *My Aim Is True* was released—Costello was making much the same kind of music that his father was singing while he was establishing a musical identity of his own.

North begins well, with a gray-hued orchestral prologue reminiscent of Leonard Bernstein's "Chichester Psalms," and most of what follows remains in the Bernstein mode, straddling the poles of serious concert music and serious popular song. The former clearly exerts the stronger pull upon Costello these days, as it did upon Bernstein in his later years. Stephen Sondheim has said that his *West Side Story* collaborator contracted "importantitis," a condition to which age increases an artist's susceptibility; and Costello is apparently not immune to it. His music on *North* has a self-consciousness that tends to overwhelm its humor (mainly in the lyrics) and its spontaneity (care of the jazz soloists Lee Konitz on alto saxophone and Lew Soloff on muted trumpet).

There are ten songs on *North*, and purchasers of the CD also get individual passcodes to allow them to download one more selection—the title song, as a matter of fact. (The gimmick proved to be moot, since the whole CD immediately showed up on Web sites for free downloading.) The songs have a common sound: all are ballads, most of them exceedingly slow, and their style is an angular sort of quasi-recitative, out of tempo. They are much like the contemporary musical-theater writing of young composers such as Adam Guettel, in which melodic phrases wander, abruptly halt, jerk about, and take acrobatic leaps with little provocation, and in which the natural cadence of the words does not necessarily fit the music with the kind of precision fundamental to earlier theater-song craftspeople such as Guettel's grandfather Richard Rodgers and his main collaborators, Lorenz Hart and Oscar Hammerstein II. Costello sings, "But . . . if-I'd-only-known . . . that this would BE the last lov-ING remark . . . you left me IN the dark." In contemporary pop music, such erratic phrasing is the norm; indeed, it is arguably an essential attribute, part of the music's treasured unsophistication. I presume that Costello does not hear his jagged writing as untidy—or, if he does, that he prefers to keep things a little messy as a matter of generational pride.

Costello need not have explained that he composed all the pieces on *North* at the piano. Listening to the music, one can picture him at the keyboard, following the scales with his hands cupped in place. In "You Turned to Me," for instance, he moves down the scale in C major, making impressive-sounding augmented chords with small variations on simple triads. Costello has gone all mushy for augmented chords, which sound jazzy and sophisticated, and he is nearly as charmed by the Dorian mode, which can have an eerie quality. His mastery of these devices is still developing; at points Costello's harmony is arbitrarily complex. Compositionally, much of *North* sounds like exercises, although that is to Costello's credit, in one sense. (He and I are roughly the same age, and I find it progressively more difficult to get myself to do exercises of any sort.) That Costello has the wherewithal to try a new musical instrument and to learn a new set of skills is remarkable in itself, and the resulting music is far more interesting than hearing him play "Pump It Up" for the jillionth time. (Costello plays piano—in a manner so spare it is nearly absent—on two tracks of *North*, and his longtime keyboardist Steve Nieve plays much the same way on all the others.)

Lyrically, *North* has Costello's most disciplined writing—not his most dynamic (*This Year's Model*) nor his most imaginative (*Imperial Bedroom*), but his most conversational, his simplest. Habitually verbose, Costello barely sounds like himself here. Each song on *North* has fewer than half the words of a typical selection on any previous Elvis Costello album, and they are employed with uncommon restraint. Only once does Costello use Tin Pan Alley clichés, in "I'm In the Mood Again," and he does so with a theatrical wink: "I lay my head down on fine linens and satin/Away from the mad-hatters who live in Manhattan/The Empire State Building illuminating the sky/ I'm in the mood, I'm in the mood, I'm in the mood again." The language is mostly personal and intimate, with Costello assuming fewer roles than usual. He is singing as himself, celebrating love and bemoaning its futility, and ruminating on the passage of time: "I never did what I was told/I trampled through the amber and the burnished gold/But now I clearly see how cruel the young can be."

Modulating his voice to accommodate the material, Costello sings his sedate new songs in a more tempered version of the mellow baritone into which he has shifted for ballads since he crooned "My Funny Valentine" on the B-side of a single in 1978. Some of his old fans have belittled him for trying to be Frank Sinatra, but the classic pop singer to whom he is most indebted is Billy Eckstine, the original musically adventurous jazz-pop vocalist with a bad-boy reputation and a throbbing vibrato. I know Costello is an admirer of the late "Mr. B" because I saw him sitting with his mother and studying Eckstine in performance at the Blue Note nightclub in Manhattan sometime in the late 1980s. It was a strange, grim evening. Eckstine, while vigorous and in good voice, had fallen into disfavor and was struggling to reclaim his lost glory. As his finale, he fumbled through a pandering medley of recent pop hits far beneath an artist with his gifts—"Love the One You're With" and "Walk a Mile in My Shoes," I remember, and something else of that ilk, maybe "Gentle on My Mind." *North* may be a flawed effort, but its defects are aspirational, and I would rather suffer them than watch another great artist go south.

Brian Wilson and the Lost Masterpiece

No masterpiece is so great as a lost one—a symphony unfinished, a painting painted over, a novel shredded or suppressed. Largely or wholly unheard, unseen, or unread, such a work derives its life, as most objects of legend do, from scraps of generative evidence and the accretion of romantic speculation about them, and it takes its lasting if ethereal form in the creative imagination of the public. The lost masterpiece is the only artwork that is perfect, the fulfillment of all our artistic dreams, because it exists primarily or solely within them.

Incomplete or perished works have loomed as large as (or larger than) extant creations since the Renaissance, when Michelangelo's greatest achievement was thought to be not the ceiling of the Sistine Chapel, nor the Pieta, but his painting of the Battle of Cascina—an unfinished work already mythologized during the sixteenth century. (Cellini wrote of the Cascina painting that "nothing survives of ancient or of modern art which touches the same lofty point of excellence. . . . He never rose half-way to the same pitch of power.") In our own time, the salvage departments of the arts have only expanded to accommodate ever more forms and new claims. Yes, Orson Welles did well enough with *Citizen Kane*; but might he have contributed something comparable in the field of nonfiction film had he finished his documentary *It's All True* in 1942? (Welles, the Buddha of the Coulda, left a rich legacy of aborted or sabotaged masterworks, from *The Magnificent Ambersons* through *Chimes at Midnight* and *Touch of Evil* to the countless scripts he claimed to have written and discarded.) Did Bruno Schulz really have the Great Jewish Novel in his unread *Messiah*, or were the accounts of his writing it the greater fiction? How many unpublished manuscripts did the NKVD steal from Isaac Babel's apartment? What if the Reaper had not defeated Duke Ellington in his race to complete his jazz opera, *Queenie Pie*?

Such questions are sometimes best left unanswered, as Joseph Mitchell found when he discovered the unseemly truth about Joe Gould's once glorified but never finished (because it had scarcely been started) "Oral History of Our Time." Harold Brodkey, who dined well for some thirty years on the reputation of a novel always in progress, could have learned from Gould and left bad enough unpublished. To rephrase the words of the rummy newspaperman in *The Man Who Shot Liberty Valance*, when the facts spoil the legend, don't print anything.

In 1967, Brian Wilson, the principal composer and producer for the Beach Boys, cut short work on an album for the band first titled *Dumb Angel* and renamed *Smile*, which would promptly and henceforth be regarded as the lost masterpiece of rock. One was due. Rock 'n' roll, then about fourteen years old, was approaching the end of a pop-music style's usual life cycle, with its original audience entering adulthood. It had to change (as swing music had, transmuting into bebop, for the previous generation) or give way to something new. Rock musicians, emboldened by an emerging school of serious-minded rock critics, grew progressively adventurous, and their records became more conspicuously artful—more complex and sophisticated, but idiosyncratically so, drawing upon the ability of recording technology to conjure the volatile multiformity of the drug experience.

In May 1966, the Beach Boys had released *Pet Sounds*, the group's resourceful venture into sonic experimentation and lyrical introspection, which Paul McCartney, duly provoked, would call "the album of all time." Three months later, the Beatles issued *Revolver*, the eclectic forerunner to *Sgt. Pepper's Lonely Hearts Club Band* (and its superior, song for song, for all *Sgt. Pepper's* invention). With *Smile*, Wilson would later explain, he set out to surpass everything that he and his bandmates and the Beatles and every other rock musician had ever done. He said he wanted to make the greatest album in rock history, "a teenage symphony to God." The cultural economy had entered an inflationary stage.

Looking back after more than four decades, knowing as we do that some rock musicians of the late 1960s and 1970s lost their way in the fantastical land of pointy hats and the London Symphony Orchestra, we may be quick to dismiss grand aspirations such as Wilson's as misplaced for a pop artist. We saw punk come along in the 1970s and yank rock 'n' roll back into the garage, where it sounded primal and true again. But ever since then, we—critics, especially—have tried to keep the music locked there, effectively containing it in an orthodoxy as formal and rigid as that of chamber music or bluegrass. No wonder so many rock bands sound dull today; imprisonment deadens. In the face of countless new bands of neo-punks replicating the thrashing of their parents' era like karaoke, who wouldn't find relief in one with the true nerve to try writing a teenage symphony to anybody? Therein we might find the same exuberant naïveté, freshness, and restless fumbling that gave both *Smile* and early punk their power.

Smile was impossibly ambitious and unwieldy, but it was not pretentious—at least not in its original incarnation, and decidedly not in its music. (The nonsensical smugness of the lyrics contributed by Van Dyke Parks is another matter.) *Smile* was sincerely, perhaps naïvely, over-reaching, but it didn't ring false. In fact, the music that Wilson conceived and recorded in 1966 and the beginning of 1967 endures as a testament to postwar popular music's capacity to resist conformity, and defy category, and indulge the personal, and alienate the masses. Although most of the *Smile* sessions that Wilson produced for the Beach Boys have yet to be released officially, dubs have circulated in high-quality, annotated bootlegs for decades, and they almost justify the music's reputation.

The tracks are consistently inventive and varied, and most of them are lovely. Some are well known from versions released on official Beach Boys records over the years, such as "Good Vibrations," a marvel by any standard, so durable that it survives Parks's clunky alternate lyrics ("I—I love the colorful clothes she wears/And she's already workin' on my brain/I—I only looked in her eyes/But I picked up something I just can't explain"); "Surf's Up," a majestic piece of music, despite Parks's cold, obtuse lyrics ("columnated ruins domino!"); "Vegetables" (or "VegaTables"), a delightfully goofy riff about healthy food, one early recording of which had a rhythm track of Wilson and Paul McCartney munching on celery and carrots in tempo; and "Heroes and Villains," a daring collage of tonal effects and shifting tempos. Other tracks from the early sessions have yet to be issued officially as they were originally recorded, including "Do You Dig Worms" (aka "Do You Like Worms" and "Roll Plymouth Rock"), a tuneful echo of Stephen Foster; "Child Is the Father to the Man," a charming little thing (its title drawn from Wordsworth) built in layers of syncopated lines; and "Mrs. O'Leary's Cow" ("Fire"), a cartoonish instrumental. There are more, and most are fascinating; still, the original sessions remain just that: sessions, experiments unfinished. (Some of the key recordings have no lead vocal tracks, and others stop abruptly, without resolution.)

Wilson, in his prime during the time of *Pet Sounds* and *Smile*, was a composer and producer whose very aesthetic was based on a melding of the two roles. He made records rather than absolute music. As he told an interviewer in 1967, "Spector started the whole thing. He was the first one to use the studio. But I've gone beyond him now." Actually, the otherwise contemptible Mitch Miller preceded Phil Spector in employing studio technology and sound effects (a cracking bullwhip, honking geese) to create an aural sphere wholly distinct from that of live performance for the pop-music audience, and avant-gardists such as Pierre Schaeffer, Karlheinz Stockhausen, and John Cage outdid them both conceptually. Still, Wilson, like Spector, the Beatles, and others prominent in 1960s rock, used the studio as a compositional instrument, and an unfinished recording of a piece was, for Wilson, a piece unfinished.

Wilson's reasons for abandoning *Smile* have never been clear. Indeed, the open questions about the project's collapse have contributed mightily to *Smile*'s legend: it has a great death narrative. By some accounts, the other Beach Boys—Wilson's brothers Carl and Dennis, their cousin Mike Love, and their childhood buddy Al Jardine—felt uncomfortable with the material, especially the lyrics, and drove Parks to quit prematurely, leaving the composer without a collaborator to whom he could relate. "He's a genius, to say the least," Wilson has said of Parks. (One wonders what is the most Wilson would say of him.) "With amphetamines pushing a freight train of ideas through our brains," Wilson has said elsewhere, "Van Dyke and I enjoyed a compatibility that was inspiring."

Wilson, who has said that he wrote much of the music on hashish as well as amphetamines, has blamed the drugs for undermining *Smile*, or at least its market potential. "I thought [Smile] was too weird," he told the *New York Times* in late 2004. "I thought it was too druggie-influenced, I thought the audience wouldn't get it." Cynics have speculated that Wilson and the band pulled *Smile* as a tactic to negotiate for higher royalties from Capitol Records. Others have suspected that Wilson broke down under the strain of reaching too far beyond his grasp.

Word spread that Wilson had suffered a nervous breakdown—a plausible prospect, considering his history of mental illness; he had long suffered from depression and had been prone to erratic behavior, problems no doubt exacerbated by his hardy recreational drug intake. Around the time of *Smile*, Wilson had an enormous sandbox constructed in his living room to house his grand piano so that he could wiggle his toes in the sand for inspiration, and when a building across the street from the recording studio burned down a few days after the sessions for "Mrs. O'Leary's Cow," Wilson blamed the song, which he believed to have telekinetic powers.

To evade inquiries about the record's status, Wilson would claim that he had destroyed the tapes. This, conflated with reports of the building fire and widespread talk of Wilson's psychosis, would provide the tragic climax of the *Smile* myth: the mad genius burns his masterpiece in an oblational pyre. Subsequent unearthing and dissemination of the tapes in the bootleg underground would give the recordings an aura of sacred texts, while Wilson's reclusiveness and volatility would feed the hoariest adolescent notions about the duality of insanity and inspiration. Brian Wilson, enshrined by his fans as the pop Nietzsche, would never again attempt anything nearly so ambitious as *Smile*, which no one in the rock audience could legally hear.

I had an uncle who gave me dating advice when I was single. "When a girl stops her train of thought and says, 'Oh, never mind,'" he told me, "leave it alone—don't ask what she was going to say. You don't want to know." The rule applies to both genders and transcends courting, I have learned, and I thought of it when I heard last year that Brian Wilson had had a sudden change of heart about *Smile*.

With his brothers Carl and Dennis dead, and with Mike Love toting around a tribute band under the Beach Boys name, Wilson had in recent years been performing and recording as a solo artist. His mental health had stabilized, by all accounts. After a successful tour of the *Pet Sounds* music—with the Wondermints, a California power-pop band, covering for his old bandmates—Wilson was encouraged to follow up with live performances of *Pet Sounds'* intended successor, *Smile*, and he assented. Wilson, then in his early sixties, re-united with Van Dyke Parks, a year his senior, to make something of the pieces that they had left scattered in 1967. "There are intimations of mortality here, intimations about the end of [Wilson's] performing cycle," explained Parks in a 2004 interview. "I get the impression that Brian knew he was running out of time."

In concert appearances, members of Wilson's troupe held him by the arms and guided him to and from the chair he sat in when he sang. To prepare *Smile* for presentation, many of the same colleagues provided the composer with essential musical support. Darian Sahanaja, keyboardist for the Wondermints, scored musical passages to connect the disparate bits of *Smile* material, and he smoothed out the endings of pieces and their tempos to give the myriad bits cohesion. Parks, a composer and arranger in his own right—he wrote the scores for the Jack Nicholson movies *Goin' South* and *The Two Jakes*—also contributed ideas to complete the elements of *Smile* and organize them as a coherent unit. In addition, Parks brought in quite a few lyrics not in the original recordings, perhaps reconstructed from memory or old notes, perhaps newly written.

Despite Wilson's fanciful description of the project, it was never a symphony any more than it was an expression of teenage identity or a message to God. (Only "Good Vibrations" evokes the adolescent experience; and just one piece, the lush wordless opener "Our Prayer," is overtly connected to faith, although one could arguably call just about any composition a kind of sacred communication.) The *Smile* archaeologists who have been generating the bootlegs, fanzines, e-mail lists, and scrapbooks on the subject (including a 299-page paperback collection of news clips and miscellany, *Look! Listen! Vibrate! Smile!*, edited by the "*Smile* historian" Domenic Priore) largely agree that the original record was to be packaged as a relatively conventional collection of discrete songs, along with one suite to be called "The Elements." (Around 1980, one of several times Wilson revisited *Smile* for possible completion and release, he talked about wanting to organize all the tunes in three sections.)

The version prepared for concert performances and adapted for CD, by contrast, is something more advanced and elaborate: a three-movement work of components arranged to flow as of a piece; themes recur, as in formal music— almost always in the new interstitial segments and orchestral flourishes that are the result of recent collaborating by Wilson, Sahanaja, and Parks. The work seems reverse-engineered not only to fulfill the historical promise of the original but also to satisfy the larger myth that has grown around it. The CD is a compelling argument for *Smile*'s singularity as a masterwork of long-form pop; but it should not be mistaken for evidence of it.

Unlike the early Beach Boys records that made Wilson's outsized reputation, the new version of *Smile* is essentially a performance piece documented on CD, rather than a work inextricable from the recording medium. The basic tracks were taped in segments over five days' time, with all the musicians, including those in the horn and string sections as well as the rock players, performing live together in the studio. In 1966, Wilson and the Boys spent six months to make the ninety hours of tape that provided the three minutes and thirty-five seconds of "Good Vibrations." The mise-en-scene of the new *Smile* is the concert hall, not the studio; and so the CD denies *Smile* the essence of Wilson's aesthetic.

The biggest problem with *Brian Wilson Presents Smile*, released in 2004, is the absence of the group for which the music was composed. "The thing is," Wilson explained in an interview in 1966, "I write and think in terms of what the Beach Boys can do." *Smile* was conceived for and geared to their voices—the exquisite blend of their literally related vocal instruments, the muscular grace of Carl Wilson's lead singing, and Mike Love's contrapuntal bite. The Wondermints, who are highly proficient musicians, do not have the personality of the Beach Boys; they have a personality of their own, a snarky one that gives their CDs of original material an ironic kick, but they keep it in check here. What they are doing on *Smile*—superbly—is mimicry, which is a difficult job, but something intrinsically devoid of the veracity and the individuality that made the Beach Boys wonderful. Brian Wilson was never the best singer in the group, and he is trying to carry all the lead vocals some four decades after his prime. His voice, a game old soldier too weak for duty, trudges through the new *Smile*, struggling to stay in key, swallowing words.

For all the hazards inherent in the task, artists such as Wilson certainly have the prerogative to return to old work years after the fact. Hell, they're the artists, and it is their work. If Manet could go into people's houses and repaint sold canvases, an aging Beach Boy can re-record "Heroes and Villains." But another question remains: does a different person have the right to take up another artist's incomplete work and attempt to finish it or to restore it? That is closer to the point with *Smile*.

Brian Wilson is a different man today than he was when he left the music unfinished. We all change over time, though rarely as much as Wilson has as an artist. A few months ago, he released the most recent of his solo CDs, *Gettin' in Over My Head*, an assemblage of new recordings so bland, formulaic, and corny that they are irreconcilable with the work of the man who set out to create *Smile* years ago. They were done by someone else, and that person is clearly not functioning on the same creative level as Wilson was in 1966. It is no wonder that Wilson relied upon colleagues to help bring *Smile* to the stage and now to CD. What they did is well meant, but it is also at once indistinctive and excessive, like the scene of *Turandot* added by another composer after Puccini's death.

Toscanini famously dropped his baton when he reached the last bar that Puccini wrote. We could do something roughly comparable and listen only to the original *Smile* recordings—if a legitimate record company would release them. In the meantime, we have only *Brian Wilson Presents Smile*. Brian Wilson's *Smile*, masterpiece or not, is still lost.

Sting the Lutenist

R ock 'n' rollers, as they age, sometimes find themselves outgrowing a music they cannot outlive. Rock, a style invented for teenagers—or, more precisely, one adapted from an older style made originally for adults, the blues—endures as a bluntly, rudely cogent expression of adolescent anxiety, rage, and sexual fantasy. *Long live rock 'n' roll! The beat of the drums, loud and bold!* Over the decades since Chuck Berry wrote that pithy, hard-driving couplet, Berry has sustained a career into old age by serving as a nostalgist. As I've discussed in another context, Berry denies the calendar and sings about high school and dating and cruising down empty highways in V-8s, evoking an always romanticized image of teen life in the 1950s for multiple generations of listeners who seek to experience rock 'n' roll in the extant form closest to its essence. Berry's chief acolytes, the Rolling Stones, ply a kindred nostalgia for the 1960s and 1970s, as do various Motown acts that are on perpetual tour in the arts-center circuit. For musicians disinclined to work in self-tribute bands, however, it is not easy to rock and age. Rock, at its crude best, is a music of disgrace, anathema to aging (or doing anything else) gracefully.

In the past few years, several prominent rockers of a certain age have pursued a novel solution to the problem of growing too old to rock 'n' roll—an approach more ambitious, if less remunerative, than self-imitation, and better, if more conspicuously unnatural, than Botox. They are backdating their careers, repositioning themselves so as to be associated with styles of music that preceded rock. Bruce Springsteen, with his Seeger Sessions revue, put aside the E Street Band and shore-bar rock to do old-timey barn-dance music, nearly completing his transformation into a folksy troubadour of the Depression era. Bob Dylan, on *Love and Theft* and *Modern Times*, mingled rock and blues songs with softly lilting numbers that sound like the Victrola curios that his old Greenwich Village friend Tiny Tim used to warble. Dylan croons this disarmingly cornball material in a sweet croak—half Rudy Vallee, half cement mix; and, on the road, he and his band dress in matching rhinestone-cowboy outfits, like a group decked out for its Grand Ole Opry debut in the late 1940s. Eric Clapton, once an innovator of hard-rock guitar, has, on recent albums and tours, focused on the blues of Robert Johnson and B. B. King (with a side trip into the 1960s for a set of concerts with the reconstituted Cream). A tier or two down the ranks of the rock hierarchy, meanwhile, the great doo-wopper Dion followed Clapton along the road to Johnson-style country blues; and Rod Stewart, confronted with the fact that few of us under fifty think he's sexy, has been trying to become a Rat Pack–style swinger, singing approximations of the treasured melodies of pop standards; and Donovan, the archetype of 1960s hippiedom, attempted a comeback as an Ike-age coffeehouse beatnik.

Each of these efforts represents not just a detour from rock but also a claim to higher ground. Since we like to think of aging as advancing, and since rock is elementally a milieu of the young, the styles of work taken up by aging pop musicians are supposed to be more advanced or elevated than rock. It is telling that so many older rockers are turning to the past, looking not outside of rock but before it to find music that seems in some way superior—ostensibly purer in its primordial quality, as we conceive of the blues; supposedly more authentic in its ruralism, as we consider folk music; or presumably more refined in its formal sophistication, as we think of Tin Pan Alley. Springsteen, Dylan, Clapton, and their colleagues in backdating are submitting to a kind of pop prelapsarianism— a belief that, in key ways, music was better before their own time. The proposition has a justifying patina of classicism and a discomforting tinge of self-abnegation.

Among the members of this camp, the winner of the badge for longest distance traveled backward in time goes hands down to Sting. In late 2006, the onetime front man for the Police and longtime paragon of pop-rock seriousness, then fifty-five, told an interviewer of his midlife disenchantment with contemporary music. "Rock has come to a standstill—it's not going forward anymore," he said. "It only bores me." The claim itself, which Bono has echoed, is of little note; pop music has always had periods of lull. In 2006, there was fine, probative new music from at least half a dozen young bands, such as Comets on Fire, the Mars Volta, and Coheed and Cambria. More interesting is Sting's response to the stasis that he described, and that was not to try moving in the forward direction he advocated, but to spin around and head backward in musical time—past Rod Stewart, Cream, the Stones, and Chuck Berry . . . past Sinatra, B. B. King, and Robert Johnson . . . past Irving Berlin, past Stephen Foster, past Beethoven . . . all the way back five centuries to the first broadly popular music in the English language, the songs of the lute-playing minstrels of the Renaissance.

The resulting CD, which hovered around the top of the classical-music charts for months after its release in October 2006, is an album devoted to the words and music of John Dowland, the late sixteenth- and early seventeenth-century composer. A lutenist, songwriter, and singer celebrated throughout much of Europe as well as in his native England during his lifetime, Dowland was a contemporary of Shakespeare (the former probably born a year before the latter), and his music has the gleeful worldliness and intermittently sorrowful bouyancy that we have come to know as Elizabethan. He composed approximately a hundred instrumental pieces, most of them for solo lute (along with some consort works for viola and lute), and roughly the same number of songs intended for lute and voice—although, as always in the case of itinerant musicians who drew from folk sources, precise attribution of work associated with Dowland is impossible. Created during the early flowering of English-language vocal music, Dowland's songs are tuneful, elegant, and widely varied in style and mood. They have been recorded many times since the rise of the early-music movement during the 1920s and 1930s, though Sting, in interviews to promote his new CD, has suggested that Dowland had been largely unknown before he discovered him and rescued him from obscurity to rival that of, say, Andy Summers or Stewart Copeland.

Like many children of the postwar years, I first heard Dowland's music in recordings by Julian Bream, the English concert guitarist and lutenist who had a sizable popular following in the 1960s, when an escalation of scholarly interest in early music coincided with the hippie culture's romance with things vaguely evocative of the Renaissance, such as flowing hair, froufrou, dirt, and archaic Old World instruments. All a rock band needed to impart a song with that *now* sound was a harpsichord or a lute on the chorus and a recorder solo. What were the Stones doing with a harpsichord on "Dandelion"? They were evoking a musical past so distant, so weird to ears of the jet age, that it seemed spacey. The original *Star Trek* television series employed the same juxtaposition of the Elizabethan and the futuristic by having various characters, including Spock, strum sci-fi lutes. The one time I saw Bream in concert, at Town Hall in the early 1970s, while I was an undergraduate, I went with two other members of a pretentious jazz-rock band I was playing in, and Bream's encore was a Beatles tune.

With his new CD, then, Sting is not simply exploring the Renaissance but also revisiting the 1960s (and the early 1970s, which, after all, were essentially still the 1960s)—the period that predated his own coming of age. This is scarcely the first time an artist has enacted a public struggle with his creative identity by poking around the world in which he was made.

The album is called *Songs From the Labyrinth*. While John Dowland had nothing to do with labyrinths, as far as I can tell, Sting has one of them in the backyard of his castle. It is a replica of the famous labyrinth at Chartres Cathedral, naturally. When the guitarist Dominic Miller commissioned a customized lute for Sting, he had the luthier carve the instrument's sound hole in the pattern of the labyrinth at Sting's house/Chartres. The CD's title suggests that the album is one of songs from Sting's lute. Yet it is not quite that.

The front cover shows Sting clutching his lute and looking magnificently chiseled, and in four more photos in the booklet he is either playing the lute or posing with it. On the recording itself, however, Sting plays on only two of the twenty-three tracks; one of them is only twenty-eight seconds long, and the other is a duet with the CD's principal lutenist, Edin Karamazov. Sting's abstinence from the instrument is no great detriment, fortunately. When he does play the lute, his attack is unduly harsh and percussive—a rocker's approach to a stroller's instrument. On nearly all the tracks, Karamazov, a skilled lutenist and guitarist from Sarajevo, handles the lute playing, and his work on the CD bursts with life. Karamazov is inclined to gypsy-style busyness, fancy shows of speed and facility. His style may not please all scholars of Elizabethan music, but it is fun.

Dowland's music is intimate, made for performances in close quarters to fairly small gatherings of patrons and their guests. In a few surviving scores of Dowland's quartet pieces, we find all four parts printed on one sheet of paper; each set of staves runs parallel to one of the four sides of the sheet, so the musicians could sit around a small table and read from the music. For me, the prospect of Sting attempting to perform such quiet, delicate music was tantalizing. His own songs, including the many ballads that he recorded both with the Police and on his own, have tended to aim for grandness, if not grandiosity. Reduction would not diminish his music. It could give it human scale.

Unfortunately, Sting oversings Dowland's songs, spoiling them with the same outsized smugness that has often infused his own music. Early on in his career, the detachment that he exudes worked well with his material. "Don't Stand So

Close to Me" is, after all, a paean to distance, as is "Walking on the Moon." "Roxanne" is about a lover ill-disposed to intimacy, a prostitute; and in "Every Breath You Take," the singer is not engaged with the object of his desire, he is stalking her. These songs are less about love than about its denial, and it is wholly fitting to sing them from a cool remove. Sting's voice has always had a forced, mannered quality as well, though that seemed in keeping with the affected Caribbean inflections of his early music, a white English adaptation of reggae. On *Songs From the Labyrinth*, however, Sting comes off as haughty and strident when he should sound as if he is, for once, standing close to us.

In addition to songs associated with Dowland and his era, *Songs From the Labyrinth* includes excerpts from Dowland's correspondence, read by Sting. This text is, for the most part, obsequious flattery, boasting of status, and obligatory politesse from a servant of various courts to his patrons. In one letter to Sir Robert Cecil, Dowland wrote:

> And according as I desired ther cam a letter to me out of Germany from the Duke of Brunswicke, wherupon I spoke to your honor and to my Lord of Essex, who willingly gav me both your hands (for which I wold be glad if ther wear any service in me that yor honors coulde command). When I cam to the Duke of Brunswicke he usde me kingly me, and gave me a rich chaine of golde. . . .

That sort of thing. Sting intones this benign arcana with austere gravity and little apparent regard for the words themselves. Every excerpt sounds the same, another excuse for Sting to speak in the formal cadences of Olde English—to impress without expressing anything in particular.

With *Songs From the Labyrinth*, Sting has given in fully to his critics' worst charges. Perhaps becoming a minstrel of Elizabethan lute songs will liberate him and free, free, set Sting (and us) free from his labyrinthine pretensions. Then again, Sting may well feel perfectly at ease with Dowland's grandiloquent bids for favor with the aristocracy of his day. *Songs From the Labyrinth* earned Sting an invitation to sing and play his lute for the present-day Queen Elizabeth. If some admirers of his early rock records have felt betrayed by Sting in recent years, one reason consistent with the coldness and pretense of his music is a sense, magnified by images of him luting for the queen, that he would like to abandon rock royalty for the real thing. One might expect him to be gratified enough to have been knighted, but—I'm sorry. I forgot: that hasn't happened just yet. My mind jumped ahead a bit.

Joe Sacco and Daniel Clowes

Comic books, the rock 'n' roll of literature, have always been a rigorously disreputable form of junk art for adolescents of body or mind. Hyperenergetic, crude, sexually regressive, and politically simplistic, comics—like rock (and, in recent years, hip-hop)—give fluent voice to their audience's simplest impulses. These are their virtues, arguably, as outlets for emotional release and as social counteragents.

In the late 1960s and early 1970s, some young musicians developed grander notions and concocted a wholly different sort of rock, a bombastic, pretentious monster of musical crossbreeding (the mind of Little Richard combined with the heart of Richard Wagner) too colossal to be contained on a 45 rpm single or even on just one 33 rpm album. Record shelves buckled under with extravagant multidisc "concept albums" and "rock operas" laden with pulp mythology and inchoate mysticism, performed by rock bands such as Genesis and King Crimson, accompanied by the likes of the London Symphony Orchestra and its chamber choir. Pop music, inflated beyond recognition, nearly suffocated under its own weight.

Over the past fifteen years or so, something similar has been happening in comics. A generation of ambitious, serious artists and writers have been applying vast amounts of their creative energy into a milieu which is essentially the visual equivalent of the rock opera: the supernatural graphic novel—that is, a full-length book in comics format (cartoon drawings with word balloons for dialogue) printed between hard covers or glossy soft-cover. The idea is not new. In Europe, books such as Frans Masereel's *Passionate Journey* and Otto Nuckel's *Destiny* had told stories intended for adults in expressionistic woodcuts or drawings as early as the 1920s, although they were only a distant ancestor of the comics we know. The first self-proclaimed graphic novel in the United States, Will Eisner's *A Contract with God*, was published more than three decades ago, in the same year as *The World According to Garp*. No one seemed to pay much attention to what Eisner and a handful of others inspired by him were trying to do until 1992, when a special Pulitzer Prize for letters went to a graphic novel, *Maus*, a two-volume Holocaust allegory by the underground comics (or comix) artist and writer Art Spiegelman, an acolyte of the gonzo master Robert Crumb.

Since *Maus*, more than a thousand graphic novels have been published, and they are, on the whole, grandiose mutant spawn of mainstream comics, overloaded with faux mythology and mysticism suitable to Seventies rock. Eisner and Spiegelman, like Bob Dylan and the Beatles during the Sixties, had experimented with grown-up themes and complex modes of expression in efforts to take their art form out of the realm of junk, whereupon a legion of less-gifted imitators reduced the notion to baroque parody.

With few exceptions, the creators of the graphic novels published in recent years have been ignoring Eisner and Spiegelman's innovation, which was not one of scale, but of kind. The thick covers, the extra pages, and the heavy paper stock—even the highfalutin graphic novel label—are secondary. Both artists' breakthrough works in book form were a significant departure from comics' tradition in being intimate and personal at their heart. In *A Contract with God*, Eisner rendered his memories and family lore in vignettes, and in *Maus* Spiegelman illustrated his father's oral history of the death camps with bleak veracity. Spiegelman changed nothing in his father's account other than the participants' species. Jews became mice, Germans, cats, but only nominally so.

How could the comic book, whose very name is sometimes used as pejorative synonym for the outrageously fantastical, do any justice to the real world? Can a medium so good at depicting the overblown and the infantile really pare itself down and grow up?

Joe Sacco, a Malta-born writer and artist who lives in New York, has taken nonfiction comics onto untested ground. He is doing journalism—first-hand depth reporting on hard-news subjects—in ink drawings and word balloons.

There is virtually no precedent for what he does, aside from the rare newspaper editorial cartoon drawn in the field. (In the early 1940s, a comic-book series called *London* portrayed events of the Second World War as they happened, but its artist, a Columbia University student, Jerry Robinson, was working in Manhattan from news clips. The "true" crime comics that dominated the candy-store racks in the late 1940s and early 1950s were hack sensationalism, like the pulp magazines that bred them.) Among comics artists, a society of ostensible iconoclasts mostly imitating one another, Sacco is legitimately unique.

His two books, *Palestine* (1996) and *Safe Area Gorazde* (2000), are similar in conception. Each has as its subject a group of people enmeshed in ageless, intractable ethnic and political conflicts: in *Gorazde*, Muslims in a village of mixed ethnicity in eastern Bosnia, during several years immediately after the Bosnian War, and in *Palestine*, Palestinians in the Occupied Territories near the end of the first intifada of the early 1990s. In concentrating primarily on Muslims in both cases, Sacco has entrusted his sympathies with the side he considers underrepresented in the mainstream American press and television. "I've heard . . . the Israeli side most of my life," he argues in an internal dialogue in *Palestine*. "It'd take a whole other trip to see Israel. . . . I'd like to meet Israelis, but that wasn't why I was here." The people in his books, as he portrays them, are disempowered—the worst fate imaginable to the super-powered populations in conventional comic books. While their Serbian neighbors are forewarned of military intrusions in time to organize and vacate their towns, Muslims, whom Sacco interviewed, find their phone lines dead and hide in their homes, watching machine-gun fire from their bedroom windows. In *Palestine*, Israeli soldiers chop down the olive trees in a Palestinian area, eliminating its residents' main source of income.

Sacco, who studied journalism in college, immerses himself in the lives of his subjects as a participant observer (like Orwell with a sketch pad, down to the anticolonial politics and the absorption with the underclasses), and he has a clear eye for detail. In *Gorazde*, the more intimate and vivid of his books, we follow him (or, rather, his stand-in, a self-caricature who is a homely, awkward version of the man with the piercing glare pictured in his author photograph) as he talks, eats, and travels with Muslims in the divided town of Gorazde who have survived the ethnic-cleansing horrors of the Bosnian War. He takes us to a makeshift dance club with a group of disarmingly Westernized Muslim young people, and we witness their obsession with the banalities of American popular culture (Levi's jeans, basketball, the Eagles). We walk the dirt streets still cleaved with Serbian tank tracks, and we see in the passersby the pallor inflicted by not enough food and too many cigarettes. In *Palestine*, much the same, we walk with Sacco as he shops at the street markets, earns his subjects' confidence (greeting a wary vendor with some practiced Arabic), and visits Palestinians' homes and refugee camps to conduct his interviews. Bags of stones hold down sheets of plastic on rooftops, and stains on the exterior walls mark floods from overflowing sewage.

More a diarist than a journalist, Sacco presents us with an essentially declarative record of his experiences and conversations. He lets his interview subjects talk, often at great length; we get their views and recollections largely unfiltered. "Too much has happened, too many family members killed," rants a Bosnian Muslim woman, scowling angrily:

> I used to have many Serb friends. I had a close friend named Miro, and it's possible he was a sniper shooting at my daughter, that he was one of those people who raped and slaughtered. . . . I can never trust those Serbs again, that's obvious, and not only that, my relationship with Serbs who remained in Gorazde has changed, too. . . . Things can never be the same.

Sacco's point of view comes across mainly from the facial expressions he draws on his cartoon self, which veer from sympathy to alarm. Almost a quarter of both books is devoted to pictorial recreations of events which Sacco's interview subjects describe: in *Gorazde*, descriptions of methodically executed atrocities by Serb forces, dramatic escapes, street fighting, and submedieval conditions in ravaged Bosnian hospitals; in *Palestine*, accounts of street fighting and of harassment, detention, and interrogation of Palestinians by Israeli hard-liners. Dedicated to providing a forum to those he considers unjustly neglected, Sacco clearly sees himself as something of a liberator of his subjects' stories. As such, he's the superhero in his comics, the person with powers beyond those of everyone else, who hides behind a mild-mannered façade.

Much as the protagonists of his books feel at odds with their surroundings, displaced or unsettled, Sacco renders his subjects and their environments as if they occupied separate planes, like the moving characters superimposed upon stationary backgrounds in animated cartoons. Heavy brush lines outline the human figures. Their status as occupants of the land beneath them is an artful illusion, Sacco seems to be reminding us; they could be torn away as easily as sketches on a tissue-paper overlay.

The only literally comic element in Sacco's work is his treatment of faces. His use of caricatures avoids the more realistic portraiture one might expect in books presented as journalism. Love-starved young Bosnian girls ogle at Sacco with ballooning fish eyes. The nose on a Palestinian man is bigger than another character's head. (In mainstream comics, there is little caricature, but only exaggeration; everything is enlarged equally and indiscriminately in a childish glorification of the idea of bigness.) Most of Sacco's characters are a bit grotesque, but funnily so—except for political leaders and his subjects' antagonists, whom Sacco renders with cold, meticulous contempt. Indeed, the comical ugliness of a character is visually a measure of Sacco's affection for him. In this, he suggests the world of male adolescence, where boys express their affection for fellow males in the code language of outrageous ridicule.

Traditionally, the physical settings have been incidental to character in the comics—so much so that bylined artists would frequently not bother with it at all; they would ink the figures zooming and flexing, and the task of filling in the frame with, say, Clark Kent's office furniture or Wonder Woman's jungle house would be left to uncredited apprentices called "backgrounders." Sacco, by contrast, is not merely attentive to the backgrounds; particular settings occupy the thematic foreground of his books. Both *Gorazde* and *Palestine* are principally concerned with the loyalties of his characters to their homelands. People describe how the wars have felt from their sides, and Sacco shows us the evidence in meticulous specificity: in the streets of Gorazde, laundry hangs from the frames of missing apartment-house windows, and kids play with toys made from the parts of burned-up, abandoned cars. In the West Bank, shards of cloth dangle from barbed-wire fences. Unlike the characters in Sacco's books, who are drawn in strong, thick cartoon lines, the streets and buildings are sketched in delicate, reverential, occasionally tentative lines. Sacco treats places as their residents talk of them, as something sacred that human meddling can too easily destroy.

He works in black ink and adds no gray half-tones or colors, at once connecting his drawings to the centuries-old tradition of political cartooning as well as to the radical underground comix of the 1960s and their progeny, the low-budget independent or alternative comics of recent vintage such as *Weirdo* and *Drawn and Quarterly*. Their stark black-and-white line drawings signal that Sacco's books are serious and they aspire to be art. Created by one person with a sensibility evident in both drawings and text, these words and pictures are works of personal expression, as opposed to the glossy commercial comics generated by production-line teams of writers, pencilers, inkers, letterers, and computer colorists.

All comic-book panels are cinematic; they look like cleaned-up and primped versions of the storyboards that directors use as guidelines for film production. Being a kind of visual journalism made in black and white, Sacco's books have something in common with documentary film. However, they are composed and paced more like feature movies, particularly films of the studio era, prior to the rise of television, video games, and the Internet. Sacco's approach to graphic sequencing—his "shot language"—is disciplined and traditional. Images follow one after another gracefully, as they do in a film by a Hollywood craftsman such as Howard Hawks or Michael Curtiz: landscapes put the subjects in perspective; figures are often shown at full length and in groups, so we can see their body language, watch their interaction, and examine their relationships; the close-up is used sparingly, for impact. Once the common vocabulary of film as well as comics, these principles now tend to be seen as old-fashioned in both forms, where barrages of close-ups and jump cuts are taken for stimulation.

By the comic-book conventions of today, making language so high a priority is an archaism as startling as using title cards for dialogue in a movie. It has become commonplace for comics artists to generate complete stories, leaving empty word balloons in the panels; only when the art is finished does a "writer" come in, filling the blanks with dialogue to accommodate the imagery. Sacco is so detached from the stylistic orthodoxy of his medium that his books actually have lengthy passages of text handwritten in columns and books, as well as in word balloons—transcripts of interviews, usually—with drawings added for amplification.

* * *

Beyond the journalistic terrain Joe Sacco has been pioneering, there is another realm of nonfiction in contemporary comic books: a subgenre of confessional memoirs and intimate, quasi-fictional realism. Once again, the work has a parallel in popular music, in which young singers and songwriters have been recording modest, gentle tunes about quotidian goings-on. An early hit among them, Norah Jones's trifle "Don't Know Why (I Didn't Call)," won five Grammys, and it exemplifies the category. Jones, talk-singing in a pretty wisp of a voice, tells us that she never got around to doing something that she doesn't seem to have been particularly intent on getting done—specifically, dialing a telephone number— and she doesn't know why not. It's a song about virtually nothing, an anthem of inconsequence and impassivity.

In comics, a group of artist-writers of Jones's generation such as Adrian Tomine and Matt Madden has been poking around the same territory, making prosaic autobiographical books about hanging out with friends, developing crushes (generally unrequited), doing temp jobs, or "whatever." The Web has provided a related phenomenon in blogs, which put their writers' daily lives up for public display in numbing detail.

The comics artist and writer Daniel Clowes would seem similar if his taste for the mundane were not so refined. He is the prolific author of short pieces, some of them autobiographical ("Art School Confidential," a story about his college years that he adapted to the screen), most of them drawn from his own experience ("Immortal, Invisible," inspired by his childhood memories of trick-or-treating, or "Like a Weed, Joe," in which his frequent stand-in, Rodger Young, suffers a dreary summer with his grandparents), others more fully imagined. In a sort of noirish magical realism set in mall society, "The Gold Mommy," a character who happens to look exactly like Clowes forgets to bring money to the barbershop and ends up murdered for no good reason.

Clowes has written several graphic novels that combine these different veins (most notably, *Ghost World*, which was made into a film in 2001). Throughout his work, Clowes's strength is his wry, affectionate way with the trite minutiae of everyday life (theme restaurants, licensed-character toys, frozen snacks, sitcom reruns) in a culture infused with commercial artifice. He has as sharp an eye for atmospheric detail as Sacco does—under the table at a yard sale in one sequence, we see the TV actress Patty Duke's long-playing album "Don't Just Stand There," an obscure artifact of Sixties plastic culture (wherein an adult who portrayed a teenager on television was repackaged as a pop singing star, thanks to studio wizardry)—and the landscape Clowes renders so acutely, commercial America, is despoiled and impermanent, too. Clowes's characters, like Sacco's, can't help but love it just the same because it's all they've ever known.

Ghost World, Clowes's most affecting book, is a languid story about a pair of teenage girls, best friends, during the summer after high school. They wander about the middle-class neighborhood of their childhood, killing time, jaded and fearful of losing their cool and each other. One of them might go to college and then again might not, and the other may follow her there. It's a warm, human book set in a landscape of vulgarity and falseness. Clowes has described the relationship of the protagonists, Enid Coleslaw and Becky Doppelmeyer, as the conflict between the id (Enid, whose full name is an anagram for Daniel Clowes) and the superego. Indeed, Enid is mercurial and lost, Becky more social and solid, although both characters are more nuanced than that—and they develop over the course of the book: breaking out of their childhood interdependence, Enid leaves town, while Becky turns to the boy they both loved.

Clowes, who is in his forties, understands the confused identities of young people on the cusp of adolescence and adulthood. "If you were to wake me up in the middle of the night and ask me how old I was, I would probably say I was eighteen," he told Terry Gross on NPR's *Fresh Air*. No wonder he excels in graphic novels, a medium teetering on the line between juvenilia and adult literature, too sophisticated for children but too closely associated with youth for the average grown-up.

Ghost World, like most of Clowes's other work, is drawn in black-and-white brush strokes, the figures rendered in the self-consciously awkward style that many alternative comic artists employ to impart a quality of anti-commercialism—yet some of Clowes's drawings, particularly the close-ups of Enid, have a tender delicacy, suggesting that he might be a more skillful draftsman than he lets on. His art looks naïve, while also conveying a sense of hidden potential, hinting again at the tension between youth and maturity. For this book, Clowes shaded his drawings with a pale aqua tone, making everything look as if it were a reflection of television, as most everything in the media-infused world of the book is.

Although it is a comic book, fictional, and absorbed with the ephemera of popular culture, *Ghost World* is ultimately concerned with the real world—that is, the peculiar reality of artifice as a defining force in a society dominated by the media and marketing. Enid loves a TV comedian who has adopted a forced "weirdo" persona because she considers him authentically phony. Her favorite restaurant is one of a chain of paltry recreations of 1950s joints, which she calls "the Mona Lisa of the bad fake diners" because it is so pitifully unconvincing. In a throwaway gag within one scene, a man perched on the second-story window ledge of a building overlooking a crowded sidewalk announces the television character whom each passerby resembles: "You look like Eddie Munster . . . you look like Homer Simpson . . . you look like Julie from the Mod Squad . . . ," echoing the theme of the dominance of television, but it's wholly inappropriate to Enid and Becky, because they themselves are nothing like characters from TV sitcoms, cartoons, or other comic books. The people they do remind me of are my daughter Torie and her high school friends: real young people struggling to find their place in the adult world.

I asked Torie if she had read *Ghost World*, Joe Sacco's books, or any other graphic novels, and she was insulted. She's seventeen, she reminded me—why would she read a comic book? It was exactly what someone in *Ghost World* would say.

The White Stripes

Rock 'n' roll has a quality of incompleteness that connects it to young adulthood. The music is formally underdeveloped. The lyrics do not need to hang together; the chords are not supposed to follow harmonic convention; the playing need not be precise; and if the singing is dead on pitch, it sounds wrong—that is, it sounds too right, too grown-up. Immanently unfinished, the music, like its audience, exists in a state of permanent adolescence and carries an implicit critique of adult society's esteem for maturity, effectuation, and refinement. Rock musicians have employed and periodically updated this aesthetic (or conspicuously rejected elements of it) for more than five decades, though few have done so as rigorously and as successfully as the White Stripes.

The band is not a band in the usual mode, but a duo of guitar and drums whose creative scales are heavily tipped on the side of the guitarist, Jack White. Born John Gillis in Detroit in 1975, he took the surname of his first wife, Meg White, a former shop assistant and barmaid who started playing the drums two months before they had their first gig as the White Stripes, in 1997. The Whites divorced at some point, but continued working together. They have maintained a creepy ambiguity about their relationship, referring to each other as brother and sister while trading in sexual innuendo on stage and in lyrics to songs such as "Sister, Do You Know My Name?" Jack White writes virtually all the material, words and music. (Although the first three of the group's six albums credited their compositions vaguely to "the White Stripes," subsequent releases of the same songs on DVD attribute them solely to Jack White; on the last three albums, all original songs have been credited to him alone.) He does nearly all the lead singing, save for two Meg White solo numbers, one of which is only thirty-five seconds long. And he plays the duo's dominant instrument, guitar, as well as some piano and, on their fifth album, a bit of marimba. The White Stripes is essentially a two-person, one-man band.

A new class of youngish singer-songwriters working under band aliases— Bright Eyes (Conor Oberst), Onelinedrawing (Jonah Sonz Matranga), Eels (Mark Oliver Everett), and Pedro the Lion (David Bazan), among the more prominent—has emerged in recent years, since desktop recording software such as ProTools has lowered the cost and the skill level necessary to make impressive-sounding multitrack recordings. Nearly anyone with some talent can now make a CD, alone, in his or her room. Digitally armed, solo artists have crossed into the terrain of bands and started taking their names. In due course, they have laid claim to the cool that comes with being in a group, while escaping (or postponing) the taint of wussiness inherent in being a singer-songwriter like James Taylor or Jackson Browne.

The White Stripes are radicals of this class, in part because they reject the technology that facilitates the music-making of most other one- and two-person groups of the day. (Quite a few guitar-and-drum duos, such as Nice Nice, Two Gallants, and Scissormen, have sprung up in the past several years, many in the Stripes' wake.) They play retro instruments—at a White Stripes concert at Manhattan's SummerStage several years ago, Jack White was playing a decades-old Kay archtop guitar, a starter instrument—and they record quickly, live in the studio, the way the Beatles did before they learned to exploit the studio and make the recording, not the composition or the performance, into the art form. A note in the booklet of the White Stripes' *Elephant*, which appeared in 2003, proclaimed in red italic type: "No computers were used during the recording, mixing, or mastering of this record." That is to say, no romantic notions about the analog past were harmed for the production. The statement was not so much a disclaimer as a claim to higher ground in a realm of pop recording perceived as authentic, and therefore superior, mainly because most other young artists aren't doing it that way today. So in truth its real claim is not to authenticity, but to exceptionalism—the enduring aspiration of adolescence.

Unlike Conor Oberst and the rest, Jack White has no interest in synthesizing the sound of a band. Synthesis is scarcely his interest. White uses a minimal number of instruments—on most tracks on the majority of the White Stripes' albums, just guitar (sometimes piano), drums, and voice: no bass to lay a harmonic foundation for a song and flesh out the rhythm section; no second guitarist to add counterpoint or stimulate his own playing; with very few exceptions, no additional musicians at all. The intent is clearly to sound not like an ensemble but like an ensemble part, a piece of something unfinished whose larger form is uncertain and irrelevant. White Stripes tracks sound like demos— or, occasionally, rehearsals for demos, the work of a couple (or a former couple, or a sister and a brother, or whatever) trying out ideas in their rec room. The recordings are bonus tracks of outtakes for albums never meant to exist. Few artists have taken the fractional nature of rock 'n' roll so to heart as Jack White and his ex-wife, the drummer who plays the same rudimentary beat to almost every song.

The White Stripes had released two albums to little effect in the United States when, in the summer of 2001, they went to England and were acclaimed there as the next new thing, largely because they reminded English critics of past next new things that had come from their own country: Led Zeppelin, the Rolling Stones, and the Beatles. "Believe the White Stripe Hype: Jack and Meg White Are the Story of the Moment," announced a rather self-referential headline in *The Independent*. Like Jimi Hendrix and the Ramones in olden days, the White Stripes returned to America legitimized by England, and they broke through here with their third album, *White Blood Cells*. The American musical climate was hospitable: pop was nearing the end of an overtly commercial phase, the era of boy bands and Britney Spears. The White Stripes seemed an antidote to the corporate thinking and technical artifice infusing the airwaves.

The English critics were on to something. The White Stripes do sound a lot like Led Zeppelin (and other groups that came up through the English electric-blues revival of the 1960s). On many tracks on their first few albums, Jack White sings almost exclusively in a pinched laryngeal squeak that seems almost a parody of Robert Plant, down to the hiccupping into falsetto and the abrupt, arbitrary wailing. His guitar playing, much the same, amounts to a reconfiguration of chordal effects and riffs that Jimmy Page and Eric Clapton (in his Cream days) adapted from vintage American blues. Compositionally, too, many of the White Stripes songs feel patched together from vinyl swatches: "Fell in Love With a Girl" (from *White Blood Cells*, which has been covered, as in obscured, by Joss Stone) uses the chorus of the Pretenders song "Middle of the Road"; "Hypnotize" (from the White Stripes' fourth album, *Elephant*) cribs the melody of Johnny Rivers's "Secret Agent Man"; and "As Ugly As I Seem" (from the Stripes'

2005 CD, *Get Behind Me Satan*) lifts the tune of Bob Dylan's "I Believe in You." Other songs appropriate more generally: here, a generic punk number ("Jumble Jumble" from the second album, *DeStijl*, named for the Dutch modernist movement); there, a playground chant ("We're Going to Be Friends" from *White Blood Cells*) or a country thing ("I'm Lonely" from *Satan*). Of course, all this comes in reduced form, as quick sketches—a couple of power chords, a few notes of lead guitar—that trace the outlines of earlier, more fully realized work; mnemonic devices for better things.

Meg White plays so sparingly that on some songs, such as "Sugar Never Tasted So Good" (from the first album) and "As Ugly As I Seem," Jack White feels compelled to add percussion fills by tapping patterns on his guitar. One way to think of her playing is economical. As such, it has an economy comparable to that of Baltic and Mediterranean Avenues, the dark-purple properties in Monopoly: it's the closest thing to bankruptcy, but only a game. Her ex-husband uses her as a found musical object, because her naïve, repetitive tapping in 4/4 time counterbalances his flailing and screeching, and also, I suppose, because she is incapable of getting in his way.

Jack White's various explanations of his partner's function are endearingly fanciful. "She brings a child-like quality to the music, an innocence, which is perfect for what we do," he said in an interview with the *Los Angeles Times*. In 2004, he told the *London Observer*, "I love the fact that it's hard for people to understand. We've said before that it's always been a great thing to get certain people to go away thinking, 'Oh dear, she can't play the drums!' 'Fine, if you think it's all a gimmick, go away!' It weeds out people who wouldn't care anyway."

Care about what? He didn't say. I would think that evidence of incompetence and gimmickry would weed out people who care a great deal about aesthetic integrity and honesty. White Stripes fans, whose numbers keep growing, must have a stronger appetite for contrivance and gamesmanship—or a more acute sense of irony—than Jack White is willing to admit. From the studied theatricality of the duo's public relationship, through their fetishization of old technology, to the rigid constriction of their music and their highly codified stage presentation, the White Stripes are a small circus of gimmickry.

In concert, the Whites wear only red, black, and white, and their stage sets invariably utilize the same motif. Every one of their albums (and singles) has been packaged in these three colors, evocations of which also lace through the words of their songs ("Broken Bricks," "Apple Blossom," "Black Math"). Graphically, this color scheme is elemental and severe, like the White Stripes' music. The visual components work together through sharp contrast and have a dynamic, kinetic effect. In this group of three visual elements, only one, red, is really a color. As an allusion, the scheme evokes early twentieth-century constructivist art and Soviet propaganda posters, in which extremism and delusion found vivid expression.

The fifth White Stripes album, *Get Behind Me Satan*, appears at first to be a significant departure from the duo's past music. Just three of the thirteen songs (the opening cut, "Blue Orchid," and "Instinct Blues" and "Red Rain") have Jack White's thrashing, distorted electric guitar, and only two of them give us White in his Robert Plant voice. On the first selection, White adopts a chirping 1970s funk falsetto, and the color in the song title isn't even red, white, or black! Most of the tracks have White strumming or fingerpicking an acoustic guitar, blocking chords on a piano, or tapping on a marimba, while he sings in a nasal, conversational tenor. Meg White's presence is often spectral; on some tunes, there are no drums at all, just some dinging on a triangle or ringing bells. (The tambourine-playing on the album is by Jack White.) The record—which is literally a record, released on vinyl LP as well as CD—is quieter and more varied in texture than the previous albums.

But finally it is of a piece with them, and ultimately less satisfying. Beneath its textural surface, *Get Behind Me Satan* is another collection of homages or larcenies ("The Nurse" ends like half a dozen John Lennon songs, the piano part to "White Moon" comes from Dylan's "Dear Landlord"), conspicuously arty gestures (a toy piano on "Red Rain," coy references to Rita Hayworth and studio-era Hollywood throughout the album's lyrics), and perfunctory musical ideas weakly or partially executed. As Jack White has said in interviews, he went into the recording studio without having finished the album's songs. He came out the same way.

Like most of the White Stripes' output, *Get Behind Me Satan* has the character of work tapes, the sound of music very much in progress. It disappoints more than its predecessors because the musicianship is poorer. Jack White is a skilled rock guitarist; mimicking Jimmy Page is not an easy thing to do. (That is why every teenager plays "Whole Lotta Love" to show off in the guitar store.) But White can barely execute simple triads on the piano; and his marimba playing is not exactly playing, it's learning on studio time. In a way, then, *Get Behind Me Satan* represents a triumph for Meg White as a musical force. The White Stripes' scales are now leveling to a point of equilateral amateurism.

Usually described as minimalism or primitivism, the aesthetic of the White Stripes is also a kind of formalism, in that they have always made themselves work within a set of carefully defined structures that matter more than their contents. They are obsessed with form, as well as with the dissembling of forms into smaller, essential units: a couple of instruments, a few chords, three colors. "The band is so special and so boxed in, and there are so many limitations," Jack

White told the *Ottawa Citizen* in 2003. "It's such an art project, in one sense. . . . I think eventually it's going to burn itself out. It can only go so far."

Two years later, he made *Get Behind Me Satan*, White's agrument for survival: an album that attempts to retain the specialness of the White Stripes by keeping the box, retaining the limitations, and changing only what is inside. The White Stripes still fetishize the past—*Satan* sounds as if it were recorded in Sun Studios after Elvis's sessions, and the CD booklet has a staged black-and-white photo of Meg and Jack White as members of a rockabilly band that could have been in Memphis in 1954. They still play all the instruments themselves, with Jack handling most of the creative work, and nearly all their songs are still variations on the same three models: electric blues, country blues, and children's music. Now they're doing so with acoustic instruments.

The White Stripes remain contemporary rock's masters of malformation. They have produced a body of work characterized by nothing so much as a refusal to be whole. All notions and whims, experiments and fits, their music begs for resolution and denies it. No wonder the band is so popular with young America: the White Stripes create the music of the IM age, the sound of tossed-off partial thoughts, blurted out and blithely replaced with more of the same, never concluding. Jack White may think of his work as a protest against the proliferation of digital technology, but his music is its leitmotif.

Abbey Lincoln and Mark Murphy

Near the end of 1956, two young jazz singers made their first albums: *Abbey Lincoln's Affair . . . A Story of a Girl in Love*, released by Liberty Records, a quality-conscious shoestring operation, and *Meet Mark Murphy*, issued by Decca, then a major jazz-pop label. Lincoln was twenty-six and black and a woman, Murphy twenty-four and white and a man, and both had talent and looks. For half a century, they followed separate and circuitous but roughly parallel career paths. Both started out singing in traditional modes, soon developed quirky original styles, indulged their inclinations to extremes, pushed the tolerance of the general public, moved out of Manhattan (Lincoln to California, Murphy to Europe), and bought time by doing some acting and teaching; and then both returned to the New York jazz scene and made a great deal of mature, sophisticated music.

Now in their seventies, Lincoln and Murphy have both survived bouts of grave illness and in 2007 released new CDs on the Verve label: Lincoln's *Abbey Sings Abbey* and Murphy's *Love Is What Stays*. Both of the albums are works about aging—or more precisely, about having grown old and looked death in the face; and they stand as companionable testaments to jazz's capacity to accommodate ideas all too rare in mainstream music, primary among them the notion that the end of life is a part of life worth the attention, the respect, and even the affection of serious artists and their audiences.

It is startling to find singers taking up the themes of old age and mortality, and even more surprising to find the artists treating these subjects honestly and intelligently, with no pretense of enduring youth nor cheap sentiment—especially in the summer of 2007, a season of slick, overdone, feel-good summer concert tours and music festivals. To watch Roger Daltrey and Pete Townshend parading under the good-because-it's-bad name of the once young and scary Who, or Mick Jagger prancing about with his beknighted sixty-four-year-old tongue stuck out, is to submit to a spectacular delusion of the pop-music world, wherein old age exists not as a natural phase in the cycle of life and death, but as a state of freakish artificial youth generated to sustain the feedback loop of narcissism spinning from the stage through the stands and back again.

Pop culture abhors the old as a matter of good business. After all, as we age we do tend to grow set in our ways of thinking and feeling—and therefore in our ways of buying. We are not great consumers anymore, and one reason we buy less is that we do less. (I should probably note here that I'm now over fifty.) The old may still have active lives, as the commercials never fail to remind us; but with the years, more and more of the activity becomes of the mind. This fact may serve more than anything else to alienate the old from the rest of America. To spend more time thinking than doing is one of the few things held in greater suspicion than to spend time not spending. Thus *Abbey Sings Abbey* and *Love Is What Stays*, both of which are sedate and pensive works, speak so eloquently in the milieu of age that they sound radical—more genuinely radical, certainly, than the pseudo-adolescent posturing of Daltrey and Townshend.

Jazz has long been a music hospitable to aging because it requires technical mastery of complex forms, it prizes individuality of expression, and it calls upon musicians to come to the bandstand with ideas worth expressing. Experience helps considerably in all these challenges—experience in living as much as in playing or singing. Several years ago I discussed some of these issues with Lena Horne, when she was recording her first album in more than a decade—her own statement on aging and mortality, which she did in the form of a musical message to departed loved ones, titled *We'll Be Together Again*. I asked her why she had let herself lie fallow for so long, and why she decided to dig back into work in her late seventies. "I was going through the motions. I thought that being a nightclub singer was a dumb thing to be," she said of the period when she had last performed and chose to hang up her sequins. And what happened during her years of self-imposed exile on Manhattan's Upper East Side? "I took long walks around the park, and I stayed at home by myself and read books," she said. "I learned how dumb I really was. Now, that's what I call getting smart."

Abbey Lincoln, who has acknowledged Horne as an important influence, has similarly cited uncertainty as a strength acquired late in her career. After a hypnotic, languorous performance at the Blue Note in New York a few years ago, she spent a bit of time with fans and reporters outside her dressing room, and someone asked her what she thought the young Abbey Lincoln would have made of the woman who had just performed. Lincoln said her youthful self "wouldn't understand her." Beaming, she added, "I don't understand her." Indeed, a kind of cryptic wisdom, an odd quality of mature naïveté, has given much of Lincoln's late-life music its unusual power.

The young Abbey Lincoln had been doing something more conventional, though doing it well, and the conventions of her time and place were sufficiently daunting. While the liturgy of the Rock and Roll Hall of Fame teaches us that old-fashioned popular music was so atrocious in the mid-1950s that Elvis had to come forth for pop's salvation, 1956 and 1957—the years of Presley's sensational ascent and the explosion of rock 'n' roll—were in fact a time of extraordinary achievement in Tin Pan Alley–style vocal music. Frank Sinatra, at the peak of his interpretive powers, released *Songs for Swingin' Lovers* and *Close to You and More*, contrasting gems of romantic bravura and sweet intimacy. Ella Fitzgerald began recording her now legendary *Songbook* series of records devoted to the canonical popular songwriters, releasing three double-album sets covering the works of Cole Porter, Rodgers and Hart, and Duke Ellington within two years, with time left for an album's worth of duets with Louis Armstrong. Billie Holiday gave her valedictory performance at Carnegie Hall, accompanied by a narrator reading excerpts from her (largely ghostwritten) memoir, *Lady Sings the Blues*. Lambert, Hendricks and Ross, the dazzling exemplars of jazz "vocalese," recorded their debut LP, *Sing a Song of Basie*. And singers such as Sarah Vaughan, Johnny Hartman, Carmen McRae, and Kay Starr were all doing some of the best work of their lives. The truth is, jazz-oriented popular music reached a creative peak at the time of rock's emergence. Adult pop had become an art music, better suited to listening and thinking than to dancing and necking, a fact that no doubt contributed to its abandonment by teenagers. Rock 'n' rollers, the victors in the end, have written the other side's early triumphs out of history.

Such was the musical environment that Abbey Lincoln and Mark Murphy dared to enter half a century ago, and their first albums showed their eagerness to prove themselves, if not to distinguish themselves, by the prevailing standards. *Abbey Lincoln's Affair* and its follow-up, *That's Him*, are of a piece: aggressive efforts to exploit Lincoln's beauty by packaging her as a doe-eyed, man-hungry sexpot. The jacket of the first album showed Lincoln lying on her back, waiting, laid out as if she were hanging upside down, and the songs on both albums were compatible messages of submission or paeans to male gratification: "Warm Valley" (a lyric version of the programmatic instrumental that Duke Ellington composed to suggest a woman's vagina), "When a Woman Loves a Man" (in which the singer is a fool in the "one-sided game" of romance), and other pieces such as "I Must Have That Man," "Strong Man," and "Don't Explain." Lincoln played the role, but she could not pull it off. There was too much bite and muscle in her singing for her to sound persuasively compliant and dim.

Like Murphy in his debut recordings and countless other musicians in their early work, Lincoln sounded more like her role models—here Billie Holiday, there Lena Horne or Dinah Washington—than herself. For Murphy, the main influence was Sinatra, followed by Nat Cole and Sammy Davis, Jr. Like many young singers, too, both Lincoln and Murphy fixed on technique to show off their vocal equipment and to establish their right to the big time, rather than employing it in the service of personal expression, as they would learn to do in a few years. Both initially focused on tonal production, making full, round notes and sustaining them over two or three bars at a time for all to behold. And both would soon leave the making of pretty sounds to Jo Stafford and Vic Damone, and shift their attention to lyrical content. In the phrase of another fine singer, Barbara Lea, they learned "not to be afraid to sound bad"—that is, not to sacrifice deeper meaning for surface beauty.

It helped Lincoln greatly to work with lyrics meaningful to her, as she began to do in 1959 with her album for the jazz label Riverside, *Abbey Is Blue*, which included Kurt Weill and Langston Hughes's "Lonely House," several tunes by the under-appreciated Oscar Brown Jr., and, significantly, the first of her own original compositions committed to record, a piercing blues called "Let Up." In the 1960s, Lincoln was devoted to civil rights and taken up with issues of African American identity. She worked closely with the gracefully probative drummer and composer Max Roach, who married Lincoln, later parted from her, and in 2007 ventured before her into death. Under Roach's direction, Lincoln sang and co-composed (with Roach and Oscar Brown Jr.) parts of a manifesto of black pride and defiance, a rhythmically multilayered musical collage for LP titled *We Insist: Max Roach's Freedom Now Suite*. Her enthusiasm for music waned in sync with the jazz audience's diminishing appetite for her politicking, and Lincoln relocated to Los Angeles, where she made a living acting, primarily for television, and teaching drama at California State Northridge. Although she made a few recordings in the 1970s and 1980s, most of them under patrons in Rome and Oslo and Tokyo, Lincoln did not commit herself fully to music again until the 1990s, when her career as a singer and songwriter finally came into bloom. Lincoln was a woman in her sixties, essentially starting over.

Murphy, in the 1960s, grew progressively committed to the hipster bebop that Lincoln left behind. For a white singer at the time, this was at once a mark of respect for African American musical culture and a jarring sign of outdatedness. Murphy, whose early promise as a jazz-pop crossover star was such that producer Milt Gabler predicted that he would "scare Frank Sinatra," abandoned any hope of mainstream success; his increasingly loopy scat solos and hepcat vibe scared the audience. Murphy moved to London, where he concentrated on acting for BBC television until the mid-1970s, when he returned to America and began performing and recording vocal music more deeply committed to bop, more retro, and more kooky than ever. Decades removed from the Beat era, Murphy no longer seemed a few years behind the times; he began to come across as fully a classicist, an artist committed to a sensibility born of another time but justifiable as more than kitsch or nostalgia.

Lincoln and Murphy have been revered elders of jazz singing for more than a decade now. Lincoln, in nearly a dozen albums as a leader, has produced a late-life body of strange and delightful sing-songy original compositions, freewheeling ruminations on her life, which she has performed with a sure, unaffected voice indifferent to nicety. Murphy, a true improviser with a sense of abandon, a strength of personality, and a melodic inventiveness rare in vocal jazz these days, has produced nearly twice as many CDs as Lincoln—all of them wildly ambitious, some of them just wild. Being an improviser, he comes off best in live performance, and his frequent shows in Manhattan jazz clubs are intoxicatingly, almost frighteningly unpredictable. I would rather watch Murphy sing, on the good chance of getting caught in the slipstream of one of his spacey vocal rides, than see nearly any of the hundreds of performers who call themselves jazz singers because they learned "How High the Moon." Murphy knows how high the moon is, and the way there, and he's taking passengers.

Their latest CDs find both Lincoln and Murphy in the ripest stages of their creative maturity. On *Abbey Sings Abbey*, Lincoln revisits many of the best original songs she recorded over the past decade, including "Bird Alone," "Throw It Away," "The Merry Dancer," and "Should've Been." These familiar pieces sound new here in part because Lincoln's producers and musicians have provided a new setting: in place of jazz veterans such as Hank Jones and Charlie Haden on traditional jazz instruments, the group here is composed of genre-crossing players such as Larry Campbell and Scott Colley, who accompany Lincoln on acoustic guitar, pedal steel guitar, mandolin, accordion, and such. The feeling of the record is earthy, of course, and warm and unhurried. The more significant change is Lincoln's singing, because her voice is nearly shot, ravaged by age and illness—but she uses all the liabilities of her vocal equipment as assets, croaking and cutting notes short, taking in breaths, almost moaning, with her head high, shoulders back, and stomach out. This is a record by a woman who is not only unafraid to sound bad but proud of it, and it is beautiful to hear.

On *Love Is What Stays*, Murphy is concerned mainly with departing. Nearly all the songs are reflections on loss—"Too Late Now," "Did I Ever Really Live," "What If" (the Coldplay song, done seriously and well), "Stolen Moments" (the Oliver Nelson instrumental with Murphy's lyrics, a signature tune of his), and nine more in their spirit. Murphy's voice is throaty and dark-hued but limber, and he sounds spontaneous, as always. He seems not to be singing the lyrics but thinking the words, and his thought has an unexpected quality of contentment. He gives us a take on loss—on death, really—without anguish or self-pity. If, as James Wood has remarked, reading literature like Saul Bellow's is "a special way of being alive," hearing music such as *Love Is What Stays* is to share in a special way of dying.

Three Women in Pop
Taylor Swift, Beyoncé, and Lucinda Williams

I
f you're going to run around with peacocks, which is what people generally do in the pop-music business, you could have no better training than Lucinda Williams had at the age of five. Her father, the poet Miller Williams, taught college in Macon, Georgia, during the late 1950s, and every two or three weeks he would take his daughter on a short drive to visit Flannery O'Connor, who loved peacocks—she had a small flock of them in her backyard and another flock in her writing. O'Connor let the little girl chase the magnificent, noisy birds, and Lucinda Williams would for the rest of her life carry a child's memory of the writer lady and her bizarre pets. After all, to have played with the peacocks in O'Connor's yard is kind of like having swatted butterflies at Nabokov's house.

In her three decades as a singer and songwriter, Williams has lived among the preening, extravagantly colorful creatures of the pop world, and she has remained a species apart. She has never taken up the manic showing-off, the strutting and crowing and sexual baiting which have been standard practices for popular singers, male and female, for ages. She is famously smart and steel-willed, though she can seem, even after all her years of touring, a bit nervous on stage; and she has always been sexy, although her particular allure involves something more advanced and adult than baiting. Her music is profoundly womanly. Williams gives the impression that she would take you home in a blink, if she thought you wouldn't bore her, and that you would bore her if you haven't read Flannery O'Connor. Posing neither as hen nor as cock, Williams is a woman rare among pop stars for her unfeathered intelligence, untheatrical carnality, and uncompromising humanity.

Now in her mid-fifties, more than twenty years older than O'Connor was on those afternoons in 1958, Williams is in the full bloom of her creative maturity. Late in 2008, she released a new studio album, her ninth since 1979. Called *Little Honey*, it is a big-hearted record—buoyant but reflective, a states-manlike work of rock 'n' roll music appropriate to its artist's age. I played it and enjoyed it when it came out, but I began fully to grasp how mature a work it is only after I uploaded the album onto my iPod, clicked "shuffle" while doing some puttering and heard one of the *Little Honey* tracks, "If Wishes Were Horses," play immediately after Taylor Swift's "Love Story," one of the hits from Swift's latest album, *Fearless*. Three or four songs after "If Wishes Were Horses," the iPod's random-choice algorithm served up a Beyoncé track. I clicked out of shuffle and sat down. Then I listened to the whole Swift album, and then to *Little Honey*, beginning to end, and then I played the latest Beyoncé release, the double-CD *I Am . . . Sasha Fierce*. (I couldn't sit through all eighteen tracks of the Beyoncé project, which is a kind of testament to it, since the music is not intended for sitting.)

A bit of imposed randomness helps to put Williams and her new work in proper perspective. It shows that *Little Honey* is an object lesson in how to be a grown woman in popular music—not merely a big girl or a bad girl, but a grown-up female person. The lesson is one of considerable (if not precisely equal) value to performers in all the realms of pop. Taylor Swift, the country star, who was nineteen when she released her second album in November 2008, will have to learn this lesson soon—ideally, tomorrow morning. She is just about on the verge of being too big, in terms of both age and fame, to be playing a girl. And she could find the challenges of her near future enacted in the tracks of *I Am . . . Sasha Fierce*, in which we witness Beyoncé, at twenty-seven, going bipolar in an effort to establish a new "bad" image without abandoning a "good" one that, at her age, may no longer work so well.

Like Lucinda Williams in her fifties, Taylor Swift in her teens has made music that seems wholly suitable to her age—or, in Swift's case, her age as it is imagined, glorified, and diminished in the tradition of teen-oriented pop. Swift, who started playing guitar and singing before she reached her teens, released her first CD, a self-titled album of original songs, when she was sixteen. (One of the tunes, "The Outside," was a trunk piece that Swift had written when she was twelve.) The songs on both of her first two albums evoke a sweet and largely outdated dream vision, prettified and petrified, of teenage life. It is a world in which the fragile adolescent id lives and dies by the crush, a place where love is all and sex is trouble. Swift writes confessional pillow-book songs centered on the old-school high-school themes of romantic aspiration ("Forever & Always"), the fulfillment of that aspiration ("I'm Only Me When I'm with You"), inevitable broken-heartedness ("Teardrops on My Guitar"), and the cruelties of teen society ("The Outside," "Fifteen").

Sex, in the songs of Taylor Swift, is a secondary, though hardly incidental, effect of amorous attachment. It is neither the be-all that it is in most pop music nor the commonplace that it is in the rec rooms and cars where that music is played. The kids in Swift's songs don't hook up, like real young people; they dream about going out on dates together and becoming couples, and they fear breaking up, like Stephanie Meyer's characters but without the fangs. It is evident from her music that Swift was home-schooled. She doesn't seem to know what is going on in the junior highs of America—or, perhaps, she has a special understanding of some need on the part of her young audience to counterbalance the hyper-sexualization in contemporary teen life with a kind of hyper-romanticization in teen culture.

The big hit from *Fearless* is a marvel of toothlessness called "Love Story," in which Swift retells *Romeo and Juliet* truly fearlessly, changing all the stuff about dying that the morbid original writer had in there. "I wrote this song because I could relate to the whole Romeo and Juliet thing," she explained to an interviewer. "I was really inspired by that story. Except for the ending. I feel like they had such promise, and they were so crazy for each other, and if that had just gone a little bit differently, it could have been the best love story ever told."

If positivity were a paramount measure of value, as Swift suggests it is, she would be the greatest American musical artist since Hannah Montana. Swift's music is uncommonly, irresistibly catchy—pop very much like soda, fizzy and bracing and so sweet that it makes you lightheaded and thirsty for more. I can enjoy what Swift does, the way I like a Pepsi in the afternoon. Her music can be faulted on multiple grounds—for its frivolity, its essential archaism, its denial of the coldly erotic, and of the tragic, in adolescent experience—but not on the grounds for which it is most frequently derided: for not being real country music. Both of Swift's full-length albums (she also released a Christmas EP better left unmentioned) qualify as country for reasons unrelated to their ritual, and largely gestural, use of Nashville musical clichés—a bit of bluegrassy fiddle, a dose of steel guitar near the bottom of the mix, and so on—the ingredients mandatory for the music to merit a country *hekhsher*. (Swift, who was born near Reading, Pennsylvania, and lived there until her early teens, when her parents moved to Tennessee for her career, has a hint of untraceable Southern color in her voice; and because Swift has actually lived in the South, her soft accent is considerably more convincing than the sketch-comedy twang that Bruce Springsteen somehow picked up on the Jersey Shore.)

The music that Swift makes is indisputably country in a Danto-ish way: it is music that country-music listeners listen to. It is pop, of course—but country music is, by tradition, pop. It is the popular music of audiences in rural and Southern communities, as well as in cities in the North, where radio listeners in the 1950s would pull in megawatt stations such as WWVA (out of Wheeling, West Virginia), and would, in their urban parochialism, mistake the country hits of the day for something ancient and primitive. Jimmie Rodgers and Hank Williams were pop stars in their time and place; and Williams adjusted his music, drawing more freely from Tin Pan Alley song structures and expanding his instrumentation, in a conscious effort to attract a broad national following. (On a boxed set of rare Williams radio broadcasts, *The Unreleased Recordings*, we can hear him playing western favorites with spare instrumentation for rural audiences at milking time, and the relative slickness of his better-known studio releases is striking by comparison.)

The unapologetic commercialism of Taylor Swift's music has roots at least as deep as the ostensible classicism of the Americana music movement that began to take form in the late 1970s and early 1980s, when Lucinda Williams was beginning to emerge as a singer and songwriter. By recategorizing music made in the vein of old-style country, the marketers of Americana sought to dissociate the work from Nashville and position it for a younger, broader audience, much as, a generation earlier, the record industry had replaced the established term "hillbilly music" with "country and western" to escape a set of limiting associations. Williams never fit the Americana label. While the recordings of her first decade were arranged and produced with an old-timey feel, Williams's best songs have always had the cryptic, anti-linear unconventionality of mid-'60s Dylan, and she has always sung with a rocker's bite. Over the years Williams's music has steadily moved further and further from the anachronistic, faux-natural artifice of the Americana scene. She has created a category of her own, as original artists tend to do.

Swift may well know that she, too, has to grow up. She is already wrestling publicly with the meaning of that proposition. In concerts, Swift sometimes breaks from her original material and sings what may seem an unlikely choice for a cover selection: a song by Beyoncé (and a team of five of Beyoncé's song-writing collaborators) called "Irreplaceable." The tune, from Beyoncé's second solo album, *B'Day*, is a taunt to a soon-to-be-ex, a reminder of a once-favored's disposability. Swift strums the tune's chunky rhythm on her acoustic guitar, and she barks, in full voice, "I could have another you by tomorrow/ Don't you ever for a second get to thinkin' you're irreplaceable."

* * *

How can a popular artist avoid being replaced, discarded, or forgotten, when popularity is essentially ephemeral? How can a girl singer not merely prevail, but also endure to do woman's work? Lucinda Williams could have been celebrating Taylor Swift's impenitent commercialism when she told an interviewer, in October of 2008, that "I didn't want to make a video when everybody else was making videos. I didn't want to sell out. I was horrified at that. Over the years, I've gotten more confident. I'm not so worried about fans thinking I've sold out if I make a video or, God forbid, if I get on the cover of *Rolling Stone*." And Swift could have been describing the absurd repositioning strategy of Beyoncé's latest album when she said, last November, that "I think when people make a record with a goal in mind like taking it to the next level or making them seem more mature, that gets in the way of writing great songs."

At a career crossroads, Beyoncé has chosen to go both ways, splitting herself into two musical personalities: the good-girl sexpot we have come to know as Beyoncé, and a newly revealed alternate identity, a bad-girl sexpot called Sasha Fierce. I have not checked this, but I presume the latter name is licensed from a drag queen. The persona that Beyoncé has constructed for Sasha Fierce—a slithery, dolled-up parody of a club girl—would certainly make a fine drag act if it had a glimmer of self-awareness or irony. It has none. As Sasha Fierce, Beyoncé offers her body parts—she has always relied upon them—but barely flirts, and when she flirts, she never winks.

As Beyoncé explained in press materials for *I Am . . . Sasha Fierce*, the album is "about who I am underneath all the makeup, underneath the lights, and underneath all the exciting star drama." Fierce "takes over when it's time for me to work and when I'm on stage, this alter ego that I've created that kind of protects me and who I really am." Fierce is "the party girl, she's bootylicious. She is, but I'm not. She's my alter ego. I'm finally revealing who I am."

The music provides little in the way of further clarity. While the album is packaged to present two sides of Beyoncé, one on each of two discs (or sets of files for downloading), the songs are largely interchangeable. There are more ballads on the first half of the album, the Beyoncé part, though many of them are danceable; and there are more out-and-out dance tunes on the Sasha Fierce half, though Beyoncé sings them and the would-be ballads with the same lusty bravura. Lavish and proficient, sleek but utterly cynical, *I Am . . . Sasha Fierce* is a jittery expression of careerism passing for complexity, a dumb show of sex play posing as adult business, a lurching attempt at professional advancement in the name of growing up.

Among the themes of Lucinda Williams's recent songs are the vagaries of the pop-music industry and the daunting odds of survival in it. She has watched the peacocks come and go, dazzle and fold up their feathers. Three of the songs on *Little Honey* ("Little Rock Star," "Rarity," and "It's a Long Way to the Top," a cover of the AC/DC song) deal explicitly with musicians and the music business, and at least one more could easily be about a fallen singer ("Jailhouse Tears," a tune about self-destruction in the mode of Williams's earlier "Drunken Angel," which was about the Texas songwriter Blaze Foley). The surprise among them is the AC/DC number, a blustering anthem that Williams sings straight, without self-glorification or self-pity. The treasure is "Rarity," an aching eight-minute message to a young woman with a musical gift, perhaps the singer's younger self. "They'll call you little honey," Williams sings in a dry hush.

And write you a check
Seduce you with money
And fuck your respect
'Cause you, you're a rarity
Your eyes say wisdom
Your skin says frailty
Your mouth says listen

Much of what Williams brings to bear on *Little Honey* speaks of wisdom, and little of it suggests frailty. Williams's voice, worn from hard use on the road (and abuse off-road), is a jagged instrument, not a weak one, and Williams wields it with casual surety.

After writing hundreds of tunes (and singing many more by other songwriters), Williams knows well how to work within the conventions of American vernacular music without slavish obedience to those conventions. The twelve original songs on *Little Honey* are precisely original enough to sound familiar and surprising. For instance, "Honey Bee," with its salty-sweet lyrics—"Oh, little honey bee, I'm so glad you stung me/Now I've got your honey all over my tummy"—has the retro sass of a Big Mama Thornton song, along with an almost punkish capacity to kick the listener's ass. One can only hope the song pops up on Taylor Swift's and Beyoncé's iPods.

PART V

Cultural Machinery

The Blogging of American Pop

Johnny Mercer, one of the master artisans of pre-rock popular music, was driving with some friends to the Newport Jazz Festival one summer in the early 1960s when a Chuck Berry song came on the radio. Mercer listened closely and grinned, as one of his car mates, the filmmaker Jean Bach, recalls. Soon he was singing along, beaming. Mercer leaned his face into the rushing air and slapped out the beat of the song on the side of the car that Bach's husband had rented for the weekend—a big red convertible, ideally suited to the moment. Bach isn't certain what record was playing, but she recalls it as something in the vein of "School Days" ("Hail, hail, rock 'n' roll!") or "No Particular Place to Go," the latter of which was a top-ten hit in the summer of 1964. Nor does she know what Mercer was thinking as he rocked and rolled up Interstate 95, although she remembers the occasion as "a picture of freedom."

While the author of "Autumn Leaves" and "The Days of Wine and Roses" found momentary liberation in Berry's freewheeling odes to teendom, the rising generation of young people had taken up rock around the clock because the music seemed anathema to everything that Johnny Mercer and his milieu represented—refinement, maturity, professionalism. Berry, like Mercer, made his reputation as a lyricist, the words of his breakthrough songs being the active ingredient that turned rhythm and blues into rock 'n' roll. Berry gave kids a music about their world (or dominant elements of it as imagined by a man in his mid-thirties), a hostel from adult society and its serious goings-on, a quotidian limbo ordered by the routines of attending school and killing time. "Up in the mornin' and out to school," he sang (in "School Days"), or (in "Too Much Monkey Business") "Same thing every day, gettin' up, goin' to school/No need for me to complain, my objection's over-ruled," or (in "No Particular Place to Go") "Cruisin' and playin' the radio with no particular place to go."

Much of the musical genre that Berry wrought—that is, the sounds on car radios for more than five decades now—has retained that absorption with the common rituals of everyday life among those living (literally or otherwise) outside the grown-up sphere. It was there in the beach music of the 1960s, reaching an early peak with Brian Wilson's myopic "In My Room." It permeated the Beatles' youthful songs about writing letters and holding hands. It waned with the rise of inflated styles such as psychedelia, heavy metal, and art rock, but returned with the punk of the Ramones, who brought American pop back to high school, and with the New Wave of Talking Heads, with all those songs about buildings and food. There were strains of it in grunge and alt-rock, which are descendants of punk and New Wave and deal in large part with the internal minutiae of dysfunction. (Hip-hop has little interest in the ordinary or in smallness of any kind, and revels in grandiosity and ostentation.)

Now pop prosaism has reached full bloom with the work of a school of young (and youngish) singer-songwriters whose aesthetic is based upon having no particular place to go and nothing in particular to say. This is a phenomenon as yet unmeasured, as far as I know. Billboard has not yet introduced a tedium chart, despite the success of practitioners of the discipline such as John Mayer and Aimee Mann (and sometimes Dave Matthews). I have heard a few dozen albums of this sort—collections of simple, modest tunes centered on workaday events and small moments. Many come from singer-songwriters with cultish followings, such as Sam Beam (a multi-instrumentalist who records under the name Iron and Wine), Mark Oliver Everett (another multi-tracker, who records as Eels), F. M. Cornog (who uses the name East River Pipe), and Mark Linkous (who, along with other musicians, plays various instruments to record as Sparklehorse). I have also seen at least twice as many lesser-known performers of their ilk in the clubs of Manhattan's Lower East Side over the past couple of years. The numbers amassing on this tiny piece of musical terrain are overtaxing its limited resources.

One evening in the summer of 2004, I went to the Living Room on Ludlow Street to hear Jill Sobule (who is quite another story, as I will explain shortly) and saw four acts before she came on. Three were essentially interchangeable singer-songwriters, two women and one man. The first murmured songs that seemed to be about students hanging out in student hangouts such as the Living Room and the cafes surrounding it—hearing the songs, one feels as if one were in them, an effect that is flattering and interestingly referential, but ultimately depressing. The second artist, who crooned with an ambiguous Eastern European accent but spoke like my cousins in New Jersey, did similar-sounding tunes (meaning numbers that sounded like their predecessors as well as one another) that were also about social inertia; one song described not wanting to talk to a stranger in a park who was reading a magazine and may or may not have wanted to talk to anyone anyway. (That is a paraphrase, but close to the actual lyrics.) The third had more of a country-and-western approach, but still sang meandering story-songs with little in the way of stories to tell; her hallmark was to do so in a monotone that had a twang.

The name of the club notwithstanding, this is hardly living-room music. Deeply solitary in point of view and mode, it feels inappropriate to a setting even nominally social. Its home—its universe—is the dorm room. The thoughts in the lyrics often seem like just that: thoughts, rather than language filtered, selected, and organized for public consumption. They are things most of us would say aloud only if no one could hear us. As Mark Linkous of Sparklehorse sings in his tune "Pig":

> I wanna try and fly
> I wanna try and die
> I wanna be a pig
> I wanna fuck a car
> I wanna new face right now
> And I want it bad
> I wanna new body that's strong
> I'm a butchered cow

Like Sam Beam, Linkous often sounds all alone on his CDs, occasionally singing in a hush so soft that the microphone barely picks up his voice. (The credits to the Iron and Wine CDs note, "Recorded, produced and written by Sam Beam. Recorded at Sam's house in Miami, Florida." Much the same, F. M. Cornog has recorded the bulk of his output in his apartment in Astoria, Queens.) Of course, every modern (or modernist) songwriter is engaged in personal expression, and the sentiments of most popular songs have always been intimate. But Everett, Beam, and their peers are doing something that transcends self expression—or, rather, that precedes it. The sounds they make, just barely, are the closest thing to not expressing themselves at all and keeping everything inside.

The obvious corollary to this genre is Web chatter. In the work's formless, unmediated presentation of highly personal yet largely generic trivia, it is musical blogging. The lyrics tend to be heavily laden with detail: descriptions of lovers (usually lost), friends, parents, siblings, passersby, neighbors, pets. We follow the songwriters as they walk or drive around, absorbing the scenery with them. Just as often, we sit or lie with them as they imagine things never done. As Mark Oliver Everett sings in "Fucker":

> *Could go to a party*
> *But I don't really want to*
> *For now I'm sitting out here on my porch*
> *Writing in the dark air*
> *Listening to my little black cat meow*

In a set at the C Note on Avenue C in Manhattan early in 2004, a singer-songwriter used nearly half of his allocated twenty minutes on stage to do one song about how the audience looked from the stage the last time he was there. I wrote some phrases from the lyrics in my notes: "spotlight glaring like the sun," "clang of plates and glasses," "faces looking back at me." Below them I wrote, "What am I doing?" I had begun to feel that I was giving the song more thought than the composer had.

Owing to its randomness and its excess, the ostensible richness of specificity in such music, like the yammering in a blog, is impoverishing. The indiscriminate details in songs like John Mayer's, with their couplets about standing in line at CVS, ordering take-out food, or sitting around watching CNN, fail to illuminate; they obscure. By telling us everything he sees and does, no matter how banal, the songwriter reveals nothing of himself (or herself, in the case of Mann) and the world he mutters about. There is a real-time quality to this work: instead of compressing experience, it simply reiterates it. It denies the distinction between experience and art. No music could be more appropriate to the wired culture of e-mail and texting, wherein every moment appears to warrant recording, one way or another.

When Bob Dylan released his song "Positively 4th Street" as a single in the mid-1960s, the venomous assault on an unnamed friend or lover (likely a stand-in for the folk purists who had accused Dylan of apostasy for shifting to rock 'n' roll) seemed as liberating in its way as "School Days" had been. "You've got a lot of nerve," Dylan snarled, "to say you are my friend." Composers working prior to and outside of rock (in art song, musical theater, the blues, and many of the world's folk musics) had long exercised the license to write about anything. Still, Dylan still stretched his listeners' ears. He seemed to break apart the frame of rock songwriting in music that is surely the model for most of today's singer-songwriters.

Unfortunately, Dylan's breadth exerts no more appreciable influence than his prolificity. Liam Clancy, the Irish folksinger, once told his young Greenwich Village compatriot, "Bobby, you have a great gift. Those wonderful words just flow out of you. But do there have to be so many of them? All those verses!" Dylan's young descendants—songwriters such as Mayer, Everett, and Linkous, as well as Devendra Banhart, Joanna Newsom, Adem (just Adem), and others, are writing not just about anything, but about everything. As such, they tend to communicate nothing except self-absorption.

I have to wonder if that isn't the point, to some degree, for at least a few of them. These are not artists without talent or intelligence. To the contrary, Sam Beam and Mark Linkous in particular are skillful musicians, each with a knack for evoking mood, and their lyrics have moments of subtle potency. ("We found your name across the chapel door/ carved in cursive with a table fork/muddy hymnals and some boot marks where you'd been," sings Beam in Iron and Wine's "Muddy Hymnal.") Why would they and so many of their contemporaries devote themselves so zealously to mundanity if not out of some kind of shared conviction? The incessant sameness and vacancy of their music certainly mirrors the environment in which today's young people grew up, a landscape of chain outlets and theme restaurants scrolling over and over like the background in a Hanna-Barbera cartoon. Perhaps they mean their prosaic, soundalike songs to reflect their world and at the same time to protest it, as if to say, "Look at all the nothingness everywhere, and listen to what it has made of us."

Jill Sobule, a singer and songwriter who has released five albums on nearly as many labels since 1990, seems to be working in the same genre of prolix vapidity, but she is not. She writes songs fixed on the domestic realm, and she sings them in a pretty, girlish voice. In her hands, however, neither the material nor its execution is as simple as it first seems. Sobule is a deft ironist. She is smart and original, a treasure undervalued by inevitable association with countless lessers who also happen to be singing about going to the laundromat in Brooklyn. Once a teenage rocker who sang and played lead guitar in bands in her native Denver, Sobule was signed to MCA Records when she was twenty-three and tossed into the mitts of Todd Rundgren, who produced her first album as if it were his own (and not hers), applying thick coats of his pop gloss onto Sobule's earnest youthful tunes. The record (*Things Here Are Different*) failed to justify the cost of Rundgren's misplaced excesses, and Sobule was dropped from the label. Five years later, she made the first CD of her creative maturity, an eponymous album of sharp, wry songs about life on the fringes. One of the tracks, "Supermodel," a punkish trifle that toyed with the cliché of impossible dreams, made it onto the *Clueless* soundtrack, and another, "I Kissed a Girl," a rocker about a fling with another woman, became a hit single. The latter was a breakthrough in pop history and a source of great pride to Sobule, although it ended up pigeonholing her as a lesbian artist. "I've been with women, and I've been with men," Sobule has said, "and they both suck, actually." (The biography on Sobule's Web site recounts her early life with her parents, the "Flying Sobules" circus troupe; her duty in a Marine Corps special forces unit in Vietnam; and other fanciful imaginings instead of factual data.)

In 2000, Sobule released a wonderful little album, *Pink Pearl*, which, like all her music after the Rundgren project, has deserved more attention. A pearl indeed, it uses to its advantage everything that undermines the music of her peers. It is full of very small moments—watching a woman working out at the gym, downing grits at a roadhouse in the South, making weekly visits to an old-lady friend—but they are discerningly selected, vividly observed, and ripe with multiple meanings. Musically, it is simple—melodies of a narrow range set against a few chords played by a small band or Sobule alone on acoustic guitar— yet it is tuneful, clever, and pithy. It expresses its share of impassivity—one song, "One of These Days," is a dance tune for people too lazy to get up—but never romanticizes it. The record also has a couple of attributes lacking in a great deal of contemporary music of every style: it is fun and it is dark, frequently at the same time. In "Guy Who Doesn't Get It," for instance, Sobule sings:

> *Say I'm in the tub with a razor blade*
> *You'd walk in and ask me, "How was your day?"*
> *Then you'd lather up and start to shave*
> *As I bleed on the new tile floor*

Sobule's 2004 CD, *Underdog Victorious*, refers to a childhood friend who is the subject of the title song, to the TV cartoon hero voiced by Wally Cox, and, obliquely and most ironically, to Sobule herself. It is of a piece with *Pink Pearl*— a lovely, charming, and often disturbing album. The mood is a bit grayer and bittersweet; one song, "Tel Aviv," tells of a woman hijacked to the Middle East for sex; another, "Last Line," stunningly interlaces the desperation of clinging lovers with their craving for cocaine. The highlight, "Strawberry Gloss," likewise recalls the summer of a young girl's coming-of-age as a time of entwined exhilaration, bafflement, and terror.

In the set she did at the Living Room that summer, Sobule mentioned that she had just returned from serving as the opening act for Don Henley. She had been booed by his audience in Atlanta, she said, because she had been wearing a T-shirt that read, "My bush would make a better president!" (Sobule now offers shirts like it for sale on her Web site.) She is not crude, as a rule; in fact, she generally comes across as sweetly demure, both on her recordings and on stage. She is impish, though, and no longer seems to give a fuck about public approval. She appears to have given up on mainstream success. This, no doubt, is a source of her work's power—it is devoid of affectation and careerism—and the reason she may well remain deserving of more attention for some time.

MySpace

A shamelessly goofy band of street musicians performs in and around the subway station at Union Square in Manhattan—a banjoist, a washtub bassist, a percussionist who plays cookware, and someone doing something else, as I recall. Not long ago, I took the group's business card, which says "No Music, No Party," and then gives a phone number. I wondered if the phrase was the name of the ensemble or a terse statement of philosophy. If it is the latter, the fellows have a point that is borne out through cultural history. A great deal of human social interaction has always been conducted to music, notwithstanding Adorno's protests that social function stains the "purity" of music. A wealth of treasured and enduring music, formal and informal (as well as aptly forgotten background noise), was originally created for get-togethers of all sorts, from Mozart's divertimenti and serenades to Louis Armstrong's New Orleans stomps to Bill Monroe's barndance bluegrass to Sly Stone's dense polyphony au go-go. No party, no music.

Every kind of socializing calls for its own music, and most of the action in social interaction transpires among young people, enslaved by their hormones to the service of meeting and attracting one another, thus perpetuating not only the species but also its popular music. At the moment, MySpace is enacting a transformation in the social behavior of teenagers and people of college age (in addition to some younger and older). In the process, the site has already had a stunning effect on the music of youth culture. MySpace is rapidly establishing a new system for hanging out and hooking up—a kind of new paradigm for young life; and, like all the old paradigms, it carries with it hazards, only one of which is its impact on music.

Founded in 2003 by Tom Anderson, who was twenty-seven at the time and who handles the creative end, and Chris DeWolfe, then thirty-seven and the money man, MySpace is a hybrid site, part networking forum, part music resource. The idea, a primordial one transported to cyberspace, was to use music to bring young people together. Anderson, who was playing guitar in an alternative-rock band called Swank when he began developing MySpace, thought it would be way cool to have a place on the Web where ambitious, unknown musicians such as himself could try to attract a following by posting their portraits, bios, information on upcoming gigs, and sample music files. But unlike several dozen sites that already did all that, MySpace encouraged users to interact with participating musicians, as well as with one another—to chat through text messages and to exchange digital pictures, building a community of people connected by an interest in new music.

Anderson had the wisdom to enlist some acquaintances, gorgeous female club kids, to be among the first MySpace users to post their photographs, imparting upon the site a patina of phototropic cool. He created what is essentially the biggest nightclub in the incorporeal world, open all day and night. It is open to virtually anyone and to anyone virtual. The only velvet ropes, thin and malleable, are MySpace's token restrictions: the site is prohibited to those under fourteen, though MySpace requires no proof of age. (It has a bouncer at the door but does not card.) MySpace also forbids the use of "personally identifiable information," though it permits messages that might contain hints of a member's identity, such as the person's name, hometown, and birthday.

As I type this, MySpace has some 55,667,000 members, and the number is no doubt higher by this point in the sentence. More than a million bands and solo musicians now have profiles on the site. On a typical day, MySpace receives two and a half times the traffic of Google. The popularity of Anderson and DeWolfe's venture among young people is such that Rupert Murdoch appropriated it in 2005, buying a controlling interest in MySpace's parent company and access to another generation for $580 million.

Open, loosely policed, and populated almost exclusively by young people presenting themselves as attractively as possible, MySpace offers abundant temptation to voyeurs and sexual predators. The site provides free and easy access to a vast and constantly replenished supply of teenage girls and boys, many of whom have posted images of themselves in various stages of undress, along with messages describing their tastes in sex as well as in music. Since anyone can pose as someone else on MySpace, it is impossible to measure the lurking. Fifteen-year-old Kimberly, the girl on a farm in Wisconsin, could really be fifty-two-year-old Buck, the parolee in a trailer in New Jersey, hiding behind a scan from a high school yearbook and a few convincing phrases of teenage jabber. At least two cases of sexual assault of underage girls have been traced to initial meetings on MySpace, according to newspaper reports.

As a social environment, MySpace is a sexual minefield, and this troubling fact is not mitigated by the fact that, as a musical resource, the site presents a set of problems of another sort. Much has been made of the Internet's effect on the music business. Everyone knows that, thanks to file-sharing and paid downloading services such as iTunes, CD sales have been declining for years. Apple (Steve Jobs's company, not the Beatles' record label, the latter of which now profits nicely from its trademark license to the former) has become one of the top three suppliers of music in the country. Yet MySpace represents something other than a new delivery system or a different economic model for the music industry. It is altering the dynamics of the relationship between the two groups of young people involved in popular music: the musicians and their audience. And so, in due course, it is changing the music itself.

MySpace, in its essence, seems like the realization of a democratic, almost utopian ideal. It eliminates or marginalizes the traditional bodies of mediation between those who make popular music and those who listen to it. A band does not need radio play, nor a video in rotation on MTV, to find an audience through MySpace. It does not need a record contract. It does not have to play a single gig. It needs only a Web page with a few song samples—though good photos and bio text, along with a willingness to chat with fans online, can help considerably. The way MySpace works is that members log on and message back and forth, exchanging thoughts on topics of the moment, including music. If they want to know more about a particular band, they click to the group's page and listen to (or download) a song; and if they like what they hear, they can spread the word among MySpace members on their list of "friends." Some MySpace users have as many as six thousand friends. As Greg McIntosh, the guitarist for a Michigan-based band called the Great Lakes Myth Society, said in an interview, "It's like being at a giant music conference twenty-four hours a day every day."

Emerging as it has in the wake of Clear Channel's domination of radio stations and rock concert halls, MySpace appears to be a grassroots counterbalance to the wholesale absorption of the music industry by a handful of entertainment-industry conglomerates. At the same time, it is yet another monolith—born of the people, yes, but owned by Fox.

MySpace has begun to spawn a breed of its own rock stars, bands that have made their reputations mainly through the site: Fall Out Boy, a punk-pop quartet that was nominated for a Grammy for Best New Artist in 2006; Hawthorne Heights, another punk-pop group; Panic! at the Disco, a kitschy techno ensemble; and Arctic Monkeys, a quartet of nineteen- and twenty-year-olds from Sheffield, England, who were already famous, largely through MySpace, before they signed with Domino Records in 2005. When the group released its first CD, *Whatever People Say I Am, That's What I'm Not*, the following January, the album entered the British pop charts at number one, and the single "I Bet You Look Good on the Dancefloor," was the fastest-selling record in English history. Arctic Monkeys, whose music is tuneful punkish pop, performed in the United States for the first time the following spring.

Through MySpace, some bands have built ardent followings so quickly that audiences know the words to their songs before the musicians know how to play them. Fall Out Boy headlined the Warped Tour of punk acts in 2005, and I caught one of the shows in Milwaukee, during a vacation with my son, who was a senior at the University of Wisconsin. Fairly impressed by the group's second CD, *From Under the Cork Tree* (an album with some good juvenile thrashing), I was looking forward to seeing the band and was surprised to find it utterly inept on stage—and I mean really inept, not inept in accordance with the anarchic conventions of punk. The singers (guitarist Joseph Trohman and bassist Peter Wentz) never used the microphone, and the band stopped and started in the middle of tunes, struggling nervously to find its place. (Not caring would have been punk. Struggling nervously was incompetent.) I heard most of the words, though, because the audience chanted the lyrics.

One band wildly popular on MySpace, Hollywood Undead, never played in public before becoming a sensation online. The group formed early in the summer of 2005 and posted a MySpace page adorned with mysterious-looking photos of the seven members of the band, their faces hidden behind hockey masks and gimmicky shrouds, along with three songs, each a listenable amalgam of hip-hop and heavy metal. As one of Undead's singers, Jeff Phillips, told the *New York Times*, "We were just a bunch of loser kids who sat around our friend's house all day, and we started making music and recording it on computer. . . . In a matter of weeks it got huge, and it kept on getting bigger and bigger. . . . If you look at our page, it's like we're a huge band that's toured a hundred times." By

March 2006, Hollywood Undead has had more than 2 million plays on MySpace, and it had yet to tour.

The instant fame conferred by MySpace is becoming the standard practice of our time, of a piece with American Idol and its variants on television, which pit amateurs against one another in competition for celebrity as spectacle, granting us viewers the dual pleasure of glorying in the ascension of one of our own and wallowing in the humiliation of those to whom we relate more closely, the losers. MySpace fills most of the space on its music pages with the work of awful bands, hundreds of thousands of them, and trolling among them provides a kind of perverse entertainment. The music is searchable by five criteria: band name, band bio, band members, influences, and "sounds like." After an hour or so of using the search mode to find something worth the effort, I got punchy and, after the words "sounds like," typed "shit." Pages for more than three hundred bands popped up, and the first five, I can attest, were well categorized.

So much of the music on MySpace is so grossly underdeveloped that listening to it is almost an act of aesthetic pedophilia. Thanks to MySpace, young bands no longer need to start out by gigging, playing one-nighters, making mistakes in near anonymity, learning what works, finding their voice through a dialogue with their audience—I mean a musical dialogue, not a chat. Good bands have no need, and no time, to get better before they get famous. Surfing MySpace, I listened to a few of more than two hundred groups that listed themselves as sounding like the Beatles, and I began to consider what the moptops themselves sounded like in their apprenticeship, when they were working out their style by labor and trial, playing six sets a night for dancers in Hamburg. Then I remembered having heard Bruce Springsteen when I was a kid and he was just starting out: he sounded like a garage-ish cross between Van Morrison and Bob Dylan, but not yet like Bruce Springsteen.

The boggling scale and speed of MySpace conspire to inhibit originality, while rewarding familiarity and accessibility. The site attracts innumerable groups that sound like other acts successful on MySpace, and it engenders mediocre music that makes a quick, positive impression. Lost in the blitz of clicking on MySpace is challenging music that might be off-putting at first but could grow on listeners, stretching their ears and provoking their minds. All the bands to rise from MySpace so far, including the talented but madly overpraised Arctic Monkeys, are good, but there is not a great one among them. One cannot help but wonder if MySpace is screening out the great ones, or failing those with the capacity for greatness.

As a measure of musical tastes, MySpace is skewed by its social character. MySpace members generally discover bands through recommendations by other members. But like all information disclosed among parties inclined to impress one another, the data is loaded, likely to reflect social expectations as much as, perhaps more than, musical passions. For instance: the son of mine with whom I saw Fall Out Boy loves not only punk rock but also the music of Ella Fitzgerald and Stephen Sondheim, yet he says that he would never admit as much on MySpace. If many of the site's members are to a significant degree mouthing what they hope will make them seem cool, they are saying only what they are hearing (or typing only what they are reading). Once again, the famously raucous individualism of the Internet results in crass conformism. The spiral effect, accelerating to tornado intensity, surely accounts for the almost instantaneous emergence on MySpace of bands such as Hollywood Undead, which are simply nothing special.

So MySpace is finally not quite as democratic as it seems, and its ostensibly democratic systems are as susceptible to corruption as any in non-cyber societies. MySpace has not eliminated mediation from the music business, it has merely supplanted the old modes with new ones. There are powerful instruments of influence in this allegedly free terrain. Webmasters have the power, once consigned to concert promoters, to lure crowds to a band. (On the day of this writing, the most listened-to artist on MySpace was the sexy electro-pop vocalist Tila Tequila, and the lead photograph on her page showed her sitting on the ground, her lips pressed to the end of the picture frame, kissing something that we cannot see but which would fall at the height of a standing man's crotch.) A whole new industry of "viral marketing" employs surreptitious e-mail techniques to spread messages about paying clients to music enthusiasts online. And acts such as Hollywood Undead, a phony band hidden behind funny masks and elaborate concealments, have mastered one of the most effective ways to prevail on MySpace: pretending to be what others would like you to be. The sexual predators have figured that out, too.

The Music of Starbucks

About fifty years ago, when the Soviets who survived Stalin began to accept the gift of his death, the state's cultural overlords started to loosen their choke hold on the country's music. The Communist Party–controlled Composer's Union consented to music other than programmatic works about collective farming, and Pravda acknowledged merit in modernist compositions of Shostakovich that it had previously declaimed as "chaos rather than music." The golden era of musical totalitarianism, a time when the libretto to *Tosca* could be re-written as *The Battle for the Commune*, was passing.

Simultaneously in the United States, the postwar atmosphere of sprawling conformity and eight-cylinder conservatism sparked in the offspring of the World War II generation a countervailing interest in all things bohemian. Dark little coffeehouses inspired by European cafes began to open around the country, and their music was part of their appeal. In Cambridge, the prototypal coffeehouse of the era, Tulla's Coffee Grinder, had only a tabletop radio, but the thing was on all day and night, tuned to the Harvard station, which played a lot of bebop. Live jazz (or spirited approximations thereof) flourished in the coffee-houses that followed, the sax and bongo playing sometimes mixed with Beat poetry or broken up by a few songs from a folksinger strumming a guitar.

By the mid-1950s, folk music came to dominate the coffeehouse scene. Earthy, old-fashioned but also trendy, easy to play without training and to sing passably without talent, left-leaning, and held in suspicion or overt contempt by many adults, folk songs fit companionably with the espresso and the imported cigarettes in the musty clubs that young patrons saw as hostels of cultural dissent. By the late 1950s, there were coffeehouses with music in every major American city and college town: half a dozen in Cambridge and the surrounding area (including the Cafe Yana, the Golden Vanity, and Club Mt. Auburn 47); more than three times as many within a few blocks in the bohemian mall of America, Greenwich Village (among them the Gaslight, Cafe Figaro, Cafe Rienzi, Cafe Wha?, and the Hip Bagel); and kindred joints in Berkeley (the Blind Lemon), San Francisco (the Drinking Gourd), Los Angeles (the Gas House), Tampa (the House of Seven Sorrows), Denver (the Green Spider), and St. Louis (the Laughing Buddha), among others.

About fifty years later, there are dozens of coffeehouses in every major city in the United States—more than eight thousand in this country now, plus more than three thousand elsewhere around the world. They are all called Starbucks. That is to say, there is a single coffeehouse duplicated some eleven thousand times. The replicant spawn of Tulla's Coffee Grinder, mutated through savvy marketing, Starbucks exploits the egalitarian, outré cool of the postwar coffee-houses in a low-key empire of flawless, impermeable elitism and conformity.

Like its ancestors in Cambridge and Washington Square, Starbucks approached music casually at first. Its outlets always played albums in the background—initially favorites of the stores' sales personnel, and later CDs that Starbucks began offering for purchase through displays on cash-register counters and on swiveling racks in the corners of its outlets. Since 2004, when the chain had a major hit in Ray Charles's final Grammy-winning album of duets, *Genius Loves Company* (co-produced by Concord Records and Star-bucks, and promoted heavily by the latter), the organization has been engaged in a grand campaign to expand its business in music. The Starbucks entertainment division (the largest part of which is Hear Music, the company's CD label) has come to employ more than a hundred people, and it moved from the parent company's home base in Seattle to Santa Monica. In 2005, Starbucks sold 3.5 million CDs, many of them albums conceived, produced, and marketed with such authoritarian rigor and with such a narrow conception of their listeners' good that they represent nothing less than the return of state-sponsored music.

Starbucks is a state for our day, a commercial society organized within psychographic, rather than geographic, borders—parameters that are now more meaningful than the old rivers, mountain ranges, roads, and lines of longitude and latitude that cable TV, the Internet, and cell phones render moot. For its citizens, Starbucks serves as an all-in-one marketplace/social center/hideaway, a corporeal version of the Internet, where they can meet and make friends, date, write notes, pay bills, conduct business meetings, even find solitude in the cocoon of iPod earplugs. While they are in their new habitat, they also purchase some 4 million drinks per day.

The Starbucks habitués are united in part by age (under thirty, or so they generally appear), race (more Anglo than otherwise, it seems in outlets outside ethnic neighborhoods), and class (middle and above, presumably), though what most unites them is the aspiration to belong to the young, white, moneyed community that we all perceive Starbucks to be. The company does not post its demographic statistics—wisely, for to do so would be to relinquish its allure. The whole point of paying $4.90 for a frappuccino is not to spend twice the reasonable price for a glass of chilled fat and sugar, but to do so as if such an outrageous act comes naturally, as if money means nothing and the word "frappuccino" means something. It is not in conventional measures of value, but in their absence, that Starbucks's customers find worth, particularly self-worth.

As the company's chairman, Howard Schultz, explained the expansion of Starbucks's music business, "Our customers have given us permission to extend the experience." How did they do that, I wonder. Did they sign a slip? Or has Schultz conflated acquiescence with will, as autocrats in coffee, music, or politics are inclined to do?

The "experience" to which Schultz refers is that of the consumption of taste, be it in coffee, creamy fruit drinks, pastries, or CDs. Indeed, he is leading his company to become an official arbiter of taste in the arts as well as in foodstuffs, an institution interested less in satisfying the tastes of its customers than in instilling them. In the realm of its first business, drinks and snacks, Starbucks displayed a belief in the malleability of judgment that approached contempt for the individual's will. Why call a small drink its opposite, "tall"? Why trademark a word for a size, such as "venti"? Why insist on referring to your salespeople by the Latinate term "baristas," with its evocation of both legal counsel and guerrilla warfare? Why, if not to press your authority to the limits of irrationality and to test the boundaries of your targets' passivity?

Starbucks produces and markets several lines of CDs, one of which, the Opus Collection, picks up the company's principles of linguistic obfuscation and tactical packaging and carries them into music. The series title appropriates the classical-music term for a collection of concert pieces, in order to conjure gravitas, while meaning, essentially, the Collection Collection. Small matter. The greater problem with the series is its manner of reducing musicians with complex bodies of work to simple images to which young consumers of venti frappuccinos can relate. The Opus Collection takes important artists from jazz and popular music—Louis Armstrong, Tony Bennett, Nat "King" Cole, Miles Davis, Ella Fitzgerald, Marvin Gaye, Billie Holiday, Etta James, Elvis Presley, Sly Stone, Jackie Wilson, and others—and makes them brands.

A great many of the CDs in the Collection focus solely or largely on the musicians' early work, with cover photos that show them young and sexy. (Even when albums include work from late in the artists' careers, as in the Tony Bennett and Ella Fitzgerald CDs, the covers usually present the artists' youthful selves; a notable exception is the Louis Armstrong release, which has a charming photo of a grandfatherly Armstrong mopping his brow.) The Elvis CD, titled *Boy from Tupelo*, draws from his primordial sessions for Sun Records in Memphis and his earliest recordings for RCA in New York, the second batch made while he still had the Sun sound in his bones. The music is ragged and kinetic, irresistible no matter how many times one may have heard it. The Etta James album, much the same, captures the singer in her early twenties, recording her sultry gospel-blues for Chess Records in Chicago. (The final track on the CD, a rocking version of Randy Newman's "Let's Burn Down the Cornfield," comes from a later session for another label.) The Miles Davis record presents the trumpeter fairly early (though not straight out of Juilliard) in pieces of muted beauty recorded for Columbia between 1954 and 1959.

The music is fine, the CDs vexing for the way in which they package every artist as an overly simplified cliché: Elvis the wild country boy, Etta the oversexed blues babe, Miles the sensual mysterioso. Youth comes across as an exalted state. But what of the various other Elvises—the sad zombie of all those interchangeable movies, the aging master of "Suspicious Minds" and "In the Ghetto," the tragic self-caricature of his final years? They are in many ways as fascinating as the Sun-era Elvis, yet they have no place in the Opus Collection. And Miles Davis—he just started to get wiggy and baffling in the early 1960s, with all his experiments in funk and electronics and even hip-hop to come. Marvin Gaye? We get only the boyish Motown wizard, none of the mad satyr who later wanted to name an album *Sanctified Pussy*.

These CDs make no claim to be encyclopedic, though the very idea of the Opus Collection clearly suggests an intent to be definitive. And therein lies their tyranny. According to the promotional text on some of its CDs, Starbucks is "dedicated to helping people discover great music." But discovery is precisely what these discs discourage. There is nothing to discover in a predictable collection of highlights from the glory days of a canonical artist. On the Starbucks

CDs, the listener escapes discovery, and is insulated against the challenge and the thrill of listening with open ears to artists of all sorts trying—possibly struggling, perhaps failing—to break free of the golden prison of what they do best and what their audiences expect of them. I have no doubt that Howard Schultz would claim that the Opus Collection CDs should serve as a starting point for listeners, and so they should. But I suspect that they rarely will. The CDs do their job too well. In their limited definitiveness, they are likely to be the end of the Elvis or Miles experience, not the beginning.

If that seems an odd criticism, I can amplify it with a brief story. Having copies of all the tracks on the Ella Fitzgerald Opus Collection from their original releases, I gave the Starbucks CD to a neighbor of mine who is a young rock singer. About a week later, I saw her in the lobby of our building, and she said that she enjoyed the album, a solid anthology of standards including "Lullaby of Birdland," "Miss Otis Regrets," and "Don't Be That Way." I brought up the fact that Ella Fitzgerald loved to experiment and stay up-to-date, and that she even did some rock recordings, including a killer version of Cream's "Sunshine of Your Love." I asked her if she would like to hear it. "God, no!" she said. "Don't burst my bubble." In music as in blender drinks, Starbucks is in the bubble business.

*   *   *

Enacting a twist on the notion of branding popular musicians, Starbucks also markets a series of CDs called Artist's Choice, in which big-name performers present favorite songs recorded by others. The idea is to show the stars as fans, sharing mix tapes with fans of their own. Predictably, some of the choices seem obligatory or designed to impress. Willie Nelson included Django Reinhardt's "Nuages"; Tony Bennett chose the Juilliard String Quartet's recording of Ravel's String Quartet in F Major, II and the Abyssinian Baptist Gospel Choir singing "I Want to Ride That Glory Train." Then, too, a few mild revelations popped up. Sheryl Crow admitted loving Elton John's saccharine "Someone Saved My Life Tonight," and Ronnie Wood of the Rolling Stones included Brian Wilson's delicate "I Just Wasn't Made for These Times." Unfortunately (though predictably, again), none of the Artist's Choice CDs I have heard manages to hang together as a set.

As a class, Starbucks's various compilation CDs are the audio equivalent of those trade paperbacks that impart the hundred and one things a person needs to know to be culturally literate. They provide talking points for potential future interaction with other Starbucks patrons—capital in the social economy of young adulthood. "How cool was Jackie Wilson?" "I know—'Saaay you will!'" "Too bad he died so young—you know, after a heart attack onstage." "Yes . . . so young—like Sam Cooke!" "How cool was he?" With each CD, a listener is granted enough to stay for the duration of one grande latte, and with luck, enough to earn an exchange of phone numbers.

Starbucks's music business also includes a small handful of original CDs produced by the company, although they offer little more to discuss. An album of duets between Herbie Hancock and pop stars such as Paul Simon, Annie Lennox, John Mayer, and Christina Aguilera—a brazen attempt to duplicate the formula of *Genius Loves Company*—was a misbegotten waste of the considerable but terminally mismatched talent involved. As for the pair of debut records by young artists—the mopey singer-songwriter Sonya Kitchell and the folk-rockish quintet Antigone Rising—they hint at promise that time might help fulfill.

By 2006, Starbucks's only new album of significance, Bob Dylan: *Live at the Gaslight 1962*, was new only as a commercial release. Bootlegs of rough, unedited versions of the recorded performance have been sold on Bleecker Street for years. The CD captures Dylan during a tentative period between his eponymous first album, an earnest recording of traditional songs about death (along with two Guthrie-inspired originals), and its stunningly mature follow-up, *The Freewheelin' Bob Dylan*, released one year later. At twenty-one, on *Live at the Gaslight*, Dylan is just beginning to come into bloom as a songwriter. He has delivered one of his first major pieces, "A Hard Rain's A-Gonna Fall," and he is nearly done polishing "Don't Think Twice, It's All Right." His set is still filled with traditionals such as "The Cuckoo," "Handsome Molly," and "Barbara Allen," though he sings and plays them with such quirky fire that they seem his own.

The performance on this CD is so dynamic that it is a bit hard to believe that Dylan dreaded playing the Gaslight, as his old friend, the late Dave Van Ronk, relished saying. The titular Mayor of MacDougal Street and host of the popular hootenannies at the Gaslight, Van Ronk used to say that Dylan never liked any of the coffeehouses. In fact, Van Ronk said, Dylan didn't even like coffee.

Rick Rubin and Kayne West

On the seating chart of the creative fraternity, record producers occupy one of the rows behind film directors and in front of book editors. In recording, it is the performers who are the "artists," as the music press and the people who run the Grammys like to remind us. Producers, as a rule, are hired by record companies to produce in a fundamentally commercial sense: to supply product. The task involves extraction (from the artists), organization and supervision (of those artists and their work), and collaboration (with the artists), in varying measures; the producer's job is essentially sustentative. Still, with every movement in popular music—and, on occasion, in other kinds of music—we tend to find at least one celebrated producer, whose output is distinctive and individualistic enough to foster claims of nothing less than authorship.

Since the first years of rock 'n' roll, when Sam Phillips of Sun Records dissuaded Elvis Presley from recording the gospel standards and romantic ballads that the young singer loved in favor of the country blues that Phillips preferred to hear him do, the notion of the ministerial, even wizardly producer has become a fixture of pop-music iconography. After Phillips came Phil Spector in Brill Building pop, Berry Gordy at Motown, George Martin with the Beatles, Billy Sherrill in Nashville, Gamble and Huff in Philly soul, Robert Stigwood in disco, Brian Eno in new wave, and countless others revered in the innumerable substrata of recorded music. More than a few have hopped several rows ahead of the performers whom they have produced, in critical esteem if not in fame. Indeed, we are now in a day when one of the most acclaimed figures in popular music, the producer Rick Rubin, does not perform, and one of the most successful performers in pop, the rapper Kanye West, made his reputation as a producer of other acts.

Rubin who won an award from *Esquire* for being the "Best Visionary" of 2006, has become the preeminent producer of the day by employing an aesthetic that pre-dates recording. His primary concerns as a producer are composition and performance, and his main objective is to capture the sound of people in the act of music-making. He thinks of recording as Edison did, as the documentation of an art made by others rather than as a creative act in itself. To Rubin, the performance, not the record, is the art form. In this, he is more a reactionary than a visionary.

By the age of forty-three, Rubin had made more than seventy albums, and from the first, his work has been an act of self-abnegation. He began producing singles for a record company that he formed with a friend, Russell Simmons, while he was still an undergraduate at New York University. Rubin ran the label, Def Jam Records, out of room 712 in Weinstein Hall—paltry quarters, even by New York City dorm standards. (I know, because I had a girlfriend on the same floor of Weinstein a few years earlier, when I was living around the corner in Rubin Hall.) And Def Jam's recordings were more spartan still—prototypal hip-hop, undoctored, unadorned.

Rubin, a Jewish kid from Long Island welcomed into the society of African American street music because of his ardor for and knowledge of the genre, made restrained, unprepossessing records in service to the musical culture he found. "I wondered what it would be like if a record felt and sounded like being at a club instead of trying to sound like a record," he has explained. The results, which included LL Cool J's breakthrough, "Radio," presented hip-hop as it was then being created, by a rapper working with no more than a turntable and a drum machine. The label on "Radio" said "Reduced by Rick Rubin." But what Rubin did was not an act of reduction; it was a refusal to inflate—or to intercede in any way. It was clearly a mark of respect, even selfless passion, and also the surest way to share in the glory of a daring new music without the risks inherent in attempting to make an original contribution.

Before long, *The Village Voice* enthroned Rubin as "the king of rap." As such, he was an heir to Alan Lomax and John Hammond, white advocates of black music who had recorded blues and jazz, and became renowned for their good taste, prescience, and egalitarianism. As rap evolved into hip-hop, taking up sampling, growing denser and more complex sonically, its *mise en scéne* shifted from the street to the studio, and Rubin lost interest. "My goal is to just get out of the way and let the people I'm working with be their best," he later said. When hip-hop began requiring a great deal more of its producers than affectionate impassivity, Rubin got out of its way, left Def Jam and New York, and started a new record company called Def American (later renamed American Recordings) in Los Angeles. Through the 1990s, he concentrated on arena rock, recording the music that he loved first as a boy in Long Island, making blunt, gutsy records for the likes of Slayer, Danzig, and AC/DC, as well as albums for somewhat more venturesome bands such as Rage Against the Machine and the Red Hot Chili Peppers. Rubin focused primarily, but not exclusively, on touring bands who were devoted to live performance, and who worked in modes so overwrought and extravagant that what they needed most was to be reduced by Rick Rubin.

Like Phil Spector, "Shadow" Morton (Spector's Brill Building colleague and the producer of the top-forty soundscapes "Leader of the Pack" and "Society's Child"), and many rock producers to follow, Rubin maintains a fastidiously crafted aura of eccentric genius. He has a frazzled, nesty beard that hangs down to his ample belly, and he nearly always wears dark sunglasses, old jeans, and baggy T-shirts—"clothes that would make a wino proud," as Johnny Cash wrote in his memoirs. Rubin's face is nearly impossible to read behind all that cover. A practicing Buddhist, he embodies the asceticism at the heart of his music and his adopted faith. He neither smokes nor drinks, and he says he has never used drugs. When Rubin takes on a recording project, he starts spending time with the musicians before the songwriting, taking walks along the beach, sharing natural food and drinking herbal tea, talking about "anything." By the time he and the musicians enter the studio, his work is largely done; he has inspired the artists by his presence, and the players are now ready to go forth and justify his faith in them. In the recording booth, he never touches a knob. Indeed, he professes to care nothing for the technicalities of recording. As John Hammond was known to do, Rubin often lowers his head and closes his eyes while his artists play; unlike Hammond, Rubin is understood to be in a state of meditative rapture, not sleep.

"I want to be touched by the music I'm making," Rubin has explained. And "luckily, other people have shared that response to my work over the years." Apparently his selflessness has not undermined his perception of the recordings he has undertaken as *his* work, the music that *he* has been making. The secret meaning of Rubin's professional altruism, clearly, is what in the film world is called auteurism.

Since the mid-1990s, when Rubin began recording Johnny Cash, he has been best known for his seemingly sorcerous ability to revive waning careers. He has become the re-animator of American music. With Cash, Rubin did not have to do much, fortunately for them both. Cash's appeal had always been uncommonly broad for a country artist, and his brooding outlaw persona had long helped him connect to the rock audience; on the television variety show that Cash hosted from 1969 to 1971, he sang his country hits and did comedy sketches, and also pulled off duets with Bob Dylan and Joni Mitchell. When Rubin took on Cash, he sat him down in the studio with his guitar and had him run through songs—dozens and dozens of them, with little rehearsal. To augment Cash's vast old repertory, Rubin suggested some recent material by young writers, such as "Hurt," by Trent Reznor of Nine Inch Nails.

The idea was scarcely radical; Cash had been doing tunes by rock-era songwriters (such as Dylan's "It Ain't Me, Babe," Robbie Robertson's "The Night They Drove Old Dixie Down," Harry Chapin's "Cat's in the Cradle") for decades. Still, the new recordings helped to introduce Cash to another generation of listeners, and the tracks had a rare poignancy. Cash was aged and ill with Parkinson's disease, and he nearly whispered the songs in a fragile croak, salvaging thin material through patination. In 2006, nearly three years after Cash's death, another CD of Rubin's recordings of Cash was released as *American V*. From resuscitating the careers of fading artists, Rubin had advanced to reviving the dead.

Rubin's effort to rejuvenate the Dixie Chicks, by steering them away from the sound of contemporary country toward music indebted to traditional bluegrass, rose high on the record charts in 2006; meanwhile, Rubin was working on a new album to reposition Justin Timberlake. Both of these projects, like the CD that Rubin made for Neil Diamond the previous year, called *12 Songs*, are acts of revivification through purification; they are cleansings, deeds of atonement for past sins of musical excess, artifice, or commercialism. Of a piece with the popular ritual of opulent transgression, public apology, and purging, they are the musical equivalent of a good cry on *Oprah* or *Larry King Live*.

Rubin's work is a fetishization of authenticity, which he conflates with simplicity and ruralism. For *12 Songs*, he persuaded Diamond to accompany himself on guitar (for the first time on record since the 1960s), and he augmented Diamond's singing and playing with just a few acoustic instruments, strummed and plucked quietly in the background. The record includes snippets of studio chatter and ambient noises. It is a sedate, homey album—and nothing like Diamond's usual work, a fact that raises crucial questions about Rubin's conception of authenticity. On the first night of Diamond's series of concerts at Madison Square Garden last summer, I sat a few seats behind and to the right of Rubin.

Diamond appeared on stage, in a flash of laser light, to the pounding electronic beats and synthesizer strains of "America." He was standing on the top of a tower in the center of the stage, bedecked in black and silver glitter, with his right fist thrust high in the air. I looked over at Rubin, who was shaking his head in disapproval. About an hour into the show, Diamond did a brief acoustic set ("And the Grass Won't Pay No Mind" and "Look Out, Here Comes Tomorrow," the latter written for the Monkees), and I noticed Rubin leaning a bit forward in his seat. There was no doubt which Neil Diamond appealed to his record producer. But which is the truer one, the more authentic? That is a separate matter.

Having listened to "Shiloh," the early Diamond song about his imaginary friend, the only one in his life whom he could ever trust, I am inclined to suspect that Diamond's demons are such that he will never reveal to us the inner Neil. The Diamond of "America"—the glitzy, mannered, and grandiose self-parody, the Jewish Elvis—is the Neil he has devoted a lifetime to devising and presenting to the public. If the artist's own intention has any connection to authenticity, Rick Rubin has done his client a disservice. The synthesizers of "America" are as authentic in their intentional artifice as the acoustic guitars of *12 Songs* are artificial in their enforced authenticity.

With few exceptions—among them *Oral Fixation 2*, the delightful, hard-grinding dance album that Rubin produced for Shakira in 2005—most of Rubin's recent productions have the pristine raggedness of Abercrombie's "Ezra Fitch Premium Destroyed Boot Jeans," which are factory-made to appear worn, dirty, and ripped, and are sold at $168 per pair. For all their apparent earthiness, Rubin's records are calibrated to precise specifications, and every loose thread, every hole, is there by design.

Kanye West is the anti-Rubin. He revels in excess, and appears to care less about authenticity and spontaneity than Rubin does about equalizing filters. A proud dropout from Chicago State University, where his mother was chair of the English department, West began producing (in collaboration with others) in 1997. He had his first hit as a solo producer, "Chyna Doll" for Foxy Brown, the following year. West relishes sampling—indeed, he has played a key role in the return of sampling to prominence in hip-hop—and he is a relentless, insatiable tinkerer. For "Bring Me Down," a song he produced for the singer Brandy, West utilized 107 tracks of samples, instruments, effects, and vocals. Forty of those tracks were takes of Brandy's voice, all of them used in the finished recording. "The way he works, he just isn't content until he's tried recording and mixing a song every conceivable way," an engineer told a music magazine. "I was getting calls [from the record company] saying, 'We have to stop him. We have to cut him off.'" West treats production as composition, and, like Charlie Mingus and Gil Evans in jazz, his artistic method is trial and error.

As a producer, West has created a small body of hip-hop records that are orchestral in their density and textural complexity: "You Don't Know My Name" for Alicia Keys, "Slow Jamz" for Twista, and "Izzo (H.O.V.A.)" and "Takeover" for Jay-Z, the rapper and impresario who headed Rick Rubin's old label, Def Jam, for three years. The lyrics are banal—mostly about sex or macho posturing, like so much hip-hop—but they are decidedly secondary to the swirling, extravagant music and the beats, which are fresh and exciting.

As a rapper West is good, though not as good as he thinks. (No one is as good at anything as West believes he is at everything.) He has a soft, boyish voice, and his words are perfunctory, not remotely as poetic and inventive as the jagged layers of sound behind them. I caught him performing at a university concert in April of 2006, and the highlight was a set of his renditions of tunes that he had produced for others, including "You Don't Know My Name" and Brandy's "Talk About Our Love." The music was luxurious and full of surprise—exhilarating tangents, strains of irresolution, delightful incongruities. It was also generated electronically: the only musicians on stage were a turntable artist and a seven-piece string section (three violins, two violas, and two cellos), whose playing was buried deep in the mix. Was it, for that reason, inauthentic? No: it was new and lavish, and neither trait makes it bad or wrong.

Open-Source Remixing

The urge to make the work our own is elemental to the act of encountering art, and we try to satisfy it in many ways. We look at a painting or listen to a piece of music and take it in, hoping that it will prove to be not only an expression of human feeling but also a stimulus to it; we expect art to move us in a personal way. Or we buy the artwork or a copy of it, making our ownership literal (if not always legal, in case of downloading bootleg digital files). Or we wear our esteem for the work like a fashion label, for the social or professional status it confers. Or we draw inspiration from the work and apply it to things we make ourselves, using whatever of it serves our needs. In one way or another, to experience art of any kind is to appropriate it, and to be a devotee of any art or artist is to be a claimant.

In the music world, recording technology has greatly complicated the issues of ownership, authorship, and proprietary rights by simplifying the acquisition of creative property. Since the rise of sampling and downloading, digital technology has transferred many of the privileges of authorship from what was once an elite of professional musicians to the iPod-ed masses. Anyone with a laptop and home mixing software such as GarageBand (a substitute for both the garage and the band) or Pro Tools (an electronic kit to help amateurs sound as if they are not) can put together technically impressive multitrack recordings. To generate the music for those tracks, home producers have for some time now been able to extract snippets from any recordings in the digital domain, doctor them electronically, edit them, and perhaps even use traditional instruments and vocal tracks. The exponential growth in the popularity of such home recording over the past several years has helped fill the pages of MySpace with fragmentary sound-alike songs, while providing countless musical neophytes with gratifying quasi-creative experiences and inflated conceptions of their musical talent. As the record industry burns to ash, record-making is thriving in the same sense that moviemaking, of a sort, is booming on YouTube—that is, in the diminished form of derivative, perfunctory goofing around, the products of which may have momentary entertainment value, especially to their creators.

Some rock acts that made their reputations as sonic experimenters a long decade ago, such as Radiohead and Nine Inch Nails, seem humbled in the presence of the shape-shifting creature that popular music has become in the digital age. Both those bands have made high-profile attempts at Web innovation that are essentially acts of capitulation, if not desperation. Radiohead made lots of news when the band released its first album since 2003, *In Rainbows*, through its Web site in a plan that allowed downloaders to pay whatever price they chose— a great publicity stunt in the form of a vast, universal tip jar. After too many listeners decided to drop in too few coins, the band released another version of the album, priced conventionally. More recently, Trent Reznor made the new Nine Inch Nails album *The Slip* available through the band's Web site in early 2008, for free. In an announcement of the release on his site, Reznor wrote, "thank you for your continued and loyal support over the years—this one's on me." A "limited edition" CD release of *The Slip*, at a price of $24.98, followed it in July of that year, at which time Reznor and the latest incarnation of his band were beginning a national tour, for which seats cost at least four or five times the price of a CD.

There is nothing wrong with—or new about—giving away samples to entice customers to pay for other, profitable goods. The technique has long been common in the narcotics trade and in the marketing of supermarket cheese cubes. More interesting than the fact that Radiohead and Nine Inch Nails have provided albums to listeners for free or for cheap are the efforts that both bands have made to come to terms with the phenomenon of home record-making. Radiohead and Nine Inch Nails have each ventured into "open-source remixing," a growing sphere of digital play in which enthusiasts are granted access to the stems of a song—the individual parts of a multi-track recording, each of which might have, say, the drums or the bass line or a guitar part—in order to manipulate them or add to them at home. In differing ways and to differing degrees, both bands are opening up their processes, making public the component parts of their music to give fans the feeling of collaborating with their idols—shadow-dancing with the rock stars. Through open-source remixing, music fans who might have been just listeners are assuming a kind of ownership which is, on its face, revolutionary, but which is, ultimately, illusory.

Radiohead, in April 2008, made available for purchase through iTunes the five stems, one for each of the five band members' instruments, which make up "Nude," a single from *In Rainbows*. (Side note: in the group's native Britain, more than half of all singles are still released as seven-inch vinyl records, as well as on CD and as downloads; it seems to me that the survival of 45s there has to do with both an English reverence for the tradition that vinyl represents and a frugal English reluctance to throw away perfectly good record players.) With each of the stems going for iTunes' usual per-song price of 99 cents, "Nude" costs five times as much to buy in parts as it costs as a song. This is to be expected. To break anything sellable into bits is to grant each of those bits a value that justifies a price.

"Nude," like several of the songs on *In Rainbows*, is one that fans of the band have long known in multiple earlier incarnations. At concerts in 1998, the tune was a soul ballad framed around the sound of a Hammond organ. By 2005, Thom Yorke was doing the song in solo performances, strumming it gently on the acoustic guitar and murmuring it like an emo navel-gazer. On *In Rainbows*, it opens with a swirling cloud of synth effects and settles into a shuffling bass-driven groove. (The terse lyrics center on the phrase "Don't get any big ideas/They're not gonna to happen," a blunt plea to resist the sexual imagination.) A wisp of a piece unaligned to a fixed arrangement, it is suited to remixing; indeed, Radiohead has itself been toying with the song for ten years.

To encourage remixes of "Nude" (and purchases of its stems), Radiohead sponsored a competition and started posting submissions on the band's site. By mid-May 2008, more than 2,200 remixes of the song had been posted and voted on by fans (and, presumably, also automatic-voted on by the digital ringers that hackers can conjure and viral-marketing services can provide for pay). I started listening to the posted remixes (and casting votes, nay and yea, for some of them) shortly after they first went up in April, and over a month's time I got to hear about two hundred versions of "Nude." I did the listening in spurts, taking in a post or two when I felt in the mood, to prevent the repetition of the tune from having the effect of torture.

A great many of the "Nude" remixes I have heard are attempts to change the overall mood of the song by doctoring the tonal colors and redistributing the weights of the musical elements. In a high number of cases, the bass line that dominates the *In Rainbows* version recedes, and new beats of all sorts take over: intricate and realistic-sounding drum patterns are among the easiest things to generate with software such as GarageBand. The gently pulsing waltz pattern of the official release gives way to heavy beats, often in the propulsive 4/4 basic to rock and hip-hop. Since GarageBand can change the time signature, the tempo, or the key of a song with a few mouse clicks, all those features of the composition get transformed in various "Nude" remixes, with results that can only with a snicker be called mixed. Much of the alteration and ornamentation in the "Nude" remixes seem arbitrary, stunty, or inappropriate. In nearly a dozen of the hundred remixes ranked highest on the Radiohead site, fans added keyboard tracks that oversimplified the already simple chords of the tune or simply got the chords wrong. Re-harmonization is not at all uncommon in the realm of interpretive music; but its point is generally to reconsider, rather than to reduce or to misrepresent, the original music.

The way GarageBand works, the process of personalizing music is highly regimented—that is, depersonalized. For each creative decision involved in customizing a track, the software provides a handy drop-down menu of options. What kind of guitar sound would you like, "Arena Rock" or "Glam" or "Clean Jazz"? What sort of vocals, "Female Basic" or "Epic Diva"? The system transforms music-making into shopping, and it provides the same illusion of individual expression that we find in the mall. Now we can make our sound in the same way we create our own look—by mixing and matching a handful of items from the racks of the same stores that everyone else in America is choosing from. After all, what does "Clean Jazz" mean, other than "Banana Republic"?

Trent Reznor, in a grand gesture of magnanimity, made the stems of the last several Nine Inch Nails albums (including *White Teeth* from 2005 and *Year Zero* from 2007) available for remixing, at no cost, through the NIN site. A longtime hero among rock techheads for the loving noisy artifice of his one-man-band recordings, Reznor is so eager to be aligned with the home-remixing phenomenon that he sponsored a compilation album of fan remixes of songs from *White Teeth* and *Year Zero*. Called *The Limitless Potential*, the album of twenty-one selections is free for downloading, although the individual stems of the tracks that the fans contributed are not accessible for further remixing through the Nine Inch Nails site. (Evidently the "open" in open-sourcing has its limits.) Most of the Nine Inch Nails remixes posted, like the "Nude" remixes, are efforts to move the songs from one mode—industrial rock, the style Reznor practically invented in the 1980s—to some other style:

house music, or psychedelia, or an approximation of funk. The remixes tend to take lateral steps, hopping across category lines from stylistic box to box. They do not, as a rule, try to differ from the originals in point of view or depth or aesthetic value; they seek to differ primarily in kind.

Despite its obvious debts to the Web era, home remixing in one sense suggests a return to the musical culture of the days before sound recording on wax cylinders, around the turn of the last century. In their capacity as remixers, members of the musical public are again assuming participatory roles, interpreting compositions at home, much as late Victorians played sheet music in parlor musicales. There is also a social component to both spheres of participation, as remixers post their efforts, listen to one another's, and vote on them. I spent a good part of a weekend making my own remix of "Nude." (For the record, I added some wan obbligato lines on guitar and concocted a vocal countermelody, which I sang with the essential assistance of a pitch-correction plug-in.) Dissatisfied with the results, I decided not to post them, and I feel as if my remix, as one unposted, is not real in the same way that the worst remixes on the Radiohead Web site are. In the ballooning community of remixers, as in the rest of the Web universe, to post is to be.

I was further deterred from submitting my remix to the "Nude" competition by the "terms and conditions" of submission. Despite the fact that remixers can not only amend the elements of the Radiohead recording but also add tracks of their own devising—new beats, different chords, additional melodies (such as the admittedly weak guitar and vocal lines I made up), even whole new sets of lyrics (or spoken language)—Radiohead claims full ownership of every part of the remixes sent its way. Every part: not just the original stems, but every bit of music anyone might add to a submitted track. The fine print specifies, "All rights in and to any remixed versions ('Remixes') of the song 'Nude' ('the Song') created by the Entrant shall be owned by Warner/Chappell Music Ltd ('WCM') and to the extent necessary the Entrant hereby assigns all rights in the Remixes of the Song to WCM throughout the World for the full life of copyright and any and all extensions and renewals thereof. . . . Thom Yorke, Jonny Greenwood, Colin Greenwood, Ed O'Brien and Phil Selway will be registered and credited as the sole writers and WCM the publishers of the Remixes of the Song created by the Entrant."

If this is legal, it is also extortionate and an act of terrible hypocrisy—a revocation of the promise of creative ownership that is drawing people to remixing, the promise that Radiohead has been eager to exploit, in large print, to sell its stems. The very idea of remixing implies remaking, and that carries with it a legitimate claim of ownership—aesthetic, ethical, and legal. If most of the remixes on both the "Nude" site and Nine Inch Nails's *Limitless Potential* album speak unpersuasively for remixing's potential, they are not definitive proof of remixing's limits. For the moment, Yorke and his band have a message for fans loaded with GarageBand and an urge to own a part of Radiohead: Don't get any big ideas. They're not going to happen.

More troubling even than the hypocrisy of a few rock stars is the narcissism at the heart of the phenomenon of home remixing—the notion that to take a work of creative expression and make it "ours" is to improve it. It is a colossal mistake to coerce an expression of others into an expression of ourselves. The premise of open-source remixing is that finally we can admire nobody so much as ourselves. But in music, as in all art and love and politics, there is usually more to gain in trying to understand what belongs, uniquely and idiosyncratically and serendipitously, to somebody else.

PART VI

Life With the Lions

Woody Guthrie

Ramblin' Man

The folksinger Arlo Guthrie likes to tell a story about his father, the legendary Woody Guthrie, who died in 1967, at the age of fifty-five. When he was a toddler, Arlo says, Guthrie gave him a Gibson acoustic guitar for his birthday. Several years later, when the boy was old enough to hold it, Guthrie sat him down in the backyard of their house—they lived in Howard Beach, Queens—and taught him all the words to "This Land Is Your Land," a song that most people likely think they know in full. The lyrics had been written in anger, as a response to Irving Berlin's "God Bless America," which Woody Guthrie deplored as treacle. In addition to the familiar stanzas ("As I went walking that ribbon of highway," and so on), Guthrie had composed a couple of others, including this:

> *One bright sunny morning, in the shadow of the steeple*
> *By the Relief Office, I saw my people*
> *As they stood hungry, I stood there wondering*
> *If God Blessed America for me.*

"He wanted me to know what he originally wrote, so it wouldn't be forgotten," Arlo Guthrie has explained.

Like the defiant, vaguely socialistic original words to his best-known song, much of what Woody Guthrie was and did during his lifetime has been forgotten, supplanted by the stuff of nostalgic sentiment. "This Land Is Your Land," purged of its earthy contrarianism, shows up with "God Bless America" on albums of patriotic music and in concerts by pops orchestras that accompany the fireworks on the Fourth of July, and its author's face has been put on a United States postage stamp. Woody Guthrie, a contradictory man who vexed his family and his closest friends as much as he challenged the authorities—"I can't stand him when he's around," Pete Seeger, his friend and also a bandmate for a time, once said, "but I miss him when he's gone"—scarcely registers as a creature of human dimension. In the popular imagination, where he endures, more than half a century after his creative prime as a writer and singer, Guthrie seems more like Gypsy Davy, Rocky Mountain Slim, and other colorful folk heroes of the songs he sang. He functions as the embodiment of gritty American authenticity, the plainspoken voice of a romanticized heartland.

Guthrie was never really so authentic, as Ed Cray shows in *Ramblin' Man: The Life and Times of Woody Guthrie*, a work of tempered debunking that is the first notable Guthrie biography since Joe Klein's *Woody Guthrie: A Life*, which started unraveling the Guthrie lore in 1980. The Klein book, fans of classic rock will recall, was the beneficiary of a sweet plug on Bruce Springsteen's 1986 boxed set of live recordings; in a halting, Okie-inflected voice, Springsteen complimented "this fella named Joe Klein," before moving into an acoustic-guitar version of "This Land Is Your Land." Springsteen was then in the process of molting his leather jacket and his urban ambitions to become a Guthrie-style troubadour of the mythic hinterland, a change that signified his maturation within the rock world.

John Steinbeck—"the Woody Guthrie of American authors," as he has been called—revered his musical compatriot in polemical realism. In his introduction to *Hard Hitting Songs for Hard-Hit People*, a book of Depression-era folk tunes compiled by the folklorist and activist Alan Lomax, Steinbeck praised Guthrie's music for capturing "the American spirit," and noted, "He sings the songs of a people and I suspect that he is, in a way, that people."

Guthrie's people were in fact the upper-middle-class American elite. His father, Charley Guthrie, was a prosperous real-estate speculator and aspiring politician (a conservative Democrat and vehement anti-Communist) in Okemah, Oklahoma, a boomtown in the oil territory of the newly annexed state; at one time, he and his wife, Nora, owned as many as thirty rental properties, and they were the first people in town to purchase an automobile. Their third child, Woodrow Wilson Guthrie, was born on July 14, 1912, twelve days after that year's Democratic Presidential Convention, and named for the freshly nominated candidate. "Papa . . . swapped and traded, bought and sold, got bigger, spread out, and made more money," Woody Guthrie recalled accurately in his often fanciful memoir, *Bound for Glory*. "We all liked the prettiest and best things in the store windows, and anything in the store was [ours] just for the signing."

The hard times of the early 1920s devastated the Guthries, claiming the family's property and the children's buying privileges. Unpersuaded by his parents' faith in capitalism, Guthrie eventually fell sway to the socialist utopianism that was attracting the attention of intellectuals, the young, the poor, and other disillusioned or idealistic Americans during the late 1920s and early '30s. He was a convert to disenfranchisement and always advocated the underprivileged with a proselyte's zeal.

"Woody Guthrie," like "Bob Dylan," was essentially a self-invention made for the electronic media: after a few years of scrounging, singing for change, and passing himself off as a seer and a faith healer, Guthrie made his name doing a comedic hillbilly act on Los Angeles radio in 1937. He had moved to the city in the mid-thirties, a time when outlandishly hokey cowboy singers were a novelty craze—a way for the music and movie industries simultaneously to exploit and ridicule rural culture for the pleasure of the urban audience. Cray describes a Los Angeles "awash in country-hillbilly-cowboy-western music," with radio stations broadcasting the likes of the Stuart Hamblen Gang, the Covered Wagon Jubilee, the Beverly Hillbillies, the Saddle Pals, the Bronco Busters, the Saddle Tramps, and the Sons of the Pioneers. Woody Guthrie rode the marketplace like a saddle-sore poke on a long-tailed dogie (or some such), crooning cowboy songs with his cousin Oklahoma (Jake Guthrie) and a cowgirl, Lefty Lou (his friend Maxine Crissman), playing the spoons, spinning tall tales, and reciting what he called his "cornpone philosophy" in a theatrical Okie drawl that he employed to disarming effect for the rest of his life.

Guthrie's inchoate socialist leanings grew into a deep commitment to the labor movement and to the social and political adventurism of the American Communist Party. (Guthrie never joined the Party—his independence was such that he "was not affiliated with anything," according to his sister Mary Jo; he did follow the Party line, however, down to belittling Roosevelt as a warmonger during the period of the German-Soviet non-aggression pact, and he wrote a column called "Woody Sez," in hillbilly dialect, for the CPUSA organs *People's World* and *Daily Worker*.) The first of Guthrie's three wives, Mary, lamented his politicization as "his downfall as an entertainer," and she had a point: the more he focussed on rousing the masses, the less he pleased the crowd. Guthrie's modest popular following diminished; at the same time, through politics, he found his voice.

"I never did make up many songs about the cow trails or the moon skipping through the sky," Guthrie wrote in *Bound for Glory*, "but at first it was funny songs of what's all wrong, and how it turned out good or bad. Then I got a little braver and made up songs telling what I thought was wrong and how to make it right, songs that said what everybody in the country was thinking."

In a letter to Alan Lomax quoted (with its creative grammar and spelling) by Klein, Guthrie expanded on this thought:

> A folk song is what's wrong and how to fix it, or it could be whose hungry and where their mouth is, or whose out of work and where the job is or whose broke and where the money is or whose carrying a gun and where the peace is—that's folk lore and folks made it up because they seen that the politicians couldn't find nothing to fix or nobody to feed or give a job of work.

Indeed, folk music has traditionally served as an outlet for native discontent, often expressed in coded language (the boll weevil stands in for field hands, the farmer's son is the government). Still, there is a great difference between the folk songs that circulated in Woody Guthrie's day and the music he wrote; that is, the very fact that he wrote it. Folk music (including country, blues, and other vernacular styles) was supposed to be anonymous—a collective art passed along orally from singer to singer, generation to generation, sometimes culture to culture. From the vantage point of today, when kids with their first guitars start writing songs before they learn to play other tunes, it is difficult to process how exceptional it was for a folk artist such as Woody Guthrie to have created a vast repertoire of deeply idiosyncratic works. (Many Tin Pan Alley, Broadway, and Hollywood songwriters of the thirties and earlier were as skilled and prolific as Guthrie, but they were working in a different vein, writing to order for professional singers.) Guthrie helped to bring the authorial imperative to vernacular music in America.

Guthrie, like most major white musicians in America, was immeasurably indebted to black music. In an unpublished manuscript quoted by Cray, he recalled that one of his earliest childhood memories was of hearing a "Negro minstrel jazzy band blowing and tooting and pounding drums up and down our street," a sound that inspired him to "sing out the first song I ever made up by my own self." At the age of thirteen, he discovered the blues; according to what Guthrie told Lomax in an interview for the Library of Congress (released on a three-CD set in 1989), he studied a "big ol' colored boy" shining shoes in front of a barbershop and singing what Guthrie found to be "undoubtedly the lone-somest music I ever run on to in my life." Each experience informs one of the two main categories of Guthrie's songs. His light tunes (many of them, such as "Car Song" and "Jiggy Jiggy Bum," written expressly for children) have a free, joyful, improvised feeling; his ballads of hard life have the impenitent rawness of Mississippi Delta blues, along with the blues' harmonic structure (three chords, tonic, subdominant, and dominant) and, in many cases, the blues' meter:

> *Down in Texas, my gal fainted in the rain*
> *Down in Texas, my gal fainted in the rain*
> *Had to throw a bucket of sand in her face*
> *Just to bring her back again.*

The Popular Front saw artistic refinement as a mark of bourgeois elitism, and so did Guthrie. "Woody believed in simplicity like people in the Bible Belt believe in their scripture," Guthrie's schoolmate Matt Jennings told Cray. Guthrie seemed to think of musical complexity as corrupt, and he wrote most of his songs with just a few chords, in the key of G. (He would slide a capo up the neck of his guitar to change keys, much as his nemesis Irving Berlin, who could play only in F-sharp, used a special mechanism built into his piano to transpose his songs.) Guthrie's melodies, many of which were adapted from traditional sources, are as basic and memorable as schoolyard chants, and the words are just as biting. (The music to the opening phrase of "This Land Is Your Land" simply follows the first four notes of the major scale, making the tune a model exercise for beginning musicians.) His lyrics, similarly, seek to convey a guileless clever-ness and intensity—a pridefully untrained intelligence. Grammar and syntax give way, rhymes miss, and accents fall awkwardly, all contributing to the songs' effect of unadorned veracity, as in "The Biggest Thing That Man Has Ever Done," one of Guthrie's many tunes about the Grand Coulee Dam:

> *I climb the rocky canyon where the Columbia River rolls,*
> *Seen the salmon leaping the rapids and the falls.*
> *The big Grand Coulee Dam in the State of Washington*
> *Is just about the biggest thing that man has ever done.*

Once Hitler ventured into the Soviet Union and Stalin joined forces with the Allied powers, Guthrie became patriotic; he supported the United States' involvement in the Second World War and pasted a handpainted sign onto the front of his guitar: "This Machine Kills Fascists." He kept it there after the war, in reference to another target: the cultural power brokers who, in his view, oppressed folk artists by rewarding sleek professionalism. Guthrie, now living in New York, challenged the commercial aesthetic of the pre-rock era through a performance style that was not merely plaintive, like that of countless singing cowboys in the movies, but almost combatively anti-musical. In the dozens of recordings that he made between 1940 and 1952 (many of which have been re-issued by Smithsonian Folkways in conscientiously engineered and annotated CDs), his singing and playing are jarring: his voice bone-gray, dry and stiff, and indifferent to pitch; his guitar work spare and ragged, and frequently out of tune. Aesthetically, Guthrie was less a socialist than an anarchist, contemptuous of the prevailing rules and standards.

For all his advocacy of the common man, Guthrie sought to be recognized as someone exceptional. Agnes (Sis) Cunningham, his sometime bandmate (along with Seeger, Bess Hawes, Millard Lampell, Lee Hays, and others) in the Almanac Singers, the leftist vocal group of the forties, told me several years ago that Guthrie was "determined to become a legend in his own time." (Cray quotes Hawes as saying that Guthrie was "desperate" to become "a big, important person.") After all, he did not call his autobiography *Bound for Obscurity*, and the book is dense with folksy anecdotes that dramatize his innate superiority to government officials, businesspeople, other authority figures, and most of his friends. *Bound for Glory* captures Guthrie vividly; he was fearsomely gifted and ambitious, and also egalitarian—a most uncommon man.

Woody Guthrie succeeded in becoming a legend in the last years of his life, as young people of the postwar era, seeking their own cultural identity, veered away from the coolly sophisticated, urbane pop on their parents' hi-fis in favor of more idiomatic music grounded in rural America—folk, country, the blues, and their hybrid, rock 'n' roll. Students by the thousands massed in Washington Square Park each week to strum along to "This Land Is Your Land," and to look for Woody Guthrie, the exemplar of the folkie ideal. He was unable to take active part in his newfound idolhood, however. Debilitated by Huntington's disease, a degenerative disorder of the nervous system, Guthrie became a tragic figure to his young acolytes: an American original cut down before his time, seemingly gone mad (wildly erratic behavior being a symptom of the disease). When the nineteen-year-old Bob Dylan arrived in New York from Minnesota in January of 1961, he told his friends that he was going to meet his god, Woody. "He's the greatest holiest godliest one in the world," Dylan said of Guthrie around that time—a "genius genius genius genius."

Reflecting on the period later, Dylan explained, "Woody turned me on romantically.... What drew me to [him] was that, hearing his voice, I could tell he was very lonesome, very alone, and very lost out in his time. That's why I dug him. Like a suicidal case or something. It was like an adolescent thing—when you need somebody to latch onto, you reach out and latch onto them."

With today's rock and pop feeling homogeneous, and with hip-hop now more than twenty-five years old, popular music is ripe for something new. Whatever comes will surely be something that challenges the complacency of the mainstream; something from disreputable sources; something critical of the status quo, harsh, simple, seemingly anti-musical, and doable without formal training—that is to say, something much in the vein of what Woody Guthrie did. If few nineteen-year-olds today think of latching onto Guthrie, his spirit may be closer than they know.

Will Eisner

The pages of most comic books are battlefields for hypertrophied mutants and space aliens raging gaudy supernatural war. This has been the case for generations now, the norm in a junk-entertainment genre whose elemental function has always been to commodify the testosterone delirium of male adolescence. To scan the racks of a comics shop like, say, Jim Hanley's Universe in midtown Manhattan is to be assaulted by costumed mercenaries such as Darkchylde and Hellboy in stories like "Seed of Destruction." Look closely, and you may recognize some of the old heroes—Superman, Batman, Wonder Woman, the Fantastic Four, and their superfriends—still fighting in increasingly pumped- and sexed-up transmutations. Poke around the middle of the store, and you'll find a mix of subgenres: reprints of vintage comics; the arty (and often raw) "comix" indebted to the underground movement of the 1960s; and Japanese titles based on the hyperactive animé cartoons. If you make it to the back of the last aisle on the far right, alongside the wall where the T-shirts are hanging, you'll find a display of hard and paperback covers startling for their incongruity, with images of Jewish immigrants in the Bronx of the Depression years, slumped old men, ranting neighbors, a squabbling family. . . . You're in the Will Eisner section, where the comics medium becomes something naturalistic, wry, introspective, and literate—that is, in the comics universe, something truly otherworldly.

Eisner, who started writing and drawing comic books straight from high school in 1936, is one of the original inventors of the form, although that fact alone hardly confers much distinction. The fledgling comics business was a sweatshop trade for creative hopefuls too inexperienced, too socially ill-equipped, or, more often, too minimally talented for the established avenues of hackdom, the pulps and commercial art. Mostly shoot-'em-ups maladroitly adapted from crime and adventure magazines, the first comic books were sexless pornography for kids, incompetently scripted and drawn. The medium changed a great deal in the years hence, of course; today's comics are drawn and written with sleek proficiency. That the form grew more significantly to become, at its best, something intelligent with rewards for grown-ups, testifies to Eisner's contributions.

Among comics professionals and enthusiasts, Eisner, eighty-four at this writing in the spring of 2001, is revered as more than a charter elder of the ultimate boy's club, but as a model of seriousness, ambition, and achievement. "I find it difficult to argue that Eisner is not the single person most responsible for giving comics their *brains*," comics writer Alan Moore has said. The author of the first literate comic book, *The Spirit* (1940–1952), two texts on the theory and practice of his discipline, and more than a dozen graphic novels over the past twenty-three years, Eisner is not merely the recipient of innumerable illustration and comics-art awards (including the National Cartoonists Society's "Best Artist," four times). The most prestigious honor in comics is named for him: the plaque bestowed each year upon one of his progeny is the Eisner.

Unsatisfied, Eisner still works obsessively, creating reflective and somber autobiographical works while tending the preservation of his legacy through a new series of hardbound reprints of his most popular creation, the Spirit comics. He drives every morning from the home he shares with his wife, Ann, in south-eastern Florida to the studio he keeps about a mile away, and he puts in eight to ten hours, six days a week. "I've been trying to prove what the medium can do my whole life," Eisner said recently. "If I thought my point had been made, I don't know what I'd do."

The fact that he has spent his whole life working in comics, striving to advance the medium from within, long undermined Eisner's prospects for recognition outside the insular society of comics buffs. Raised in the tenements of the Bronx, Eisner has surely learned the rule of every ghetto, literal or aesthetic: Anyone can come in, few can get out. It was one thing for gallery artists such as Lichtenstein and Warhol to draw upon the style of the comics as a resource; it has been quite another for comics specialists to try elevating both their medium and the way it is perceived. (In jazz, a kindred American popular art form, indigenous creators suffered from a parallel imbalance when orchestral composers such as Stravinsky and Milhaud were praised in high-brow circles for employing "jazzy" touches in their concert works while the jazz masterworks that served as their inspiration were going ignored or dismissed as low-class entertainment.) Eisner recalls being invited, along with several other comics artists, including Harvey Kurtzman and Joe Kubert, to attend the opening of a Pop Art show at the Brooklyn Museum in 1974. "At first, I thought, 'Oh boy! This is great! We're finally being invited into the arena,'" he recalled. "Then I realized we were brought in for novelty value—the weird guys who do those crazy comic books." He cringed from the wound more than thirty years later.

As Eisner remembers things today, he already had lofty visions for the comics form when he created the Spirit after several years of generating now-forgotten comic-book features such as "Muss 'Em Up Donovan" (a series about a vicious law enforcer, a proto–Dirty Harry) for various publishers. The Spirit is an independent detective who has no superpowers and wears no costume (aside from a token mask Eisner treated as a blue skin graft around the eyes). "I had long been convinced that I was involved with a medium that had real 'literary potential,'" he wrote in the introduction to the first volume of *The Spirit Archives*, each of which reproduces six months of Spirit stories (on good paper but in slightly reduced scale and with computer-generated colors that lack the texture and accidental vibrancy of the cheaply printed, off-register originals). What gave him such faith in a medium so disreputable and juvenile, he can't recall. From the earliest episodes of the Spirit, however, Eisner's aspirations are clear. The characters are memorable and human, including the Spirit (despite his name). The stories are intimate fables about desperation, loss, and human folly, developed from gestural crime situations; the pacing, graceful; and the drawing, naturalistically bravura.

The Spirit had the benefit of special provenance. When the character appeared in 1940 (two years after Superman and a few months after Batman), a hitherto-unchallenged hierarchical divide separated the two forms of comics—the decades-old, enormously popular newspaper strips and the just-sprouting comic books. The one-panel daily and expanded Sunday color strips produced by the major press syndicates were presumed to be read by the whole family and, accordingly, were designed for adults as well as children; comic books, despite having the space to tell more complex stories, were distributed by candy-store wholesalers and generally treated as another unhealthy confection for kids. The

Spirit was born in neither domain; Eisner developed him under commission to create a comic book that would be distributed in Sunday newspapers, where it would reach readers of every age. Eisner wrote the feature "up," for the adults. The childhood fantasy of magically transforming into a grown-up—*Shazam!*—was a staple of comic books; with the first issue of *The Spirit*, delivered on June 2, 1940, the medium itself matured instantaneously.

There was never much to the premise of the Spirit character: private detective Denny Colt is taken for dead, although he's really alive, and he encounters (as often by accident as by intent) miscellaneous troublemakers (typically, exotics such as spies and smugglers or vampy women smitten with him). That's it—no parents from outer space, no wizards or genies, no incantations, no kit of gadgets and weapons. The Spirit never behaves spookily, and no one in the stories seems to think he's supernatural; he gets punched and kissed, and he bruises and kisses back. The idea of the Spirit is a positioning statement of objection to comic-book ideas, brazenly cursory, a mark of contempt for the gimmickry passing for characterization in the comics of the era.

There was not much crime in the Spirit stories, either—at least not after the first couple of years, when the series reached its maturity. Much as Orson Welles and Alfred Hitchcock used trash sources as excuses to explore emotional terrain, Eisner tended to focus on psychological themes such as loneliness, betrayal, and despair against a translucent scrim of cops-and-robbers doings. In "Two Lives," for instance, Eisner interweaves the stories of unrelated captives, an incarcerated hood and a milquetoast fellow trapped in a bad marriage; they both escape, are mistaken for each other, and are returned to the wrong prison. There was surely little else in that Sunday's newspaper—and certainly nothing in the comics—so cynical about matrimony. In "The Desert Island," the Spirit and a femme fatale named Sand find themselves stranded in paradise, although the Spirit is delirious with fever the whole time, sexually frustrating a woman who had tried to do him in countless times before. Before long, Eisner was dispensing with the pretense of crime situations—and with the Spirit himself. In some of the most poetically imaginative stories in Eisner's work (or, for that matter, in all of comics), the Spirit scarcely appears in his own comic book. Instead, we meet a nobody named Gerhard Schnobble on the day he discovers he has the power to fly, or we find Adolf Hitler on a secret reconnaissance mission, roaming the subways and hobo jungles of New York (in a twist on *Death Takes a Holiday*).

Both Schnobble and Hitler find enlightenment in Eisner's hands, but suffer ignobly for it in the last panel. Schnobble, reveling in his uniqueness among men, is accidentally hit by a gunshot meant for the Spirit and falls to his death before anyone saw what he could do. Hitler, converted to egalitarian niceness by his exposure to America, decides to give a speech reversing all his policies, but is assassinated by a warmongering lieutenant. Eisner's world often seems a bleak, even godless one, not so much part of an irrational or existential universe as a worse one, rigged in the devil's favor.

Like Welles and Hitchcock, again, Eisner has always been fascinated by form, and he began experimenting with the architecture of his medium in the same period as *Citizen Kane*, *The Magnificent Ambersons*, and *Lifeboat*. (Comparisons with film, comic books' moneyed cousin, are irresistible and dominate much of the writing on comics, especially the Spirit.) One Spirit story was told from the point of view of a murderer, all the images rendered in the ovals of the killer's eyes. Another one took place in the "real time" of the ten minutes Eisner calculated it would take to read it. The text for another was all rhyming verse. Another had no text at all but unfolded in pantomime. One meta-episode included scenes of Eisner as both author of the tale at hand and a key part of it. Boundlessly imaginative and fearsomely ambitious—yet, still, "a comic-book man"—Eisner seemed to be trying to push out the boundaries of the comics form, as if he were one of his own characters, another misunderstood victim of a cruel system, struggling to escape.

Much of the Spirit series was explicitly autobiographical, foreshadowing the highly personal graphic novels Eisner would begin writing in the late 1970s. The setting was Eisner's native New York, at first cited by name as Manhattan, then left vague (under pressure from a syndicator fearful of alienating readers elsewhere, according to Eisner), and later generically labeled as Central City. There was no centrality in the *mise en scène*, however; in its architecture, weather, population, and culture, the home of the Spirit was strictly Old World Northeast urban—more specifically, lower-middle-class ethnic. Like Eisner in his youth (before the success of the Spirit enabled him to move with his parents from the Bronx to Riverside Drive), the people he drew lived in tenements near elevated tracks, ate ice-cream cones, and rode the subway to work. They had strong features and wore heavy clothes that could use a pressing.

Jules Feiffer, who was one of Eisner's assistants early in his career, has written that he grew up presuming the Spirit was Jewish (despite the former Denny Colt's Irish-sounding first name), and I see his point. The character is "different" and held in suspicion by those outside his circle of compatriots. Yet I grew up presuming the Spirit was Hungarian, like everyone in my neighborhood. He's resourceful, smart, independent, and strong, as we thought of ourselves. Both views are correct, of course: the Spirit is the fantasy self-image of every outsider, a force of superior cool, strolling immunely through a landscape of malevolent "normalcy."

With newspaper circulation declining under competition from television and with Sunday papers dropping the Spirit insert to cut costs, Eisner abandoned it in 1952. He would say he had lost interest in the project anyway, and the last Spirit stories—a series of loopy outer-space adventures farmed out to free-lancers—are unnerving proof that he had. Eisner, who had employed artists and writers to help him during his World War II military service, relinquished much of the work on these episodes to Jules Feiffer, who wrote the scripts and plotted them in rough sketches, and Wally Wood, a brilliant young draftsman who had distinguished himself doing intricate science-fiction drawings for William M. Gaines's Entertaining Comics (EC) shop. The final story of the Spirit has him zooming around outer space, leading a crew of unsavory ex-convicts on a journey to the moon.

Eisner's creative attention was already elsewhere. In the years following his wartime service, Eisner had continued taking on work for the army as a civilian contractor, writing and drawing instructional comics for military publications. He found himself attracted to the notion of comics as an educational tool, which he saw as a way to experiment further with the form and to continue making comics with some seriousness of purpose. The work was also lucrative; the Eis-ners had two children. Wholly disinclined to work in mainstream comic books, a genre that had matured little since his days on "Muss 'Em Up Donovan," Eisner shifted his focus to educational work, most of it for the armed services. He stayed at it for twenty-six years.

His publishers today tend to discourage inquiry into this period, the longest stretch of sustained effort in Eisner's lifetime. Why mention work such as the special issue of *PS: The Preventive Maintenance Monthly* that Eisner prepared on the subject of "The Army's Brand New Equipment Record System and Proce-dures"? What point is there in knowing that the illustrations in *A Pictorial Arse-nal of American Combat Weapons* were rendered by a comics genius? Eisner, who veers to the left politically, professes enormous pride in his work for the military. "I never demonstrated how to kill," he stresses. "To me, the commercial comics industry was a wasteland. I have always had a conviction that the comics medium is capable of anything. I saw an opportunity to show that comics could be an effective teaching tool as well as an art form."

A good soldier, he accomplished his mission and went no further. Because the enthusiasm for Eisner among comics collectors is both great and indiscrim-inate, his educational/military arcana shows up often on eBay, where I bought a few copies of *PS* magazine published in 1962 and 1968. They're disorienting, with page after page of distinctively Eisnerian art—clever spot illustrations, masterfully composed comics panels, luxurious double-page illustrations—put to use in explaining matters such as how to repair a radio antenna or jump-start a tank. A blonde vamp straight out of a Spirit episode appears every now and then to make a pronouncement, and the effect of word-picture association makes everything she utters seem like a double-entendre. On one page, she murmurs, "Weather makes a difference in performance." (Hubba hubba!) To see all that Will Eisner effort put to such perfunctory and haphazard use is maddening.

* * *

Plenty of American lives do indeed have second acts; third acts are unusual. Had Will Eisner died at age sixty in 1977, his reputation as a comic-book pioneer would have been secure. *The World Encyclopedia of Comics* would still have praised the Spirit as "the historical bridge between the comic book and the newspaper strip" and proclaimed that "Eisner's influence on the art and development of the comic book has been tremendous and lasting." New readers would have discovered the Spirit through reprints of the original stories, which the comics artist and historian Denis Kitchen began publishing through his Kitchen Sink Press in 1972. Eisner's name would have taken a duly prominent place in comics history, somewhere between those of George Herriman and Charles Schultz, and his decades of creative exile under government contract would seem a curious footnote, like Windsor McCay's final years as a vaudeville attraction. But his most serious work, his graphic novels and other late-period books of integrated drawings and text, would never have set yet another standard for comic books.

Invited to sign autographs at a collectors' convention in the mid-1970s, Eisner was startled to see the transformation comics had undergone while he had been drawing instructions for fixing shafted injection pumps. The generation raised on Eisner's Spirit, Harvey Kurtzman's anarchic *Mad*, and the relatively sophisticated EC Comics work of Wally Wood, Al Feldstein, and a few others, had grown up and created underground "comix." One of the few literally comical offshoots of the Sixties counterculture, the stories by Robert Crumb (Mr. Natural, Fritz the Cat, etc.) and Gilbert Shelton (The Fabulous Furry Freak Brothers) that Eisner discovered were ragged, uneven, explicit in their portrayal of sex and drugs, and self-consciously primitive or retro; but they were experimental and not for kids.

Eisner, who had become prosperous enough to start declining commissions for military and educational art, shifted his attention again. He devoted most of a year to creating a book consisting of four related stories told in a free adaptation of the comics style, published in 1978 as *A Contract with God and Other Tenement Stories* (subtitled "A Graphic Novel by Will Eisner"). In sheer seriousness of intent and subtlety of execution, it was to underground comix what the Spirit was to Superman.

Set in the Depression-era Bronx *shtetl* of Eisner's youth, the four tales are tragic memory plays about Jewish immigrant life. Frimme Hersh, the protagonist of the first and longest story, makes a pact with God and feels betrayed when his cherished daughter dies. In the second tale, a vainglorious young street singer submits to a love-starved old diva for alcohol money. In the third, a pedophilic superintendent is undone by a little girl who's scarcely pure herself. Finally, vacationers tangle with their social aspirations at a Catskills resort.

The characters pepper their talk with Yiddish, and they look like working people—toil-worn and thick from too much cheap food—rather than the posed anatomy models on most comics pages. In its concern with the struggle between God and man, its faith in demons, and its echoes of Yiddish folklore, the book clearly suggests the work of Isaac Bashevis Singer, whose short story "Joy" has the same core motif as Eisner's title story. Yet Eisner never read Singer until the early Nineties, when an admirer pointed out the parallels in their work and gave him a copy of *Love in Exile*, a collection of Singer's autobiographical writings.

Visually, *A Contract with God* marked the beginning of a dramatic change in Eisner's approach. In the Spirit years, Eisner employed his virtuosity to dazzling effect with kaleidoscopic "splash pages," German Expressionist–style perspectives, and spectacularly detailed backgrounds (for which he sometimes called upon the help of an architectural draftsman). Now he made no effort to dazzle. Forsaking color for stark black pen and ink, Eisner began to use a spare, allusory visual language to match the poetically ambiguous narrative content of the stories. He learned to evoke a cityscape with a few strokes implying a skyline or suggest a tenement room with the outline of a window frame. In turn, the eye focused on the characters and the speech in the word balloons, on the emotional realm.

Like Ingmar Bergman late in his life, Will Eisner gave up film for the theater. He has taken a couple of years to write each of his recent books, working alone in Florida, and they have grown progressively more intimate and subtle. With one exception (*Life on Another Planet*, which is not a star-trotting adventure but a look at how a mere hint that we might not be alone can unleash earthly paranoia), all of Eisner's graphic novels and story collections are works of memory, most of them centered around the Bronx of his upbringing (*New York: The Big City, Dropsie Avenue: The Neighborhood, The Building, Invisible People, Minor Miracles*), others dealing with his later life. We see one or two characters at a time in an abstracted setting, as if on a stage set, and we watch as they betray their brothers, seduce their antagonists, die of heartache, and occasionally find love or solace.

Who are these books *for*? What would one of the teenager boys roaming the aisles of a comics shop think if he picked up *Minor Miracles* and flipped through the first story, in which disreputable Amos borrows money from his responsible brother Irving to open a furniture shop and drives him to ruin, or *Family Matter*, wherein wheelchair-bound Ben sits silently as his children gather on his nineti-eth birthday to fight over his estate? The answer, no doubt, is the same one Chuck Jones, the auteur of the Warner Bros. cartoon stable, gave when he was asked whom he made his films for: children or adults? Jones said neither; he made them for himself.

For the cover of the *Will Eisner Reader*, the author made a watercolor painting of an old man in Bermuda shorts, gazing in awe at a young boy blithely con-structing a mammoth building complex out of sand. The man looks very much like Eisner himself, long-faced, wide in the middle, and arch-backed from too many years at the drawing board. But the kid is doing what Eisner has done, using the stuff of child's play to make something improbably grand.

Elvis and the Colonel

Having aspired to be as famous as Arthur "Big Boy" Crudup (a gut-bucket singer and songwriter well known only to blues devotees), Elvis Presley surpassed his early ambitions by a factor of about a zillion, and after a few years the enormity of his success began to weigh upon him. He struggled to grasp how he—a poor boy from East Tupelo, Mississippi, who had failed music in high school—could become the most popular recording artist in history, an idol to young people all over the world, and a movie star. "Why am I Elvis?" he wanted to know. "Why was I plucked out of the millions and millions of lives to be Elvis?" At the suggestion of his confidant and hairdresser, Larry Geller, Elvis started reading inspirational texts and popular books on mysticism and Eastern thought, such as Paramahansa Yogananda's *The Autobiography of a Yogi*, Vera Stanley Alder's *The Initiation of the World*, and *The Impersonal Life* (by "Anonymous"). He took this spiritual inquiry so seriously that he considered devoting the rest of his life to it by becoming a monk.

Elvis would never find the answers he sought, because he was looking in the wrong place. Turning inward, as he was, he could presumably have learned something about himself and the music he created; but to understand how he became Elvis, the phenomenon, he would have had to study a different person: his manager (and something more), an outsized mystery man who went by the name of Thomas A. Parker and insisted upon being called "the Colonel."

Before Parker laid siege to the twenty-year-old Presley and assumed control of his career, early in 1955, Elvis had been a regional sensation—a big story, but local news. Performing an erotic transmutation of black rhythm and blues, white gospel, and country music (with strains of cornball humor and Tin Pan Alley schmaltz), Presley had roused Southern girls to hysterics at county fairs, and local demand for the first few records he made for the Memphis-based Sun label, beginning with a fiery rendition of Crudup's "That's All Right" and a rocked-up version of the country ballad "Blue Moon of Kentucky," overtaxed the small company's pressing facilities. Distributed mostly in the South, the records Presley made for Sun Records never made the national pop-music charts.

Rock 'n' roll was in the air; Elvis did not invent it. Teenagers, black and white, had been dancing to hard-driving "jump blues" records by black groups such as Jackie Brenston and the Delta Cats' "Rocket 88" (commonly regarded as the first rock song) since the early 1950s, and white "hillbilly cats" and western-swing musicians such as Bill Haley and Billy Jack Wills were combining elements of African American music with commercial pop and country-and-western styles around the same time. In fact, Haley had begun to make a career out of retooling black musicians' hits like "Rocket 88" for white audiences before Elvis paid Sun Records founder Sam Phillips four dollars to cut his first record. In doing so, Haley followed an old American custom of whitening black music for profit and glory, updating the tradition that had given us Stephen Foster; the first talking picture, *The Jazz Singer*; the first jazz record, "Livery Stable Blues," by the all-white Original Dixieland Jass Band; and the Swing era.

To judge from Presley's earliest recordings, however, it was Elvis who repre-sented rock 'n' roll at its unblushing, volatile best; he was its first master and the embodiment of every reason that adolescents of the postwar years turned to it. Elvis and his music were both young, and in their earthy unconventionality, overt sexuality, and coded blackness—Presley was white, yet, as a Southerner, still *other* to the rest of America—they implied all kinds of challenges to the conservatism and homogeneity of mainstream popular culture in the 1950s. Of course, in order to become our all-purpose symbol of postwar discontent, Elvis needed to quit his previous job as a truck driver for Crown Electric, and Colonel Parker, who had heard talk of Presley while he was promoting the country singer Eddy Arnold, made that possible by buying out his Sun contract (for a then-impressive $35,000) and taking him to RCA Records and into the big time. The Colonel's price was lifelong servitude.

Parker thought nothing of music or culture of any sort. "He really was tone deaf," the journalist Alanna Nash quotes Joan Deary of RCA Records as saying in *The Colonel: The Extraordinary Story of Colonel Tom Parker and Elvis Presley*, a commendably temperate and serious treatment of a story that could have tempted a lesser writer to sensationalism. Parker, like many people in the 1950s (including some of Presley's fans), thought of Elvis as a charismatic novelty—an exotic, unique, and therefore valuable commodity in the entertainment trade. A veteran of the lurid, freewheeling carnivals and tent shows that appeared on the outskirts of rural communities and disappeared with the townsfolk's earnings, the Colonel learned most of what he knew about show business and public taste as a sideshow barker and concessionaire. (He had a special fascination for one exhibit, a man with long hair, a beard, and a phony tail billed as "the Thing! Half Man, Half Animal!" according to Nash.)

He was also a highly developed grifter, a self-proclaimed con artist who thought every situation in life was a game to win, every person either a shill or a mark. He treated Elvis as both, accomplice and victim. He carried on negotiations with film studios as if he and Presley were collaborators and full partners, and he signed everything, even his Christmas cards, as "Elvis and the Colonel." At the same time, his contract with Presley gave Parker independent decision-making authority over nearly every aspect of Elvis's career, and he rigged the financial machinery so that he, the manager, often made more money than his client. Parker sometimes had Presley sign the bottom of blank contracts, which he would fill in later. Nash recounts an exchange between a British journalist and Parker in 1968. "Is it true that you take fifty percent of everything Elvis earns?" Parker was asked. After a moment's thought, he answered, "No, that's not true at all. He takes fifty percent of everything I earn."

He claimed that he and Presley had a commensurate division of responsibilities: Elvis made the music and the movies, and the Colonel made the deals. The truth was knottier, as it often is with creative artists and their managers. Parker's machinations dictated or limited most of Presley's professional activities—the kinds of songs Presley could record, and when, where, and with what musicians, which movies he could make as well as many of his personal moves, down to the friends he could see, how they would spend their time, and even the woman he would marry. (The Colonel pressured Presley to wed Priscilla Beaulieu, the daughter of an army officer, whom Elvis met while he was stationed in Germany and who had been living with Presley in Graceland since she was sixteen, in order to avoid a career-damaging scandal exposing him as the seducer of a minor.) "Look, it's pretty easy," Parker told his client. "We do it this way, we make money. We do it your way, we don't make money." Elvis ended up doing almost everything the Colonel's way, frequently to his career's and his own detriment and, in time, to his frustration.

Like the managers of two other dominant figures in twentieth-century popular music—Irving Mills, who represented Duke Ellington, and Albert Grossman, who managed Bob Dylan—Colonel Parker recognized the profitability of music publishing and tried to maximize his artist's participation in it. Mills and Grossman nurtured their young clients' urges to compose, while Parker exploited Elvis's trust and inertia, confining his repertoire almost exclusively to songs from a malleable old country-music publishing company he could manipulate, Hill and Range Songs, which "cut in" Presley (and, by extension, Parker) on the royalties. Elvis Presley's name appears on the copyrights of dozens of tunes he recorded, including "Don't Be Cruel," "Love Me Tender," and "Heartbreak Hotel." As Dylan, the Beatles, and their peers elevated the standards for rock songwriting, Hill and Range's offerings seemed ever more pale and dated. By the mid-Sixties, Elvis was recording goofy tripe such as "(There's) No Room to Rhumba in a Sports Car," "Do the Clam," and "Petunia, the Gardener's Daughter."

Like Doris Day's manager-husband, Marty Melcher, who took a sultry jazz singer and reduced her to pandering infantilism, compelling her to sing only "bouncy tunes," Parker imposed a rigid code on Hill and Range songwriters. An "Elvis song" had to have simple, accessible words, a first-person point of view, and a happy ending—like the standards of children's books. Composers were also prohibited from meeting Elvis, restricting their conception of him to his ever-more-wholesome public image and insulating them from his own indifference toward their contributions to it.

No other manager of a noted artist has ever been so cynical of his client's talent, as Parker demonstrated in his pitiless lordship over Elvis's tenure in Hollywood. Presley, a movie buff since boyhood, had committed whole scenes from *Rebel Without a Cause* to memory. Fearful that his music might prove to be the passing fad of his early critics' predictions, he was enormously gratified when in 1956 Parker succeeded at parlaying Elvis's early fame into a movie contract with Paramount, and he hoped to begin a substantial screen career, like those of pop-music stars of preceding generations such as Bing Crosby and Frank Sinatra. As he told the producer Hal Wallis, "My ambition has always been to become a motion picture actor—a good one, sir." Parker, never confident of Elvis's acting ability (or of the money in anything smacking of art), made sure Presley never had the chance. The studio contracts which the

Colonel negotiated gave Parker approval over all of Elvis's prospective movie projects, which he saw strictly as cross-merchandising vehicles for soundtrack records, tie-in singles, and souvenirs.

In doing so, Tom Parker was one of the inventors of the contemporary entertainment industry, in which the movie is the promotional device, and the baseball cap with the title logo is the main product. Every Elvis movie had to include at least four songs, and they would inevitably come from the Hill and Range catalog. Parker refused to allow Elvis to appear in *Thunder Road*, *West Side Story*, or *Midnight Cowboy*.

Indeed, Parker effectively kept Elvis out of the film world; although Presley starred in thirty-one movies (or, more accurately, made one movie thirty-one times), they have always existed in a self-contained, unchanging sphere all their own, unrelated to developments in film during the same years. (In 1956, a year before *Love in the Afternoon*, Presley appeared in his first title, *Love Me Tender*; thirteen years later, when *They Shoot Horses, Don't They* was released, he made *The Trouble with Girls*.) Elvis movies, with their interchangeable titles *(Girls! Girls! Girls!*, *Girl Happy*, *Easy Come Easy Go*, *Live a Little Love a Little*) and story lines (young race-car driver/pilot/speedboat driver with guitar confronts gangsters/politicians/businessmen, thereupon getting girl), have a genre to themselves: the Elvis movie. Ostensibly set in vacation locales like Acapulco or Hawaii, suggested by cartoonish, backlot sets, they are as exotic as the foreign foods in a mall food court, and in their manufactured predictability, they provide the same kind of cheesy comfort. "They'll never win any Academy Awards," Parker admitted. "All they're good for is to make money." Presley called them "travelogues" and came to resent not being entrusted with more serious material.

Like Brian Epstein, who took a band of working-class rockers in pompadours and leather jackets, packaged them in bangs and Edwardian suits, and merchandised them, creating Beatlemania, Colonel Parker neatened up, softened, and promoted Elvis Presley as a brand suitable for mass consumption. Unlike the Beatles (especially John Lennon), however, Elvis failed to project a strong sense of self or a challenging artistic conception to counterbalance the accreting banality of all his marketing. While Epstein licensed the Beatles' identities for use as characters on a Saturday morning cartoon show, the boys were recording "Penny Lane" and "Strawberry Fields Forever," and Lennon was writing books of arch verse. The Mop Top hype and promotional gimmicks always felt ancillary and irrelevant to the real Beatles. In the case of Elvis, the exploitation came to define its object; indeed, it seemed to replace him. For years before Presley died in 1977, at the age of forty-two, there appeared to be nothing more to him than his detached, out-of-time presence in those movies, the throwaway songs, the garish Las Vegas stage shows, and the chintzy souvenirs—just the Elvis an old sideshow carny wanted us to have. To this day, much of what we think of when we think about Elvis is the handiwork of Colonel Parker.

How could any artist submit to such constriction for so long? For all the good their managers did them at one time, Duke Ellington fired Irving Mills once he was well established, and Bob Dylan eventually left Albert Grossman. When Marty Melcher died, Doris Day took over her own affairs (and won a landmark suit against Melcher's partner for misappropriation of funds), as the Beatles did after Brian Epstein's death. (They ended up suing one another.) Theories about the mysterious bond between Presley and Colonel Parker have been the midrash of Elvis fandom. Some believe Parker allowed Elvis to fall into drug addiction and supplied him with pills to keep him compliant, although there's no hard evidence to support this. Others, including Nash, see the Colonel as a surrogate parent. (Elvis's beloved mother, Gladys, died in 1958, and his father, Vernon, who outlived his only son by a few years, was something of a rogue and, in Elvis's eyes, betrayed him by cheating on his mama.) There may be some truth to the latter notion: after Parker arranged for Presley to sign with RCA Records, Elvis told him, in a telegram,

> You are the best, most wonderful person I could ever hope to work with. Believe me when I say I will stick with you through thick and thin and do everything I can to uphold your faith in me. . . . I love you like a father.

Bobbie Ann Mason, whose Penguin life of Presley deals knowingly with his roots in Southern poverty, defends Elvis's subservience to the Colonel as a function of his provenance. Being poor and Southern and feeling powerless and inferior, Elvis (like his parents, whose approval was crucial to Parker when Elvis was still a minor) learned deference to authority as a survival tactic. The Presleys raised Elvis to see virtue in work, and he accepted orders from Colonel Parker because he was the boss, despite the technicality that Elvis Presley employed him. Moreover, Mason suspects, if the Presleys recognized Parker as a hustler, they likely respected him as such:

> There had to be a hustle, because you knew the game was rigged against you. . . . The Presleys knew they needed a guide, someone of their own kind who could maneuver among the bankers, lawyers, company executives—none of whom were to be trusted. The Presleys

probably considered themselves lucky to find a con man who could challenge the big dudes, because they knew the big dudes would just stomp on them. That was the way life was.

Elvis and his parents all died without knowing how grand a hustle the Colonel had pulled off. He was scarcely "one of their kind," the West Virginia–born colonel he pretended to be, but an illegal alien named Andreas van Kuijk, who had fled his native Netherlands under hazy circumstances—perhaps a murder—and scammed his way through the ranks of the American entertainment industry, from the carnivals into country music to Elvis, with stops as an army deserter (discharged as a psychopath) and a game warden along the way. Parker (never his legal name) kept his identity a secret until his final years, when he thought a few details from the truth would give him a tactical advantage in a court proceeding. In her book, Alanna Nash, building upon the research of the German journalist Dirk Vellenga, tells in unprecedented and meticulous detail the full story of Parker's real history and his audacious posing.

In retrospect, it seems almost fitting that the man who transformed Elvis Presley into an icon of pop artifice should be a creature of self-invention. He knew his trade, as Bobbie Ann Mason points out. Both Presley and Parker were never what they seemed, we now know: in his youth, when Elvis terrified parents as he snarled and gyrated like something from hell, he was actually a shy, religious fellow who lived with his mother and father. When he returned from the army, looking clean-cut and demure, he began his private descent into drug abuse and sexual excess. No degree of deception could have fazed his manager, the Kentucky colonel from Noord-Brabant.

Presley "was trapped by his dependence on the Colonel," the songwriter Jerry Lieber told Alanna Nash. "He was never able to take control of his own life." One can't help but wonder how Presley's life and work might have been different had he mustered the will to leave Parker in the Sixties, as he told friends he wanted to do. Would he have made *Midnight Cowboy*, after all, or accepted Barbra Streisand's overture to appear with her in *A Star Is Born*? Could he have improved his performances? Or was he doing what he really wanted to do all along—and posing when he talked of wishing he could do more serious work?

Colonel Parker liked to stand outside the theater after Elvis had given a concert, peddling souvenirs. For Presley's fans, Parker had "I Love Elvis" buttons. For others, he also carried "I Hate Elvis" buttons. Clearly, neither was appropriate for Parker; he just liked selling the buttons. He didn't care one way or another about Elvis. In the end, sadly, his client seemed to feel the same way.

Ken Burns and the Great Men of Jazz

No other act of commemoration in the popular media confers as much authority as the infectious gravitas of a film by Ken Burns. Over the two decades prior to this writing in 2001, Burns made more than a dozen documentaries on American subjects, such as the Civil War (1990), baseball (1994), Lewis and Clark (1997), and women's suffrage (1999). Two of those films, *The Civil War* and *Baseball*, were monumental in scale and effect—each broadcast on public television in more than a dozen parts—and were hits on TV and best sellers on videocassette, as well as in the form of book tie-ins prepared by Burns and the historian Geoffrey C. Ward. Largely owing to the success of Burns's documentary, the Civil War became something close to a popular craze in the Nineties, and tens of thousands of new enthusiasts joined the ranks of those who were already costuming themselves as Confederates and Federals in reenactments of historic battles. My teenage son, Jake, joined the 14th Brooklyn and helped defeat the *faux* Rebs at Antietam. In January 2001, Burns's third epic documentary, *Jazz*, began its run on PBS, broadcast in two-hour episodes for four weeks. The book version was published in time for holiday gift-giving, and ancillary CDs—a five-disc boxed set, a "best-of" CD, and twenty-two discs devoted to individual musicians profiled in the film—were rolled out simultaneously. How long would it be before my son and his friends were reenacting the 1937 cutting contest between the Benny Goodman and Chick Webb orchestras at the Savoy?

Burns had evidently seen jazz as a great subject for some time, although he acknowledged in interviews that he knew little about the music when he began working on his film in earnest during the late '90s. In an early sequence of *Baseball*, Burns seemed to signal his future intentions with a quote from the scholar and writer Gerald Early: "When they study our civilization two thousand years from now, there will only be three things that Americans will be known for: the Constitution, baseball, and jazz music. They're the three most beautiful things Americans have ever created." (Early, an incisive thinker whose presence in *Jazz* gives the film much of its focus and spirit, has obviously had a substantial influence on Burns; he is the filmmaker's new Shelby Foote.)

In the music and the culture of jazz, Burns recognized the opportunity to explore some of his favorite themes: American identity, individuality, race, and democracy. "I think that the essence of jazz . . . is at the heart of who we are as a people," Burns told the journalist Larry Blumenfeld. "It's this notion of the tension between the individual and the collective, you know, the solo and the ensemble. It's this notion of race. It's very much, to me, the rarefied, purified idea of democracy." Here we have themes rich and sweeping enough for a nineteen-hour film—and for something equally important to a filmmaker working on Burns's scale: a grant proposal. (*Jazz* was funded by endowments from General Motors, the Pew Charitable Trusts, the Doris Duke Charitable Foundation, and the John D. and Catherine T. MacArthur Foundation, among many others.) If the pitch is the art form in Hollywood, as Joan Didion suggested, the grant proposal is its counterpart in nonfiction film, and it takes grand themes that illuminate the American experience to persuade foundations to deem expensive projects like this worth funding. From the schematic linearity of its structure to the hortative tone of its narration, the grant permeates each sequence as the blues infuses every composition by Duke Ellington.

Burns is on to something, of course. As jazz musicians and fans have known since the music's emergence in the early years of the last century—and as some in high-brow circles recognized as early as 1919, jazz has always been a potently sophisticated form of expression. Largely improvised, simultaneously cooperative and competitive, a celebration of the primacy of the individual voice, sensual, cerebral, deeply steeped in African American life, jazz is one of America's major contributions to world culture. There is no need for exaggeration such as Burns's claim that jazz is "the only art form created by Americans." (Apart from the issue of whether jazz is a form or a style like baroque or twelve-tone music, Americans also created the blues, country-and-western music, tap dance, Abstract Expressionism, the comic strip, and more.) Nor does Burns do the music and its creators justice by presenting much of the film as a series of arguments in support of his theses about American identity and such, with little space in twenty hours' time for dissent, ambiguity, or irony (Gerald Early notwithstanding). Clearly he could still learn a thing or two about expression from African American culture.

The film preceded the book, as Burns explains in his introduction to the latter; accordingly, both are structured cinematically as series of vignettes telling the life stories of the most influential and prominent musicians in jazz history. Although Burns and Ward are credited as coauthors of the book, Burns evidently contributed the organizing principles and thematic guidelines, and little writing beyond the introduction; generously, one could take this arrangement as an homage to the jazz bandleaders' tradition of "cutting in," whereby Benny Goodman attached his name to Edgar Sampson's "Don't Be That Way" and Cootie Williams split the copyright to Thelonious Monk's "Round Midnight" when they recorded the songs. Jazz, film and book, proceeds from the Great Man School of history.

As if to leave no doubt that jazz masters deserve the same reverence long accorded Bach, Mozart, Beethoven, and other composers in the European tradition, Burns presents his subjects in the terms he would have found in a music textbook three or four decades ago. There is an artistic hierarchy, headed up in descending order by Louis Armstrong, Duke Ellington, and Charlie Parker; in fact, Armstrong is directly compared to Bach repeatedly, and Ellington to Mozart at least once. (The Parker-Beethoven connection goes undeveloped, though it need not have. Stanley Crouch, the liveliest of the film's many interview subjects, once linked the two as innovators in harmonic abstraction during a lecture at Tufts University.) The ranking being chronological as well as qualitative, a paternalistic narrative is implicit; each master left his innovations—swing time, tone color, abstraction—for the next to pick up and advance.

The first sequences of the film trace the emergence of jazz as a rigorous, inventive new social music developed by Negroes and Creoles in turn-of-the-century New Orleans. We are introduced to James Reese Europe, the black composer and conductor who performed his disciplined and formal music in Carnegie Hall in 1914; while his work was scarcely jazz by any familiar definition, Europe became a model for jazz orchestra leaders such as Duke Ellington. And we meet Jelly Roll Morton, the self-aggrandizing Creole pianist and composer who laid claim to inventing jazz, and the cornetist and bandleader Joe "King" Oliver, whose group was a training ground for both the pioneering clarinetist Sidney Bechet and the cornetist who would supplant Oliver in fame and influence, Louis Armstrong. Once introduced, Armstrong towers over the remaining nineteen or so hours of *Jazz* the way Bach looms over Western music history. Just as every classical musician still plays the scale Bach established in the eighteenth century, jazz artists, we learn, continue to employ variations of the harmonic and rhythmic vocabulary Armstrong codified and brought to a level of perfection.

Each of the ten episodes of the film series has at least one substantial segment on Armstrong: we marvel as he creates the first indisputable masterpieces of the jazz canon, the Hot Five recordings of 1925; we see him take up singing, inventing "scat" improvisation; we are even granted a kind of intimacy we have with no others in the film as we follow the vagaries of Armstrong's love life until he finally finds domestic bliss in a middle-class home in Queens. (Ellington's *amours* would have made much more interesting viewing.) There are penetrating segments on Armstrong's schism with the founders of the bebop movement and on the charges of minstrelsy he unjustly suffered in his late years (with, once again, refreshingly frank and lucid commentary by Early). None of this is excessive: such is the depth of Armstrong's genius and the breadth of his influence.

The film pushes matters only in tethering Armstrong to virtually every subsequent innovator in jazz history. The critic and biographer Gary Giddins, who gets more screen time than anyone else interviewed and serves as the film's tempered voice of authority on all aspects of jazz, describes Charlie Parker's landmark "KoKo" as "shocking, the way Louis Armstrong was shocking in the 1920s." Nat Hentoff compares the thrill of discovering Thelonious Monk at Manhattan's Five Spot to the imagined exhilaration of seeing Armstrong and the Hot Five in a Chicago nightclub (despite the fact that the Hot Five was a recording-studio ensemble and never performed in clubs). Sonny Rollins, Giddins explains, "has that ebullience that I associate with Louis Armstrong." Even John Coltrane is characterized in relation to Armstrong, in his case by the fact that he appears to have nothing in common with him. The threads of that paternalistic narrative weaken under the strain.

The second Great Man in Burns's account, Edward Kennedy "Duke" Ellington, is treated almost as hagiographically as Armstrong, though less accurately. The creator of some five thousand distinctive works of music (from blues riffs to orchestral suites, ballet and film scores, and Broadway musicals), Ellington is characterized as "an African Stravinsky" who "erased the color line between jazz and classical music." Music "flow[ed] effortlessly from his pen," we hear, as the narrator describes Ellington composing alone in his locomotive sleeper while the members of his orchestra slept. He wrote "Mood Indigo" "in fifteen minutes while waiting for his mother to finish cooking dinner," and his compositions were so fully wrought that "even the solos in 'Reminiscing in Tempo' were written."

While Ellington did indeed compose incessantly, including when he was alone in his sleeper car, a core element of his genius and an aspect of a creative process deeply indebted to the African tradition is his extraordinary method of creating music collaboratively with his musicians. The main theme of "Mood Indigo" was actually an improvisation he had heard his clarinetist Barney Bigard play. Yes, Ellington composed the solo that trumpeter Cootie Williams performed on the recording of "Reminiscing in Tempo," the masterpiece he wrote in memory of his mother. In truth, precisely the reverse was not only more typical, but integral to Ellington's music-making technique: his musicians' improvised solos became part of their leader's compositions. Ellington worked with the members of his orchestra cooperatively and motivated them to contribute ideas.

An inspiring stimulus and a profoundly gifted editor, he kept his ears open during the countless thousands of solos his musicians played on the road, and he plucked the musical gems among them to refine and expand into fully formed compositions: from Otto Hardwick he found the basis of "Sophisticated Lady" and "Prelude to a Kiss"; from Cootie Williams, "Do Nothing 'Till You Hear from Me" (originally "Concerto for Cootie"); from Johnny Hodges, "Don't Get Around Much Anymore" and "I'm Beginning to See the Light"; from his son Mercer, "I Got It Bad (and That Ain't Good)." (This process is mentioned briefly in the *Jazz* book but never suggested in the film, which points out only that Ellington wrote *for* his musicians, not necessarily *with* them.) Billy Strayhorn, Ellington's "writing-arranging companion" from 1939 until Strayhorn's death in 1967, contributed "Take the 'A' Train" and dozens of other masterworks in the Ellington Orchestra repertoire.

These facts scarcely argue that Ellington was any less a composer than, say, Stravinsky; the resulting music holds up comparably. They demonstrate, however, that he was a radically different sort of composer—not another lone genius tapping his own resources (though Ellington composed rather well that way, too), but a brilliantly exploratory creator working largely in an inclusionary, communal tradition.

Burns's distortion of the way Ellington composed his music is defensive and patronizing. To ignore the collaborative aspect of Ellington's method is to demean the culture he devoted his life to celebrating, and to remake him in the mold of the Western classical icons is to propagate their sovereignty. Why do we need to think of Ellington as another Mozart or Stravinsky? He was the first Ellington, and that is quite enough.

There are subtle hints of racism and anti-Semitism in other profiles in the film. We keep hearing how ideas "seemed to flow effortlessly" from musicians such as Armstrong and Ellington, an echo of the discomforting notion that African-Americans are instinctual musicians. By contrast, we learn elsewhere that Artie Shaw rehearsed so strenuously that his lower lip bled and that Benny Goodman practiced religiously every day of his life. There is no suggestion that black artists have also labored to master their art. According to Burns, Goodman and Shaw (born Arthur Arshawsky), both Jews, seem to have taken up jazz largely for the glory and money in it, anyway. The film speaks of Goodman deciding to pursue music full time because he found himself making $15 per night, three times his father's daily earnings at the Chicago stockyards. When Shaw first heard a saxophone player, the narrator tells us, "That did it—music would be his way to fame and fortune." Goodman was "fiercely ambitious" and Shaw a "professional," but neither of them, apparently, an artist worth discussing in aesthetic terms.

In its pride in jazz as a reflection of America, the film veers toward cultural xenophobia. Jazz began as and remains an American art—specifically, an African American art, composed and performed predominantly by people of color evoking their lives in musical terms. It is elementally black music, although whites and others have always played it and have contributed to it, just as people of all backgrounds have composed and performed in the Western classical tradition. Since the second decade of jazz history, however, the musics of other cultures have increasingly exerted influence upon jazz, and jazz has infiltrated countries around the world.

The most notable form of this musical cross-fertilization is Latin jazz, which is all but ignored in Burns's film and given passing nods in the book. This is not an easy error to make. The Puerto Rican valve trombonist, composer, and arranger Juan Tizol joined Duke Ellington in 1929 and appears prominently in still photos and movie footage of the Ellington Orchestra in *Jazz*: his collaboration with Ellington, "Caravan," plays on the soundtrack. Tizol contributed a whole book of Latin-tinged compositions to the Ellington repertoire, including "Perdido," "Moon Over Cuba," "Conga Brava," and "Jubilesta." At the same time, the Cuban trumpeter Mario Bauzá was soloing in the Chick Webb orchestra, and the Anglo-Cuban composer Chico O'Farrill was doing arrangements infused with Latin rhythms for Benny Goodman. By the 1940s, the rhumba fad made Cuban big bands a rage in Manhattan, with Bauzá, the percussionist Machito, and others leading their own highly successful orchestras. (The big-band leaders Xavier Cugat and Desi Arnaz had jukebox hits with a pop version of work in this vein.)

Meanwhile, swing was so pervasive a force that it wafted into unexpected pockets of the musical landscape, including the South and the West. There had been novelty hillbilly-jazz groups such as the Skillet Lickers of Georgia recording as early as 1925, and by the 1940s Western swing was a popular style; musicians such as Milton Brown, Bob Dunn, and Tex Williams were improvising to rural music set to swing time. Two of the best bands in the genre, Bob Wills and His Texas Playboys and Spade Cooley and His Western Dance Gang, recorded extensively and competed for a reputation as the hardest-swinging band, much as Benny Goodman and Chick Webb had. They even had a Savoy-style cutting contest in Venice, California, in 1943. (Spade Cooley won, and his was the band with multiple stringed instruments and no horn section.)

There is virtually none of this in *Jazz*. (Machito's name appears on a theater marquee in a couple of still photos, and the subject of "Caribbean rhythms" finally comes up during a discussion of Dizzy Gillespie's explorations in Afro-Cuban music during the 1940s.) Why? Is jazz less authentic when it reflects Puerto Rican or Cuban experience? Duke Ellington, Chick Webb, and Benny Goodman thought not. Does jazz become something other in the hands of country musicians using stringed instruments? Perhaps. That would have been a provocative question for Gerald Early. Still, Latin jazz and Western swing *happened*; they are facts of music history. Ignoring them because they fail to accommodate the filmmaker's agenda is something worse than bad history; it's politics.

Most troublingly, *Jazz* (film and book) gives up on the music forty years too early. The film employs nine of its ten episodes, a full seventeen hours, to get to the 1960s, then it rock-skips over the last four decades in one episode and abruptly sinks. Entire movements such as "free jazz" and major artists of the past thirty years such as Ornette Coleman and Cecil Taylor are all but dismissed in comparatively short, tentative segments. Neither of them gets the series' full profile treatment: *Ornette Coleman was born and raised . . .* , like that. Instead, the narrator quotes Ellington musing over the arabesque web of styles that came to shroud jazz by the early 1970s: "I don't know how such extremes as now exist can be contained under the heading of 'jazz.'" The film's narrator adds gravely, "The question was whether jazz, the most American of art forms, would survive at all." The real question was whether jazz would survive as a mostly American art form or if a growing range of influences from around the globe—especially South America, Asia, and parts of Africa—might not transform it, as they indeed have in recent years. That, in Ken Burns's schema, might be the same as death.

John Lennon
The Life

A s he said about the Maker of All Things in the song he called "God," which was really about himself, John Lennon is a concept by which we measure our pain. Lennon made a great many things both miraculous and ungodly during his foreshortened and intensely public life, and much of what he did brought us grief, in the multiple meanings of the word, or granted us the effect of grief's denial: ecstasy. Lennon and the three mates for whom he served as semi-official leader came to America just in time to provide gleeful relief from our famous post-Kennedy malaise. He proceeded to outrage conservative Christians who were protective of the bigness of Jesus; he vexed aesthetic fundamentalists who were reluctant to accept rock 'n' roll as art; he infuriated rock traditionalists who were even more reluctant to accept the conceptual avant-garde; he irritated Paul fans; he conferred upon us the irrepressibly unpleasant Yoko and released "Whatever Gets You Through the Night"; and then he abandoned us, withdrawing from public life for nearly five years. Finally, through his death at the hands of a fan in 1980, he made us face the darkest potential of the mixed-up, out-of-control feelings of love and fury that he had stirred and refracted with a smirk.

His admirers and his detractors—there are no others in this case—have been talking and writing fervently about Lennon since the first days of Beatlemania, in Liverpool, all those years ago. I do not know exactly how many books have been published about the Beatles, but I own fifty-eight, and I am not a collector by the standards of Beatle fandom. The number of newspaper, magazine, and journal articles about the group and its music is essentially unknowable; the major indexes cite tens of thousands, and those lists exclude fanzines, newsletters, teen mags, and the alternative press, in which much of the most obsessive and revealing documentation of Beatledom has taken place. (A 2008 issue of *Beatlefan*, a magazine published for three decades, had the first of a two-part interview with Ringo's former fiancée, Nancy Andrews, as well as an illustrated history of "Yellow Submarine" memorabilia.) In 1971, Dick Cavett had John and Yoko as guests on his late-night talk show, and, by way of unnecessary introduction, Cavett described the Beatles as "the most written-about, the most listened-to, and the most imitated" musicians of their time. And so, 2008 brought us 822 additional pages bound in hard covers as *John Lennon: The Life*, by Philip Norman. To note that Lennon and the band he founded have enduring capacities to ignite the public imagination is to commit an obviousness that is, quite aptly, painful.

Norman, a British journalist and author of breezy novels and nonfiction books on pop-culture subjects, is best known for another book about the mop-tops, called *Shout!: The Beatles in Their Generation*, which appeared in 1981. It was notable as a fairly serious, if flawed attempt to humanize the Beatles and to factor the elements of timing and money into their legend. *Shout!* was good on the convoluted, ultimately catastrophic business end of the Beatles' life, which Norman had once covered as a reporter, and the book was thorough in its treatment of Brian Epstein, the Beatles' deliciously eccentric business manager. (Among the anecdotes that Norman relayed was one about how Epstein, as a boy, would smash a toy rather than share it with other children.) *Shout!* luxuriated in the supposition that Epstein had been not-so-secretly in love with Lennon, and it betrayed a parallel in the heart of its own author. (If, for a writer, respectful affection can open windows on a subject, infatuation leads inevitably to closing the shades and turning off the lights.) The first sentence of *Shout!* began: "John Lennon was born on October 9, 1940 . . . ," and Norman went on to characterize Lennon as "eighty percent" of the Beatles. Throughout *Shout!*, Norman derided Paul McCartney as a cunning square, and he dismissed George Harrison and Ringo Starr as so-so musicians with luck at finding friends. Generous to marginal figures such as Lennon's first bandmates, the drummer Colin Hanton and the bassist Len Garry, who had given Norman interviews for the book (and for its follow-up, the Lennon biography), Norman smashed the Beatles he could not have all to himself.

After some thirty years covering the Beatle beat, Norman appears to have little enthusiasm left for any of the four—and least of all for the subject of his new book, the object of his old ardor. Like a submissive lover who has been in an inequitable marriage for too long, Norman seems to have had enough of John Lennon. He conducted relatively few new interviews for an ostensibly major work on a major artist of the recent past; he has summoned little in the way of revealing insights into Lennon or his time; and his prose is repetitious and, for the most part, bloodless. Such tepidity is, in this case, not just misguided but also misleading, because John Lennon was many things, but none of them was dull.

Like *Shout!*, Norman's biography of Lennon is nicely detailed on the Beatles' brief apprenticeship in Liverpool and Hamburg, as well as on the much-told story of Beatlemania. Norman is skillful at deciphering the class dynamics among the Beatles—John, the self-proclaimed working-class hero, was raised half a station above Paul, and George and Ringo were of lots considerably below the other two. ("He's a real wacker," Lennon's aunt Mimi said after meeting George, as Norman quotes her.) Norman properly casts the early success of the Beatles in England as not merely a triumph for the lower orders but also as part of a larger collapse of class structures throughout the United Kingdom in the postwar era. Yet like many British writers on the subject of the Beatles, he mistakenly transfers the function of class in the group's rise at home to their success in the United States.

For young Americans, who were scarcely oblivious to class but were attuned instead to a different system of class codes, the Beatles never "read" as lowly. Dressed in their matching Edwardian suits, dolled up with their foppish hair, and chirping in heavy accents of some kind—who knew from Scouse, in New Jersey?—the Beatles came across mainly as something English, and that put them, in American minds, a rank above Americans. In our self-conception, all Americans, relative to the English, are real wackers. (This standpoint is of a piece with Americans' beloved, insidious anti-elitism and our defensive pride in both our realness and our wackerness.) At the peak of Beatlemania as a cultural craze and licensing bonanza for Brian Epstein, King Features produced a series of Saturday-morning Beatles cartoons, and the voice actor for John gave him a clipped upper-crust accent; I watched the cartoons every weekend in the '60s, and I never noticed this until recently, when I played some of the cartoons on YouTube for my little son, Nate. When I was a kid, I conceived of the Beatles simply as English and, therefore, more sophisticated than American rock acts. As their work evolved and the Beatles took postwar pop into the realm of art music, I was just one in a country full of rock fans who mistook the Beatles, as Englishmen, for people endowed by birthright for the task.

When Elvis first saw the Beatles, he said they looked like "a bunch of faggots," and their mere Englishness was no doubt feminizing in the eyes of Americans less enlightened than the King of Rock 'n' Roll. Norman shuffles awkwardly around the issue of sexual transgression in the Beatles' early appeal, but he falls considerably short of doing it justice. Beyond the bangs and the falsetto "woo's" and the odd suits, all of which were taken as fey in the early 1960s, the spirit of Eros was palpable in the sight of John and Paul, standing face to face—a bit of stage-craft made possible by McCartney's left-handedness and Lennon's right-handedness—as they sang together into a shared microphone, their lips nearly touching. Among the specialties in the Beatles' youthful repertoire, moreover, were quite a few songs sung by or associated with women—girl-group hits such as the Marvelettes' "Please Mr. Postman," the Shirelles' "Boys," and the Teddy Bear's "To Know Him Is to Love Him," which John crooned, sometimes without changing the pronouns, and "Till There Was You," the gooey ballad from *The Music Man*, which McCartney learned from a Peggy Lee record.

For adolescent boys, then, the Beatles were far more complexly stimulating than traditional male pop stars, and for the girls who dominated the band's hordes of hysterical fans, moreover, the Beatles were more than objects of erotic desire. In the meticulous perfection of their public selves, in their sheer prettiness (Ringo excepted, although he had a *jolie laide* quality under the right lighting), and in the magnitude of their popularity, the Beatles surely served many of their young female fans as a fantasy projection, a dream image of teenage girlhood—a group prototype for Hannah Montana, in drag. Beatlemania was, in this sense, an opulent expression of self-love, and that fact alone makes it the official start of the '60s.

It is more than forty-five years now since the emergence of the Beatles in 1963—a very long time by the pop-culture clock. How long, exactly? If this were 1963, and I were writing about the singing sensation of forty-five years earlier, I would be talking about Al Jolson. Indeed, in some ways, Beatlemania seems as remote as the mania over Jolson, and "Love Me Do" sounds as hokey today as "I'm Sitting on Top of the World."

* * *

There are four thousand holes in *John Lennon: The Life*, and the one in most dire need of fixing is the absence of enlightening discussion of the creative work that makes Lennon matter. Philip Norman, who has done books on Buddy Holly and Elton John, in addition to his writing on the Beatles, is the rare biographer of musicians who has little evident interest in music itself. He concentrates on the events of his subjects' lives with an eye for personal details (John liked to conjure a romantic mood, lighting a candle by the bedside, before sex) but not much of an ear for the songs they devoted those lives to creating. When he does take up a specific work, Norman tends to characterize the song by the style or the quality of its lyrics. Thus he describes "If I Fell," the gorgeous Lennon ballad that the Beatles performed in their first film, *A Hard Day's Night*, tersely as "plaintive." Yes, the words are simple and direct; but the music is luxurious and complex, with harmony parts that purl around the melody. Song after song from record after record goes without much attention, as if John Lennon started a band called the Beatles just so he could imitate a paralyzed person on stage and kick a friend in the head after the show.

In much of what he does on the lyrics, Norman gives way to the same kind of myopia and inclination to inflation that mars a great deal of other writing on the Beatles. In a section on "In My Life," for example, he writes that Lennon "sketched out a song that would use poetic observation in the style of Wordsworth or Tennyson, recalling the Liverpool he had known as a child and lamenting how, even over his short lifetime, that old, solid world of ships and docks had all but vanished." This, for a lovely, truly plaintive song made up of gauzy generalities about "people and things that went before." In a passage on "Norwegian Wood," much the same, Norman asserts that its lyrics "are among very few [song lyrics] that can also be read as poetry or even drama," dismissing in a huff the dozens of considerably poetic and dramatic lyrics of pre-rock song-writers such as Lorenz Hart and Yip Harburg, not to mention poetic rockers such as Chuck Berry, Smokey Robinson, and Bob Dylan.

Weighted heavily on the side of Lennon's life before and during his years with the Beatles, Norman's book glances over Lennon's experimental records with Yoko Ono and his post-Beatles rock albums, two of which—*Plastic Ono Band*, Lennon's bleak, unsparing first solo album, and *Double Fantasy*, John and Yoko's joint testament of contentment in what should have been Lennon's mid-life—had as much fine Lennon music as any Beatles albums. Yoko Ono, who submitted to interviews with Norman and encouraged his book when he first proposed it to her five years ago, has, since reading the manuscript, disavowed it on the grounds that it is "mean to John." I think she has a point. Indifference to the art is a profound act of hostility to the artist. In his deafness to the music that Lennon went to such pains to produce, Norman hurts Lennon's legacy more than Lennon, his art, his politics, or his wife ever hurt anyone.

Paul McCartney's *Chaos and Creation*

T he last time Paul McCartney made an album in the vein of his 2005 CD, *Chaos and Creation in the Backyard*, John Lennon was alive to hear it. McCartney had just cast off Wings, the notoriously ephemeral quasi-band comprising his blithe novice-musician wife, Linda, and their loyal mate Denny Laine (augmented on some records by a floating assortment of players varying in ability) after nine years, ten LPs, and countless critical gibes at the slyly criticism-proof "Silly Love Songs." With the benefit of nine days of stock-taking in a Tokyo jail on a charge of marijuana possession, McCartney retrenched; he re-grouped without a group, playing all the instruments on an album called *McCartney II* in 1980. "He sounds depressed," Lennon told a writer for *Playboy* not long before he was murdered. Indeed, with the exception of the intricate, bouncy single "Coming Up" and the grating "Temporary Secretary," most of the songs on the record were startlingly, uncharacteristically, almost refreshingly lugubrious and dull. McCartney was ready to re-claim his musical identity, if only he could find it.

The album was a titular sequel to his first solo venture, made ten years earlier, immediately after McCartney had left his previous band. *McCartney*, much like the records John Lennon, George Harrison, and Ringo Starr each made immediately after the Beatles disbanded, was an act of purging. Yet unlike Lennon's *Plastic Ono Band* (a Janovian scream of self-defined genius in pain), Harrison's *All Things Must Pass* (a creative awakening in the name of pop mysticism), and Starr's *Sentimental Journey* (an outrageous attempt to croon standards, with some elegant arrangements by Oliver Nelson and Chico O'Farrell), *McCartney* was less an effort to establish an individual identity as it was an attempt to purge the Beatles of its group identity. *I don't need those other three—nor anyone else besides my wife*, McCartney seemed to be saying. *I can do it all, just as well, by myself, in the backyard of my estate in Scotland.* The album was something of a cheat: supposedly homemade on lo-fi equipment, it was only partly so. Several of the most striking tracks, including "Maybe I'm Amazed," "Junk," and "Every Night," were recorded in secrecy, over time, in top London studios, and the best songs ("Junk" and "Teddy Boy") had been composed years earlier, with the Beatles in mind.

Still, *McCartney* was impressive and appealing. It was also flawed by an excess of fragmentary, slipshod tracks—harbingers of Paul's long solo career. By making proudly Beatles-esque music all by himself, writing every word and playing and singing virtually every note (Linda contributed some background vocals, though not many notes), McCartney shook off Lennon, Harrison, and Starr to try to prove that what remained without them, Paul McCartney, was the Beatles. By simultaneously corrupting the effort, mingling the sophisticated, burnished moments with others of maladroit noodling, he laid claim both to the esteem of the Beatles' achievements and to the license to coast off them as he chose.

Chaos and Creation is essentially *McCartney III*. It brings McCartney playing nearly all the instruments—various guitars, piano, organ, bass, drums, miscellaneous percussion, autoharp, recorder, even cello, flugelhorn, and toy glockenspiel. (Several tracks have additional string and brass sections, and a few guest soloists handle specialty instruments such as the duduk, an Armenian woodwind.) As with *McCartney* and *McCartney II*, this effort is an attempt at redefinition—in this case, a clarification of McCartney's creative identity after more than a decade of diffusive fiddling, sidesteps, dalliances, and half-hearted experiments. For his previous album, released four years earlier, McCartney wrote the songs hastily, in some cases finishing them in the studio, and he recorded the music with unfamiliar young studio musicians under Los Angeles producer David Kahne. The result, *Driving Rain*, was even weaker, more scattershot than his preceding recording of original material, *Flaming Pie*, from 1997, a toy chest full of colorful, misshapen playthings, including two songs written while they were being recorded: a duet with Steve Miller and a nonsense tiff called "Really Love You," co-credited to Ringo because he supplied the back-beat. McCartney explained that working on the Beatles' *Anthology* of obscurities had inspired him to make *Flaming Pie*, which not only derived its named from a vintage *bon mot* by John Lennon but whose music sounds very much like Beatles rejects, demos, and outtakes. (They were nominally improved by Jeff Lynne, their producer, who tried brushing the album with that metallic ELO sound.) Both records had notable high points, though: *Driving Rain's* "She's Given Up Talking," a cryptic story-song, and *Flaming Pie's* "Calico Skies" and "Heaven on a Sunday," a pair of lovely ballads.

Between the two albums, in 1998, McCartney lost his wife to cancer and wrestled with the grief, recording a raw, simple album of early rock 'n' roll numbers (and a few originals in their style) with a tight little pick-up band. Named *Run Devil Run* for a sign that he saw on a New Orleans drug store, the record is a small triumph, but it is essentially not Paul McCartney music. A month later, he released a collection of short pieces in the classical mode, *Working Classical*, his third CD of concert music, following the well-meaning work of apprenticeship, "Liverpool Oratorio" in 1991, and the overwrought "Standing Stone" six years later. Like every one of his pop albums, including the worst, *Working Classical* is, by turns, uncommonly tuneful and pleasant (most notably in a pair of sweet, pretty tone poems, "A Leaf" and "Spiral") and numbingly trite (as in the string-quartet versions of "My Love" and "Lovely Linda").

He sees every musical venture as a rail journey, McCartney explained in an interview to promote *Chaos and Creation in the Backyard*. "It's like sort of stepping on a train," he said. "I don't worry about other trains I've been on, just this new train, and that's exciting. You just have to realize that perhaps you can't always have as great a journey as you had in the past." Of course, riding a locomotive is a passive experience. It is not much like the active and often arduous creative processes that composers and musicians typically describe. If McCartney thinks of himself as a mere passenger in the course of his work, one wonders: who, then, is steering? Who, or what, is running the engine? His producer? His collaborators? His audience? Each of them influences him, sometimes mightily. But the primary traits of his music—its casualness, its buoyancy, its disarming juvenility, its caprice, its wild unevenness in quality—suggest that McCartney tends to entrust his destiny to only one driver: himself. His own talent took him so far for so long that he has become content to go along for the ride.

For *Chaos and Creation in the Backyard*, McCartney hired the producer Nigel Godrich, because he liked the textured clarity of the albums that Godrich recorded for Radiohead, Travis, and Beck. It was Godrich who persuaded McCartney to avoid his penchant for winging it, in a phrase, and urged him to pare down, to concentrate on song craft, to play as many instruments as possible himself, to re-claim his musical personality. "He wanted to keep it really simple, really straight, really direct and very me instead of 'Let's get modern, let's get gimmicky' or 'Let's do this because it's the latest groove,'" McCartney said. The album succeeds at that: it has a plaintive, organic feeling. The songs, all but one of which are mid-tempo ballads, flow smoothly and have affecting melodies. There is less filler than usual for McCartney—only "Friends to Go" (a song about wanting people to leave the house, "Let 'Em In" reversed) and "Follow Me" (which says that and little more) are outright throwaways. There are three treats—"Fine Line" (the single, and vintage McCartney pop), "Jenny Wren" (a lyrical folkish number, a close cousin to "Blackbird," inspired by the Dickens character from *Our Mutual Friend*), and "Riding to Vanity Fair" (Paul in a petulant, arty mode). The rest of the music—eight more songs, plus a "bonus" instrumental jam (McCartney having fun with himself) tacked on at the end but not listed on the credits—is quite good, but hardly exceptional; catchy, but not memorable. On the whole, the album has the confidence and the veracity missing from *McCartney II*, but it falls far short of *McCartney* in both chaos and creation.

Uncommonly deft as a musician, McCartney has played multiple instruments since he was a Beatle and overdubbed all the parts to "Why Don't We Do It in the Road?" In fact, he worked alone to make a few of the most durable recordings of his Wings and solo years—"Oh Woman, Oh Why" (the superior flip side to his first post-Beatles single, "Another Day"), "Arrow Through Me" (credited to Wings in 1979), and "Return to Pepperland" (recorded for an album intended to commemorate the twentieth anniversary of *Sgt. Pepper's Lonely Hearts Club Band*, in 1987, but never issued commercially), as well as two CDs of techno experiments that he released in the 1990s under the pseudonym the Fireman. Still, as *Chaos and Creation in the Backyard* reminds us, assuming responsibility for the whole has a way of diminishing McCartney's commitment to each part. In the Beatles, his playing was frequently most inventive when his role on a track was limited, as in his bass lines on George Harrison's "Something" and "Old Brown Shoe," his drumming on John Lennon's "Dear Prudence," and his electric guitar solo on Harrison's "Taxman." The musicianship on *Chaos and Creation* is merely functional—dazzling only in concept, only if you read the credits. Unless the music works as well as that of a group with more than one member (as some past McCartney efforts have), the one-man-band scheme is a banal gimmick, anyway. An application of the King Buffet aesthetic, it measures value by quantity—by all you can play, not by how good any of it is.

The ego at the heart of every do-it-all act was already rife for parody in 1921, when Buster Keaton (a cinematic multihyphenate himself) directed *The Playhouse*, a stunning silent short (intended to be accompanied by live music) that shows a stage full of performers, all portrayed by Keaton (thanks to a special effect executed by rewinding a hand-cranked camera, removing strips of tape from the lens, one by one, and exposing the film multiple times). "This Keaton fellow seems to be the whole show," jokes a character, through a title card. Six decades later, McCartney made a music video presenting himself playing all the instruments on "Coming Up," an update of *The Playhouse* done with a blue screen and no irony. A promotional documentary DVD packaged in a special edition of the *Chaos and Creation* dispenses with the effects, but fixes on McCartney's versatility, cross-cutting scenes of him at the grand piano, him strumming his guitar, him behind the drum kit—making clear the message that the fellow is the whole show.

This mandarin idealization of music-making as craft marks a fall from the elevated place to which McCartney helped to bring pop music as a Beatle. While many of the Beatles recordings were multitracked, performed by only one or two members of the band ("The Ballad of John and Yoko," for instance, has only John and Paul playing all the instruments), they were done in the larger context of an approach that challenged the rock audience to think of music as an expression of creative intelligence rather than an exercise in technique. "Yesterday" features only one Beatle, Paul, and a string quartet; "Revolution #9" is an aural montage of found-object recordings; "Being for the Benefit of Mr. Kite" has a tape of a calliope cut apart and re-arranged—yet their fans came to understand this work as Beatles music, because the band members were the source of its ideas, whether or not they had their hands on the instruments or used conventional instruments at all.

Despite its Grammy nomination for album of the year, *Chaos and Creation in the Backyard* disappoints, as much of McCartney's solo music does, because it is good and not great; that is, it fails to meet the standard McCartney established for his own work some forty years ago. Asked about "Yesterday" in an interview with Robert Shelton, Bob Dylan remarked that "if you go into the Library of Congress, you can find—there are millions of songs like that written in Tin Pan Alley." John Lennon, asked late in his life about the same song, said, "Wow, that was a good 'un!" Both of them were correct. "Yesterday" is indeed like millions of older songs in kind, but it is also superior to a great many in quality. McCartney is a genre composer, as Irving Berlin was; and at his best, as a Beatle, McCartney drew upon a handful of compositional models to create exemplary specimens in his own voice—the musical-hall tune ("When I'm Sixty Four," "Honey Pie"), the screeching rocker ("I'm Down," "Helter Skelter"), the love ballad ("Yesterday," "Michelle," "The Long and Winding Road"), the folk ditty ("Mother Nature's Son," "Two of Us"), and a few others. This is not to say that he was incapable of breaking ground as a composer; he could and did in the Beatles (his conception for *Sgt. Pepper's*, his work on the medley on *Abbey Road*) and occasionally in his solo work ("Talk More Talk" and "Pretty Little Head" from *Press to Play*, the Fireman albums). For the most part, though, Lennon's specialty was invention, and McCartney's was refinement. In the 1960s, McCartney stood as the postwar generation's defense against the then-vociferous attacks on the ostensible inadequacies of rock songwriters. Even those of us who preferred Lennon and considered his music more important could hold up Paul and say, *Look, here's one of ours, and he's as good as Irving Berlin*. It remains difficult to accept that as a delusion when, with every new album, McCartney taunts us with snippets of charming melody and, sometimes, even a clever turn of phrase.

I have met Paul McCartney a couple of times, and we once spent a good deal of an evening together—on September 10, 2001, not that the date meant a thing to us then. We talked for a while about his father, an amateur musician, and about his childhood in Liverpool. I was taken aback to find that McCartney, one of the most successful men in the world, still liked to think of himself as working class (or wanted to be thought of as such). There is no doubt an element of blue-collar pride in the populism that infuses his music. At the same time, much of what he does is, in a way, a betrayal of his class. McCartney was granted an extraordinary musical gift—as an artist, he was born into privilege, and for most of his solo career, he has simply glided along, exploiting that entitlement without exerting much effort. He's always been busy and productive, but he just doesn't work hard enough.

Joni Mitchell's *Shine*

S weet bird of time and change, you must be laughing. Quite a bit of time
has passed since Joni Mitchell last picked up the guitar or sat at the piano
and wrote a song—about ten years now—and she has changed. After her
last album of new material, *Taming the Tiger*, which was composed in 1997 and
released the next year, Mitchell participated with varying degrees of engagement
in the making of six CDs or multi-disc packages: four compilations of tracks
from her old recording catalog, organized by theme or by record label; one
album of readings of Tin Pan Alley standards (mingled with two gems of her
own that have joined the popular canon, "Both Sides Now" and "A Case of
You"); and a double-CD set of remakes of her earlier work, done pre-rock style,
with a symphony orchestra. Upon making the remakes, she announced that she
would never record again, and she said that she had forgotten why she had ever
loved music. In 2007, Mitchell returned with nine new songs (and one more
remake, this one a musical update, of "Big Yellow Taxi") on a stunning album
called *Shine*, which was marketed through Starbucks by the chain's powerhouse

label, Hear Music. But the album stuns in more ways than one, and whatever laughter it has incited in that sweet bird of Mitchell's fancy could be of joy or decrial.

The news that Joni Mitchell was playing and writing again was cause to let out a hearty crow. One of the most serious and ambitious songwriters to make pop for adults in the rock era, Mitchell has earned the ardor of a worshipful following, whose members include other serious and ambitious musicians such as Björk, Elvis Costello, Prince, and Caetano Veloso. Her fans among performers respected for their edgy intelligence could, without any outside help, fulfill all the music programming needs of NPR. How her late-life absence from performing and composing has affected her standing among the larger public is unclear, though it has no doubt diminished her name recognition at least as much as it has enhanced her mystique. In pop music, ten years is forever— longer than the entire recording career of innumerable acts, including the Beatles, and longer than the life cycles of most pop-music trends, including the folk-rock craze of the 1960s, through which Roberta Joan Anderson turned herself into Joni Mitchell.

She has never liked being thought of as a folkie—or at least not liked it since she stopped being a folkie. In the early 1970s, when I was in high school, I saw Mitchell in concert for the first time. Touring to support *Blue*, her latest album, she did a brooding show, accompanying herself on acoustic guitar, mountain dulcimer, and piano. (In a review for my school paper, I described Mitchell as an "aging princess of folk-rock music"—she was twenty-eight.) Before beginning "A Case of You" that evening, she explained how she had been inspired to play the Appalachian instrument by the dulcimer-strumming folkie poet Richard Farina. (The song itself is about Mitchell's affair with a superior folkie poet, Leonard Cohen.) Twenty years later, when I was doing some research on Farina, Mitchell and I chatted over smokes in the bar at the Blue Note, the jazz club in New York. Mitchell had come to see the drummer Brian Blade, though she could not see him at all and could not hear him very well from our spot near the exit, which was the only place in the club where she was allowed to smoke. "I was never a folksinger," she told me, emphatically. "I was always a jazz artist."

Okay. But . . . what about the music on the first four Joni Mitchell albums— all those tunes in the folk vein, like "Michael From Mountains," "Song to a Seagull," and "Chelsea Morning"? They were not folk, Mitchell insisted; they were jazz. She told me to go home and listen to the songs again, paying special attention to the harmony. In her guitar accompaniment, she said, she had been playing "jazz chords."

That is true but incomplete information. There have always been strains of several kinds of music, including jazz, in Mitchell's guitar playing and in the writing that she has done on the instrument. She is an intuitive composer, indifferent to music theory and formal conventions. As such, she has a great deal of illustrious company among composers in folk, rock, and blues, though not so much company among jazz masters (notwithstanding the boggling Erroll Garner and a few lesser geniuses of the naïve). Impatient and impulsive, Mitchell has employed a method of writing on the guitar that simplifies the work of composing while nicely complicating the results. She retunes the strings to make an open chord that has a sound she likes, in the manner of Delta blues players, and she produces variations and modulations with fairly simple fingering up and down the fretboard. This process has helped Mitchell create a songbook of instantly recognizable pieces united by their odd character of found harmony. In the songs that she has written at the piano, an instrument for which retuning the strings is prohibitively time-consuming, Mitchell's harmonic conception is more conventional, though still intuitive and occasionally suggestive of postwar Third Stream jazz for its moments of liquid, puddling chromaticism.

Liberated by her intuition but also limited by it, Mitchell could make jazz chords—the opening of "Jericho," for instance, shifts hiply from an F major ninth to a B minor seventh over E; but she struggled to compose fully wrought jazz compositions, and then, in the late 1970s, she dove headlong into jazz fusion with the albums *Don Juan's Reckless Daughter* and *Mingus*. (On the latter, Mitchell contributed two pieces of her own, in addition to her collaborations with Charles Mingus, who died before the recording was complete.) A defining trait of Mitchell's life and work is her insistence on not fitting in—not with other pop stars, nor with most others of her generation. In a culture in which every performer in music or politics poses as an outsider to get inside the centers of power and glory, Mitchell has always sought a place not just outside, on the same plane, but significantly above her competition and their audience. If the folkies were strumming G chords and hooting union bromides, Mitchell wanted to make artful stacked chords and murmur cryptic ruminations. If everyone was rocking out, Mitchell wanted to do jazz fusion. Anyone can do the alienated-artist act; only someone profoundly ambivalent about power and glory can so blithely ignore the risk of alienating the public.

When she found that she had hit a wall trying to do jazz, Mitchell changed direction and turned to synthesizers and electronics in another attempt—one born of Mitchell's tenacity, for certain, but also, it seemed, of some desperation—to stay ahead of her fellow baby-boomer pop artists and their public. Between 1982 and 1998, she made six albums of songs buried under manic, garish electronic noise. These recordings had fine moments, such as the exquisite "Love," based on Corinthians 1:13 ("Although I speak in tongues of men and angels I'm just sounding brass and tinkling cymbals without love," set to a gorgeous, purling melody), on *Wild Things Run Fast* (1982); "Two Grey Rooms," about her divided mind; and "Cherokee Louise," a dark memory play about a tortured childhood friend—the last two of which appeared on the exceptional *Night Ride Home* (1991). The latter album and its follow-up, *Turbulent Indigo* (1994), revealed Mitchell's delicate compositions through less cluttered electronics, and Mitchell recoiled, hiding in a fancy cage of studio gimmickry on the bloodless *Taming the Tiger*. A pattern had emerged: the weaker the songs, the weirder the synthesizer settings. "I have this need for originality," she explained to an interviewer. When she could not provide it, she synthesized it, conflating creativity with novelty.

Around the turn of the century, Mitchell signed with a new label, the temperately arty Nonesuch, and she decided to pause for a moment and reconsider what she had done, at her best, in the past. (The head of Nonesuch, Robert Hurwitz, is understood to have exerted considerable influence here.) With Nonesuch funding the mammoth undertaking, Mitchell re-recorded twenty-two of her most durable songs, from "The Dawntreader" (1968) through "Just Like This Train" (1974) and "Amelia" (1976) to "Borderline" (1994), with a seventy-piece orchestra and the jazz musicians including Herbie Hancock. The very idea of doing remakes was antithetical to Mitchell, as she once made clear to a concert audience after someone in the stands dared to call out a request for an old song. Drawing a contrast between the visual arts and the performing arts, Mitchell, who also paints, said, in a somewhat petulant lecture in 1974, preserved on her live album *Miles of Aisles:* "A painter does a painting, and he does a painting—that's it, you know. He's had the joy of creating it, and he hangs it on some wall. Somebody buys it, somebody buys it again, or maybe nobody buys it, and it sits up in a loft somewhere till he dies. But . . . nobody ever says to him—nobody ever said to Van Gogh, 'Paint a Starry Night again, man!' You know, he painted it. That was it."

The album of remakes, *Travelogue*, turned out beautifully, in part because the orchestral settings reinforced the depth and the timelessness of Mitchell's finest music, and also because she sang the songs with affection and care, in a fragile, grandmotherly voice that betrayed the effects of age and chain-smoking. (Mitchell claims that the transformation of her voice from airy and bright to husky and low is the result of laryngeal disease, unrelated to her smoking.) For the first time in her life, Mitchell approached her work in the spirit of classicism, dispensing with the futurism. The act seemed a bittersweet valedictory, and after it she packed up her instruments.

What could we expect from her in 2007, after a layoff of ten years? A return to her prime—another masterpiece like *Blue* or *The Hissing of Summer Lawns*? Of course not. Those albums were made many years ago by someone other than the woman Mitchell was at sixty-three. No, the fair thing to hope for—and the greater achievement—would be an album that speaks with those early records' veracity of what it is like for that new person to be living the life of a sixty-three-year-old. After all, one of Mitchell's most important contributions to American popular music was her key role in making pop an outlet for deeply personal expression. She once recalled as an epiphany the first time she heard "Positively 4th Street," a venomous rant at an unnamed party who had betrayed Dylan somehow. "Oh my God," Mitchell said to herself, as she later recalled, "you can write about anything in songs!" Mitchell's own innovation was not to write about just *anything*—Paul McCartney had a corner on that—but to delve into her inner life and render those which are not things: inchoate hopes, sexual imaginings, nightmares, the impulses to love and to mother and to hurt.

With songs such as "Blue," "Woman of Heart and Mind," "Troubled Child," "Sweet Bird," "Hejira," and dozens more, Mitchell brought an almost psychotherapeutic candor and intimacy to the record bins. She internalized popular music and made it something personal, idiosyncratic—modernist. In Mitchell's songs, as in work of the high modernists as well as the modernists in lower quarters such as Furry Lewis and Charles Mingus, individual expression and its necessary structure had primacy, and accessibility was secondary at best. It is a testament to the beauty of Mitchell's voice, as well as to the charm of her tunes (when she chose to write charming tunes), that she kept getting record contracts for so many years. Unfortunately, self-examination and self-command could slip sometimes into self-absorption and self-indulgence, and her songs could be overlong, meandering, droning, and repetitious.

If only those were the sins of Mitchell's new CD. *Shine* is a lovely album, full of listenable music. Mitchell wrote most of the songs on the piano, as instrumentals, and later added lyrics. The music is warm and elegiac, for the most part—vaguely evocative of the Rachmaninoff that Roberta Joan Anderson loved as a girl. There are synthesizers—all played by Mitchell, who generated most of the music on the album (including some of the bass parts) on various keyboards; but they are programmed to sound like traditional instruments, and Mitchell employs them with taste.

The stunning puzzlement of the album is the near absence of its author in the words. Of the ten songs on *Shine*, one, "If," is adapted from the Rudyard Kipling verse, and another, as I mentioned, is a remake of "Big Yellow Taxi," one of Mitchell's most tuneful and least personal songs. The eight new pieces with words and music by Mitchell are nearly all outward-looking considerations of political and social issues such as over-development and the exploitation of natural resources ("This Place"), over-population ("If I Had a Heart"), pollution ("Bad Dreams"), militarization and war ("Strong and Wrong"), and all of the above ("Shine"). In its lyrics, which frequently fight the gentle music, *Shine* is, on the whole, polemical, utterly predictable in its hippie utopianism, shrill, and cold.

In a late-life fit of nostalgia, Mitchell has gone all the way back to the liberal pamphleteering that she never liked in the 1960s and that Dylan, with "Positively 4th Street," led her to reject. She wags her finger and pokes it in the chests of the big bad boys, but she never touches herself to risk breaking her own skin. Indeed, she professes on the album to have no heart anymore. I find this impossible to accept. If Mitchell has indeed lost the ability—or the will—to reveal herself, that is a major loss to her art, to its audience, and, I suspect, to its creator. *Shine* is a kind of revelation, but of the saddest kind, and it proves, definitively, that you don't know what you've got till it's gone.

Wynton Marsalis

M anhattan is empty during the last week of August, and the kind of emptiness it achieves is like that of the mind during meditation—a temporary, unnatural purity. On a Tuesday evening in late August of 2001, I was wandering around Greenwich Village and ended up at the Village Vanguard. After sixty-some years of business the illustrious little jazz haunt hasn't changed; it remains one of the inexplicable constants of the Manhattan landscape. Its midtown cousin, Birdland (named for the bebop saxophonist Charlie "Yardbird" Parker), closed down decades ago and was replaced by a strip joint, Flash Dancers, which has been in business longer than Birdland was; a theme nightclub near Times Square now uses the Birdland name. There's still a Cotton Club in Harlem, but not in the original location, and now it's a seedy disco. The Vanguard has somehow survived in its primordial basement and has retained all the bohemian eccentricities that have always helped make it cool: the fence-post marquee, with performers' names handwritten vertically; the treacherously angled stairwell; no food served; no credit cards accepted. Lorraine Gordon, the Vanguard's owner and the widow of the club's founder, is a Medici of the jazz world, a patron and king-maker. Among jazz fans and musicians the Village Vanguard is clearly a paragon of the music's own kind of purity—one that's neither temporary nor unnatural.

I walked in on a set in progress and took the next-to-last seat on the burgundy-leather banquette that runs along the east wall. The end table, Lorraine Gordon's, was vacant, indicating that Gordon was probably in the kitchen, where she does the books and where musicians congregate between sets. (Although foodless, the Vanguard has one of the most venerable kitchens in New York.) A small combo was running through the bebop classic "Blue 'n' Boogie" at a duly vertiginous speed. There was no mistaking the bandleader: Charles McPherson, an alto saxophonist who was a protégé of the late bassist and composer Charles Mingus. McPherson is a venturesome musician who upends the jazz repertoire on the bandstand, and he composes pieces built on surprise, as Mingus did. Although he is a superior talent, he's not a top jazz attraction, which is why he was scheduled for the last week in August. For his second tune after my arrival McPherson, in homage to his mentor, played Mingus's homage to Lester Young, "Goodbye Pork Pie Hat." The performance was languid, and my eyes drifted, settling eventually on the trumpet player, because he was turned away from the audience and even from the rest of the band, staring at the floor. Although I couldn't place him, he looked vaguely familiar, like an older version of Wynton Marsalis.

During the third song, Charlie Parker's "Chasin' the Bird," the trumpeter stepped to the center of the bandstand to take a solo. "Excuse me," I whispered to the fellow next to me (a jazz guitarist, I later learned). "Is that Wynton Marsalis?"

"I very seriously doubt that" he snapped back, as if I had asked if it was Parker himself.

Stylishly dressed in an Italian-cut gray suit, a dark-blue shirt, and a muted blue tie, the soloist had the burnished elegance that Wynton Marsalis and his musician brothers have been bringing to jazz for two decades. If this man was not Wynton, he looked like what "Marsalis" means—but older and heavier, and not just in appearance. There was a weight upon him; he didn't smile, and his eyes were small and affectless. I could barely reconcile the sight before me with the image of youthful elan that Wynton Marsalis has always called to mind.

The fourth song was a solo showcase for the trumpeter, who, I could now see, was indeed Marsalis, but who no more sounded than looked like what I expected. He played a ballad, "I Don't Stand a Ghost of a Chance With You," unaccompanied. Written by Victor Young, a film-score composer, for a 1930s romance, the piece can bring out the sadness in any scene, and Marsalis appeared deeply attuned to its melancholy. He performed the song in murmurs and sighs, at points nearly talking the words in notes. It was a wrenching act of creative expression. When he reached the climax, Marsalis played the final phrase, the title statement, in declarative tones, allowing each successive note to linger in the air a bit longer. "I don't stand . . . a ghost . . . of . . . a . . . chance . . ." The room was silent until, at the most dramatic point, someone's cell phone went off, blaring a rapid sing-song melody in electronic bleeps. People started giggling and picking up their drinks. The moment—the whole performance— unraveled.

Marsalis paused for a beat, motionless, and his eyebrows arched. I scrawled on a sheet of notepaper, MAGIC, RUINED. The cell-phone offender scooted into the hall as the chatter in the room grew louder. Still frozen at the microphone, Marsalis replayed the silly cell-phone melody note for note. Then he repeated it, and began improvising variations on the tune. The audience slowly came back to him. In a few minutes he resolved the improvisation, which had changed keys once or twice and throttled down to a ballad tempo, and ended up exactly where he had left off: "with . . . you . . ." The ovation was tremendous.

Lorraine Gordon had come in shortly before the final notes. Leaning over to me, she said, "What did I miss?"

That was a good question, and I had others. What was Wynton Marsalis, perhaps the most famous jazz musician alive, doing as a sideman in a band led by a lesser-known saxophonist in the slowest week of the year? Where were the scores of fans who used to line up on the sidewalk whenever Marsalis played, regardless of whether he was billed and promoted? Why did he look so downtrodden, so leaden . . . so different that he was scarcely recognizable? How could his playing have been so perfunctory (as it was for most of that evening) and yet so transcendent on one bittersweet song about loss and self-doubt? *What happened to Wynton Marsalis?*

That may be like asking *What happened to jazz?* For twenty years the fates of Marsalis and jazz music have appeared inextricably intertwined. He was a young newcomer on the New York scene at a time when jazz seemed dominated and diminished by rock-oriented "fusion," marginalized by outre experimentation and electronics, and disconnected from the youth audience that has driven American popular culture since the postwar era. Extraordinarily gifted and fluent in both jazz and classical music, not to mention young, handsome, black, impassioned, and articulate, especially on the importance of jazz history and jazz masters, Marsalis was ideally equipped to lead a cultural-aesthetic movement suited to the time, a renaissance that raised public esteem for and the popular appeal of jazz through a return to the music's traditional values: jazz for the Reagan revolution. In 1990 *Time* magazine put him on the cover and announced the dawn of "The New Jazz Age." Record companies rediscovered the music and revived long-dormant jazz lines, signing countless young musicians inspired by Marsalis, along with three of his five brothers (first his older brother, Branford, a celebrated tenor saxophonist; later Delfeayo, a trombonist; and eventually the youngest, Jason, a percussionist) and his father, Ellis (a respected educator and pianist in the family's native New Orleans). By the 1990s, Wynton Marsalis had become an omnipresent spokesperson for his music and also one of its most prolific and highly decorated practitioners (he was the first jazz composer to win a Pulitzer Prize, for *Blood on the Field*, his oratorio about slavery)—something of a counterpart to Leonard Bernstein in the 1950s. He took jazz up and over the hierarchical divide that had long isolated the music from the fine-arts establishment; the modest summer jazz program he created won a full constituency at Lincoln Center. In 1999, to mark the end of the century, Marsalis issued a total of fifteen CDs—about one new tide every month.

In the following two years he did not release a single CD of new music. In fact, after two decades with Columbia Records, the prestigious and high-powered label historically associated with Duke Ellington, Thelonious Monk, and Miles Davis, Marsalis had no record contract with any company. Nor did his brother Branford, who just a few years earlier was not only one of Columbia's recording stars but an executive consultant overseeing the artists-and-repertory direction of the label's jazz division. (Branford formed an independent record company.) Over several years, Columbia drastically reduced its roster of active jazz musicians, shifting its emphasis to reissues of old recordings. Atlantic folded its jazz catalogue into the operations of its parent company, Warner, and essentially gave up on developing new artists. At the end of the twentieth century, Verve was a fraction of the size it had been a decade earlier. In addition, jazz clubs around the country had been struggling, and the attacks of September 11 hurt night life everywhere; New York's venerable Sweet Basil closed in the spring of 2001, after twenty-five years in operation, and later reopened as a youth-oriented world-music place. In the institutional arena, Carnegie Hall discontinued its in-house jazz orchestra at the end of the 2001–2002 season.

For this grim state of affairs in jazz Marsalis, the public face of the music and the evident master of its destiny, has been declared at least partly culpable. By leading jazz into the realm of unbending classicism, by applying the Great Man template to establish an iconography (Armstrong, Ellington, Parker, Coltrane), and by sanctifying a canon of their own choosing (Armstrong's "Hot Fives," Ellington's Blanton-Webster period, Parker's Savoy sessions, Coltrane's *A Love Supreme*), Marsalis and his adherents are said to have codified the music in a stifling orthodoxy and inhibited the revolutionary impulses that have always advanced jazz.

"They've done a lot to take the essence of jazz and distort it," the composer and pianist George Russell told the *New York Times* in 1998. "They've put a damper on the main ingredient of jazz, which is innovation."

A former executive with Columbia Records who has worked intimately with five Marsalises says, "For many people, Wynton has come to embody some retro ideology that is not really of the moment, you know—it's more museum-like in nature, a look back. I think as each day passes, Wynton does lose relevance as a shaper of musical direction. He's not quite the leader of a musical movement any longer. That doesn't mean he's not remarkable, or without considerable clout, or that he's not the leader of a cultural movement. But within the record industry the Marsalises are no longer seen as the top guys."

Six weeks after he played in Charles McPherson's band at the Village Vanguard, Wynton Marsalis turned forty. (His publicists will have to come up with a nickname to replace "the young lion.") Marsalis had been struggling, clearly. In addition to the rest of his troubles, he and his fiancée broke off the engagement that might have brought stability to his notoriously mercurial romantic life (he has three sons by two single women, one on each coast), and Jazz at Lincoln Center suffered a setback shortly after Marsalis's birthday, when the chairman of its board of directors was murdered in his home. In February of 2003, Marsalis returned briefly to the spotlight, when he, his three musical brothers, and their father joined forces on their first CD together, *The Marsalis Family: A Jazz Celebration*—released on Branford's new label, Marsalis Music, and supported by a high-profile PBS special and a brief national tour starting a few days later. But this effort to celebrate the Marsalis legacy was seen by some in the jazz world as just another exercise in nostalgia. It's a criticism that familiarly echoes the one that has bedeviled jazz as a whole for some years. Yet if the lives of this man and America's great indigenous music are indeed entwined, their predicament calls for fuller scrutiny and better understanding. It's too easy to dismiss Marsalis's condition as a midlife crisis.

Every icon needs an origin myth. Born in the same city as jazz, Wynton Marsalis was blessed with a signifying provenance. "I'm from New Orleans," he has told an interviewer, as shorthand for his musical background. "We don't need a concert hall for jazz." In many ways Marsalis's story is so neatly connected to jazz history that it defies credulity. Had a screenwriter created Wynton Marsalis, a cynical producer would have sent back the opening scenes for rewrite: too perfect. Not only did he come from the cradle of jazz but he plays the trumpet, the instrument that originally defined the music. "The first jazz musician was a trumpeter, Buddy Bolden," Marsalis once said, "and the last will be a trumpeter, the archangel Gabriel." Moreover, Marsalis rose to prominence in the mid-1980s, just as jazz was approaching its centennial. "There's a tremendous symbolic resonance that has always been a part of what Wynton's about," says Jeff Levenson, a veteran jazz writer who also worked as an executive at both Columbia and Warner Bros. Records. "This kid emerges who's a hotshot . . . and the whole thing has a kind of symmetry to it Louis Armstrong starts things off—trumpet player, New Orleans, turn of the century. Wynton closes it out—a trumpet player from New Orleans."

Dolores and Ellis Marsalis still live in the house Wynton left when he moved to New York on a scholarship to Juilliard, in 1979. It is a nice, modest place of green-painted clapboard, in a neighborhood that used to be nicer. To enter the house one goes through an iron gate and past a patch of lawn with manicured shrubbery and a statue of a black madonna in the center. The interior looks large without six boys frolicking in it at once. (Only Mboya, who is autistic, lives at home now.) Dolores Marsalis keeps the house, her husband tells me with a pride they obviously share: everything is just so, and communicates to the visitor in a gracious way. The chairs have pressed crocheted doilies pinned to their backs: they are not for horseplay. The walls are covered with paintings and graphics portraying African-American themes: they are not decorations but art. The table next to the front door holds a display of photographs of women in the family: everybody counts.

Ellis Marsalis is a sturdy man, sixty-eight, who moves with a deliberate bounce. A lifelong educator who has taught music on every level from elementary school to college, he held a chair in jazz studies endowed by Coca-Cola at the University of New Orleans until his retirement, in 2001. When he speaks, his words have the measured authority of a lesson. Wynton Marsalis is very much like his father in the way he holds himself (hunched a bit, as if he were reading from a music stand), sits (legs spread), gestures (forward and in tempo), and speaks (with a disarming touch of New Orleans patois).

To Ellis Marsalis, the work ethic his own father taught by example is primary to success, be it in commerce or in art. "When I was teaching [high school]," he says, "I used to see a lot of talent that didn't particularly go anywhere, and at first it was really mysterious to me. I couldn't really understand it—I mean, to see a seventeen-year-old kid who's a natural bass. Those are born. You don't learn to do that. And to hear coloratura sopranos who couldn't care less. I was forced to reappraise what my understanding of talent is. Then I eventually began to discover that talent is like the battery in a car. It'll get you started, but if the generator is bad, you don't go very far."

A musician by aspiration who took up teaching by necessity, Ellis Marsalis was ambivalent about his own decision to stay in New Orleans and raise his children, rather than to pursue a big-time career in New York. "At the time Wynton was growing up, I still had a lot of anxiety about going to New York," he recalls.

I asked him if he thought Wynton had recognized his frustrations and had set out to aim higher by making New York his home base. Was he trying to fulfill his father's dream? "Could be," Ellis said, nodding slowly. "It could be."

In *The History of Jazz*, Ted Gioia wrote, "[Wynton] Marsalis's rise to fame while barely out of his teens was an unprecedented event in the jazz world. No major jazz figure—not Ellington or Armstrong, Goodman or Gillespie—had become so famous, so fast." The facts are impressive: while still at Juilliard, Marsalis was invited to join another kind of conservatory, the Jazz Messengers, a band led by the drummer Art Blakey; soon after, he was appointed the group's musical director, at age nineteen. As Ellis Marsalis says, "He called up and said, 'Man, I have a chance to join Art Blakey's band. What do you think?' I said, 'Well, one thing about Juilliard, man,' I said, 'Juilliard's going to be there when they're shoveling dirt in your face. Art Blakey won't.'" By 1982, when he turned twenty-one, Wynton had toured with the jazz star Herbie Hancock and had played with distinction on half a dozen albums, leading "the jazz press to declare him a prodigy," Jon Pareles wrote in the *New York Times* in the mid-1980s. Columbia Records signed him in an extraordinary contract that called for Marsalis to make both classical and jazz recordings, and he started a collection of Grammys in both categories. No jazz musician has had such success since.

* * *

To a degree Marsalis's aesthetic, which draws reverentially on the African-American traditions of the blues and swing, seems to repudiate the style of the previous era. Swing was a rejection of traditional New Orleans jazz, bebop a rejection of swing, cool jazz a rejection of bop, free jazz a rejection of the cool, and fusion a rejection of free jazz. (Though reductive and Oedipal, this theory bears up well enough if one ignores the innumerable overlaps, inconsistencies, and contradictions, and also the entire career of Duke Ellington.) Wynton and his young peers were rejecting fusion, an amorphous mixture of jazz and pop-rock, which they saw as fatuous and vulgar, and which they thought pandered to commercialism.

As the composer and trumpeter Terence Blanchard, a childhood friend of Wynton's who followed him to New York and into Blakey's band, recalls, "In the early eighties we had to fight for our existence in the music war. The fusion thing was real big, and we were trying to get back to, like, just the fundamental elements in jazz"

But for all fusion's attributes as a target (it was slick, ostentatious, cold, and elementally white, much like the big-band "innovations in modern music" of Stan Kenton and the "third-stream" pretenses of the 1950s), the style scarcely dominated the New York jazz scene when the Marsalis brothers and Blanchard started out. In fact, when Wynton Marsalis played at the club Seventh Avenue South in the last week of January 1982, to promote his eponymous first solo album, nearly every jazz room in town featured bebop (or older styles of the music): Kai Winding was at the Vanguard, Anita O'Day at the Blue Note, Dizzy Gillespie at Fat Tuesday's, Archie Shepp at Sweet Basil, George Shearing at Michael's Pub.

"There was a whole lot of jazz in New York then, and it was straight-ahead [bebop], by and large," recalls the pianist and educator Barry Harris. "You had all the work you could do [as a bebop musician], and nobody was doing fusion but the kids. Now, they made the festivals and whatnot for the younger crowd. That was where that was at. It was no big thing. That was a good time for straight-ahead [music] in New York."

Although marginal to the core jazz constituency, centered in New York (as it had been for decades and continues to be), fusion had a voguish appeal to college audiences and other young people. The Marsalis revolution was especially radical, then, in rejecting a style popular among musicians of the revolutionary's own age, rather than the music established by his elders; it was subversive methodologically as well as aesthetically, and the ensuing polarization in jazz circles on the subject of Marsalis and his music was uniquely intra-generational.

The musical landscape Marsalis entered in full stride and soon dominated was far more complex than most accounts have suggested—as is the actual music he has made. Marsalis was never a nostalgist like the tuba player Vince Giordano, who re-creates jazz styles of the early twentieth century. The improvisations on the first few Wynton Marsalis albums employed elements of the blues and swing (along with other styles, including free jazz), but in the service of personal expression; and Marsalis's earliest compositions, with their harmonic surprises and their lightning shifts in time signature, were less homage than montage. In the image his detractors like to paint (over and over), Marsalis single-handedly halted jazz's progress. "Wynton has the car in reverse," the trombonist and composer Bob Brookmeyer has said, "and the pedal to the metal"; if so, the vehicle was already in gear. Over the course of the 1970s, a movement to elevate esteem for jazz and protect the music's heritage was emerging in one sphere at the same time that fusion and the music of the living bebop masters coexisted in their own spheres. The Smithsonian Institution began an effort to preserve the musical archives of Duke Ellington and other jazz masters; the bandleader and trumpeter Herb Pomeroy was leading a repertory jazz program at the Berklee College of Music, in Boston; the saxophonist Loren Schoenberg was working with Benny Goodman to revive his big band; the bassist Chuck Israels formed the National Jazz Ensemble; the musicologist and conductor

Gunther Schuller was conducting vintage jazz works and writing about them as if there were a canon; the impresario George Wein founded the New York Jazz Repertory Company. "I just felt like it was time," recalls Wein, who later produced the neo-traditional concerts of the Carnegie Hall Jazz Band. "There was a lot of that percolating at the time, and that's the atmosphere that Wynton and the others came into."

The revival movement itself was a revival. Back in the late 1930s, when the "From Spirituals to Swing" concerts at Carnegie Hall gave American jazz the imprimatur of the cultural establishment, the music had changed course and languished in a contemplative state. Writers and musicians of the period rediscovered the artists and styles of the music's (relatively recent) past—a respite, time has shown us, during which jazz began metamorphosing into bebop.

The debate over classicism that has swirled around Marsalis is nothing new, either. The enduring issue is, of course, not which work is entitled to a place in the canon—Manet's Dejeuner sur l'herbe? Jelly Roll Morton's "Black Bottom Stomp"?—but who is empowered to confer that distinction. Marsalis has compounded things substantially, not only by making music that he expects will be taken seriously but also by defining the terms, and by challenging white critics and white-dominated institutions to yield authority over such matters.

The scholar and author Gerald Early, a professor at Washington University in St. Louis, says, "Wynton Marsalis is a target for criticism because, unlike a lot of artists, he's become a quite outspoken critic himself, and he has articulated a historical theory and an aesthetic theory about jazz music. I think that critics feel kind of threatened and rather uncomfortable when an artist comes along who's capable of doing that pretty well—well enough so that a critic has to respect it. Indeed, most of the early press about Marsalis was laudatory, until he dared to use his platform to advance ideas about jazz history and black identity. Ever since, jazz critics, most of whom are white, have tended to treat Marsalis more severely.

"The fact that these critics are white, that a lot of the audience for jazz music is white," Early says, "I think is a source of tension for many of the artists who are black. White critics basically codified and structured the history of this music and made the judgments about who is significant in the music and so forth, and I think in this culture that can't help but be a real source of tension for many black jazz musicians."

Stanley Crouch, a critic and a long-standing influence on Marsalis, is quick to expand on the theme. "I think a lot of the criticism of Wynton's music is based upon a hostility toward him. Marsalis, any way the critics look at him, is superior to them. He's a greater musician than any of them are writers. He's a good-looking guy. He has access to and has had access to a far higher quality of female than any of them could ever imagine. He doesn't look up to them, and that's a problem."

Wynton Marsalis lives in an airy eight-room apartment on the twenty-ninth floor of a high-rise tower a few dozen footsteps from the stage entrance to Alice Tully Hall, where Lincoln Center's jazz orchestra has been playing since it started, in 1987. His home is as conscientiously detailed as the house of his parents. On a visit in 2002, I asked him if his mother had helped him decorate it, and he laughed. "Maybe she should have," he said. "She knows what she's doing." But he has his own taste. The living room, which is so spacious that at first I didn't notice the grand piano in the corner, is done in vivid colors; Marsalis says that he likes Matisse for the "positivity and affirmation" of his work, and that he picked up the artist's vibrant palette in his appointments. Patterns on the carpeting and the fabrics suggest crescents, the symbol of his home town. Sunlight floods the room from banks of windows at the room's outer corners. "I like the sun," Marsalis told me as we sat on sofas opposite each other. "The source of life. There's a lot of sun in New Orleans." An enormous lithograph of Duke Ellington hangs over one of the sofas, and other prints and photographs of Ellington, along with those of Armstrong and Blakey, line the hall leading to the other rooms.

Gerald Early has commented on Marsalis's sense of style: "Whether he is at the cutting edge of what's going on in jazz now is neither here nor there. He represents a certain kind of image, which I think is enormously important, of the jazz musician as this kind of well dressed, extremely sophisticated person, and a person who lives well—a person who reads books, a person who, you know, enjoys a kind of *GQ* sort of life."

Until recently Wynton Marsalis seemed physically unaccountable to time. His good looks were the boyish kind. Full-checked and bright-eyed, he was adorable. At the same time, he always carried himself with a poised surety, a masculine grace, that tended to make women straighten up and men start poking their toes at things. The nickname "young lion" seemed appropriate, Marsalis being a creature of fearsome beauty who is also nocturnal, combative, and nomadic. As he approached forty, his body began its midlife thickening. He projects a quieter, softer, slower presence now, although he still plays a tough game of basketball.

For most of the past twenty-five years he has been on view in his natural state: working. Marsalis is living by the work ethic that his father passed on from his grandfather, with a determination that would seem pathological if it weren't utterly normal for him. He is not manic; he works at a moderate pace but never stops. Indeed, although Marsalis has not been recording much lately, he is constantly working with the Lincoln Center Jazz Orchestra. From his office in the headquarters of Jazz at Lincoln Center he oversees its creative and educational activities. He practices the trumpet for several hours every day. He plays with his sons when they are with him. And in the evening he goes out—leaving just a few hours a night for sleep. When we spoke at his home, I asked him what the man in the lithograph over his head, Duke Ellington, meant to him.

"Indefatigable worker. He loved music and people and playing. He played a lot, and he loved jazz, and he loved the Afro-American people."

"Do you have a performance philosophy?"

"I've always tried to be respectful of my audience. I always sign people's autographs, always acted like I was working for them. I try to play people's requests, try to come up with a way of playing that I thought people would want to listen to—never thought I was above them. I'm here to do a job. I always try to be professional, and many times, in halls across the country, I'm the last one to leave—all the crews are gone.

"For me to tell people who are spending their money and have worked their jobs and are going on a date with their husbands or their wives, tell them, 'I know you all are here, and you should be honored that I'm here'—that's just not my philosophy."

He keeps a dressing room full of elegant clothing—closets of dark suits and formal wear, and a rack of hats. The bedroom has a long cabinet with framed family photos and other memorabilia on display; when Marsalis sits up in his bed, they are what he sees.

He flopped onto his mattress and focused on the task of cleaning and lubricating his trumpet. "I should properly do this all the time," he said, shaking his head at himself. "I keep playing till it's so filthy all you hear when I play it is the dirt." Marsalis pulled his instrument apart and began a consuming procedure that involved massaging a viscous fluid onto each of the parts. As he worked, he talked about music, which is what he seems most at home doing wherever he is.

"My daddy said to me, when I was leaving high school, you know, debating whether I would go to New York, should I go into music, and the whole thing was, 'Well, you don't want to go into music, because you'll end up being like your daddy.' He struggled his whole life. He said, 'Man, I can tell you one thing. Do it if you want to do it and if you love doin' it. But if you don't want to do it for that reason, don't do it. Because when it really, really gets hard, you have to tell yourself, This is what I want to do.' My father told me, 'Don't sit around waiting for publicity, money, people saying you're great. Son, that might never happen. If you want to do it and you love doin' it, do it. But if you don't . . .'" Marsalis shook his head.

For all his success and acclaim, Marsalis is vexed by his critics in the jazz establishment. "My relationship with the jazz critics has never been good," he said, pausing for some time, at least half a minute. "It's never been a great relationship. I've never been portrayed accurately—not at all. The whole thing was always, like, trying to water down your level of seriousness, always trying to make you seem like an angry young man and all this. Man, you know—that was just bullshit.

"When I hear that term, 'classicism,' it's hard for me to figure out what people are talking about. There are so many musicians playing today—like, the way Joe Lovano plays, the way Marcus Roberts plays, the way that Joshua Redman plays, the way that Danilo Perez plays, the way Cyrus Chestnut plays. There are a lot of musicians playing a lot of different styles. In any period of any music a vast majority of the practitioners sought some common language, and then there are people who do variations on that language. I think we need to delve deeper into the tradition, not run away from it. See, musicians are always encouraged to run away from it. You know, if you're a musician, you want to run from it, for a basic reason—because you don't compare well against it."

In 1992, *The New Yorker* ran a cartoon depicting a middle-aged white man lying in bed. Two young children are bursting into the room. "Dad! Dad! Wake up!" one of the kids yells. "They just discovered another Marsalis!" As each of his musician brothers—and their father—followed Wynton onto the national jazz scene, the Marsalis era took a shape that began to seem dynastic. The family looked like musical Kennedys, from the strong-willed patriarch to the pair of handsome, charismatic sons who led their generation to the younger siblings struggling to fulfill impossible expectations. Eventually all five musicians ended up working at Columbia Records—back under the same roof but in a variety of roles.

Easily reduced to clichés of sibling contrast, Wynton and Branford have personified the duality Wynton sees in the world of the arts: purity versus corruption. In its cover story on Wynton and the young lions, *Time* emphasized the brothers' polar attributes.

> Wynton, extraordinarily disciplined and driven by an insatiable desire to excel, was a straight-A student who starred in Little League baseball, practiced his trumpet three hours a day and won every music competition he ever entered. Branford . . . was an average student, a self-described "spaz" in sports and a naturally talented musician who hated to practice.

Branford has played with rock and pop musicians such as Sting and the Grateful Dead; Wynton has derided pop-jazz players as "cult figures, talking-all-the-time heroes, who have these spur-of-the-moment, out-of-their-mind, left-bank, off-the-wall theories about music which make no sense at all to anybody who knows anything about music." Branford has performed and recorded funk music under the pseudonym Buckshot LeFonque (derived from a pseudonym that the saxophonist Cannonball Adderley used in the 1950s). Wynton told a Kennedy Center audience in 1998, "There's nothing sadder than a jazz musician playing funk."

They maintain a respectful distance, playing together on occasion and rarely explicitly criticizing each other in public. "I love my brother, man," Wynton told me emphatically. "That doesn't mean we talk every day. We might not get a chance to talk to each other at all for a long time, and we might not agree on everything when we do talk—or when we don't. But I love my brother Branford, man. I love all my brothers."

Branford toed the same line when I interviewed him in 2002, and yet he promptly drew a distinction between his work and Wynton's. "I love my brother," he said, "but we're totally different. I don't agree with some of the statements that he makes when he says jazz lost the world when it stopped being dance music. One of the things that attracted me to jazz was the fact that it wasn't dance music. I wouldn't want to play jazz and have people dance to it. That's not my thing."

Although at first praising Wynton's efforts to carry on the legacy of jazz, Branford couldn't seem to resist taking a thinly veiled shot. "I think it's something that should have been done a long time ago and has to be done," he said. "I use classical music as a role model. There are classical musicians who preserve music. There are people who play madrigals. There are people who only play in their Baroque chamber orchestras."

Some of those who know the two brothers well see sibling dynamics as an explanation for every step in their careers. "They have tremendous love and tremendous respect for each other, and they will fight to defend one another when speaking to outsiders," Jeff Levenson, the former Columbia executive, says. "But I really do believe that for Wynton and Branford, each of their achievements has been a competitive strike against the other. They've channeled all that rivalry stuff into their own motivational energy."

Branford's career has largely followed pop-culture convention—he's been a musical anti-hero. He exudes a lusty nonchalance, an Elvis quality, that also infuses his saxophone playing. His music is muscular and aggressive. Thoroughly aware of his bad-boy reputation and its market value, he has sustained it into his forties through practice. "They [writers] think I'm an arrogant cuss, which I am," he told me. When Wynton speaks of being mistaken for "an angry young man," the man might be his older brother. Branford's success, coursing through the turbulence of pop-music stardom, network television, and best-selling genres including funk, seems, if not inevitable, at least easy to understand.

Wynton, for his part, rose on a bubble made from an unprecedented mixture of seemingly incompatible ingredients: youth culture, history, the African American experience, mass marketing, and the ideals of fine art. He was a young man who honored his elders, promoted higher standards in a cynical business, and played a black music thought to be in decline to become a national sensation. How long could he float like that?

*   *   *

When jazz musicians teach improvisation, they often start with a basic assignment: Go home and listen to a recording you like. Take one musical phrase that appeals to you, and use it to construct a composition of your own.

The record industry spent the 1990s on a similar project: the big labels heard what Wynton Marsalis was saying, took from it what appealed to them, and used it to build a new business of their own. In seeking to elevate the public perception of jazz and to encourage young practitioners to pay attention to the music's traditions, Marsalis put great emphasis on its past masters—particularly in his role as director of Jazz at Lincoln Center. Still, he never advocated mere revivalism, and he has demonstrated in his compositions how traditional elements can be referenced, recombined, and reinvented in the name of individualistic expression. "It's a mistake when people say about Wynton that what he's doing is recapitulating the past," Gerald Early says. "I really think that what he's doing is taking the nature of that tradition and really trying, in fact, to add to it and kind of push it forward." But record executives came away with a different message: that if the artists of the past are so great and enduring, there's no reason to continue investing so much in young talent. So they shifted their attention to repackaging their catalogues of vintage recordings.

Where the young lions saw role models and their critics saw idolatry, the record companies saw brand names—the ultimate prize of American marketing. For long-established record companies with vast archives of historic recordings, the economics were irresistible: It is far more profitable to wrap new covers around albums paid for generations ago than it is to find, record, and promote new artists.

As Bruce Lundvall, the head of the Blue Note recording company, acknowledges, "The profitability of the catalogue is a mixed blessing. Let's say [consumers] buy their first jazz record when they hear Wynton or Joshua Redman or whoever it might be. Then they want to get the history. They start to buy catalogue, and that's exactly what the active, current roster is fighting. I remember [the saxophonist] Javon Jackson saying to me, 'I'm not competing with Joshua Redman so much as [with] Sonny Rollins and John Coltrane and Lester Young and Stan Getz's—the whole history of jazz saxophone players, which is available [on CD]." Jeff Levenson adds, "The Frankenstein monster has turned on its creators. In paying homage to the greats, Wynton and his peers have gotten supplanted by them in the minds of the populace. They've gotten supplanted by dead people."

But dead people make poor live attractions, and thus jazz clubs have suffered commensurably. "You know, I really love Duke and Louis and Miles and Ben Webster and all those guys, but I like jazz best when I can hear it live—it is supposed to be spontaneous music," says James Browne, who ran Manhattan's Sweet Basil. "They've been saying jazz is America's classical music, and it deserves respect. Well, now it's America's classical music. Thanks a lot. What do we do now?"

No longer signed to major record labels, Wynton, Branford, and other jazz musicians of their generation are taking stock (and they now have the leisure to do so). The focus of the discourse in jazz has shifted from the nature of the art form to that of the artist.

Both Wynton and Branford describe their departures from Columbia Records as an opportunity for self-evaluation. "I'm not with Columbia," Wynton said soberly in his apartment. "It was not vituperative. It's just time for me to do something else. It's just time, and it's a good thing. It's just time for me to figure out how I can forward my identity, to say, 'This is who I am.'

"The record companies should have abandoned us a long time ago. They should have saved us the trouble. It's not going to be healthy for our pocketbooks, but it's healthy for jazz. Through that void there is opportunity. Somewhere in that void is an opportunity for somebody to come up and start signing jazz musicians and letting them make the records they want to make."

Within Lincoln Center, Wynton Marsalis's jazz program has always had a status much like that of black culture in America: it is of the whole, yet other. Jazz at Lincoln Center began as a way to fill blank dates on the calendar at Alice Tully Hall, the smallest of the institution's four major theaters. "I didn't think it was important at the beginning," Marsalis says. "They called me and said they wanted to do some concerts with dead hall space in Lincoln Center, and did I have any ideas about what they could do? Because I had played classical music, I was a person to call. So I called Crouch—'What do you think? What could we do?' So we got together. It wasn't that big a deal—it was just three of us in a room [Marsalis, Crouch, and Alina Bloomgarden, of Lincoln Center], talking. Then I started to take it seriously."

* * *

Although Jazz at Lincoln Center became the institutional equal of the Metropolitan Opera, the New York Philharmonic, and the New York City Ballet, most of its concerts are still being held in Alice Tully Hall. In the fall of 2004 Jazz at

Lincoln Center moved into a sprawling multipurpose compound at Columbus Circle, a few blocks south of Lincoln Center proper. There, at the Frederick P. Rose Hall, it is part of the Time Warner Center, which houses not only the corporate headquarters of Time Warner but also a hotel, a condominium tower, and various stores and restaurants. It is the only one of Lincoln Center's fiefdoms to be based "off-campus." Still of the whole, yet other.

Marsalis was deeply involved in the planning of—and the fundraising for—this new home for Jazz at Lincoln Center, which he talks about with a keen sense of "the spirit of place," the phrase he once used as the title of a concert of Duke Ellington's travel music. In a piercing wind on a January afternoon in 2002, we walked around the construction site, a beam skeleton more than ten stories high at that point, and he described the philosophical underpinnings of the project.

"This is going to be the House of Swing, and we want everything in it to swing, even though the only thing swinging around here now is girders—watch your head," Marsalis said calmly. Against the cold he and I were both wearing long topcoats, woolen scarves, and hardhats, but he looked comfortable; he seemed to know every unmarked area in the maze of steel and most of the men working in it. Marsalis guided me to the center of an open space, about 250 square yards, which would someday be one of Jazz at Lincoln Center's two main performance venues—this one large enough to stage one of Ellington's symphonic suites; the other one about half its size, for small groups and solo recitals. "They're like two sides of the same thing, like night and day or man and woman," he said.

"Sound is very important" Marsalis continued. "So are the people. The people are as important as the musicians here." The stages will be lower and closer to the seats than they are in typical theaters, and the spaces will be designed to carry, not diminish, the sound of the audience. "We want to hear the audience answering us back—the call and response, we want that."

On our way to a makeshift elevator used for shuttling the work crews and materials, a foreman approached Marsalis, accompanied by several construction workers. "Excuse me, Wynton—I want you to meet Moose," the foreman said. "He's a hell of a singer."

A stocky fellow stepped forward tentatively. He had a stiff-lipped, nervous grin that he spoke through. "Hi, Wynton," he said.

Marsalis shook his hand. "Why don't you come over some time and do some tunes with us—sing with the band?" Marsalis said, waving a hand northward in the direction of Lincoln Center.

"No kidding?" the aspiring singer said, still grinning (but less nervously).

"Come on over—we'll do some tunes."

Like Louis Armstrong and Duke Ellington, both of whom toured the world under the auspices of the U.S. State Department during the Cold War, Marsalis has a feeling for people and a passion for his art that in combination make him a potent political force. No one denies his importance as a global ambassador of jazz. "He has never moved me as a trumpet player," Whitney Balliett, a well-known jazz critic, says. "But God—watching him in the Burns thing [Ken Burns's 2001 PBS documentary about jazz], it's phenomenal! All he has to do is open his mouth, and out it comes." According to the composer and conductor David Berger, who has been associated with the Lincoln Center jazz program since its inception, "Duke Ellington probably had more charisma than anybody I ever met—I mean, he was amazing. But Wynton, he's got it too. When you talk to him, he makes you feel good—just his presence, his energy. It elevates you and makes you want to be a better person."

I accompanied Marsalis to an event at the Cross Path Culture Center to benefit Barry Harris's jazz-education institute, and I lost him in the crowd of several hundred people. Dozens of jazz musicians, including Randy Weston, Kenny Barron, Allan Harris, and Jeffery Smith, were milling around the loftlike open space. When a camera flash went off, I spotted Wynton having his picture taken. Shortly after that another flash popped, ten or fifteen feet away from the first, and I saw Wynton posing again. I realized that all I needed to do to find him at any point during the evening was to look out at the crowd, and a camera flash would mark him.

To an institution like Jazz at Lincoln Center, Marsalis has been an asset of immeasurable value. "What strategy does the board of directors have for raising funds?" I asked the board chairman, Lisa Schiff, in her office, a few blocks south of Jazz at Lincoln Center's future home. "Wynton," she said.

For years Jazz at Lincoln Center was savaged by charges of mismanagement, racism, elitism, ageism, cronyism, and sexism, but these days it is more inclusive, forward-looking, and professional. Indeed, the concert schedule put together for the 2001–2002 year by Marsalis and his reorganized staff (including Todd Barkan, the artistic administrator, an independent-minded impresario who joined Jazz at Lincoln Center two years ago) was practically a manifesto against canonical rigidity. Emphatically multicultural, eclectic, and even contemporary, the program presented the music of Brazil (Pixinguinha, Cyro Baptista), of women (Abbey Lincoln, Barbara Carroll, Rhoda Scott), of white people (Woody Herman, Lee Konitz), of the French (a tribute to the Hot Club de France), and of young adventurists (Greg Osby, Akua Dixon). Perhaps Marsalis really did have a plan for Moose the construction worker to sing with the Lincoln Center Jazz Orchestra.

"One of my problems with Wynton used to be that he drew such a hard line many times," the composer and saxophonist Greg Osby recalls. "He doesn't seem to be that firm anymore. A lot of it I recognize as youth. He's a lot more accepting of varied presentation now. Not to say that he loves it, but he's a lot more tolerant of it."

Jazz's public advocates, Marsalis among them, like to talk about the music as a democratic art, a form of communal expression founded on the primacy of the individual voice. In recent years the conversation about the future of the music has focused on the global expansion of the jazz community and the integrity of the voices in that expanded community. But if the effectiveness of any democracy is in inverse proportion to its size, it looks—again—as though jazz may be doomed. That is to say, the music may not survive in the form we now know. Two decades after Wynton Marsalis and his troops took up arms against fusion, world music, the apotheosis of fusion, is at the gate.

"I wonder about the future of jazz, with all the music from other parts of the world floating around more and more and more," Whitney Balliett says. "Eventually that's going to be picked up in jazz. It already has been, and I wonder if there will eventually, in the next ten or twenty years, be a kind of diffusion—if the music will no longer be the jazz that we had ten or twenty years ago."

As for Marsalis, the very subject of globalism and jazz makes him choke on his words. I brought up the topic while we were eating Chinese food on the Upper West Side of Manhattan, after he had told me how much he was enjoying his spicy chicken. "World music"—he coughed out the phrase—"and all that stuff. I like people's music from around the world, and music from around the world belongs in Jazz at Lincoln Center. But for me—my music—I like jazz. I like the swingin'. I loved Art Blakey. I loved Dizzy. I love jazz musicians. Jazz has to be portrayed and brought forward for what it is—and celebrated. It can't be sold by being subsumed into the world-music market, and I'm just not willing to—I'm not willing to compromise my integrity under any circumstances. I wouldn't do it when I was twenty. I'm certainly not going to do it when I'm forty."

In 1939, Duke Ellington walked away from his contract with Columbia Records. Coincidentally, he, too, turned forty that year, and was at a career crossroads. After more than a decade of near servitude to his manager, Irving Mills, Ellington ended their association and started rebuilding his musical organization. He hired a pair of virtuoso innovators, the bassist Jimmy Blanton and the tenor saxophonist Ben Webster, and began composing with a new collaborator, the twenty-four-year-old Billy Strayhorn. "Ellington's music was marked by increased rhythmic drive and instrumental virtuosity," John Edward Hasse wrote in a 1993 biography of the composer. "[It presaged] bebop and other musical developments to come, and numerous musical explorations and innovations. With breathtaking originality, Ellington broke more and more new ground." In

1946 the jazz magazines would proclaim, almost in unison, that Ellington was passe again. Ten years after that *Time* would declare "a turning point in [Ellington's] career," saying that the composer had "emerged from a long period of quiescence and was once again bursting with ideas and inspiration."

When Wynton Marsalis turned forty, in the fall of 2001, Jazz at Lincoln Center threw him a surprise party at the Manhattan nightclub Makor, a couple of blocks away from his apartment. I had received an invitation and had been told that the guest list would be limited strictly to those who knew Marsalis well or worked closely with him, but there were hundreds of people sardined into the place: musicians and administrators from Jazz at Lincoln Center; the saxophonist Jimmy Heath; the broadcaster Ed Bradley; and others I could not see, because no one could move. Marsalis entered at 10:30 that evening, accompanied by his father and Stanley Crouch (who lured Marsalis to the club under the pretext of meeting a couple of women). The band struck up "Happy Birthday," New Orleans–style, and Marsalis waded through the crowd toward the bandstand, beaming, his arms raised high in the air.

It took him nearly twenty minutes—and thirty choruses of "Happy Birthday"—to reach the stage. "It really was a surprise," Marsalis said, and he began to cry. "Sometimes you're working so much, and this stuff just unfolds, and—I don't know. I can't say nothing."

The first piece the band played, after "Happy Birthday," was Ellington's "C Jam Blues" (also known as "Duke's Place"), and the last song of the night was Ellington's "It Don't Mean a Thing (If It Ain't Got That Swing)." Thanking his well-wishers, Marsalis eventually approached my vicinity in the crowd, and I asked him if he knew where Ellington had been on the same day in his life. "In Sweden," he said in half a beat. "Making some music—or making something!" (Ellington had indeed been in Stockholm, on a European tour.)

A few weeks later we were talking about his birthday, and Marsalis brought up Ellington again. "I have so much further to go," he said. "I'm just a baby. I'm just trying to figure out how to play. Like Duke, man—Duke never stopped, never stopped learning. Till the end, man, he was sitting at the piano every night—every night—trying to figure out how to do it better.

"I've had my ups and downs. Everybody does. I don't know what you would say about me right now. But I'm not concerned with that. You have to keep your mind on the issue, and the issue is the music. You have to look at the world around you and the things that happen to you and take them inside yourself and make something out of it. That's what jazz is. That's how I feel."

For Wynton Marsalis, fate is an opportunity for creative improvisation—another ringing cell phone at the Village Vanguard.

PART VII

Otherwise Engaged

Harry Partch

Indigent and homeless for many years, the American composer and instrument inventor Harry Partch, who died in 1974 at age seventy-three, made resourceful use of refuse. He patched together an odd musical style of his own from materials others had discarded. From the figurative dustbin of music history, Partch dug out arcane theories of tonality abandoned in the mid-seventeenth century—ideas outmoded when Bach established the "tempered" scale of twelve semitones—and he used them to develop idiosyncratic compositional systems based upon microtones, resulting in a range of tones much larger (and more attuned to nature) than the conventional scale allows. From literal garbage heaps, meantime, he took objects such as used laboratory bowls, beams from a dismantled bridge, empty liquor bottles, and surplus aircraft nose cones, and constructed instruments out of them that would produce notes on the scales he invented. Partch's peculiar junkyard art has more serious aims than the popular trash aesthetic, a celebration of rubbish as kitsch. It was not that he took ironic pleasure in bad ideas and vulgar sounds; he saw merit and beauty in musical systems and in objects others had rejected, and he couldn't bear to let them go to waste.

The experience of seeing and hearing Harry Partch's work performed on his instruments is a singular one. More than a decade after I first saw a performance of a Partch composition, a production of the composer's forty-minute *Revelation in the Courthouse Park* (conducted by Danlee Mitchell, one of the composer's young protégés), at Manhattan's Alice Tully Hall in November 1989, I can still replay *Revelation* in my mind as if it were a primal childhood memory. A theatrical spectacle, the piece draws on two parallel stories in words and music: one, Euripides' *The Bacchae*, the other an update of the same tale, this time set in postwar America, in which Dionysus is transformed into the teen idol Dion Isus. Partch's instruments, fancifully designed concoctions built to be seen as well as heard, dominated the stage, upstaging the cast of some three dozen costumed singers, dancers, musicians, drum majorettes, and tumblers.

Several of the devices were monstrous, the size of four-cylinder cars; to play Partch's bass marimba, a wood-scrap construction seven feet across and five feet high, a percussionist scurried back and forth, rapping its boards with his fists. Following the composer's instructions, the musicians swayed or twirled their bodies in time and manipulated their instruments in melodramatic gestures—"I always urge my performers to either caress or rape an instrument, never to merely use it," Partch said. Impressively, the work at the heart of all this proved worth the Herculean effort. The vocal music, which hewed closely to the inflections of spoken language, was delicate and gracefully nuanced, and the accompaniment and instrumental interludes swept around the words, buoying them up in a sea of exotic tones—the ring of glass bottles; the wavering hum of a pump organ tuned to microtones; the dry, brittle ping of tuned lengths of bamboo; Japanese bells muted inside hollowed gourds.

In the ten years after I saw that performance, interest in Partch grew considerably, largely owing to the efforts of a few Partch infatuates, music scholars of the postwar generation, and aging rock-and-rollers seeking new sources of cool. Virtually all of Partch's recorded works were issued on CD in *The Harry Partch Collection*, four volumes of material including most of his major compositions in performances originally supervised by Partch himself and released on his own private LP label (with the composer's liner notes), as well as a pair of multi-CD sets called *Enclosure 2* and *Enclosure 5*. Both are uneven collections of serious pieces and of lesser curiosities drawn from Partch's recording archives, and compiled by Philip Blackburn, the enterprising young program director of the American Composers Forum in St. Paul, Minnesota, who also edited *Enclosure 3*, a fetishistic, glossy-cover scrapbook reproducing Partch's notebook pages, drafts of music and prose pieces, doodles, and memorabilia.

Bitter Music, edited by the musicologist Thomas McGeary and published in 1991, is a more scholarly and representative anthology of Partch's writings. It includes the title piece, a diary of an eight-month vagabond adventure on the Pacific Coast with snatches of overheard talk and graffiti set to musical notation, as well as the librettos of his six major vocal and theater works, essays, and his frequently self-aggrandizing lectures on his work, the evils of the musical establishment, and their mutual exclusion.

Partch's own book *Genesis of a Music*, a quirky, prolix treatise on the history of musical intonation and his theories of pitch, acoustics, and instrumentation, initially published in 1949 and significantly expanded by the author for a revised edition in 1974, remains in print. The book is primarily written for musicians interested in playing the author's music, and includes charts listing formulas for tuning the instruments and instructions for their proper maintenance. Much of the prose is pretentious and obtuse: "The shadows of music are bred in deceit—half enticing, half forbidding, with myriad degrees of light-dark infusion—true interpretation with misinterpretation." But there's never a lack of passion. Conductors and composers of mainstream music are "kidnappers" and "traitors," and historical advocates of just intonation—that is, natural tones as opposed to those produced on a keyboard—are portrayed as fallen gods. Even the presentation of mathematical ratios in the charts feels reverential.

Finally, in 1998, the first biography of Partch, a thorough survey of his life and work by Bob Gilmore, an English writer on music and lecturer at the Dartington College of Arts, appeared, followed by a full-length documentary directed by Ray Davies, songwriter and singer for the 1960s rock band the Kinks, filmed while a group of avant-garde, jazz, and pop musicians, including Leonard Cohen and Elvis Costello, used Partch's instruments to perform music composed by the jazz bassist Charles Mingus. What makes Partch's life and work worthy of so much attention?

Partch clearly saw himself in much the same way as he saw his instruments. He projected an elegantly eccentric and exotic image, and he took pride in being self-made. He rethought and reconstructed his life and his past as often as he remade his most treasured musical construction, a microtonal pump organ he called the Chromelodeon, neither ever quite to his satisfaction. In his biography, however, Gilmore manages to extricate key facts of Partch's life from his self-mythologizing.

Born in 1901 to former missionaries to China living in Oakland, Partch claimed for a time to have been a native of China, later amending the tale to claim that he had been conceived in a Boxer prison camp in Shantung Province (which was unlikely). He studied piano as a child and proved adept enough by adolescence to accompany silent films in Albuquerque, where he learned a youthful lesson in music's power of salvation: though Partch was frail, the local toughs resisted their inclination to pick fights with him so as to preserve his fingers and good music at the movies.

After moving to Los Angeles on his own at age eighteen, Partch briefly attended the University of Southern California, picked up work on and off as a newspaper proofreader, and began composing conventional classical-style pieces for piano and symphony orchestra. He promptly rejected conventional composition—driven, no doubt, by his failure in classical music as well as, he insisted, by an impulse to make a different sort of music. "Call it intuitive," he wrote in *Genesis of a Music*, "for it was not the result of any intellectual desire to pick up lost or obscure historical threads. For better or for worse, it was an emotional decision."

Partch proceeded, nonetheless, to poke around for those threads, studying the history of intonation in Los Angeles libraries. He discovered the early proponents of just intonation: the Roman philosopher and mathematician Archytas, a friend of Plato; Euclid, whose formulas served as the foundation of Partch's scales; King Fang, a Chinese thinker of the second century BC; and Ptolemy, the Alexandrine after whom Partch would name one of his most beloved instruments. (As he makes clear in *Genesis of a Music*, Partch was also conversant with the work of later theorists and experimenters who explored the possibilities of microtones within equal temperament—that is, tones within the twelve semitones—such as R. H. M. Bosanquet and Colin Brown, both of whom predated Partch in the early twentieth century.) In later years, he would describe this process (shifting the time frame back a bit) with the characteristic arrogance of an autodidact:

> In 1919, as I recall, I had virtually given up on both music schools and private teachers, and had begun to ransack public libraries, doing suggested exercises and writing music free from the infantilisms and inanities of professors as I had experienced them. . . . Before I was twenty, I had tentatively rejected both the intonational system of modern Europe and its concert system.

Partch had a flair for characterization, especially his own, and an affection for the dramatic gesture. Following his "musical discovery" in the Los Angeles libraries, as he would recall in subsequent decades, he gathered every composition he had written to that point (including an unfinished piano concerto, a symphonic poem rejected by the Los Angeles Philharmonic, and some attempts at writing popular songs) and conducted a ritual burning on his apartment stove.

His missionary-turned-Christian-Scientist mother may have instilled his sense of sacrifice as an ennobling force; though Gilmore never addresses this theme directly, it is key to understanding Partch. Once he began work in his own systems of intonation, which employ mathematical ratios to divide one octave into as many as forty-three almost imperceptibly distinct tones, Partch found the musical establishment slow to accept his ideas, and he wore his outsider status as a badge of honor. He collected newspaper reviews of the few performances he gave at small recitals, and retyped the critical passages to which he added meticulous citations, leaving out the praise. Although he could proofread or type whenever he needed money, he took up menial labor and lived in and out of indigence, as if to dramatize his victimization. "I lay on Imperial Beach [near the Mexican border in San Diego] without food—because I was determined to have surcease from continual begging for my music," Gilmore quotes Partch as recalling. For nearly eight years beginning in 1935 (and occasionally later in his life), Partch was homeless. He hitchhiked and rode rails around the West and Midwest, worked in fields with other itinerants, and slept in transient shelters and work camps, all with his eye trained toward posterity.

Partch kept fastidious notes on his daily experiences, which he would presently use as source material for two major projects. The prose diary "Bitter Music" was the first of these (it includes some musical notation, hence Partch's inclusion of the work in some of his lists of compositions), a conventionally self-righteous, though often coarsely funny, Depression-era complaint against the period's social ills. ("Today I have bitter thoughts as I wander from one line of red tape waiting to another," Partch wrote. And, "Considering the constitution of our society, I feel that an artist might as well give up who isn't blessed either with a substantial dependable income or a substantial dependable ring dang doo.")

The second project, *U.S. Highball*, is a pulsing, kinetic twenty-five-minute text-and-music montage sometimes referred to as Partch's hobo opera, in which the composer set to music transcriptions of the speech of the homeless people he encountered, employing one of his microtonal scales, for performance by vocalists talk-singing (the ensemble can vary in size from one to a dozen, at the artists' discretion) and three of his early instruments (Adapted Guitar, Kithara, and Chromelodeon). This, Partch's "hobo period" work, invariably dominates popular press descriptions of Partch and is a potent factor in his allure as a gritty, anti-establishment artistic rebel—the Woody Guthrie of microtone theory.

Gilmore's tone is uniformly reverent toward Partch, and occasionally defensive of his lesser works, but he rarely deepens the biographical facts of Partch's life with critical or musicological analyses. (While narrowly focused scholarly papers on Partch by Thomas McGeary, Peter Garland, and others have been published, a comprehensive critical analysis of Partch's work remains to be written.) Still, Gilmore's detailed account of Partch's epic determination to mount his work, his relentless squabbling with musicians and producers over minuscule details, and his persistence in the face of ridicule, misjudgment, and rejection argue forcefully for the composer's clarity of purpose and his uniqueness in serious twentieth-century American music, a creative landscape in which quixotic misfit visionaries like John Cage, Conlon Nancarrow, and Partch himself sometimes seem the norm.

Partch's career falls into two periods. In the first, roughly from 1930 to 1950, he worked in the idiom of intoned speech, in which he said he sought to explore "the intrinsic music of spoken words" by setting verbal language to music and to accompaniment closely akin to the voice. In his theory of music, he gave precedence to unadorned organic sounds, basing his aesthetic on what he liked to call the "corporeal"—something fundamentally rooted in the specific and physical. "Corporeal," for Partch, referred to "the essentially vocal and verbal music of the individual . . . a music that is vital to a time and place, a here and now," such as epic chant, some folk music, even seventeenth-century Florentine opera—any music that is "physically allied with poetry or the dance." The corporeal was the antithesis of the abstract, which he rejected as being based on the dominance of nonverbal musical forms, like the symphony, over "the vitality of words." "Sometime between 1923 and 1928," he wrote in *Genesis of a Music*,

> I finally became so dissatisfied with the body of knowledge and usages as ordinarily imparted in the teaching of music that I refused to accept, or develop my own work on the basis of, any part of it. With respect to current usage this refusal was a rebellion; from the standpoint of my creative work it was the beginning of a new philosophy of music, intuitively arrived at. Just how old this "new" philosophy actually is has since been a continual revelation to me.

Indeed, performances emphasizing the musicality of intoned speech date to 2300 BC China and Plato's Greece, and the debate over the primacy of music or of words (*prima la musica* or *prima la parola*) had raged for centuries before Partch developed his arguments in favor of the latter.

Perhaps owing to childhood memories of his parents conversing in Mandarin, Partch had an acute ear for the cadences and the shifting pitch of speech. He heard music in words, and he set out to notate it precisely. Since very few of us employ the musical notes of the twelve-tone scale for casual chat (though some people come close: think of Bing Crosby, who talked as he sang, in tune and in swing time), Partch devised his own scales of microtones and the instruments for playing them.

It was to echo speech initially (and later to add harmony and counterpoint to the vocal phrases) that Partch began making his own instruments in the late 1920s. His first was a viola with an expanded fingerboard attached by a violin maker, followed quickly by an adapted guitar, a reconfigured reed organ (originally called the Ptolemy, later rebuilt and renamed the Chromelodeon), and the harplike Kithara, humble ancestors of Partch's progressively more bizarre constructions.

Amending his approach to intonation periodically over the years, Partch developed a variety of musical systems that made use of mathematical ratios to divide one octave into 29, 55, 39, 37, or the original 43 tones, as opposed to the twelve notes of the tempered scale. The difference between one note and the next in highly divided scales such as these is virtually imperceptible, and every note sounds sour to unconditioned ears. Phrases seem an erratic assault until the mind adjusts and begins to sense musical structure in the sound. Newcomers have the same trouble with other musical forms attentive to microscopic delineations of pitch, such as South Asian liturgical chant and contemporary hip-hop.

Partch's work in intoned speech also prefigured rap's use of raw street talk for its text. Most prominently in *Barstow* (1941) and *Bitter Music* (1943), Partch illuminated a poetic vigor in the vernacular of the fringes of mid-century American society:

> *"I have a job for the first time in five years!"*
> *"You fucking beggar! Haven't you the decency to refuse it?"*
> *"You Dog-damned fool! Are you plumb batty?"*
> *"Yes, I am. Do you care?"*

Initially composed for voice and adapted guitar, revised several times in subsequent years for Partch's growing array of instruments, *Barstow* demonstrates the deftness with which Partch used the colorative capacity of his scales and instruments for interpretative effect. He selected minutely nuanced tones to match the rage in the hoboes' language, sometimes exaggerating its vulgarity for comic value.

Though eclectic, Partch's tastes in his text sources were not catholic. Beyond the speech of the homeless, he gravitated toward literary sources: scenes from Shakespeare plays including *Twelfth Night* and *Romeo and Juliet*, *Finnegans Wake*, Yeats's "By the Rivers of Babylon," Thomas Wolfe's "God's Lonely Man," and English translations of works by the eighth-century Chinese poet Li Po. Partch said he felt a special kinship with Yeats, whom he had visited in 1934 in Rathfarnham, Ireland, to discuss his plans for setting Yeats's translation of *King Oedipus* to music. The composer would later recall Yeats's comment, "No word shall have an intonation or accentuation it could not have in passionate speech"—an affirmation of the central tenet of Partch's conception of intoned speech. No matter that Yeats was notoriously tone-deaf, Partch craved approbation, and this was, after all, Yeats. Although the poet would describe Partch in a letter to his friend Margot Ruddock as "very young, and very simple," Partch would long cling to words he treasured as Yeats's blessing: "You are one of those young men with ideas, the development of which it is impossible to foretell, just as I was thirty years ago."

Partch largely exhausted the genre of intoned speech after two decades and, beginning in the early 1950s, worked mainly in his second mode, which he called "integrated theater." This loftily redundant phrase simply means theater—already an integrated union of language, music, movement, and the visual arts, of course. (He composed very little "absolute music," that is, music without words, a notable exception being the mid-1960s suite for an ensemble of his instruments, *And on the Seventh Day Petals Fell in Petaluma*, which began with a text from various sources which was later eliminated.) "I believe in a total integration of factors," he explained, "not as separate and sealed specialties in the artificially divorced departments of universities, but of sound and sight, the visually dynamic and dramatic, all channeled into a single, wholly fused, and purposeful direction. *All*."

Partch's move toward a meta-Wagnerian theater coincided with his affiliations (mostly as an artist in residence, occasionally giving lectures) with a few universities, where abundant supplies of undergraduates all agog over Partch's bohemian weirdness were available to stage his extravagant theatrical conceptions on the cheap. When Mills College in Oakland produced Partch's setting of Yeats's *King Oedipus* in 1951, the composer's emerging reputation helped attract an impressive group of critics from the national press, including *Time* and *Theatre Arts*, the latter of which raved, perceptively if effusively, "With the production of Harry Partch's *King Oedipus* the Western theater has been given one of the most challenging and revolutionary potentials in its history."

While based for a few years at the University of Illinois at Urbana-Champaign, Partch created his two most celebrated full-length theater works: *The Bewitched* (1955), an episodic "dance-satire" in eleven movements dealing with literal and metaphoric spells in a variety of contemporary settings ("Visions Fill the Eyes of the Defeated Basketball Team in the Shower Room," "The Cognoscenti are Plunged into a Demonic Descent While at Cocktails"); and *Revelation in the Courthouse Park* (1960). Partch supervised the staging, the choreography, the set design, the costumes, the lighting, and the musica bafflingly complex, nearly sadistically demanding idiom employing a forty-three-tone scale for voice and the ballooning collection of Partch instruments.

He contended that instruments and musicians should perform dramatic roles: Partch would insist that the dozen or more instruments used in the score for a major theater piece be positioned prominently on stage, and he would lecture the musicians on their responsibility to swoon and gyrate to the mood of the music while they performed it. "When a player fails to take full advantage of his role in a visual or acting sense, he is muffing his part—in my terms—as thoroughly as if he bungled every note in the score," he chided in a manual he wrote for his musicians. "There is surely some special hell reserved for the player of one of the more dramatic instruments who insists on deporting himself as though he were in tie-and-tails on a symphony orchestra's platform (such as experimental hanging by the gonads on a treble Kithara string until he relents)."

Partch certainly built as much theatricality as musicality into the more than thirty instruments he made over four decades, largely out of the eye-catching objects he happened upon: he found the zigzagged eucalyptus bough for the Gourd Tree in a neighbor's trash pile; the Bloboy was adapted from junked automotive horns. The Mazda Marimba has tiers of burned-out light bulbs, and the Zymo-Xyl makes use of empty liquor bottles. (Partch usually had materials on hand sufficient to have constructed a new Zymo-Xyl every few days.) Mostly percussion intruments, they were each intended to contribute a particular tonal color, and all were designed with an eye for their visual as well as sonic effect: driftwood hewn in Gaudi-style curves, prism-arrays of blocks, and sheets of wound-wire strings assembled in a hybrid of primitivism and otherworldliness that recalls most uncannily the 1960s *Star Trek* episode in which Mr. Spock has a jam session with alien-race hippies. In 1966, the San Francisco Art Museum included several of Partch's instruments in a show of functional sculpture and gave their creator the Nealie Sullivan Award for design.

Partch's instruments have always been praised more readily than the work for which they were ostensibly constructed. "The instruments add atmosphere, and do it admirably," the *New York Times* noted in a 1944 review of three Partch works performed in a League of Composers concert at what was then called Carnegie Chamber Music Hall, "but the music—so-called—is of entirely secondary importance." *Time* derided his work as "goblin music." Partch responded to the frequent emphasis on his instruments defensively, insisting, "I am not an instrument-builder, but a music-man seduced into carpentry." If so, he submitted wholly; by Gilmore's account, Partch devoted far more time and attention to building, reconfiguring, repairing, and managing storage of his instruments than he did to composing, despite the fact that tethering his compositional *oeuvre* to instruments so difficult to maintain, demanding to play, and costly to ship made his work virtually impossible for most classical-music institutions to stage. Moreover, as Gilmore neglects to mention, Partch never really needed to invent instruments in order to compose forty-three-tone music; he could have used any non-fretted string instruments (violins, cellos, etc.) or non-calibrated brass (trombones, trumpets). But Partch clearly valued the range of exotic timbres he was able to manipulate with his own instruments, and he obviously loved to tinker.

Now from three to six decades old, and in most cases jerry-rigged with fragile materials that the habitually impoverished Partch could afford to buy or could find somewhere, his instruments remain the perishable heart of the composer's work. Since these creations are costly to house and keep in playable condition, Dean Drummond, a student of Partch and caretaker of his instruments, in an inversion of Partch's method of making instruments in order to play his music, has been staging concerts of new works composed for Partch's instruments to help keep them in use—and to explore their potential beyond Partch's own compositional ideas. Drummond's performance of his own eighty-six-minute film score *The Last Laugh*, at the Winter Garden theater at the World Financial Center in lower Manhattan in November 1998, featured ten of Partch's instruments, including the Cloud-Chamber Bowls, the Diamond Marimba, and the Bloboy. It was an earnest presentation of lucid, if somewhat derivative, Partch-inspired music, fairly well attended by an animated and predominantly young audience. "I love Partch," one man sitting to my right said. "His stuff is wild . . . futuristic sci-fi jazz." But such reactions betray a skewed perception of Partch's music (and much of Drummond's work with Partch's instruments), which is grounded in tradition, antitechnological, and meticulously notated with little room for jazzlike improvisation.

* * *

What is such a listener loving, then, when he says he loves Partch? In 1971, Ravi Shankar, the Indian sitar virtuoso, performed at New York's Madison Square Garden as the opening act for George Harrison, Bob Dylan, Eric Clapton, and a roster of other rockers whom Harrison had gathered to raise money for Bangladesh relief. After hearing a few minutes of Shankar's ensemble, the audience of some 20,000 roared in approval. "Thank you," Shankar replied. "If you appreciate the tuning so much, I hope you will enjoy the playing more." However ill-informed, the members of Shankar's audience may have been responding at least partly with natural enthusiasm for something startlingly new to their ears. Maybe they really did like the tuning, for the jumbled beauty of the timbres and the instruments' jolting, erratic tempi. Perhaps Partch's instruments are exhilarating in the same way that Shankar's Indian instruments are, by producing sounds of an unexpected, almost unfathomable beauty—wild perhaps, but primeval rather than futuristic, and rigorously organized rather than improvisational in form.

Decades after its composition, Partch's music remains potent, still utterly unique in its uncompromising evocation of the darker hues of the emotional spectrum—and the lighter. In Partch's numerous works dealing with hobo life, the music exquisitely complements the yearning, the rage, and the resignation (as well as the self-pity) of the text. (Paul Bowles, while he was a music critic for the *New York Herald Tribune*, commented in 1944 on Partch's skill at "expressing a kind of all-embracing unhappiness.") In time, Partch became equally adept in the realm of the ludicrous. Often mistakenly presumed to be gravely serious, the laughably outrageous work he created for the theater is *supposed* to be funny. Many of his works, such as *Revelation in the Courthouse Park*, *The Bewitched*, and *Water! Water!*, were designed as parody or satire; when they make one want to laugh—and they frequently do—they are succeeding.

Although he is typically linked with figures of the twentieth-century avant-garde such as Cage, Nancarrow, Henry Cowell, and Lou Harrison, Partch didn't think of himself as a modernist. And for all his inventiveness, Partch distrusted technology; he abhorred electronic music and saw his work not just as an alternative to its increasing prevalence during his lifetime but as a corrective to it. "The . . . individual's diminishing significance in the face of an industrial machine is not to be disputed, but nothing could be more futile (or downright idiotic) than to *express* this age," wrote Partch in a 1959 essay. "The prime obligation of the artist is to transcend his age, therefore to show it in terms of the eternal mysteries. What this age needs more than anything else is an effective antidote."

In a tangible sense, Harry Partch has transcended his age: More than twenty-five years after his death, his work was more available than before. The details of his life had been published. Chain stores carried the recordings he made; rock stars played his instruments. Can a biopic be far behind? I would like to think that the Partch revival, such as it is, speaks of more than his cult appeal as a kook. Indeed, his work seems more timely than it was during his lifetime, as a statement in protest of technology that was conceived years before our lives were computerized, and as a link to primitive and non-Western musical traditions explored long before the popularity of "world music." Time has proven *Time* wrong: there is something haunting in the music of Harry Partch, but it has nothing to do with goblins; it is the spirit of the primal, the sound of someone banging on a gourd. If it surprises, it can also fascinate for its echoes of the earliest attempts to make music, for the unnerving beauty of such strange, raw sounds, and for its reminder that one man's garbage can be another man's art.

Elmer Fudd

I get a feeling when I watch one of the old Warner Bros. cartoons, and the closest I can come to describing it is a Russian word, *razlyubit*. It refers to a certain affection one always retains for the first person one loved. Growing up in the three-channel suburbia of northwestern New Jersey during the early 1960s, when local affiliates used syndicated cartoon packages to fill the time between toy and candy-bar commercials in the after-school hours, I learned most of what I first knew about film comedy from the nearly 1,000 animated shorts produced under the Looney Tunes and Merry Melodies trademarks between 1930 and 1964. Warners closed up the bungalow clubhouse where directors such as Friz Freleng, Chuck Jones, and Robert McKimson long conspired to create Bugs Bunny, Daffy Duck, Porky Pig, and the Road Runner, abandoning production in favor of marketing and distribution, as all the studios had already done for feature films, in the same year Lyndon Johnson was elected president, the Beatles took over the record charts, Cassius Clay defeated Sonny Liston for the World Heavyweight Championship, and my sister got her first boyfriend. It was a period of tumult for us all, one way or another; fortunately, the vintage Warner Bros. cartoons, fixed in the timeless other of cartoon Hollywood, provided certain respite every day before dinner. In six and a half minutes, each of the shorts—or the better among them, since all aren't equally inspired—knowingly exploited and parodied the studio system that had, for decades, been the entertainment universe. Looney Tunes developed its own stars, the biggest being Bugs, the cavalier Brooklyn rabbit, and Daffy, the manically vainglorious duck, whose casual interaction with caricatures of real-life screen actors such as Humphrey Bogart and Edward G. Robinson served to reinforce the cartoon characters' stature and illuminate the actors' cartoonishness. (One of Bugs' animated friends sees him on a park bench next to Bing Crosby, Eddie Cantor, Jack Benny, and Al Jolson, and he says, "Bugs Bunny—why are you hanging around with these guys? They'll never amount to anything.") In ostensible behind-the-scenes stories, Looney Tunes characters would squabble over studio business with a brazen virulence unseen in contemporary newsreels of flesh-and-blood Hollywood families smiling by the pool. (Threatening to leave Warners, Porky Pig asks his boss, "What's Errol Flynn got that I haven't?" That both spent most of their time without pants goes unspoken.) Of course, Warners' cartoon studio also included a regular supporting player: a strange, lonely animated human in a realm of anthropomorphic celebrity, Elmer Fudd.

After a few years of awkward experimentation as a profoundly silly figure alternately called both Elmer Fudd and Egghead, he took full form in a 1940 Bugs Bunny short, "A Wild Hare"; from then on, he appeared as permutations of the same character in a fairly wide range of story situations. While the Looney Tunes stars (Bugs, Daffy, Porky Pig, Sylvester, and company) were virtually always featured as themselves, Elmer costarred as a hunter, a Mountie, a scientist, a hotel manager, or a farmer. In "The Hardship of Miles Standish" (1940), a knock-about twist on Longfellow's nineteenth-century poem, he portrayed pilgrim John Alden; in "What's Opera Doc?" (1957), Chuck Jones' scathing parody of Wagner's *Der Ring Des Nibelungen*, he sang ("Kill the wabbit!") as the warrior Siegfried. Elmer Fudd became the character actor among actor characters. Whatever his role, however, Elmer—like Mickey Rooney in Warners' stock-company version of *A Midsummer Night's Dream* or John Wayne in Cecil B. DeMille's Biblical epic, *The Greatest Story Ever Told*—retained his elemental Fuddness.

A grown man old enough to have gone completely bald, Elmer J. Fudd is an oversized newborn, proportionally and psychologically. His head is a fruit bowl of round shapes: honeydew cheeks, plum nose, cantaloupe eyes on a blue-ribbon crenshaw head. In a live-action film, Elmer would be Guy Kibbee (the governor in *Mr. Smith Goes to Washington*) or Henry Travers (the angel Clarence in *It's a*

Wonderful Life). His wide open, blinking eyes signal the work of a slow mind, although Fudd is not cartoon-dumb in that goofy (or Goofy) "which way did he go?" way; Elmer is an innocent, not an idiot. The only adult human in the Warner cartoon world, he is the most like a child. (Fudd's speech impediment, wherein r's and sometimes l's are spoken as w's—"You scwewy wabbit!"—occurs commonly among preschoolers.) However, Elmer's infantility does not seem designed to help children to relate to him. As directors Freleng and Jones frequently explained, their animated shorts were not made for kids. Moreover, in his supporting capacity, one of Elmer's principle functions is to enlarge the hero (say, Bugs) through self-reduction. He may be cast as a titular figure of authority or hold a kind of power (say, a shotgun) at the onset of the film—the boss to adults in the audience, the grown-up to kids—but he will inevitably lose out in the end, largely by virtue of his own inability. During the Second World War, Warner director Bob Clampett attributed a boom in the popularity of Bugs Bunny cartoons to audiences' association of the scrappy, ever-triumphant prey Bugs with American GIs and the hapless predator Elmer with the Axis powers; Elmer, Chuck Jones added, even looked something like Mussolini.

In American film, the great sentimentalists—Chaplin, Disney, Capra, and Spielberg (as well as their innumerable imitators, particularly Jerry Lewis and John Hughes)—have glamorized a romantic conception of childhood as a more innocent, that is, purer, therefore, higher state of being than adulthood; in their work, age corrupts and most of what we associate with maturity (sex, career, culture) is rendered suspect. At Looney Tunes, a contrary view predominates: Elmer, the studio's prominent symbol of childlike innocence, suffers mightily for his immaturity. (Tweety Bird, though very young, is smarter than his grown adversary, Sylvester the Cat.) By nature open-minded, trusting, sensitive, and forgiving, Elmer is congenitally ill-equipped to compete with Bugs, the image of savvy, charm, quick wit, and resourcefulness, not to mention duplicity. In Disney's hands, Elmer's puerility, like the essential simple-mindedness of Mickey Mouse, Donald Duck, Goofy, Pluto . . . in other words, virtually all Disney characters except for the villains, most of whom are awfully dumb, too . . . would, before the end credits, prove to be his redemption; at Warners, it's his undoing. I remember hearing my big brother call Elmer a "dummy" and a "loser" when I was a kid, and I'm glad he made that association between the two traits; it's one my own two children haven't gotten much from television in the 1990s.

An exceptional character in house at Warners, as well, Elmer Fudd was not voiced by actor Mel Blanc, who handled the characterizations for virtually every other male in the Looney Tunes stable and who was generally the only vocal performer acknowledged in the Warners cartoon credits. Working anonymously, comic character actor Arthur Q. Bryan devised the sad, dysphasic voice that evokes Elmer instantly and has been inextricably associated with him for seven decades—a low-energy baritone mix of croak and tremor, with wots of wowds pwonounced wike that. Bryan, who looked even more like Elmer Fudd than Mussolini did, used several voices in convincing portrayals of various sorts of dullards in countless radio shows, a handful of films (nearly all forgotten programmers such as 1940's *Millionaire Playboy* and 1944's *I'm from Arkansas*), and a few episodes of TV series, most notably an *I Love Lucy* in which he makes a rare appearance using Elmer's voice as a different character. Shortly before Bryan's death at sixty in 1959, Warners began trying out others as Elmer, including Mel Blanc (who had filled in for Bryan on a few occasions), though none brought the character quite the same helpless élan.

Chuck Jones, one of more than a dozen Looney Tunes and Merry Melodies directors who used Elmer to varying degrees, is responsible for nearly all of his most memorable appearances: those in "The Scarlet Pumpernickel" (1950), "The Rabbit of Seville" (1950), "Beanstalk Bunny" (1955), "What's Opera, Doc?" "Bugs Bonnets" (1956), and the trilogy of Daffy-Bugs hunting-season confrontations, "Rabbit Fire" (1951), "Rabbit Seasoning" (1952), and "Duck! Rabbit! Duck!" (1953). While Jones has written extensively about his life and work in two memoirs, *Chuck Amuck* (1989) and *Chuck Reducks* (1996), he scarcely mentions Elmer. "Daffy Duck is a rueful recognition of my own (and your own) ineptitudes. Bugs Bunny is a glorious personification of our most dappy dreams," Jones theorized. "We love Daffy because he is us, we love Bugs because he is as wonderful as we would like to be." What about Elmer Fudd? Neither our cartoon self-reflection nor our dream image, he is not us at all, by design; an anti-Everyman, he's The Other Guy through whom we identify ourselves only by rejection.

In the 1950s, Looney Tunes' creative use of Elmer as a negative force, a character through whom given ideas could be discredited by ridicule, approached cultural insurgency. At a time when popular entertainment reinforced the postwar ideal of cosy suburban prosperity with TV series such as the *The Adventures of Ozzie and Harriet* and *Father Knows Best*, none of the Warners cartoon characters followed that American Dream, except Elmer Fudd. His goals were the middle-class aspirations of the Eisenhower era: He tried to keep a nice house, do his job ("Oh deaw!" he cries in 1954's "Design for Leaving," "I'w be wate for wowk!"), and unwind on the weekends; even his hunting was recast as an idle pastime ("I'm a vegetawian—I onwy hunt fow spowt."). His antagonists Bugs, Daffy, and Sylvester clearly hold Elmer's conservative pursuits in contempt and zealously undermine them through street wile (Bugs), anarchy (Daffy), and connivance (Sylvester). For those of us watching at an impressionable age, the message was persuasively subversive: The only one behaving like our parents, doing everything they told us to do, was the fool.

Then there's the gay thing. Much has been made of Bugs Bunny's cross-dressing and flirting with male characters, particularly Elmer; the lead characters ponder Bugs' feminine sex appeal in the movie *Wayne's World* (1992), and animation scholar Kevin S. Sandler has written a thorough essay on the topic of Bugs' sexuality in the anthology about Warner animation he edited, *Reading the Rabbit* (1998). Bugs adopts drag thirty-six times and kisses twenty-eight male and four female figures, Sandler points out. Yet, Elmer also crosses gender barriers and in a significantly different way. For Bugs, sex is another of his tricks; he plants a surprise kiss on a male opponent's lips (whether he is Elmer or Yosemite Sam) to disarm, confuse, or humiliate him, and he dolls up and seduces foes to gain power over them. Bugs manipulates gender and employs sex tactically, but he always returns to a clear-cut male role by the end of the cartoon. When Elmer responds amorously to a male overture or dons a woman's clothes, by contrast, it is an act of submission; he is giving in to a romantic impulse, not pretending to be something he's not. Bugs and Elmer go so far as to marry in two cartoons (*The Rabbit of Seville* and *Bugs Bonnets*), Bugs the groom (retaining his male identity), Elmer an ecstatic bride. Is the animators' intent to deride homosexuality by associating it with Elmer? Probably. Then again, both of these cartoons use the image of Bugs and Elmer happily wed as their climactic, closing messages. "You know," Bugs explains with a smile, "I think it always helps a picture to have a romantic ending."

I'm surprised that there's been so little critical discourse about Elmer Fudd, what with two generations raised on TV cartoons now heading the university pop-culture (and gender) studies departments. The reference book *Looney Tunes and Merrie Melodies: A Complete Illustrated Guide to the Warner Bros. Cartoons* by Jerry Beck and Will Friedwald pictures all the popular Warners characters except Elmer on its cover and omits him from its character index. At what remains of the Warner Bros. studio, a string of new cartoons with the classic characters was produced in the 1990s, keeping the licensed merchandise franchise alive, although none features Elmer in more than token cameos. As a licensed merchandise commodity, too, he is represented on some half a dozen of the thousands of geegaws I saw for sale at the Warner Bros. Studio Store on Manhattan's Fifth Avenue. "Duh," my twelve-year-old daughter said to me, pithily. "Who wants Elmer stuff? He *is* Elmer." Well, duh, indeed. Perhaps there is some recompense in the prospect that his famous costars are who they are, at least partly because of him. At the very least, he seems to be getting what he always wanted: west and wewaxation at wast.

Walt Whitman and Fred Hersch
The Jazz *Leaves of Grass*

W alt Whitman's *Leaves of Grass* was always a work in progress—or a series of works that varied in character and grew exponentially in size over more than three decades, until the poet's death in 1892. The first edition, published 150 years ago, was something of a vanity project manufactured with typesetting assistance from Whitman himself, and it presented a dozen poems on ninety-five pages. The second, published fourteen months later, contained thirty-two poems. Over the next four years, Whitman achieved full bloom as a writer (and as a man, owing in part to a visit to New Orleans that inspired a set of fearless poems about same-sex affection), and he expanded his masterpiece to 156 poems, including revisions and new orderings of the earlier ones into thematic clusters. (The 1860 edition, arguably the richest of the lot, is no longer in print, despite the fact that the work has long been in the public domain and could be published cheaply.) Whitman would devote most of the rest of his years to reshaping and applying more clay onto this work cast from early life. By the last of the nine versions that he produced, the "deathbed edition" of 1892, *Leaves of Grass* included more than four hundred poems on more than seven hundred pages.

As a song of self, it sings of an epically mercurial and voluptuous spirit. For this reason, *Leaves of Grass* endures, while so much poetry beloved in this country during Whitman's lifetime—Joel Barlow's "The Columbiad," Timothy Dwight's "The Conquest of Canaan"—would strike us as derivative, precious, or stilted, if we could find copies to read today. Whitman's masterwork still speaks to us not least because it is among the most American of our books, not only for its much-vaunted evocation of democratic ideals, its celebrations of individualism and egalitarianism, and its quirky, vernacular radicalism, but also for the seeming inexhaustibility of its resources. It is boundlessly explicable. What better gift could a master explicator like Bill Clinton give his girlfriend than a copy of *Leaves of Grass*, which glorifies bedrock American principles at the same time that it glories in matters of the flesh? (In her thank-you note, Monica Lewinsky wrote that "Whitman is so rich that one must read him like one tastes a fine wine or good cigar—take it in, roll it in your mouth, and savor it!" But I digress.)

Composers since the turn of the last century have gone fishing in Whitman's well-stocked stream of verse. Initially condemned for blasphemy and indecency (he advanced a vague pantheism and reveled in all varieties of sensation), Whitman was a prototype of the American Artist Underappreciated in His Own Uncultured, Overly Puritanical Country But Recognized, Thank Goodness, by the Europeans. The latter drew often upon Whitman in their music, to challenge the entrenched orthodoxies of their own countries. Delius found kinship in Whitman's quasi-paganism and overt carnality, and set Whitman's poetry to music in three of his signature pieces: *Sea Drift* (1904), *Songs of Farewell* (1930), and *Idyll* (1933, based on musical material from Margot la Rouge of 1902), all of which employ shifting layers of harmony to sweeping effect, an approach roughly parallel to Whitman's use of dense clusters of language. Vaughan Williams drew inspiration from the poet's erratic, seemingly spontaneous outbursts in his serpentine Whitman homages, *Toward the Unknown Region* (1907) and *Sea Symphony* (1910). Holst also wrote several good Whitman settings, including a lovely adaptation of Whitman's famous requiem for Abraham Lincoln, "When Lilacs Last in the Dooryard Bloom'd," which Holst treated as an elegy for fallen veterans of World War I. And in the era of the next war, the German-born composers Kurt Weill and Paul Hindemith (musicians with vastly different aesthetics) both marked their relocation to the United States by writing pieces set to the verse of Whitman; the poet's iconoclasm, defiance of prevailing mores, and sheer Americanness seemed to reinforce their rejection of fascism. (Weill, following Holst, adapted one of Whitman's Civil War poems, "Drum Taps," to memorialize victims of World War II.) With the emergence of the postwar avant-garde in the years to follow, Whitman surfaced again, this time as the spiritual father of American bohemia, a proto-modernist. In 1957, Ned Rorem composed a set of angularly lyrical art songs to Whitman's verse, and in 1976 George Crumb revisited the durable "Lilacs" poems, in Apparition, setting them to a suite of bold, tonally venturesome works for voice and modified piano. (Four Rorem tunes, as well as select Whitman settings by Vaughan Williams, Weill, Hindemith, Ernst Bacon, and others appear in uniformly fine renditions by the baritone Thomas Hampson, accompanied by Craig Ruttenberg, on the album *To the Soul: Thomas Hampson Sings the Poetry of Walt Whitman*, from EMI Classics.) More recently, Whitman's vast output has been mined for its evocation of what Whitman called "manly attachment." He hinted at the theme here and there in his work, but dealt with it squarely in the "Calamus" (or "Live Oak, With Moss") poems inspired by his New Orleans jaunt— work once considered scandalous, now heroic. In 1993, Michael Tilson Thomas composed a delicate, pretty song, "We Two Boys Together Clinging," set to a excerpt from "Calamus":

> *We two boys together clinging,*
> *One the other never leaving. . . .*
> *Arm'd and fearless, eating, drinking,*
> *sleeping, loving,*
> *No law less than ourselves owning . . .*

All told, no fewer than five hundred musical compositions, works varying widely in style, scale, and intent, have been set to Whitman's words, most of them drawn from the eight versions of *Leaves of Grass*, and more Whitman inspired music keeps appearing. (Even Madonna has written a song quoting Whitman, her melodramatic "Sanctuary." But I digress again.) "The proof of the poet is that his country absorbs him as affectionately as he has absorbed it," Whitman wrote in the preface to the 1855 edition of his epic. The musical landscape's capacity to absorb Whitman remains considerable, and *Leaves of Grass* is, musically speaking, still very much a work in progress.

As one might expect from the author of American poetry's democratic manifesto, Whitman was a public champion of homegrown American sounds. He served for some time as a newspaper music critic, and he used his forum to argue the superiority of just-emerging modes of American folk music over traditional forms of Western music. In a way, he declared the culture wars a hundred years early, advancing "heart music" (earthy, declarative, informal, American) over "art music" (refined, urban, formal, European). Lauding one of the many family vocal groups popular in the decades before the Civil War, Whitman praised the music as "simple, fresh, and beautiful." He added: "We hope no spirit of imitation will ever induce them to engraft any 'foreign airs' upon their 'native graces.'"

He liked minstrel shows, too, identifying in them a high level of artistry for a "low" form of popular art. As he wrote about one minstrel group (no doubt white performers in blackface, although African Americans also participated in minstrelsy, essentially parodying whites parodying them) in a review titled "True American Singing," "Their negro singing altogether proves how shiningly golden talent can be spread over a subject generally considered low. Singing with them is a subject from obscure life in the hands of a divine painter: rags, patches, and coarseness are imbued with the great genius of the artist, and there exists something really great about them."

Whitman absorbed a great deal of music in his lifetime, and he noted in his maturity that his youthful musical encounters informed his writing deeply. As he told his late-life friend Horace Traubel (who compiled the poet's reminiscences in *With Walt Whitman in Camden*), "My younger life was so saturated with the emotions, raptures, and uplifts of such musical experiences that it would be surprising indeed if all my future work had not been colored by them." *Leaves of Grass*, in Whitman's own view, was indebted to the Italian operas that he came to love in the decade prior to the book's first publication. "But for the opera," he said, "I could never have written *Leaves of Grass*."

He was referring in this instance not to the opulent emotionality of Italian opera, an obvious corollary to Whitman's poetry, but to the flexibility of recitative, opera's freedom to dispense with rhyme and the metrical patterns of traditional song. But the music of Whitman's verse begs other analogies as well. It in its jagged, erratic lines, its unpredictable swoops and sudden eruptions, *Leaves of Grass* anticipated Charlie Parker as much as it reflected Rossini.

How strange that *Leaves of Grass* inspired no major work in the jazz idiom, at least none that I know of, until recently . The composer and pianist Fred Hersch has written a glorious setting of excerpts from the book, which I heard performed by the composer and a seven-piece chamber-jazz ensemble at Zankel Hall in New York. (Hersch and his group also toured the piece to support its CD release by Palmetto Records.) Whitman's idiosyncratic poetry certainly seems more suitable to the improvised spontaneity of jazz than it is to, say, the noble Anglicism of Vaughan Williams or the rigorous intellectualism of Hindemith. Indeed, one of Whitman's hallmarks is that his poems are not primarily intended to describe phenomena; they are phenomena. Their function is not merely interpretive: they are put forth as objects for our interpretation, much as a jazz solo is not just the performer's rendition of a composition, but a composition itself.

Structurally, too, many of Whitman's poems employ the same form as jazz pieces geared for jamming. A poem will often begin with a line stating the theme or subject—the "head," in jazz lingo—and then launch into elliptical development of that theme. Digressions are as welcome as conventional development. Details transcend the plan.

Hersch, who is gay, HIV-positive, and fed up with habitually being described as such, has said that he was drawn to *Leaves of Grass* for the centrality of the moment in Whitman's aesthetic. "It has nothing to do with Whitman being gay and me being gay or any of that shit," he has remarked. "Life is change, and the only thing we have is this moment." (The latter thought does seem connected to the fact of Hersch's living with HIV, as well as to his Buddhist faith.) His *Leaves of Grass* has a spark, a joy taken in its own being, that honors Whitman as it salvages the work from the banality of serving as a monument to him. It makes no effort to be monumental in the grand, symbolic, official, gray-poured-concrete sense. Yet, in its unaffected surety and easy-flowing originality—its fealty to the minute-by-minute impulses of a gifted composer who loves to improvise—it is a magnificent achievement.

Since he was composing an "evening-long" work from a lifelong endeavor, Hersch had to edit mercilessly. He used about 0.5 percent of the text at his disposal, by my own rough math, and his choices are telling. With the exception of the essential "Song of Myself," he passed over Whitman's best-known poems, such as "Lilacs" and "O Captain, My Captain," and he used none of the many poems about the Civil War and New York City (also Hersch's home). There seems no scheme to Hersch's selections other than his personal taste—the most appropriate criterion for doing Whitman justice—and an evident intent to veer the core idea of self toward the universal.

The self that Hersch's setting of *Leaves of Grass* celebrates is a composite of Whitman, Hersch, and a conception of the universal self that Hersch extracts from the text and accentuates through the music and the organization of materials. While Whitman began the first edition of his book with "Song of Myself," the indelible birth cry of the American ego, the first poem in Hersch's setting is "Song of the Universal":

> *Come said the Muse.—*
> *Sing me a song no poet has yet*
> *chanted.*
> *Sing me the universal.*

Hersch repeats the passage four times (Whitman used it once), and he has it sung by Kate McGarry, a versatile singer with a gentle, lilting, reedy voice—the kind we tend to associate with Irish folk songs and their funny stories about rural life and death.

Hersch employs two vocalists, McGarry and the jazz singer Kurt Elling, each to distinct effect. McGarry generally handles the transcendental and agrarian stuff; she is more prominent in the second half of Hersch's work, which grows progressively more intimate and ruminative—it gets freer in mode and calls for more instrumental improvisation. Elling takes care of the robust American self-projection that opened Whitman to charges of ungentlemanly arrogance in his day. (Whitman relished the criticism and asked for more by publishing harsh reviews of his book as appendices to some editions of *Leaves*.) "When you're singing lines like 'I celebrate myself' and 'I sing myself,' you have to own it," Hersch has said. Elling owns it; he has a steely baritone voice and good range, which he stretches to impressive effect through the force of will that infuses most of his singing. In Elling's hands, a great many lyrics communicate self-celebration. Still, much to his credit (and, presumably, Hersch's), Elling taps unexpected resources of grace and subtlety at points in *Leaves of Grass*, such as the segment titled "A Child Said, 'What Is the Grass?'"

Wisely, Hersch does not employ a period idiom; he refers to nineteenth-century music (marches, fanfares, folk tunes) sparingly, with incidental gestures. Hersch's *Leaves of Grass* is contemporary in feeling and wholly in keeping with his past work. Its debts are evident: Brazilian jazz, Monk, the harmonic concepts of both Bill Evans and Herbie Hancock; but the music is distinctively Hersch's—unabashedly passionate, rich as marzipan, and always swaying, sort of dancing to itself. As Whitman does with his poetry, Hersch uses accessible musical language that belies sophisticated, complex ideas. Under the gorgeous melodies McGarry and Elling sing in pieces such as "After the Dazzle of Day" lie puzzle patterns of harmony.

I love this piece of music, though I find it disappointing in one way. The unnerving charm of the early versions of *Leaves of Grass* is their perplexity—the disorder of the poems, their aimless and inexplicable digressions. I would have liked to hear a bit of that Whitman too, to have his brilliant indulgence also translated into jazz. Then again, I can always play a Coltrane record.

Michel Petrucciani

O ne grave away from Chopin and not far from Balzac and Jim Morrison in Pere-Lachaise, the Parisian cemetery and tourist hotspot, lies the French-Italian pianist Michel Petrucciani. He died in January of 1999 in New York, the city where he had made his reputation as a jazz tyro, and when his body was returned to France for his burial, thousands of mourners filled the streets of the 20th arrondissement. One of the French radio channels played no music but his for twenty-four hours. Chirac praised Petrucciani for his "passion, courage, and musical genius" and called him "an example for everyone."

Of what, exactly, was Petrucciani an example? Chirac was no doubt referring to what he described, in proto-Oprahish terms, as Petrucciani's "courage"—the tenacity and the inclination to defiance which seemed, in Petrucciani, triumphs of the mind and the heart over the body. Petrucciani, a musician of rare power and expressive confidence, suffered—truly suffered, in lifelong pain—from osteogenesis imperfecta, the "glass bones" disease. For most of his thirty-six years, Petrucciani could not bear the weight of his own body without leg braces or crutches. He never grew past the height of three feet, and he typically weighed about fifty pounds. He was as fragile as his art was robust, his life as tenuous as his music is durable.

Over the course of 2009, Dreyfus Jazz, the French-American label, issued remastered, repackaged, and in most cases expanded versions of the ten albums that Petrucciani recorded for the label in his last years, as well as a two-DVD set of documentary and concert footage not previously released in this country. The series is an overdue reminder of the ecstatic power of Petrucciani's music. I cannot think of a jazz pianist since Petrucciani who plays with such exuberance and unashamed joy. Marcus Roberts and Michel Camilo have greater technique; Bill Charlap and Eric Reed, better control; Fred Hersch has broader emotional range; Uri Caine is more adventurous. Their music provides a wealth of rewards—but not the simple pleasure of Michel Petrucciani's. With the whole business of jazz so tentative today, you would think more musicians would express some of Petrucciani's happiness to be alive.

The power Petrucciani communicated, as a pianist, was the force of a will, a muscularity of the mind. He admired and emulated Duke Ellington, but had to simulate the effect Ellington and some other strong pianists have achieved by using more of their bodies than their hands. (Ellington, like Randy Weston today, put his lower arm weight into his playing to give it extra heft.) Petrucciani generated power through the speed of his attack. His force was willed; but, in the determined gleefulness of his playing, it never sounded forced.

Giddily free as an improviser, Petrucciani trusted his impulses. If he liked the sound of a note, he would drop a melody suddenly and just repeat that one note dozens of times. His music is enveloping: he lost himself in it, and it feels like a private place where strange things can safely ensue. Today, when so much jazz can sound cold and schematic, Petrucciani's music reminds us of the eloquence of unchecked emotion. "When I play, I play with my heart and my head and my spirit," Petrucciani once explained to an interviewer. "This doesn't have anything to do with how I look. That's how I am. I don't play to people's heads, but to their hearts. I like to create laughter and emotion from people—that's my way of working."

Born in Orange, near Avignon, in 1962, Petrucciani was raised in Monte-limar. A two-lane highway and a rail line run parallel from the north into the village, about half a kilometer apart. In an industrial area beyond the area's residential neighborhoods, a service road lined with a few warehouses and factories feeds both transportation routes. There used to be a small, square, white-washed concrete building between a couple of the warehouses, until it was bull-dozed for commercial expansion. Anne and Tony Petrucciani, a part-time guitarist in the Grant Green mold, reared their three sons there. The bottom half of the structure was a two-car garage with one car, an old two-horsepower Citroen; the family lived above.

Essentially the Texas of France, Montelimar has a people who take fierce pride in their southern identity, distrust those northern elitists, speak with a twangy accent, and revel in the telling of tall tales. "Michel was really into bull-shitting," remembers one of Petrucciani's friends, the French journalist Thierry Peremarti. "Michel would lie to your face. That's one of the reasons he didn't get more press. He pissed off a lot of people. He was from the south—you talk, you talk, and you say nonsense." In 1980, Petrucciani told a *People* magazine reporter that he had raced Harleys with the Hell's Angels and had gone hang-gliding with eggs between his toes.

There are four categories of osteogenesis imperfecta (OI), a family of disorders involving genetic dysfunction in collagen production. The first is Type I, which is so subtle that it frequently goes unrecognized and untreated. Type II is the most severe, usually lethal upon birth; the victims' bones crumble at first touch. Petrucciani was born with a moderately acute kind of OI in a group overlapping Type III and Type IV: his bones were so weak that they fractured more than a hundred times during his childhood. Any kind of movement was difficult and usually painful. Petrucciani could not walk at all until adolescence, when his bones strengthened somewhat (like those of all teenagers, including OI sufferers). He had physical deformities typically associated with OI: distorted facial features, a protruding chin, bulging eyes, and curvature of the spine. In most cases like Petrucciani's, life span is diminished, and in those instances where the patients reach middle age, deafness usually occurs.

"He was in pain all the time," recalled his father. "He cried. I bought him a toy piano." The keyboard looked like a mouth to Michel, and he thought it was laughing at him, so he smashed it with a toy hammer, and his father got him an old full-size upright abandoned by British soldiers at a military base. From the age of four, Michel spent virtually all his free time, which was abundant, at the piano.

Petrucciani was twelve years old and looked like a toddler when his father started carrying him into jam sessions around the south of France. He was thirteen when he made his professional debut at the Cliousclat Festival in the southern district of Drome. "My European promoter told me, 'We got to do a tour with this little cat,'" remembers Clark Terry, the trumpeter. "I didn't believe him. When I heard him play—oh, man! He was a dwarf, but he played like a giant. I said, 'Listen, little guy—don't run away. I'll be back for you.'" Within two years, Petrucciani would be performing regularly in French jazz festivals, first with the expatriate American drummer Kenny Clarke and shortly after that with Terry.

During his first years performing and recording professionally, Petrucciani's specialty was youthful over-compensation. His piano playing, though already tinged with the romantic lyricism that would later distinguish it, tended toward defensive demonstrations of virtuoso technique and speed. Without having yet come to a mature understanding of what he wanted to say, he said little but did so really, really fast. He projected swaggering, roguish macho—a youngster's fantasy conception of continental virility. He called everybody "baby" and wore a yachtsman's cap. "He acted tough and pushy, and his playing was tough and pushy," says the writer and trombonist Michael Zwerin, who was living near Petrucciani and met him when the pianist was fifteen. "He knew how to say 'motherfucker' in French."

A fellow named Jean Roche lived near Zwerin and the Petruccianis, and he had experience with audio recording. (When Olivier Messiaen decided to experiment with bird sounds in his music, it was Roche who hid in trees and recorded the chirping.) Roche came into a bit of money and spent a sizable portion of it building a lavishly equipped recording studio near his home in the rural south. To give himself practice at engineering, Roche offered some nearby jazz musicians free access to the studio. Zwerin, Michel and his brother Louis Petrucciani (a bassist), and the French-Italian drummer Aldo Romano, who was vacationing at his parents' home nearby, spent most of a week there making Michel's first album, aptly titled *Flash*. "It's kind of sloppy and everything needs another take, but it swung, and it certainly shows off Michel well," says Zwerin, who served as titular leader of the sessions.

"We were sitting there wondering what to play," he remembers. "It was kind of hot. And Michel said, 'Anybody know "Giant Steps"?' Neither Louis nor I wanted to admit we didn't really know it. So there was this great silence. And Michel said, 'Well, I do!' And he pounded into a solo version of it at a very fast clip, and it was really amazing. That to me is Michel—'Well, I do!' Man, a confidence you wouldn't believe."

From the moment Petrucciani found he could excel at the piano, I think, what he could *do* overcame what he *was* as his source of identity. *I play jazz piano, baby, and I do it faster and more fancily than anybody. I do, therefore it doesn't matter what I am.*

* * *

Near the end of his life, Petrucciani looked back on his early career and called Aldo Romano his "guardian angel." The drummer, a generation older than Petrucciani, describes himself as Petrucciani's second father and remains proud of having helped Petrucciani pull away from the first one. "He wanted to see the world," recalls Romano. "But Michel was very fragile, and so everybody in his family was afraid. And also you have the problem of his father, because his father was an idiot. He didn't trust anybody. He wanted to keep him as a partner, to play music with. He was very jealous. So I had to fight to take him to Paris, because his father didn't want me to, because he wanted to keep him, like you would cage a monster."

After a brief visit to Paris and a return home in the autumn of 1980, Petrucciani moved into Aldo Romano's house in Bezons on the western perimeter of Paris and began his life as an adult professional. His music took on a new warmth and delicacy, a confidence in place of cockiness, and his grown-up personality—not just an emulation of his gangster heroes, but his own amalgam of southern French wile, musical sensitivity, and the bright, sparkling energy often associated with his genetic condition—began to emerge.

Petrucciani, who was always aware of the limited life span of OI sufferers, worked fast. Through an introduction by Romano, Petrucciani signed a recording contract with Owl Records, a French independent run by Jean-Jacques Pussiau, a former photographer, and he recorded six albums within three years. "He was always in a hurry," recalls Pussiau. "He said, 'Jean-Jacques, I don't want to lose time.'" The albums—especially the last two, *Note 'n Notes* and *Cold Blues* (both recorded in 1984)—are irresistibly precocious records, over-stuffed with ideas. Though most of this music is now difficult to find, there is an easy-to-get compilation of fifteen exemplary tracks, *The Days of Wine and Roses: The Owl Years (1981–1985)*.

"We had an exceptional relationship," Pussiau says, "because I carried Michel in my arms very, very often. That creates a very strange intimacy. You know what it is to hold your child in your arms? I could feel his heart beating against my chest. I used to go on the stage and pick him up, and he was full of sweat. I would carry him away, and his sweat would soak through our shirts and onto my skin. Sometimes, when I used to carry him, he would bite my ear. We'd walk into a restaurant, and he'd *chomp*."

Petrucciani found success easily in France. "We did a tour together (in France), and the first place we played was packed," remembers Lee Konitz, with whom Petrucciani recorded a fine duet album, *Toot Sweet*, in 1982. "I said, 'Oh, man—my time has finally come.' Then I realized this little guy was the big attraction. He had just skyrocketed." The Petrucciani-Konitz duets, reissued here on the Sunnyside label, capture the maturing Petrucciani in a mode of harmonic exploration. That is to say, he is doing his best Bill Evans (especially on the first track, "I Hear a Rhapsody," which Evans himself had done as a duet, with the guitarist Jim Hall).

In 1981, Petrucciani had himself fitted for leg braces and crutches, rendering him independently ambulatory (at short distances) for the first time in his life, and he left for America, breaking away from both his family and Aldo Romano. "He didn't feel free with me," says Romano. "So he had to kill his second father somehow to move on. He needed to escape. He needed to go very far, as far as he could go, and that was California."

Petrucciani may or may not have stopped in Manhattan for a while. Although I have been unable to find anyone who actually saw him in New York this early, musicians have circulated stories that Petrucciani would tell about his first stint in the city. In one, he scammed his way to New York on bad checks, then had to hide out in Brooklyn with the help of Sicilian family connections. In another, he played piano for trade in a midtown brothel, where he learned the secrets of love. (Music-parlor prostitution in 1981? Where were the riverboat gamblers and runaway slaves?)

In Northern California, Petrucciani met his final mentor: Charles Lloyd, the saxophonist and self-styled mystic who had dropped out of the music scene for most of the previous decade. Petrucciani, then eighteen, visited Lloyd, then forty-three, at his house in Big Sur, and they began playing together. Lloyd decided to return to the road, with Petrucciani as his pianist. "Michel was like a son, and I loved him," Lloyd told me. "In his youthful innocence I recognized a quality one does not often find in another human being. Every inch of his small frame was filled with creativity and intelligence." Put another way, "Michel kicked Charles in the ass," says Peremarti. "Michel had something special, and Charles saw that right away. It made him pick up the saxophone."

* * *

Among the things special about Petrucciani was his way with women. He had five major partners, all of whom he called his wives, beginning with Erlina Montaño, a dark beauty, part American Indian, whom he met in Big Sur. While she has not spoken publicly about Michel since the couple's break-up in 1984, Petrucciani's second "wife," Eugenia Morrison (whom he definitely did not marry) and others have enlightening views on Petrucciani's amatory *je ne sais quoi*. "He was beautiful," says Morrison, a pretty, auburn-haired visual artist who lived with Michel for five years, longer than anyone since he left his parents' home. "I think he was the most beautiful person I've ever met."

Is she speaking of an inner beauty? "No—that was there, yes. That was part of it. But he was beautiful to look at. He was beautiful to touch. He had a face like an angel. His eyes shimmered. He was warm.

"It was exciting to be with Michel—*always* exciting. Oh . . . boy! You never knew *what* he was going to do next. He would do anything—he didn't care. When you were with Michel, it was always an incredible time. It was the most fun you could ever have."

Other men near Petrucciani were baffled by his sexual magnetism. "What a Don Juan! I always marveled at that," says Alan Bergman, a New York attorney who represented Petrucciani for many years. "I asked my wife and my daughter, 'Do you see what all of these women see in him?' They said, 'Of course! He's lovely. He has more charm and charisma than anybody.'"

When he first met one woman he fancied—a friend of the ex-wife of Bernard Ivain, Petrucciani's manager in his final years, "He said, 'May I kiss your hand?'" recalls Ivain. "And she said, 'Certainly.' And he said, 'May I kiss your arm?' And she said, 'Yes.' And he said, 'May I have five percent of your heart forever?' And she said, 'Yes, Michel, certainly.' And he said, 'May I take that whole five percent right now, all in one go?' And he jumped on her."

* * *

By late summer, in 1984, Petrucciani was ready for New York, and he left California, Charles Lloyd, and Erlinda Montaño. He gigged around Manhattan for a few months, letting the jazz powers check him out. "He was one of these total natural cats who could just sit and play with anybody, any time, any tune, whatever we were playing," recalls the saxophonist Joe Lovano, who became one of Petrucciani's closest friends in New York. "Michel was the most magical cat I ever knew, man." Blue Note Records snatched him up—the first artist Lundvall signed when he revived the label. "He was a very, very proud signing for us," says Lundvall. "He was the one young artist of that whole era who had the credibility and real originality of the great artists of the past." Almost immediately after meeting Eugenia Morrison in the kitchen of the Village Vanguard, Petrucciani moved in with her.

"Everything came together for Michel quite remarkably when he came to New York," says the artists' manager Mary-Ann Topper, who took Petrucciani on as a client. "I know not only because he told me but because he told many people and it was quite apparent, that was the happiest time of his life."

The first time I saw Michel Petrucciani, a friend of his was carrying him into Bradley's, the tiny piano-jazz club in Greenwich Village where I spent most of my nights and salary in the 1980s. I had grown up in suburban New Jersey with a neighbor my age who had osteogenesis imperfecta. His name was Joey Bascai. His parents pulled him around in a wagon, but he used to like playing baseball. His father would pitch to him carefully, since a wild throw to his chest or head would have been devastating; he could swing the bat and do it well, and the rest of us kids would take turns as his runner. When I saw Petrucciani's friend walk past me with Petrucciani in his arms, I read all my old feelings about playing ball with Joey into his eyes: a vertiginous mixture of exhilaration in being part of the kicky little guy's fun and terror in the knowledge that it could end horribly in an instant. The bar crowd cleared a path from the door to the piano, and Petrucciani screamed, "Get out of my way, motherfuckers!"

Over the next few years, I saw Petrucciani a dozen times at Bradley's and the Village Vanguard. He recorded roughly an album a year for Blue Note, including some gorgeous work with Wayne Shorter and Jim Hall. *Power of Three*, the trio album they recorded live in Montreux in 1986, may well be the most robustly emotive work of jazz recorded in the 1980s. Petrucciani's music had reached full bloom. He was improvising with loving, playful winks at every style from Harlem stride to free jazz, and he was composing tuneful, idiosyncratic pieces indebted but not wholly beholden to Monk and Ellington.

"I've never been around anyone who loved to live like Petrucciani—and live life to the fullest," says Mary-Ann Topper. "He said to me, 'Mary-Ann, I want to have at least five women at once, I want to make a million dollars in one night'—things that were probably impossible. But had Michel ever thought that anything was impossible, he would have never done anything he did." As Petrucciani himself said, "I'm a brat. My philosophy is to have a really good time and never let anything stop me from doing what I want to do. It's like driving a car, waiting for an accident. That's no way to drive a car. If you have an accident, you have an accident—*c'est la vie*." Fond of wine since his early adulthood in Paris, Petrucciani was now widely known to be drinking to excess and said to be enhancing his appetite for alcohol with cocaine. "Michel had a wild streak that was almost self-mutilating," says his last attorney, Alan Bergman.

Lundvall recalls, "I had my son, who was fourteen, and my neighbor and his son—two young kids—and we went backstage to see Michel. Michel said, 'Bruce—you have a one on one [powder narcotic, equal parts cocaine and heroin]?' I said, 'Michel, I don't do that stuff.' Right in front of the kids—he was completely wild. That was Michel. He was really abusing himself a lot."

More sexually active than many people with OI (or without it, for that matter), Petrucciani had five major partners: Erlinda Montaño; Eugenia Morrison; Marie-Laure Roperch, a diminutive young French-Canadian jazz fan he met on the road; Gilda Butta, an accomplished Italian classical pianist whom he married in New York, though the union ended within weeks, and he was soon back with Marie-Laure; and Isabelle Mailé, an adoring Parisian whom he was with at the end. In 1990, Petrucciani and his third "wife," Marie-Laure Roperch, had a son, Alexandre, who inherited the same strain of osteogenesis imperfecta as his father.

In his last years, Petrucciani worked at a manic pace, performing more than a hundred solo piano concerts per year—140 in 1998 alone. Too weak to stand with crutches, he was now using a wheelchair regularly. "He was working too much—not only recording and doing concerts, but he was always on television, and he was always doing interviews," recalls Bernard Ivain, Petrucciani's manager in his final years. "He got himself overworked, and you could see it. He pushed too much." Late in 1998, Petrucciani decided to slow down. "He couldn't keep up that pace anymore—he was physically exhausted," says Francois Zalacain. A few days into the new year, he was admitted to Beth Israel Hospital in New York, and he died there, of a pulmonary infection, on January 6, 1999.

Among the musicians Petrucciani phoned in his last days was Wayne Shorter. "He and I talked, and he said he comprehended that he was sick—that was an important thing," recalls Shorter. "There's a lot of people walking around, full-grown and so-called normal—they have everything that they were born with at the right leg length, arm length and stuff like that. They're symmetrical in every way, but they live their lives like they are armless, legless, brainless, and they live their life with blame. I never heard Michel complain about anything. Michel didn't look in the mirror and complain about what he saw. Michel was a great musician—a great musician—and great, ultimately, because he was a great human being, and he was a great human being because he had the ability to feel and give to others of that feeling, and he gave to others through his music. Anything else you can say about him is a formality. It's a technicality, and it doesn't mean anything to me."

Philip Glass and Leonard Cohen
Book of Longing

s anyone who has ever balanced a salad spinner on his or her nose for
two days could tell you, the secret of getting into The Guinness Book of
World Records is to invent your own category, and the same principle
applies in the arts. Distinctiveness, which is something different from distinction, tends to lead to recognition. Accordingly, we have among the most celebrated composers of the past four decades Philip Glass, who plays the
electronic keyboard but whose virtuosity really lies in the creative disassem-
bling and re-assembling of category. Educated in the Western concert tradition at Juilliard, he first attracted attention by playing unconventional,
Eastern-sounding music on amplified instruments in art galleries, and he has
gone on to produce hundreds of genre-defying pieces of work—operas without drama; symphonies based on the themes of rock albums; foreground-steal-
ing background scores for horror movies, documentaries, Woody Allen
pictures, and other films; collaborations with Nobel laureates and pop singers.

Glass is the rock audience's conception of a classical artist and the classical audience's conception of a rock star. He is America's idea of an open-eared "world" composer and the rest of the world's idea of an American musical rebel.

In 2007, Glass had his seventieth birthday and paid only nominal attention to the occasion, at least publicly. There was no major retrospective like the city-wide celebration of Glass's tribesman Steve Reich that dominated the New York concert scene when Reich turned seventy in 2006. Glass toured the country and a few spots in Europe with his ensemble, performing a concert called *Book of Longing*, and he dismissed the birthday amiably when he was asked about it in interviews. "I'm not a great worshiper of the past," he told *The Guardian*. "Even this year I've been too busy to look back, although people seem to want me to."

Near the end of his birthday year, though, Glass released a CD of *Book of Longing*. It is a collection of vocal settings of verse by Leonard Cohen, and, in both its words and its music, it looks forward, as well as back and around, in yearning laced with strains of self-absorption, dissipation, and aimlessness. A collaboration between kindred souls—two arty, carnal, aging Jewish-born Buddhists—the album would be a fitting valedictory for either Glass or Cohen.

As an artist, Cohen has always been more conventional, less prolific, and much more affecting than Glass. A published novelist and poet of moderate note before he took up songwriting in the mid-1960s, Cohen had coveted status as a real writer at a time when musicians such as Bob Dylan (though not only Dylan) and an emerging class of rock critics were beginning to think of popular song lyrics as literature. Cohen could barely play the guitar; he constructed his long, elliptical, lyrical, wordy songs with simple folkish chord patterns; and he could not sing at all—he delivered his songs in a kind of atonal parlando. These musical limitations acted to reinforce Cohen's authenticity as a poet; they gave his music a masculine fragility; and they foreshadowed, even more than Dylan's ragged early work, the brooding anti-professionalism of later bedroom-studio artists such as Conor Oberst and Robert Pollard, who have zealous followings today. Like Glass, Cohen has always had the cachet of someone functioning outside the parameters of musical category. He is the pop world's idea of a literary figure and the literary world's idea of a pop songwriter.

Glass worked with Cohen's words for the first time in 1984, when he set Cohen's elegy to a departed friend, "There Are Some Men," to an angular melody for a cappella chorus. One of three choral pieces Glass composed for a concert to celebrate the 450th anniversary of Quebec, Cohen's birthplace, "There Are Some Men" appears on a CD of Glass's early vocal music, *Songs From Liquid Days*, which, in addition to the choral work, includes settings of lyrics by the pop and art-rock songwriters Laurie Anderson, David Byrne, Paul Simon, and Suzanne Vega—the Rat Pack of BAM. A precursor to the Glass-Cohen *Book of Longing*, the *Liquid Days* album is not the coming together of pop and avant-garde sensibilities that one might expect, but a testament to the composer's force of personality, ego, and will. Each of the quasi-melodic, droning pieces sounds much like the other, and the songs come together only as a statement of indifference to the creative personalities of Glass's ostensible partners.

Looking back on the work that he has done with various lyricists, stage directors, film-makers, and choreographers over the years, Glass has said he sees collaboration as the "engine" that has advanced his music. But what sort of advance is it that occurs through creative domination and the subsumption of others' artistic identities to one's own? This is the campaigning of a cultural imperialist. Its point is not the free trade of ideas, but creative conquest.

Glass says that he wanted for years to compose more music to Cohen's verse but had to wait while Cohen pursued a spiritual quest at the Buddhist monastery on Mount Baldy in southern California. Cohen spent five years, beginning in 1994, in retreat; ordained as a Rinzai Zen Buddhist monk, he took the name Jikan (Sanskrit for silent one) and served as an assistant to the teacher Kyozan Joshu Sasaki Roshi, cleaning and cooking meals and, in his abundant solitude, writing more verse and drawing pictures. This period has enhanced Cohen's mystique in recent years—in part, I suppose, because Cohen not only abandoned worldly life but in time abandoned that abandonment and returned to us as a resuscitated hipster with a jaunty cap drooped over one eye. Cohen's biography provides a long drop-down menu of cool images, from underappreciated poet and novelist to mystic and lustful old uncle.

Late in 2005, at the composer's request, Cohen gave Glass the unpublished manuscript to a collection of 167 poems and song lyrics—many of which dealt with Cohen's experience on Mount Baldy and his return to secular life. In "Roshi at 89," for instance, Cohen writes wittily about his teacher:

> *He's sitting in the throne-room*
> *on his great Original Face*
> *and he's making war on Nothing*
> *that has Something in its place*
> *His stomach's very happy*
> *The prunes are working well*
> *There's no one going to Heaven*
> *and there's no one left in Hell*

Like much of Cohen's writing, this is better sung, even talk-sung, than read. *Book of Longing*, which was published in 2006, also includes dozens of pen-and-ink drawings by Cohen, the bulk of them grotesquely unflattering self-portraits or sexy female nudes. As Cohen later explained, he drew what interests him.

Cohen was thrilled by Glass's attention. "It's like Bach asking if he can use your lyrics," he told a reporter for the Montreal *Gazette*. "It's his seventieth birthday, and he's just a kid with a crazy dream." What Glass proposed was a multimedia song-cycle performance piece derived from Cohen's verse and drawings, a dream planted by Glass's muse in consultation with a consortium of institutional funders whose needs clearly played a considerable role in shaping the work. As the credits in the booklet to the CD of *Book of Longing* note, the production was commissioned by the Luminato Festival of Arts and Creativity, the Adelaide Bank Festival of Arts, the Lincoln Center Festival 2007, the University of Texas at Austin Performing Arts Center with support from the Topfer Endowment for the Performing Arts, and several other such institutions. Festivals and their like, after all, are in the business of festivities—events, not mere artworks, produced to elevate the populace, bring together artists from a range of spheres, impress everybody, boost tourism, and demonstrate the capacity of the arts to justify big donations.

In its stage incarnation, which toured the eight commissioning festivals in 2007, *Book of Longing* featured Glass, his ensemble expanded by a few instruments (including two string players), four vocalists (on the CD, soprano Dominique Plaisant, mezzo-soprano Tara Hugo, tenor Will Erat, and bass-baritone Daniel Keeling), and the voice of Leonard Cohen (speaking text on recordings), as well as Cohen's drawings, which were projected on screen as visual counterpoint to the piece's twenty-two songs, instrumental interludes, and brief spoken-language sections. The two-disc CD set presents the selections in the sequence in which they were performed, in rough clusters of five or six pieces of various types: one love song, one ballad, one autobiographical, one spiritual, one comic, perhaps a spoken thing. There is no narrative line, just a notion to mix things up, although that idea is novel enough in Glass's work, much of which treats music as a static presence, essentially shapeless and uniform in texture.

Many of the sets of verse that Glass chose from Cohen's book sound as if they had been conceived as lyrics, and two sets were in fact words to songs co-written by Cohen and Sharon Robinson for *Ten New Songs*, the solo album Cohen released in 2001, two years after he left the monastery. Glass's hubris and Cohen's acquiescence in Glass's enterprise were such that both men were willing to forget about Cohen and Robinson's nicely wrought and appealing songs. To listen to the Cohen-Robinson songs and then hear what Glass did with the same words is to be dumbstruck by the coldness of Glass's music. The Cohen-Robinson song "A Thousand Kisses Deep" is a wafting R&B lament—hypnotic, though diminished a bit by the recording's Euro-pop synths and cheesy programmed drums (performed by Robinson, who played most of the instruments on the album and sang along with Cohen on most tracks). The Glass setting of the same lyrics, "You Came to Me This Morning," is rigid and strident when it should be lyrical; the chords jerk about awkwardly, and the melody follows, too closely, in kind. At more than ten minutes in length, the song, like much of Glass's music, seems endless—a thousand kisses long, but skin deep.

The Cohen-Robinson "Boogie Street," a highlight of *Ten New Songs*, shuffles and sways like the boogie number it is supposed to be. Robinson's drum machine clicks out an irresistible groove, and Cohen croons the catchy tune with a wink. The Glass version, "A Sip of Wine," is ponderous and grim, despite the fact that Glass's melody traces the broad contours of Robinson's tune; and the singer, Tara Hugo, pronounces "boogie" with the same discomfort that Gary Cooper displayed when, as a haughty professor who hires a showgirl to help him learn slang, he has to utter the same word in the movie *Ball of Fire*, made in 1941.

It is to Glass's credit that *Book of Longing* is a work short on the idiosyncratic musical devices that Glass has employed to excess throughout his career. The seemingly endless repetition, the incessant chugga-chugga-chugga rhythms, the busy arpeggio figures common to the vast majority of his compositions, no matter their genres, occur in these song settings but do not overwhelm them. Still, the music is unmistakably Glass's. As usual, Glass works with a fairly small palette of musical materials—minor keys, for the most part, simple chord patterns, predictable melodies that tend to follow the roots of those chords like connect-the-dot lines, and spare arrangements geared to his ensemble of long-time compatriots. The songs in *Book of Longing* are, without notable exception, elemental and fairly conventional.

Those are not, in themselves, failings. There are larger problems with this music, and they are the enduring vexations of Philip Glass's work: its glibness, its mechanical character, its seeming arbitrariness. The music is, on the whole, frigid. It does not evoke or stir much feeling, and this is a failure close to sin in work connected to Leonard Cohen. In his writing, Cohen is often cryptic—indirection and irresolution are important parts of what poets do—but he is elementally concerned with feeling. "I'm angry with the angel/Who pinched me on the thigh/And made me fall in love/With every woman passing by," he writes in "This Morning I Woke Up Again." And "I loved you when you opened/Like a lily to the heat/I'm just another snowman/Standing in the rain and sleet," he writes in "You Came to Me This Morning."

The singers Glass employs on *Book of Longing* scarcely help. Glass composed the melodies to fall in the lower parts of each singer's register, an approach sometimes used to discourage concert artists from over-singing. Yet the four here all over-sing, articulating the lyrics with a formality and a theatricality wholly inappropriate to Cohen's casual, intimate language. The effect is comical, sadly—in the same way that Steve Allen used to get cheap laughs by standing at a podium and reciting rock-song lyrics in stentorial tones.

In multiple ways, then, *Book of Longing* yearns in vain. "When I was a young boy, I worked in my father's store, where he sold records," Glass recently told *The Guardian*. "I listened to a lot of music and liked nearly all of it. People forgot to tell me that some stuff was better than others." Musical egalitarianism is one thing, indiscrimination another; and someone seems to have forgotten to tell Philip Glass the difference.

Jules Feiffer at the *Village Voice*

A dot-eyed, L-nosed little boy, unmistakably the handiwork of Jules Feiffer, stands in the top left corner of a *Village Voice* cartoon published in March 1965, nine years into Feiffer's forty-one-year run with the paper. In a sequence of six meticulous doodles, the kid grows from childhood to early middle age: A couple of pen strokes provide him with rolled-up jeans, and he is a teenager; a dash of ink puts a cigarette between his fingers, and he is an adult; two vertical lines crease his pants, and he is a young businessman; the outline of his torso squiggles out at the belly, and he looks about the age his creator was at the time, thirty-six. Regular readers would have recognized the fellow in the drawings as one of a small handful of recurring characters in Feiffer's weekly comic strip—a congenitally perplexed, self-obsessed New Yorker who Feiffer named Bernard Mergendeiler and who many people understood to be a stand-in for Feiffer. In a monologue hand-lettered in block capitals, vintage comic-strip style, each of the incarnations of Mergendeiler discusses a different stage in his intellectual development. "When I was little, I listened to radio serials, read comic books, and went to 'B' movies," the boy says.

"When I got a little older, I listened to big band swing, read slick magazines, and went to 'A' movies," the teenager continues.

"When I got even older I listened to FM stereo, read literary quarterlies, and went to foreign movies," the adult goes on. "And then the pop-culture movement began. Now I listen to old radio serials, read comics books, and go to revivals of 'B' movies.

"In a society without standards," says the mature Mergendeiler at the end of the cartoon, "who needs to grow up?"

It is a gleefully contradictory cartoon, and it speaks cogently of Feiffer's complicated relationship with mainstream American popular culture. Of course, all the relationships in Jules Feiffer cartoons are complicated—those of the young singles more interested in courtship fads than in each other, those of the middle-aged marrieds leading separate lives, those of the marketers and the consumers who the marketers court like lovers, those of the politicians and the citizenry who the politicians exploit like a market, and, above all, those of the people of all sorts and their distant, elusive inner selves. Feiffer, in the *Village Voice* cartoons that remain high points of his long and many-sided career, employed a pop-culture form associated with juvenilia, the comic strip, to confront the adult world in literate, sophisticated terms. In a society with low expectations for the art of his choosing, Feiffer set his own standards and helped make comics grow up, whether they needed to or not.

The craze for pop-culture artifacts of the pre-war era, having taken place in the Sixties, was mistaken for a movement. It was elementally ironic, of course— an assault, by means of wryly affectionate diminishment, enacted by the indulgent youth of the postwar generation upon the youthful indulgences of their parents. As such, it really had nothing to do with Feiffer and his cartoons. Feiffer's affection for comics was unironic, as was the work he did in the comics' medium. In an article he wrote for the *Los Angeles Times* in 1966, Feiffer contrasted his literary idols with those of Alfred Kazin; while Kazin had been influenced by writers such as Blake, Lawrence, Emerson, and Whitman, Feiffer explained, his own models were the writer Jerry Siegel (who, with his high-school friend, the artist Joe Schuster, invented Superman) and three comics artist-writers: Bob Kane (who created Batman), Jack Cole (Plastic Man), and Will Eisner (The Spirit). All four of the writers Feiffer cited had worked in the genre of costumed heroes, and Feiffer, who read their stories as a poor Jewish kid in the Bronx during the late Depression years, found solace in their blunt, fantastical but elementary tales of misunderstood outsiders bestowed with secret powers (intellectual, physical, or metaphysical). "Superman, Batman, and the rest, in my day, were anti-angst, anti-Beckett, anti-Albee," Feiffer explained. "No soul-eroding analysis for super-heroes—their solutions were drastically simple: a quick shot in the mouth on behalf of the underprivileged." At its heart, the work Feiffer did for the *Village Voice* would almost always be loyal to the early comics' ethic of moral clarity and unpretentiousness. Yet, in its growing urbanity and deepening intellectualism, Feiffer's work came to represent that ethic's necessary betrayal.

*　*　*

Feiffer got his professional start, straight from James Monroe High School at age seventeen, working as a studio assistant to Eisner. Feiffer erased pencil lines, ran errands, and ghost-wrote stories for Eisner's *Spirit* comic book, which was distributed around the country as a Sunday newspaper supplement and, accordingly, reached a fair number of adults as well as kids. Feiffer's reward for nearly three years of anonymous service to one of his idols was a one-page strip published under Feiffer's own name on the back page of the *Spirit* supplement: *Clifford*. Named for its main character, a sharp-eyed city boy around six or seven years old, *Clifford* joined what was, in 1949, already a half-century-long tradition of comic strips centered on the cutely naughty antics of kids more savvy, more reasonable, and far more alive than the adults who mistakenly thought they were in charge of things. Like the Yellow Kid, the odd little roughneck from the turn of the last century who almost single-handedly established the comic strip as a popular phenomenon, Clifford was dubious of authority in all its forms, and his juvenile transgressions—skipping school, making too much noise in the museum—were most often protests or acts of retaliation for the inequities and the rigidity of the society grown-ups oversaw. Like Skippy, the young protagonist of Percy Crosby's wildly popular strip of the prewar years, Clifford was clearly the best informed and most rational person of any age in his neighborhood, despite his utter indifference to school or books without drawings and word balloons. All these kids were essentially superheroes without superpowers—underestimated outsiders who had unorthodox ways of overcoming injustice.

Feiffer had to drop Clifford in 1951, when he was drafted. In interviews since then, he has described his two years in the army as a decisive encounter with a kind of institutional authority considerably more severe than that of Clifford's elementary school. "What changed my life and my career was getting drafted in my early twenties," he told a reporter in 1989. "I found it such a rude awakening—the sense of being thrown into a mindless, dictatorial system . . . whose whole aim was reducing the individual to a cipher. My battle against that set me up for what I was looking to do for the rest of my life."

Not long after his induction and appointment to the Signal Corps, Feiffer began, in his spare time, to work on an unusual (though not unprecedented) project—a book-length work that would look and read much like a story for children but would deal with themes more suitable for their parents. The clear antecedent for what Feiffer set out to do was *The Bear That Wasn't*, a fable of dehumanization in the sphere of industrial manufacturing written and drawn by Frank Tashlin, the genre-blind writer, artist, and filmmaker who directed Looney Tunes shorts salted with lusty innuendo ("Porky at the Crocedero," "Cinderella Goes to a Party") as well as live-action features peppered with loony sight gags ("The Girl Can't Help It," "Will Success Spoil Rock Hunter?"). Published in 1946, *The Bear That Wasn't* tells of a giant grizzly who wakes up from hibernation to find a factory constructed where the forest used to be. He is put to work, and no one—not the foreman, not one of the vice presidents, not the president—will believe he is a bear.

In Feiffer's story, *Munro*, a four-year-old boy—drawn in a casual, scratchy style, he could be a sketch-pad rough of Clifford—is inexplicably drafted into the Army and bused off to the soldier factory of boot camp. "So with a bar of soap, chocolate cigarettes and a toothbrush, Munro went to war," we learn in hand-lettered text, the language of which echoes the rock-a-bye cadences of a bedtime story. No one the tiny private meets—not the sergeant, not the camp psychiatrist, not the chaplain, not the colonel—will believe he is a boy. With *Munro*, Feiffer started to crystallize the anti-authoritarian strain that had subtly infused *Clifford*, while neatly mixing the formal elements of picture books with the content of adult conversation. He was inching away from the sphere of Siegel, Kane, Cole, and Eisner, into the realm of William Steig, Saul Steinberg, and the *New Yorker* cartoonists.

When every publisher he approached passed on *Munro*, Feiffer decided that poor branding was his problem, and he hatched a plan to get cartoons published in the *Village Voice*, then just a year old, for the value of association with a paper that had been fast to earn a reputation as a hostel of outré chic. "It was clear that once I could get in publications [that book editors] would recognize, they'd recognize me," Feiffer recalled in an interview conducted this year. "I saw on all their desks copies of the *Village Voice*, so I figured if I could be in that paper, then they might confuse me with Steinberg, Steig, or Thurber and publish me." Working for free, a rate favored by alternative media, then as now, Feiffer began in October 1956 to contribute a weekly comic strip to the *Voice*. Its original title (changed to "Feiffer" after its artist's strategy had proven successful at branding his name) was "Sick, Sick, Sick"—an allusion to the mania for the psychoanalysis that Feiffer saw as soul-eroding, in a era when hipsters who read the *Village Voice* considered something "crazy" if it was madly cool. (In the first Feiffer cartoon for the *Voice*, a man suffering a stomach ache from anxiety so irritates two strangers at a bus stop that all three end up buckled over in pain: sick, sick, and sick.)

After just a few weeks of experimentation with various graphic styles, formats, and approaches to humor—one strip would suggest Steig; another, Harvey Kurtzman, the artist and writer who had started *Mad* magazine; the next, the French-Hungarian painter and cartoonist Andre Francois; the next, Gene Deitch, an illustrator of kooky jazz record jackets—Feiffer found his cartoon voice in the *Voice*. In only the first several entries did Feiffer bother with the comic-strip conventions of word balloons for dialogue and panels (the boxes that isolate the individual moments in a strip, like the frames in a movie storyboard). By the fifth entry, published on November 11, 1956, "Sick, Sick, Sick" was all Feiffer. The strip for that week has a single character, a painter drawn in short-hand scrawls: he is wearing a white frock and a beret and a mustache, and he has a few brushes in his right hand and a palette in the left; he has a gigantic nose, like all men in French cartoons and all caricatures of the French, and his lips are pursed in a broad frown, as if he were thinking in Existential clichés. To his left is an easel. One player, one prop, no background. We see the character in full body, and our visual perspective never changes in eight drawings. The mode is theatrical, rather than cinematic in the manner of most serious comic strips of the time (which aspired, in genre-envy, to feel like movies), and its small-scale, economical theatricality is specifically that of college theater or Off-Off-Broadway. Feiffer figured out quickly how to give his *Voice* cartoons a feeling of the scrappy artiness always associated with Greenwich Village.

With that fifth strip, Feiffer established the format he would employ, with minor variations, for four decades. A one-scene play would unfold in two rows of images that would take about a minute or two to read. The painter in that early cartoon, like a great many of Feiffer's characters, faces the reader directly and does a monologue. "I'm an artist," he tells us. "But it's not really what I want to do." (He wants to be a shoe salesman, we learn.) Through his characters, Feiffer did first-person cartooning, foreshadowing not only the confessional underground comics of the late Sixties and early Seventies, but also the deeply subjective, sometimes solipsistic graphic novels popular today. Feiffer helped personalize the funny pages, abandoning the superhero for the superego.

Issues of identity would be central to countless Feiffer strips published after the tale of the shoe salesman trapped in a painter's body. Absorbed with the theme of self and also with the theme of self-absorption, Feiffer saw tyranny in the much-bemoaned conformity of the Fifties as well as in the less-examined exaltation of the individual. His cartoons are populated in roughly equal proportions by Babbitts dizzy from racing in lock-step and free-thinkers drunken with self-importance. "In between being silent, conforming, belonging, acquiring and taking care of my leisure problem, I haven't yet had a chance to seek status," says a sulking man in a gray flannel suit. "I guess I'll fit in somehow."

Created as topical commentary, one strip replaced by another one more timely, week after week, Feiffer's comics hold up oddly well decades after they were initially published. Fantagraphics, the Seattle-based publisher of neatly organized collections of vintage material by comics masters, has made a long-term project of packaging Feiffer's complete works, and the first several books, including one of a prospective three-volume series of *Complete Village Voice Strips*, are now in print. The *Voice* comics stand out among these publications as Feiffer's signal achievement. Bolder and more original than Feiffer's perfectly fine plays and screenplays (*Little Murders*, *Carnal Knowledge*), more ambitious than his sweet children's books (*The Man in the Ceiling*, *I Lost My Bear*), and wholly better wrought than his patchy novel, *Ackroyd*, Feiffer's *Voice* work is a sanctum of unapologetic intelligence and sophistication rare in American popular culture and rarer still in comic strips.

In their concern with the preoccupations of the late 1950s and '60s—conformity, psychoanalysis, the Bomb, Madison Avenue, premarital sex—the cartoons collected in the first volume of *Complete Village Voice Strips* can seem dated fifty years later, though hardly as much as a collection of Yellow Kid strips from 1908 would have seemed dated in 1958. A man in a grey flannel suit leans on a stool, puffing a smoke as he does a monologue about Castro: "Quite frankly, we may as well recognize that Americans don't *dig* revolutions anymore. After all, we've had ours! Why vulgarize it? I mean, look what's happened to Cadillacs." Did anyone ever really *talk* like that? Perhaps not exactly, though a lot of people *sounded* like that, and Feiffer's ear was attuned to the strange dialects of social and political discourse. What salvages Feiffer from irrelevance as a Cold War curio—the Mort Sahl of cartooning—is the political ambiguity and the poetic irresolution of so much of his work. "I never thought of myself as a liberal," he once explained. "I thought of myself more as a kind of unaffiliated radical."

Feiffer's *Voice* cartoons were first collected under hard covers in spring, 1958, less than two years after he started drawing them, and the book (titled *Sick, Sick, Sick*) was a sensational success, especially on college campuses. The *New York Times*, early in 1959, reported sales of more than 95,000 copies, ongoing "in the nature of a gallop" at a rate of some two thousand copies per week. In an attempt to come to terms with Feiffer's appeal, Julius Novick wrote, in *Harper's*, "All over America, men and women, and especially boys and girls, are dying to be cultured, sophisticated, high in brow . . . These are citizens of the greater Greenwich Village of the spirit; Feiffer is their unsparing but sympathetic chronicler, and sometimes also their spokesman."

College crazes come and go, of course, and the fad for culture high in brow soon went, taking with it the terms by which Jules Feiffer could be considered cool in the social economy of youth. When I moved to the Village in the early

Seventies, to attend NYU, I thought of myself as a cartoon buff. I sought out the *East Village Other*, because Robert Crumb and other underground artists drew for it, but I found Feiffer's *Voice* comics off-putting. They were elegant, rather than raw; they were subtle and often cryptic, rather than brash; they were urbane, rather than urban in the going conception of the term; and they were smart, rather than self-consciously, ironically naive. I was not alone among comics' enthusiasts of the underground generation to ignore Feiffer, but I was missing a great deal.

It is more than ten years now since the management of the *Village Voice* squeezed Feiffer out, using his salary as an excuse. He had been earning $75,000 a year, and the *Voice* told him the paper was going to cut him from the payroll and buy his strip from its syndicator for $200 an installment. Feiffer quit and pulled the cartoon from the *Voice*, but continued doing it for syndication to other papers until 2000, when he announced that he "got tired of" it and decided to concentrate on writing children's books. In his final series of comics for syndication, Feiffer featured the modern dancer in black tights who had become his signature character. As she arched and bounded around the frame, she mused about Feiffer's reasons for ending the strip (and with it, her life). She asked Feiffer if he was doing it "because no one of your generation knows you're around anymore, and young people have never heard of you?"

A Feiffer caricature of Feiffer himself appears, alongside the dancer, in top hat and tails. "This is my last strip, and now I'm dancing," he announces.

"Get out of my space," she replies. "I made you, you jerk! If I hadn't started dancing to spring in 1957, you'd still be writing scripts for Will Eisner."

The final image is one of Feiffer, tipping his hat to the reader. "Wait for my big finish!" he says. "You'll be dazzled!" It was a curious, taunting, unnecessarily defensive closing statement from an artist unique for his willingness to let characters stand still, stare straight ahead, and talk. Jules Feiffer's legacy as a comics artist is that he succeeded not in dazzling, but in engaging us.

John Zorn

Tonic, an ascetic little hostel for outre music and arty noise in the longtime cultural center of outre artiness, Manhattan's Lower East Side, closed down in April 2007 after nine years of hot-and-cold business—a casualty of engulfing gentrification and bureaucratic harassment, according to the club's owners. For their last night on Norfolk Street, they arranged to go out as grandly as possible and booked John Zorn, the fifty-three-year-old godhead of the downtown musical scene, to lead two sets of performances by an ad hoc assemblage of musicians in his sphere. The line for admission started forming more than three hours before showtime, and it stretched along two blocks before the doors opened. The evening was chilly and wet. I counted three open umbrellas, including my own.

A film crew was interviewing people on line, and one of the men in a group ahead of me waved down the camera operator. "If half these bullshit parasites came down here before this place closed," he told the film-maker, "it wouldn't have to close!" As the crew moved down the sidewalk, the piqued guy asked me if I had a cigarette, and I asked him to tell me about some of his favorite Tonic shows. He said this was only his second time at the club, although he loves John Zorn and had seen him play elsewhere.

About ten minutes before the first set was scheduled to start, Zorn came striding down the street, parallel to the queue, just a few feet from the people, glaring straight ahead. He was carrying his alto saxophone in a case and wearing baggy desert-camouflage pants and an orange T-shirt—the same clothes (or precisely matching ones) that he had worn each of the last three times I had seen him perform this year, once earlier at Tonic and twice at The Stone, the tiny storefront performance space that Zorn himself owns and operates on Avenue C. As he sped past, fans burst into a chant of "Zorn! Zorn!" He glowered in silence, and when the camera pointed at him he shook his head, declining the attention. I could only wonder what the shouting fans and the film crew had in mind. Why would they think that someone who makes a point regularly to appear dressed in camouflage and an orange T-shirt would want attention?

In the music he put together that night, Zorn made a bookend to the concerts that he had organized for Tonic shortly after the club opened in 1998, events that had helped considerably to establish Tonic's credibility as a bohemian refuge. On both occasions, Zorn served in part as a creative shepherd—selecting, organizing, and hosting the performers—and also as the special guest star of his own show, sort of a recherche hydra of Ed Sullivan and the Beatles. On the last night at Tonic, the musicians drifted in and out of the club and all around the bandstand, and their playing styles varied—more than two dozen artists performed in various configurations into the early hours of the morning—though they were connected in their common passion for free improvisation, their take-it-or-leave-it attitude toward conventional Western tonality, and their conception of noise as music.

None of this thinking has been new or radical in the domains of classical music, jazz, or hardcore rock and punk for years. But neither have the ideals of free improvisation, atonality, or noise-as-music poured out of the rarefied waters of art music into the mainstream to join the standards of value applied on *American Idol*. Indeed, the unifying principle of much of the work performed at Tonic from its opening shows to its closing ones, as with a great deal of music at other new-music venues such as the Knitting Factory and The Stone, is not really its ostensible newness or radicalism, but rather its unacceptability in popular culture. Though commonly regarded as insular and self-referential, the world of John Zorn and his peers and followers is integrally engaged with the mainstream, in that it defines itself by its conscientious alienation from it. The music is all about status.

Zorn appeared onstage after about half an hour of performances by four small groups, one of which featured the delightful pianist Sylvie Courvoisier, who produced a spirited rhythmic sound collage by rapping and strumming every part of the inside of the instrument. One of the drummers used a violin bow to play the steel rim of his snare drum. A percussionist thwacked on a Jew's harp and yammered loopy gibberish while his partner did a slow, rudimentary tap dance. It was all resolutely *different*. And yet it was all nearly identical to the neo-Dada happenings of the Warhol era—the 1960s again, but without the ameliorating benefit of the drugs.

Performing in a trio with piano and drums, Zorn played an improvisation of sound graffiti sprayed in bursts and flurrying splashes of accelerating propulsion. He began with a series of short modal phrases, but quickly abandoned modality and, in little time, dropped tonality altogether, screeching and cronking. Early in his career, Zorn began to develop an expansive vocabulary of extramusical sounds that he could produce with precision on the alto saxophone, often by using only the mouthpiece of the instrument, sometimes by playing the mouthpiece through a bowl of water. For a few years, he tried to devise a system to identify all the noises he could make and to notate them with hieroglyphic-like symbols, an effort along the lines of his idol Harry Partch's attempts to invent new scales and notational methods to accommodate the odd tones, microtones, and quasi-tones that emanated from the instruments that he constructed out of old light bulbs, empty liquor bottles, and driftwood. To the uninitiated, the sounds that Zorn produces may sometimes seem like assaultive noise blurted out arbitrarily. In fact, they are assaultive noise crafted with meticulous care. For this piece, Zorn employed the entire saxophone, though he blew into it so hard that the instrument rattled in his hands and appeared about to fly apart.

After the first set, Zorn spoke briefly—very briefly—to a small group of fans and a couple of journalists assembled near the door to the club's office. "The yuppies are taking over," he warned us in a vatic hush. "We're all fucked." He lowered his head and hurried away, presumably to prepare for the second set.

The last night at Tonic presented John Zorn—a guarded man protective of his public image—as he likes to be seen: a martyrly champion of a noble and doomed cause, a victim of institutional indifference and maltreatment. He revels in his vaunted status as an outsider and a cultural insurgent; hence the meticulous screeching and cronking, as well as the guerrilla's pants. For years, before he switched to the orange T-shirt, he performed in one printed with the phrase "Die Yuppie Scum." In the few interviews he has given, Zorn has been quick to articulate his hero worship for artistic dissidents and outcasts such as Partch, Charles Ives, Joseph Cornell, and Harry Smith—his determination to follow their example, and his fear of oppression by giant, faceless institutions. "I think the outsiders, the individualists, the people who have a messianic belief in themselves and are able to stick with their vision despite all odds . . . the people that can stick with that, they're the ones that are really going to make a difference in the world," he said in an interview with the magazine *JazzTimes*. "And they will always be a small number, and I've always aspired to be one of that number." And this: "I see enormous corporations acting like slave masters, like the return of the pharaohs. I see co-opting all around. I see McDonald's everywhere. I see the destruction of . . . the small mom and pop stores. . . . That is the big problem—the pharaohs controlling us. Sure, there will be independent artists, always. But they'll always be on the fringe."

Apart from the vainglory of such messiah talk, there is a sizable problem with Zorn's ongoing self-projection as a repressed, misunderstood, and underappreciated musical outcast. It is the fact that he is now a well-established and celebrated figure, a composer recognized not only in the downtown institutions in which he has always thrived, and in the sibling bodies that he has founded and run for the advancement of his own work and that of his kindred souls and proteges, such as The Stone and his record company Tzadik, but in major cultural institutions as well. The pharaohs of the arts establishment have bestowed honor and riches upon him. In 2006, he won a MacArthur "genius" grant ($500,000), and, in March of the following year, he received the William Schuman Award from the Columbia University School of the Arts, one of the largest grants given to an American musician ($50,000). The latter is given for lifetime achievement, and has gone previously to composers such as Milton Babbitt, Gunther Schuller, and Steve Reich.

But the achievements of Zorn's lifetime so far are a mixed lot—all of them extraordinary in one way or another, some indisputably significant, others dubious. He is certainly important and may well turn out to be historic as a symbol of musical adventurism and an inspiration to other composers—like Eric Satie, an enigmatic provocateur with an outsize mystique who stirred acolytes to do work better than his own. Over the decades since Zorn emerged as a model of the free-spirited genre-bending associated with downtown Manhattan, he has drawn countless musicians and composers into his orbit, and he has recorded or performed with dozens of them, including some fine ones, among them the composer and trumpeter Dave Douglas, the guitarist Bill Frisell, the pianists Anthony Coleman and Wayne Horvitz, the cellist Erik Friedlander, and the drummer Joey Baron.

Zorn is an exceptional artist, without question, because he prizes and seeks exceptionalism above all. This is not to say that he is exceptionally good at his art. What he is good at—so very good as to suggest a kind of genius—is being exceptional. Unfortunately, uniqueness is not an aesthetic value; it is a term of classification. To say that Zorn is one of a kind, as he certainly is, is to ignore the larger matters of his nature as an artist and, more significantly, the nature of his work, much of which is thin and gimmicky, and some of which is elementally corrupt.

Through his fiercely individualistic modes of working, Zorn deters attention to the work itself. He is obsessed with processes and systems, and he is often cavalier about their results. In the small-ensemble performances and albums that first brought him attention, Zorn led improvising musicians in what he called "game" pieces. Zorn did not compose them, exactly, but was responsible for them in that he invented and supervised the unprecedented system of rules for their spontaneous invention by the performers. He devised a set of signal cards, each of which indicated, in code, when certain musicians should play: now, the brass instruments; now, drums and guitar; now, the person to the left of the last person who played; now, nobody. . . . Further upending the standard notions of compositional authority or prerogative, Zorn left it to the musicians to call for the cards to be changed. His role was to stand in front of the group, hold up the cards, and switch them at the players' demand. The meaning of these cards changed as he added body-language cues, such as how high he held the sign and whether or not he was wearing a baseball cap at the moment.

The byzantine rules—to which the audience was never privy—were the art-work, such as it was. As Zorn explained, "What I came up with was this kind of game structure that talks about when people play and when they don't play but doesn't talk about what they do at all." Not *what*, but *when*: the content, the music itself, scarcely mattered to Zorn, who was concerned mainly with the novelty of its system of generation, a scheme not devised in service to the expression of human feelings, but brazenly indifferent, if not hostile, to them. As such, Zorn's game work was less an innovation in the creative process than a debasement of it.

Without making too much of his admiration for messiah figures, it is clear that a dominant theme of Zorn's career has been his dedication to attempting to invent new musical paradigms and launch new movements. At some point in his late twenties or early thirties, Zorn grew more interested in his Jewish heritage, as many artists (and non-artists) of all backgrounds turn to their roots as they age. The results of Zorn's ethnic awakening have included a body of more than five hundred shortish compositions with the group title "Masada," named for the famous Jewish martyrdom site of the Roman era; his record label Tzadik (tzaddik denotes a righteous person, a saintly person, in Hebrew); and an umbrella effort that is broader, more ambitious, and more nebulous, which Zorn calls Radical Jewish Culture.

Zorn has overseen the performance and the recording of the Masada pieces by ensembles of various sorts—art rockers, chamber groups, and a jazz quartet featuring Zorn on alto saxophone, Dave Douglas on trumpet, Greg Cohen on bass, and Joey Baron on drums. As compositions, the Masada pieces are simple and repetitious, inspired loosely by traditional melodies and, for the most part, constructed with the standard tools: minor keys and folk-dance rhythms. Many of the tunes are charming and elegiac, unique among Zorn's generally oppressive work; and Douglas, Cohen, and Baron are all players of uncommon sensitivity, employed well here. Zorn, too, though scarcely on the level of his bandmates as an instrumentalist, plays with rare nuance and delicacy on some of the Masada CDs.

Beyond the Masada pieces, the concerts and recording projects organized by Zorn under the rubric of Radical Jewish Culture have been a mishmash of works, some related so tenuously to Jewish culture that Zorn's application of the phrase seems less radical than cynical. An early example, and just one of many, is Zorn's multi-artist, two-CD tribute to Burt Bacharach, titled *Great Jewish Music*. The collection features a hodgepodge of artists associated with Zorn, as well as Sean Lennon, playing Bacharach hits such as "Close to You," "Do You Know the Way to San Jose," "What's New Pussycat," and "The Man Who Shot Liberty Valance." The music is delightful pop schmaltz; but apart from the Yiddish origins of that term, it is no more Jewish music than this sentence is Magyar language because its writer has great-grandparents from Hungary.

Zorn was asked, on NPR, what exactly it is that makes music Jewish. "Well, you know, I've been doing this for quite a while and I don't think I can honestly answer that question very accurately," he said. "It could be a lot of things. It could be just an intention of it wanted to be that. It could be a scale. It could be some dramatic subject or theme. It could be something historical. It could be something that's just emotional. It could [be] a lot of things. It could be nothing. I don't know." But to identify something or someone as Jewish and then accept "nothing" as a legitimate reason—surely this is in some way to deny the richness, and even the legitimacy, of Jewishness; it is, in its whatever-ism about its own identity, reckless and demeaning to real Jewish culture. Zorn, following up on the Bacharach CD, approached Dave Brubeck with the proposition of honoring his work in the *Great Jewish Music* series, and Brubeck had to tell Zorn that he is not Jewish. Thinking of "Blue Rondo a la Turk" and "Pick Up Sticks," I wonder why Zorn presumed that Brubeck is a Jew. Was it the cantorial part that Brubeck once included in a religious oratorio about social justice? But Brubeck, a Catholic, has also composed a mass. Or was it his nose?

On that last night at Tonic, Zorn headed back to the stage for the second set, and fans once again yelled out to him, "Zorn! Zorn!" Somebody hollered "Shalom!" and Zorn replied, "What it is!" *What it is?* That is a perfectly, bafflingly appropriate salutation for the living master of creative delusion.

Josh Groban

L ike Nabokov in this but in nothing else, my eldest aunt has always been indifferent to music. Yet she called me once in 2005, for the first time since my childhood, to ask if I could get her a pair of tickets for a concert at Madison Square Garden. My aunt was an eighty-three-year-old Italian-American dressmaker, and she wanted to see Josh Groban, who was a twenty-three-year-old Californian known for singing Latinate songs of enormous appeal to old women of all ages. The performance in New York on February 11, the Friday before Valentine's Day, was to be the climax of a long tour of grand venues that Groban had undertaken to promote his latest release, *Live at the Greek*, a CD/DVD of an earlier show at the Greek Theatre in Los Angeles. As such, the concerts had essentially been evocations of a document of a performance of past recordings: mementos of a memento of a memento. And thus is Josh Groban, a pop-culture phenomenon of our day whose music and image are mainly echoes of idealized fantasies about a romanticized past.

In a few years' time, Groban emerged from harmless obscurity in undergraduate musical theater to assume pointless ubiquity in the casino-and-arena circuit. He had done virtually nothing professionally when, through the recommendation of a vocal coach, he caught the attention of Los Angeles–based producer and songwriter David Foster, a contemporary Medici of pop. At his reckoning, Foster will answer for having laced the air of drugstores everywhere with the hits of (in alphabetical order) Andrea Bocelli, Michael Bolton, Chicago, Celine Dion, and Whitney Houston, among others. (It should be noted in this context that Foster is also a philanthropist and runs a foundation, named for himself, to aid children in need of organ transplants.) Of all the artists Foster has groomed, Groban is surely his cardinal achievement—a wondrously strange living amalgam of imposed ideas about pop artistry, most of them fearsomely cynical.

Through the puppet-mastery of Foster and personal manager Brian Avnet (whose prominent credit on Groban's CDs, "Management: Brian Avnet for Avnet Management," is so desperate to fill space that it is a near palindrome), Groban came up through television, which is the most efficient means of reaching his core audience: women of a certain age who stay at home watching television instead of going out with dreamy young men like Josh Groban. He appeared on a season finale of *Ally McBeal*, singing and acting, even before he made his first album, and he went on to build an audience for his recordings and concerts not through radio, the traditional pop-music means, but on the small screen. He promoted the release of his eponymous debut CD with another appearance on *Ally McBeal*, and also did stints on *Rosie*, *Larry King Live*, the *Today* show, and *Oprah*, and his record sales climbed in suit. After *20/20* aired a segment on Groban, his first CD went from Number 108 to Number 12 on the charts. *Live at the Greek*, the CD/DVD, made its premiere as a PBS special, reaffirming that public broadcasting's vestigial prohibitions against airing commercials do not preclude its programs from being commercials.

Groban's appeal begins with his delicate, boyish looks and his timid manner. He keeps his hair longish and uncombed (or, more likely, meticulously done to appear undone), beckoning anyone maternally inclined to comb it with her fingers and slip a hand in his pocket with a few dollars for the barber. Groban is not small, but he is proportioned like an adolescent; indeed, he has a softness that is uncommon in an era when even adolescents weight-train to be buff. In many of his photographs and between songs in concert, Groban tends to peer down at his feet like a grade-schooler in a recital; watching him perform, as I did not long ago at an Indian-territory resort in New York state, one cannot help but feel a bit nervous for him and protective of him. The effect is insidious. By inviting our sympathy before earning our admiration, Groban is plying the hoariest sort of theatrical psychology, transplanted from Victorian melodrama to its twenty-first-century counterparts: daytime television and the casino stages.

On Web sites and in chat rooms for his fans (who go by the name Groban-ites, like members of a Biblical tribe, and are as territorial as one), the raving about Groban focuses on his "purity" and how "sweet" and "good" and "nice" he is, especially to his fans. Groban threatens us with the complacency of virtue as most pop singers his age promise the dangers of vice. A counteragent to the hypersexualization of pretty young singers such as Hilary Duff and Lindsay Lohan in youth-oriented pop, Groban offers a kind of hyper-desexualization for an older crowd. Bluntly put, his attraction for women (and men) twice (or more times) his age has an element of sexless pedophilia—or a chaste romanticism, which has shown up from time to time in the history of popular music but has not been pervasive since the early days of Tin Pan Alley and long-forgotten songs such as "Baby Shoes" and "When You Were Sweet Sixteen."

What's startling about Groban as a singer is the power of the voice that emanates from the modest vessel. He has an airy, robust baritone, which he proj-ects with confidence and apparent ease. It is an impressive instrument, well employed mainly to impress. Having recorded accessible classical works such as Bach's "Jesu, Joy of Man's Desiring" as well as many pseudo-classical pieces of recent vintage such as Albert Hammond's "Alejate," Groban is commonly mis-taken for a classical vocalist, or a "crossover" artist applying formal technique to a repertoire melding high and low forms. Actually, he has something closer to a "legit" theatrical voice than a legitimately classical one. Groban could have been (and may well become in the many years ahead of him) a musical-theater star like his early idol Mandy Patinkin, who prevailed with less natural equipment.

The eye and the ear have trouble connecting what they get from Josh Groban. He looks young and unassuming, but when he sings, out comes a grown man, a powerhouse; he is the Clark Kent of pop. At least some of his fans are no doubt drawn to this incongruity as a self-projection. At the risk of pathologizing a group of people that I have encountered only in relatively small numbers in one theater, I think Groban's audience is, on the whole, a profoundly geeky lot, and Groban may reinforce their self-images as people with far more capacity than their appearances suggest. I can certainly vouch for my aunt, who will tell anyone interested that her main complaint about growing old is that she still feels like a bambina inside.

Several million people who are not necessarily Italian-American are respond-ing to a potent Old World quality in Groban's music. Each of his CDs includes at least a few songs sung in Spanish, Italian, or French, as well as songs in English. In addition to light classics, he does vaguely classical-sounding compo-sitions of recent vintage by songwriters from around the world, whom Foster seeks, such as Andrea Sandri, Luis Enriquez Bacalov, and Lucio Dalla. The new tunes seem built on traditional melodies or variations thereof, glammed up through dense production laden with electronic effects. They sound very much like the synth-heavy tunes piped into the lounge of a hotel on the Bosporus, appropriations of folk culture rendered opulently grotesque.

I have no idea what the non-English songs are about, since the booklets of Groban's CDs print the lyrics in their original languages rather than in translation, providing no help to his listeners who do not happen to read Spanish, Italian, or French, while giving them a keepsake of their fandom as a brush with exotica. The accompanying pictures reinforce a neatly crafted image of Groban as a generic continental: he wears a black turtleneck, he stands in a field alongside a tiny sports car, he walks below a concrete bridge that seems to have watchtowers. Then again, in one setting, he has on a T-shirt with a "New York" logo. Then again, Groban is from Los Angeles, and New York is the most European of American cities. So what exactly is the location of these photographs? They bring to mind nothing more than the indefinite foreignness of all the made-up countries in the old television show *Mission Impossible*, in which the guest star who looked like Groban always ended up with Barbara Bain before getting shot under that concrete bridge.

With his globalist leanings and his classical (or quasi-classical) orientation, Groban might seem antithetical to the temper of his time, the Bush era. His music draws upon the folk traditions of Europe, the Middle East, and Africa, and his lyrics (at least the English ones) are rarely grounded in this or any particular culture, but speak in universal platitudes of mountains and seas and time and sand and sky. Groban might appear to be making a kind of populist world music, customized for PBS and NPR, primed for Rush Limbaugh to tar as elitist and Eurocentric. In truth, however, Groban's work is wholly of a piece with the George W. Bush–era political climate. Its aesthetic doctrine is not globalism but imperialism, and the Europe it evokes, for the wish-fulfillment of Groban's more lonesome fans, is the idealized, homogenized Europe of old travel brochures—Europe as an adult theme park, where vacationing Americans could find romance to the sound of a zillion violins.

Grandiosity and artifice are the core attributes of Josh Groban's music. David Foster, who came up in the West Coast music business under the shadow of Phil Spector, works on an epic scale. The CDs that he has produced for Groban, like many of his records for Bocelli, Celine Dion, and his other clients, have been constructed through the accretion of big sounds—voices layered over string orchestras over choirs over rock bands over synthesizers over more synthesizers. Foster loves the synthesizer the way Spector loved sleigh bells. (Groban's CDs include credits for synth programming and sound design.) The music has the same grandness as a Las Vegas buffet, a vulgar luxuriousness. Musically, there is nothing inherently wrong with bigness, of course; without it, we would have neither Gotterdammerung nor "River Deep, Mountain High." Foster's mistake is to so distrust his material and to so underestimate his audience that he strips tunes of their charm by inflating them, while obscuring the instruments (and sometimes Groban's voice) under tiers of superfluous digital noise.

The synthetic unorthodoxy of Groban's CDs makes them right at home on Billboard's "Classical Crossover" chart, which the music trade instituted to cleanse the classical chart of the likes of Groban, Hayley Westenra, Sarah Brightman, and Bond (an all-sexpot string quartet whose musicianship is hard to gauge from the electronic mush on their recordings). Traditional classical musicians, among them Yo-Yo Ma and Joshua Bell, also show up on the crossover chart, presumably because their appeal extends beyond the core classical audience, "crossing over" into the larger public. Otherwise, little unites the acts in the crossover list—even less than unites those in the pop category or in jazz. Some, such as Bocelli, draw largely from the classical repertoire; others, such as Westenra, mix it up (some Schubert, some Sondheim, some Bach, some Arlen); others, such as Bond, play instruments associated with classical music (although Bond's work is not remotely classical). Nearly all the above are simply too young and too pretty, as well as too talented, for savvy producers such as Foster not to exploit for their mainstream potential. (Meanwhile the classical charts are peppered with CDs that stretch the definition of classical, such as *Classic Meets Cuba* by the Klazz Brothers and *Cuba Percussion*, and *Beautiful America*, a suite of music-therapy pieces by Tim Janis, a New Age specialist in "uplifting" music.)

Considering how insular music audiences tend to be, I cannot help but wonder how much crossing over is really going on these days. Are the Grobanites developing a taste for Bach now and moving on to "Weichet nur, betrubte Schatten"? Is Bond luring chamber music buffs into the sonic wonderland of Radiohead? Or does "crossover," like the inverted language of legislative titles, really mean "dead end"? The best term for music such as Josh Groban's is surely the "semi-classical" of my parents' day. It precisely denotes the work's essential fractionality, reminding us that this music can be serious, but only in part.

On a thematic level, this notion of crossing from one realm to another, particularly from the earthly to the celestial, runs deep in Groban's music. His songs are ripe with images of transcendence and orchestral crescendos that conjure the opening of the skies. "Let this be our prayer/As we go our way/Lead us to a place/Guide us with your grace/To a place where we'll be safe," Groban bellows in "The Prayer," composed by his producer. (Foster previously had the song recorded by Bocelli and Celine Dion as a duet, and had the same track released on separate albums by each of them.) While some songs (particularly "My Confession") evoke Catholicism explicitly, most have a nondenominational but overt religiosity, implicitly Christian and often conflated with romantic sentiment. When Groban sings of the "echoes of our souls," or when he intones, "When I am down and, oh my soul, so weary. . . . You raise me up, so I can stand on mountains," love and salvation are indistinct. In the end, both feel cheapened by the songs' glib sanctimony.

No matter. The fealty of the Grobanites shall not wane, because their idol loves them back. Groban and Avnet go to uncommon lengths to nurture a congregational sense of community among the singer's admirers. He devotes time to "meet and greets" with fans before his concerts, he corresponds with them regularly by e-mail, and he acknowledges them generously on his CDs. For curiosity's sake, I'd love to hear what other Josh Groban albums a different fan base—and a different producer—would make possible. It would be interesting to hear this exceptional voice applied to earthier, more substantive, less calculating music. I would love to see him come down off that mountain and hear him do *Carousel*. And I wonder what he would like to do.

Marjane Satrapi

The eons-old culture of the place we now call Iran first inspired comic-book artists as early as 1949, when the late Disney-studio veteran Carl Barks wrote and illustrated a twenty-four-page adventure fantasy titled "In Ancient Persia" for Dell Comics. Lightly peppered with Middle Eastern arcana, the story makes reference to the historical cities of Kish and Susa, and it depicts the fictional Ali Cad scurrying to find the capital of Persia—Persepolis, which he recalls as a "roaring boomtown." Three time-honored cartoon gimmicks inform the narrative: a mad scientist, uncanny resemblances, and talking fowl. Ali Cad just so happens to be a double for the book's protagonist, Donald Duck, who is mistaken for the wholly caddish Ali and trapped (along with the former's nephews, Huey, Dewey, and Louie) in a nominal Persia that functions mainly as a source of whimsically grotesque exotica.

Comic books were not the place to look for more enlightened views of Iran, past or present, until recent years. In late 1998, Marjane Satrapi, an expatriate Iranian woman living in Paris, began writing and drawing what would become a series of quirky, veracious memoirs in comic-book form. Collectively titled *Persepolis*, they may well represent the first notable use of the word in comics outside the context of Donald Duck. While the books are named for a city of the first millennium BC, they are utterly contemporary and intimate accounts of Satrapi's life in and out of Iran. The first, published in America in 2003, details her childhood in Tehran in the years prior to, during, and after the Islamic Revolution of 1979. The second, issued here the following year, follows the author to school in Vienna, where she suffers a traumatic indoctrination into Western society and young adulthood, and then back home to Tehran, where she struggles to find her place in both a stultifying, bifurcated society and a doomed marriage of convenience.

Employing a pop medium associated with America to portray a complex, ancient culture of the Middle East, Satrapi has made her country—at least her loving view of it as a land of noble traditions and human passions misrepresented by fundamentalist extremism—appealing to Western eyes. She has upended the worst American stereotypes of Iranians as humorless jihadists on the axis of evil, putting a new face on her homeland: namely, Satrapi's doodle-like caricature of herself. With thick curlicues of black hair and a capital L of a nose (a couple of ovals with adroitly placed dots inside), the cartoon girl in the first *Persepolis* could have been an Iranian exchange student in Charlie Brown's class. *Persepolis* has now appeared in a dozen or so European countries in addition to the United States, and the two volumes have found a welcoming readership, particularly among those around college age who take their generation's wealth of ambitious comics and graphic novels as seriously as their parents took classic-rock albums. (None of Satrapi's work is available in her native Iran, where comics have been banned by religious authorities who view them as decadent.)

Much as *Persepolis* defies widespread preconceptions of its subject matter, it also challenges long-held prejudices against its medium. The books are not juvenile, but sophisticated, even in the first volume's referential use of its child narrator's often naive point of view; they are not hyperactive and do not glory in violence, but progress at the mercurial pace of memory and depict the horrors of life under the Shah and the Islamic Revolution as a way of protesting them; they are not male-oriented, but absorbed with matters of womanhood (particularly the sexual inequity of Islamic fundamentalism); and they are not overblown or self-consciously arty, but simple, elegiac, artfully unaffected. At the same time, they are proudly comics and good at the things comics do best: The drawings have punch and clarity (the Guardians of the Revolution, who nab the young Satrapi for wearing a denim jacket and Nikes, look like ghouls; the shrouded school girls are interchangeable), and the story takes fanciful flights (at the start of the revolution, when Satrapi suddenly feels groundless, we see her float into outer space; God visits Satrapi from time to time to have a glass of milk or talk about the weather).

Satrapi was promptly acclaimed in Europe, where arts institutions carry on a vaguely Marxist tradition of advancing parity between the high and the low. She won Spain's Fernando Buesa Blanco Prize for a literary work furthering peace, as well as most of the important honors for comics' art in Europe, and pages from her books have been exhibited at museums and galleries in Paris, Berlin, and Lucerne. She has lectured on her work at the Royal Academy of Fine Arts in Naples and spoken at the elite Tschann Libraire in Paris. In the United States, it has been much the same; the first *Persepolis* book was praised in the book-review pages and made several best-seller and best-of-the-year lists. Soon after its publication, Satrapi began receiving commissions from the same sort of venues, including one for a *Times* Op-Ed-page comic about the 2003 Nobel Peace Prize, which had been awarded to the rights activist Shirin Ebadi, a fellow Iranian woman for whom Satrapi had served as translator on the day the prize was announced.

The *Persepolis* books entwine the stories of Satrapi's first twenty-five years and her country's contemporaneous history. The first words above the first book's first drawing—one of the author at age ten, a year after the Islamic Revolution—are "This is me. . . . " But the art depicts what fundamentalism had brought upon her: Posing dutifully for a class photo, she is sitting with her arms folded, wearing the mandatory black veil and a plain, long-sleeved, button-down dress; in the second panel we see four of her classmates, all positioned and attired identically. This is my country, Satrapi tells us in pictures with as much value as words. Near the end of the first book, as Satrapi prepares to leave Iran for the journey to Europe and womanhood that makes up *Persepolis 2*, her father implores her, "Don't forget who you are and where you come from." Her books are proof that she listened.

The young Marjane Satrapi was a bright and troublesome girl, having been educated during the last years of the Shah's reign in relatively liberal, bilingual (French/Persian), secular schools. As she depicts herself in the first *Persepolis*, she was something of an Iranian Pippi Longstocking, a free spirit who challenged authority in all forms that affected youthful life, be they parental, academic, religious, societal, or governmental. Initially sympathetic to the "cultural revolution" against the Shah, she defied her parents' orders to stay safely clear of public protests and joined a demonstration with her maid, only to be caught and roundly punished by her mother. After the fundamentalists imposed rigid new standards for dress and conduct (public and private), the adolescent Satrapi dared to ignore them, and (a) went out in public alone, (b) to buy bootleg cassettes of

Kim Wilde and Camel, (c) wearing Nikes and a jean jacket adorned with a Michael Jackson button. (Nabbed for the last transgression, Satrapi was taken off the street and interrogated, although she escaped punishment by claiming that she wore the shoes for school sports and that Michael Jackson was really Malcolm X.) Defiant beyond recklessness, she was expelled from one school for striking the principal in a fight over a forbidden bracelet, then dared to question her subsequent overseers on matters of political dogma. Her parents, seeking to protect her from punishment worse than expulsion, sent her to school in Austria. She was fourteen.

Thus begins *Persepolis 2*, wherein Iran starts becoming a spectral presence in Satrapi's life. Seduced by Western pop culture and its romantic idealization of loners, outlaws, and the like, Satrapi goes through a series of phases much less common in Iranian culture than they are in the average American high school or college. She discovers sex and suffers betrayal; she makes gay friends; she takes up smoking and drinking; she does drugs and even deals a bit for a time; she becomes a punk. . . . Exhausted by it all, Satrapi returns to Iran four years later, studies art, and, desperate for male companionship, submits to a marriage that she regrets before the end of her wedding night.

"The books are about me, and they are about my country, but we both change in the books, and I'm still changing—look, now I'm married again, and I'm happy, and I was so miserable before," Satrapi explains, relaxing in the front room of the airy, third-floor apartment in Paris's Marais district where she and her second husband, Mattias Ripa, a Swedish émigré, have lived for four years. Relaxing is a relative notion to Satrapi; she had worked all day on a Sunday, as she docs nearly every day and most evenings, because she revels in it.

"It's not that I think working is the best thing in the world—I'm really passionate about what I do," she says. "If I cannot do it, I would die by my own hand. I'm very lucky that my husband understands." (Satrapi, in turn, has no interest in what he does for a living—nor the least knowledge of it. "Nobody wants to believe me, but I don't know," she says with a wink of a smile. "I prefer not to know. My first husband and I knew everything about each other, and we did everything together, and it was awful. This way, I can imagine, 'I wonder what he's doing,' and I think that's better.")

She teeters on the edge of the seat cushion of a brown leather armchair, seemingly prepared to lunge across the coffee table if need be. She smokes as she talks—and smokes as she snacks on sweet pistachios that her mother shipped from Iran—occasionally using one cigarette to light the next. "The point of the books is not just to say, 'Oh, look at me—I was cute, and I had black hair, and my parents, they were nice.' The point of the books is to show what a person is really like who comes from my country, because nobody outside of my country knows that there are normal people in Iran. I shit and fart, and I laugh and I make love.

"I don't really care what people think of me," Satrapi, now thirty-four, says. "But I care what they think of my people. I love my people, even though the ones in power right now are idiots."

Her parents, Taji and Ebi Satrapi, prosperous social idealists who deplored the oppression of the Islamic revolution but came to accommodate it, take pride in having instilled in their only child a devotion to independence that they have compromised in their own lives by remaining in Iran. "The most important thing for us was definitely independence," her mother says, responding to questions relayed and translated by her daughter. "We always wanted her to grow up as an independent woman with all that this may mean. In a country like Iran, with its patriarchal culture, a woman with an economical independence may also often be a happier person than a woman who is financially dependent on her husband.

"I remember her always saying, 'If I don't try to do it, how would I know if I can do it or not?' The word fear is something she doesn't know the meaning of."

Like her work, Satrapi's apartment is a mosaic of Middle Eastern and Western, high and low—a willful testament to cultural and aesthetic heterogeneity. Hanging from one wall are a small handwoven rug, a diorama of figures from Persian mythology, and a painting of one of her great-aunts—a Jean Harlow look-alike, posing in the nude; on another wall are a couple of vintage American advertisements with the slogans "The Man for Me is a Pipe-Smoking Man" and "I'm your best friend. I'm your Lucky Strike." On a third wall is a poster of one of Roy Lichtenstein's comics-inspired paintings, and on another is an array of palm-size stones onto which photographs of Satrapi's parents have been glued, gifts to the daughter in Paris from her mother's maid. An appetite for kitsch appears to run in the extended family.

Despite having read no superhero comics in her youth—and few other comics besides a Soviet-published title, *Dialectical Materialism*—Satrapi has been inclined to hero worship, as well as grand ambition, from an early age. Her book portrays each of her parents much as she sees herself today, as a flawed champion of a virtuous minority position. Her parents once fought to preserve their values of Marxist secularism; Satrapi, through her books, seeks to challenge the Western caricature of Iranians as malevolent zealots. "I always thought, I will grow up and I will fight for the freedom of the people—I will be like Che Guevara!" Satrapi says. "The fight that I'm making now is to show the people in other places of the world that a person in Iran can be very much more like them than they think."

The very fact that an Iranian female has written a graphic novel shatters perceptions, Satrapi has found. "A lot of people can't believe that a woman from my country could do such a thing—they think we're all idiots or maniacs and don't know about anything except how to hide behind a veil," she says.

The deftness with which she has lifted that veil to reveal herself, as well as Iranian life as she has seen and felt it, distinguishes Satrapi from the many artists of her generation who have done intimate memoirs in cartoon form. According to the comics historian Trina Robbins, author of *The Great Women Cartoonists* and other books, "What most women, like most guys in the independent comics field, do is very boring, because an awful lot of the indie cartoonists, unfortunately, really have very boring lives, and they make these really boring real-time comics that say, Oh, I hang out at the coffee shop, and then I go to my job at the used record store. . . .' Whereas the story that Marjane has to tell is so incredible and so powerful, and she tells it magnificently. It's a privilege to hear her story, and not another one about 'I hate myself because my thighs are fat and my boyfriend left me.'"

After her failed first marriage, Marjane Satrapi left Iran for the last time (so far) to study illustration at the Strasburg School of Decorative Arts. Following graduation, at age twenty-four, she moved to Paris with aspirations of writing and drawing children's books. Having grown up without much exposure to comics, she had not given them much thought one way or another. "I started reading comics late, really," she recalls.

In that, she has much in common with those around college age who have made *Persepolis* and other graphic novels a popular phenomenon, embracing a form many of them likely see as something new and their own. They are, on the whole, the first young adults since the invention of the comic book to have grown up without much connection to traditional comics; in essence, today's graphic-novel audience is the postcomics generation. Because of a radical change during the '70s in the way comic books were distributed and sold and, commensurately, how they were created and read—comics largely disappeared from magazine racks and re-emerged in hobby shops, where they mutated into specialty items for obsessives engaged in collecting and trading them (ideally, wrapped and unread). Publishers facilitated this shift into "direct sales," which liberated them from magazine distributors' irksome policy of returning unsold titles for credit. Although many kids have continued to buy comics (and sometimes read them), absorption with comic books has not been a common rite of American childhood for decades. Video games, being more kinetic as well as more suspect in the eyes of adults, have taken comics' place. Accordingly, when readers in their twenties today pick up graphic novels, they are inclined to do so without the prejudice of entrenched childhood associations.

When Satrapi first tried to create books for children, she failed magnificently; she wrote and illustrated fourteen titles for young readers and received 187 letters from publishers rejecting them all, she says. Satrapi remained blithely unimpeded. "She always had this self-belief," says her Swede husband. "She was famous when I met her. Nobody knew it, of course." (Since the success of *Persepolis*, Satrapi has published four children's books in France, most of them revisions of her once unaccepted ones.)

Meanwhile, at her shared studio, five French artists, all about her age, were thriving in comics. Thanks to a friend of one of her friends, Satrapi had landed in L'Atelier des Vosges, an exquisitely decrepit space on the perimeter of the Place des Vosges that French comics enthusiasts regarded as the Parisian Bloomsbury of the art form. "It was an accident that I was lucky enough to be in the same studio with the best comics artists in France," Satrapi explains, sitting at her drawing board in the atelier late on a weekday morning. "The miracle of the thing was not that these people decided that they were going to make a movement—it happened that all of us were in the same studio, all of us around thirty years old, and I end up there. We were all talking all the time," Satrapi says, miming chatter and rolling her eyes. "I was telling my friends there about my life in Iran and the Islamic Revolution. They didn't know anything about my culture, and I didn't know anything about comics before I met them. One of them, and then two of them, then three of them, said to me, 'Come on, come on, come on—you should do a comic out of that.'"

L'Atelier des Vosges was and is a somewhat fluid assemblage of French comics artists who share working quarters, provide mutual stimulation and support, and publish themselves in a cooperative called L'Assocation, through which the *Persepolis* books originally appeared. Its membership has included some of the most esteemed names in European comics' circles, including David B., Christophe Blain, Emile Bravo, and Joann Sfar. "We came, most of us, from fine art, from modern art, and we were trying to do comics," explains Sfar, whose children's book, *The Little Vampire Goes to School*, was a best seller in the United States. "We were learning our job together—there was no master and pupil. We are still learning, and we try to play together. Sometimes, we have two people draw the same story at the same time, to see the difference. We play and experiment and, most of all, please ourselves. But Marjane thought comics books were vulgar and something for kids. She was not interested until she realized, 'Okay, it's not a genre, it's a medium.'"

As Satrapi recalls, "Suddenly I started doing it, and they helped me a lot. I didn't know the language of comics. I had the drawings follow from right to left, like in my mother language. They all gave me advice. Emile Bravo told me, 'When you are drawing, be like a lizard—be perfectly still, but aware of everything around you. Don't waste your energy with a lot of movement while you're working. Be like a lizard.' There were things that I didn't know how to draw. Cristophe said to me, 'A hand is like this. . . .'"

Satrapi roughs out a one-page opinion comic about the Iraq war, commissioned by the Italian newspaper *Il Manifesto*. She has just begun and is testing designs for a panel depicting a grid of invading aircraft. Dispensing with drawing-class convention, she uses a marker rather than pencil; the ink, being less forgiving, "forces me to concentrate," she says. "Otherwise I would sit here all day and draw shit." At the same time, she employs a counterbalancing ritual to prevent her work from becoming overly self-conscious: She draws on the most inexpensive paper she can find. "If I use very good paper, I feel like I have to make a masterpiece," she says, "and the best way to make shit is to feel like you have to make a masterpiece. I feel now like the world is waiting for a masterpiece every time I put a brush in my hand, and that is a bad thing. Cartoonists shouldn't have to be too good.

"I never thought that I was good and that I had talent—I still don't," Satrapi says as she draws. "My understanding of anatomy has always been zero, because in the anatomy class I took in Iran, the woman was fully clothed. I didn't even know how an arm bends. I'm not really a very good drawer—I'm a good budgeter. I do the best with what I have."

Satrapi finishes her page, looks it over, shrugs her shoulders, and reaches for a cigarette. "The technical quality is not the thing that matters," she says, darting her eyes at the page on the table. "Cinema is reality, but reality is obvious. Nothing is more truthful than a drawing, because it's an interpretation.

"I like black and white better than anything, because there's no bluff in black and white. To me, color is extra information, and when you add color, whether or not the drawing is naive, it makes something real about it. I write a lot about the Middle East, so I write about violence. Violence today has become something so normal, so banal—that is to say, everybody thinks it's normal. But it's not normal. To draw it and put in color—the color of the flesh and the red of the blood, and so forth reduces it by making it realistic. Black and white makes it abstract and more meaningful." Satrapi picks up the page she has finished and looks again at the maze of jet fighters she has drawn. She turns it upside down and gently pounds her fist on the back of the paper.

* * *

It is hardly a bad reflection on comic books that it took decades for the medium to be accepted as suitable for adults; to the contrary, it seems a testament to comics' resilience and adaptability. About a quarter of a century ago, the pioneering American artist and writer Will Eisner published one of the first book-length comics drawn from personal experience: *A Contract with God and Other Tenement Stories*, a collection of four loosely related stories about tenement life in the Bronx of the Depression years, inspired by Eisner's childhood. While American precedents for adult-oriented, long-form comics date back to the era of *God's Man*, the wordless "novel in woodcuts" that artist Lynd Ward rendered in 1929 (antecedents for which can be traced all the way to hieroglyphics, if you want to get technical about it), *A Contract with God* prompted a generation of artists and writers to experiment with long-form comics, because the idea was good enough for the revered Will Eisner. "He was the most credible and loudest evangelist in the early years," recalls Paul Levitz, the president of DC Comics, who was a twenty-two-year-old comics writer and editor when *A Contract with God* was published. "Will was the guy who was an established figure, who stood up and said, 'This is the way of the future—these things are going to be for adults, and they are going to tell stories of intellectual worth.'"

Eisner's approach to making comics for grown-ups was vigorously transformative. "I believed that the medium had a capacity to go beyond the joke-book usage," Eisner has said. Unremitting in their determination to prove the point, his books have been serious above all—virtually purged of humor, in fact.

Satrapi and many of her peers, like the underground artists before them, see seriousness of purpose and lightness of execution as mutually compatible—indeed, the tension between the two, pulled to extremes, is the essence of their aesthetic. Robert Crumb's early influences included Little Lulu comics and talking-animal cartoons, and the ghosts of nursery school in his artwork make his darkly comic tales of drug trips and sadomasochism all the more disturbing. Art Spiegelman, much the same, extricates the Holocaust from the realm of abstract evil, thereby magnifying its horror, by rendering the Nazis and Jews as accessible cartoon cats and mice. Satrapi takes on adult subjects (Islamic fundamentalism) in sophisticated ways (interlacing her narrative with Iranian history, demonizing no one), while also exploiting the expectation of a good time integral to what used to be called "the funnies." (Her cartoon self trades jibes with God, whom she depicts as a look-alike for Karl Marx, but with curlier hair.)

When Satrapi looks up from her drawing table, she sees a found-object collage of novelty items: a poster of Bruce Lee, an assortment of children's stickers from a flea market, an "A for Anarchy" logo made out of a varnished sausage, a Russian circus poster depicting performers engaged in inexplicable feats. "What is he doing?" she asks, pointing to a contorted painted figure in something like a Gypsy space costume. "Or these people over here—you don't know really what is happening, either. If they do what they're doing, they are going to die, they are going to be like hamburgers. It's not possible. The artist took people for idiots. I think this is very, very funny." A short while later, Satrapi picks up a cell phone from her drawing table and starts carrying on a terse business conversation, during which a spray of water shoots onto my shirt from the phone, which I realize is a gag water toy. Satrapi roars.

Several days a week, Satrapi likes to sit in a sidewalk café around the corner from her studio and watch for amusing passersby. "This is the best place in Paris, because you can sit here and watch all the fancy people as they walk across the street," she says, squirming to get comfortable on the tiny iron seat. "You can tell this is becoming a fancy area, because the food shops are closing, and they are being replaced by clothing shops, because the rich people, they don't need to eat. The rich people, they eat air, and they shit bubbles. The rich people, all they need are make-up and clothes and shoes.

"I have to move, because it's become too fancy," Satrapi says. "Sometimes, I need to go out and buy something other than shoes."

Where would she go? No further than a "not so good" neighborhood in Paris, she says. Despite her fascination with American pop culture, as an artist, Satrapi feels bound to live in France. (Crumb has been living in Sauve, a medieval village in the south of France, for years, and his American friend and fellow comics artist Peter Poplaski is a neighbor there.)

"In France, comics are taken seriously, yes—but, at the same time, they are not such a big deal," Satrapi says. "Here, as a comics artist, you have respect, but at the same time, you are allowed to do some foolish stuff—they will excuse you.

"I know that I'm a very serious person, but I don't want to be thought of as a serious person. The fact of not being taken for serious, for me, gives me freedom. That's the only thing that I care about—being free, acting free, thinking free," she says as she snuffs out her cigarette. "That is the hardest thing and the most important thing."

Acknowledgments

I am profoundly grateful to several editors who welcomed these essays into their first homes: Leon Wieseltier of *The New Republic,* to whom this book is rightfully dedicated; Robert Silvers and the late Barbara Epstein of *The New York Review of Books*; Robert Vare of *The Atlantic Monthly*; David Remnick and Daniel Zalewski of *The New Yorker*; David Friend and Graydon Carter of *Vanity Fair*; Steve Wasserman of *The Los Angeles Times Book Review*; and Eric Banks of *Bookforum*.

My deep thanks go to Ben Schafer of Da Capo Press and my agent Chris Calhoun for their enthusiastic advocacy of this book. Thanks, also, to cover designer Georgia Feldman and Lori Hobkirk of The Book Factory.

I'm very grateful to David Yaffe for writing the Foreword.

I thank Nicholas Lemann, Alisa Solomon, and Samuel G. Freedman, among my many supportive friends and colleagues at Columbia University.

Special thanks to Sarah Brown for her editing and research. For additional research, I thank Deirdre Cossman and Anna Brenner.

Thanks to the helpful members of the staffs of the Lincoln Center Library for the Performing Arts, Butler Library at Columbia, Bobst Library at New York University, and the Institute for Jazz Studies at Rutgers University.

Above all, as ever, thanks to my best collaborator, my wife, Karen, and the kids, Jake, Torie, and Nate.

Credits

The chapters on the following subjects were originally published, in different form, in *The New Republic*: the Blogging of American Pop, Ray Charles, Elvis Costello, Philip Glass and Leonard Cohen, Josh Groban, John Lennon, Abbey Lincoln and Mark Murphy, Alan Lomax, Paul McCartney, Susannah McCorkle, Joni Mitchell, Mos Def, the Music of Starbucks, MySpace, Anita O'Day, Open-Source Remixing, Michel Petrucciani, Rick Rubin and Kanye West, Sting, Three Women in Pop (Beyonce, Taylor Swift, and Lucinda Williams), the White Stripes, Walt Whitman and Fred Hersch, Brian Wilson, and John Zorn.

The chapters on these subjects were first published, in different form, in *The New York Review of Books*: Will Eisner, Elvis and the Colonel, Harry Partch, Joe Sacco and Daniel Clowes, Rodgers and Hart, and Dinah Washington.

The chapters on the following subjects were published, in different form, in these publications: Wynton Marsalis and Bobby Darin, *The Atlantic Monthly*; Marjane Satrapi, *Bookforum*; Sammy Davis, Jr., *The Los Angeles Times Book Review*; and Woody Guthrie, *The New Yorker*.

The chapter on Billy Eckstine is based in large part on research for an unpublished article written for *Vanity Fair*. The chapter on Jules Feiffer was not previously published. Nor were significant portions of the chapter, "A Hundred Years of the Blues." (Other parts of that chapter appeared, in different form, in *Mother Jones*.) The chapter on Elmer Fudd was written for the book *O.K. You Mugs: Writers on Movie Actors*, edited by Luc Sante and Melissa Pierson.

All text used by permission.

Index

and recording technology, 97, 99
and reinvention, 48
and *Revolver,* 97
and rock 'n' roll, 90, 203–204
and songwriting, 190, 205
and studio, 117
and youthful songs, 138, 204
Beauchard, David (David B.), 301
Beautiful America (album), 293
Bebop
    and Armstrong, 197
    and coffeehouses, 151
    and cool jazz, 224
    and Eckstine, 4, 7, 8, 11
    and Ellington, 235
    jazz begins metamorphosing into,
        226
    as jazz's dominant style, 4
    and MacManus, 93
    and McPherson, 219
    and Murphy, 126
    and Parker, 218
    and swing, 97, 224
    and Wynton Marsalis, 224, 225
Bechet, Sidney, 197
Beck, Jerry, 254
Beethoven, Ludwig van, 105, 196
Belafonte, Harry, 5, 13
Bell, Joshua, 293
Bellow, Saul, 127
Bennett, Tony, 49
    and Charles, 84
    and Eckstine, 5, 13, 16–17
    and Opus Collection and Artist's
        Choice, 153, 154
Benny, Jack, 251
Benson, Hugh, 36
Berger, David, 234
Bergman, Alan, 267, 268
Bergman, Ingmar, 185

Berle, Milton, 12
Berlin, Irving, 105
    and *Annie Get Your Gun,* 32
    and Eckstine, 16
    and F-sharp, 175
    and "God Bless America," 171
    and McCartney, 210, 211
    and McCorkle, 53, 54
    and Tin Pan Alley, 22, 23
    and Washington, 76
Bernstein, Leonard, 28, 93, 221
Berry, Chuck, 89, 103, 105, 137–138,
    205
Betsy (musical), 29, 53
Beverly Hillbillies, 173
The Bewitched (musical), 246, 249
Beyoncé, 129, 132–133
Beyond the Sea (movie), 45, 81
Beze, Dante, 24
    See also Mos Def
Big Daddy Kane, 24
Bigard, Barney, 198
*Billy Eckstine Now Singing in 12
    Great Movies* (album), 16
Billy Eckstine Orchestra, 4, 8–10
Bitter Music (Partch, ed. McGeary),
    241, 243, 245
Björk, 213
Black on Both Sides (album), 24
Blackburn, Philip, 240
Blade, Brian, 213
Blain, Christophe, 301, 302
Blake, William, 277
Blakey, Art
    and Eckstine, 4, 8, 10
    and Pittsburgh, 6
    and Wynton Marsalis, 224, 227,
        235
Blanc, Mel, 252, 253
Blanchard, Terence, 224, 225

Brodsky Quartet, 92
Bronco Busters, 173
Brookmeyer, Bob, 225
Broonzy, Big Bill, 84
Brother Ray: Ray Charles' Own Story
   (Charles and Ritz), 82
Brown, Charles, 81
Brown, Colin, 242
Brown, Foxy, 160
Brown, Milton, 200
Brown, Oscar, Jr., 125
Brown, Ray, 6, 91
Browne, Jackson, 117
Browne, James, 232
Brubeck, Dave, 288
Bryan, Arthur Q., 253
Burns, Ken, 194–200, 234
Bush, George W., 292
Butta, Gilda, 268
Byers, Billy, 16
Byrne, David, 73, 272

Cage, John, 99, 244, 249
Caine, Uri, 262
Calloway, Cab, 25
Camel, 298
Camelot (musical), 30
Camilo, Michel, 262
Campbell, Larry, 126
Cantor, Eddie, 251
Capitol Records, 99
Capra, Frank, 252
Captain Newman, M.D. (movie), 46
Carmichael, Hoagy, 32, 84
Carnal Knowledge (movie), 281
Carnegie Hall Jazz Band, 226
Carousel (musical), 28, 294
Carroll, Barbara, 234
Carroll, Diahann, 30
Carson, Johnny, 35

Carter, Maybelle, 75
Carter, Nell, 21
Cartoons, 115
   animé, 178
   and Barks, 295
   Beatles, 203
   and Eisner, 179
   and Feiffer, 276–282
   and "graphic novels," 109, 280,
      300
   and Marsalises, 229
   and *New Yorker,* 279
   and Sacco, 110, 111–112
   and Satrapi, 296, 300, 302, 303
   talking-animal, 303
   Warner Bros., 186, 250–254
   See also Comic books; Comic
      strips
Cash, Johnny, 86, 93, 158, 159
Cassotto, Walden Robert, 46
   See also Darin, Bobby
Castro, Fidel, 281
Cavett, Dick, 202
Cecil, Sir Robert, 107
Cellini, Benvenuto, 96
Centennials, 27–28, 29, 59
Chamber music, 98, 293
Champion, Gower, 15
Champion, Marge, 15
Chaos and Creation in the Backyard
   (album), 206, 207, 208–209, 210
Chapin, Harry, 159
Chaplin, Charles, 252
Charlap, Bill, 262
Charles, Ray, 81–86, 151
Charnin, Martin, 32
Chess, Leonard, 75
Chess, Philip, 75
Chess Records, 153
Chestnut, Cyrus, 229

in Hanley's Universe store, 178–179
as junk art, 108, 178
and language, 113
Little Lulu, 303
and Sacco, 109–113, 114, 115
and Satrapi, 295–304
and sensationalism, 110
and settings, 112
underground, 112, 178, 184, 280, 303
Comic strips
creation of, 196
and Eisner, 180–183, 184
and Feiffer, 276–282
and kids' antics, 278
and movies, 280
Communist Party, 173
Como, Perry, 15
Complete Village Voice Strips (Feiffer), 281
Comstock, Eric, 33
Concord Records, 151
Connor, Chris, 43
A Contract with God and Other Tenement Stories (Eisner), 109, 184–185, 302–303
Cooder, Ry, 73
Cooke, Sam, 5, 155
Cooley, Spade, 200
Cooper, Gary, 274
Copeland, Stewart, 90, 105
Copland, Aaron, 27, 90
Cornell, Joseph, 285
Cornog, F. M., 138, 139
Corporeal music, 244
Costello, Elvis, 89–95, 213, 241
Cotton, James, 61
Counterculture, 47, 51, 105, 184

Country music
and Americana music, 131
and Cash, 159
and Charles, 84, 86
and Costello, 91, 93
creation of, 196
and Darin, 46, 81
and Dixie Chicks, 159
and folk music, 174
and heartbreak, 74
and jazz, 200
at Living Room, 139
and Presley, 188, 190, 193
and Swift, 129, 130–131
and Washington, 79
and Woody Guthrie, 173, 176
Courvoisier, Sylvie, 285
Covered Wagon Jubilee, 173
Cowell, Henry, 249
Cox, Wally, 142
Cray, Ed, 172, 173, 174, 175, 176
Cream, 62, 104, 105, 118, 154
Crissman, Maxine, 173
Crosby, Bing, 3, 10, 36
birth of, 59
and Bugs Bunny, 251
and Hit Parade, 67
and love songs, 4, 11
and movies, 190
singing style of, 7, 59
and talking, 244
Crosby, Percy, 278
Crouch, Stanley, 196, 226, 232, 236
Crow, Sheryl, 66, 67, 154
Crudup, Arthur "Big Boy," 187, 188
Crumb, George, 257
Crumb, Robert, 51, 109, 184, 282, 303, 304
Crystal, Billy, 35
Cuba Percussion (album), 293

Love and Theft (album), 104
Love in Exile (Singer), 185
Love Is What Stays (album), 122, 123, 127
Love Me Tender (movie), 191
A Love Supreme (album), 221
Luce, Henry, 13
Lundvall, Bruce, 231, 267, 268
Lynne, Jeff, 208

Ma, Yo-Yo, 293
Maazel, Lorin, 90
Machito, 199, 200
MacManus, Declan, 93
    See also Costello, Elvis
MacManus, Ross, 93
Mad (magazine), 184, 280
Madden, Matt, 113
Mademoiselle (magazine), 53
Madonna, 48, 257
The Magnetic Fields, 23
The Magnificent Ambersons (movie), 182
Mailé, Isabelle, 268
Malcolm X, 298
A Man Called Adam (movie), 38
The Man in the Ceiling (Feiffer), 281
The Man Who Shot Liberty Valance (movie), 97
Manet, Edouard, 102, 226
Mann, Aimee, 93, 138, 140
Mars Volta, 105
Marsalis, Branford, 221, 222, 229–230, 232
Marsalis, Delfeayo, 221
Marsalis, Dolores, 223
Marsalis, Ellis, 221, 223–224
Marsalis, Jason, 221
Marsalis, Mboya, 223
Marsalis, Wynton, 219–236

The Marsalis Family: A Jazz Celebration (album), 222
Marsalis Music, 222
Martin, Dean, 17, 34
Martin, George, 157
Marvelettes, 204
Marx, Karl, 303
Masada (albums), 287–288
Masereel, Frans, 109
Mason, Bobbie Ann, 192, 193
Master P, 64
Mastin, Will, 35–36, 38
Matisse, Henri, 227
Matranga, Jonah Sonz, 117
Matthews, Dave, 138
Maus (Spiegelman), 109
Maxwell, Elsa, 27
May, Billy, 23
Mayer, John, 138, 140, 141, 155
Mazzolini, Tom, 63
MCA Records, 141
McCartney, Linda, 206, 207, 208
McCartney, Paul, 216
    with author, 211
    and Beach Boys, 97, 98
    and *Chaos and Creation in the Backyard,* 206, 207, 208–209, 210
    and Costello, 91, 93
    and *Driving Rain* and *Flaming Pie,* 207–208
    and "granny music," 52
    and Lennon, 201, 203, 204, 210, 211
    and *McCartney* and *McCartney II,* 206, 207, 209
    and music-hall songs, 91
    and rock 'n' roll, 90
    and *Run Devil Run* and *Working Classical,* 208
    and *Shout!,* 202

Mr. Smith Goes to Washington (movie), 251
MTV, 146
Muldaur, Maria, 32
Munro (Feiffer), 279
Murdoch, Rupert, 145
Murphy, Mark, 122–127
The Music Man (musical), 204
Musical theater, 29, 31, 59, 94, 141, 246, 247, 290, 291
Mussolini, Benito, 252, 253
My Aim Is True (album), 91, 93
My Fair Lady (musical), 30
MySpace, 145–149, 163

NAACP, 35, 37
Nabokov, Vladimir, 128, 289
Nancarrow, Conlon, 244, 249
Nash, Alanna, 189, 192, 193
National Jazz Ensemble, 225
National (record company), 11
Navarro, Fats, 4
Nelson, Oliver, 127, 207
Nelson, Willie, 86, 154
The New Danger (album), 24
New Wave, 91, 138, 157
New York: The Big City (Eisner), 185
New York Amsterdam News (newspaper), 21
New York Herald, 59, 249
New York Jazz Repertory Company, 226
New York Post, 47
New York Public Library, 54
New York Times
  and Brian Wilson, 99
  and Feiffer, 281
  and Hollywood Undead, 147
  and O'Day, 40–41
  and Partch, 247

and Satrapi, 297
and Wynton Marsalis, 222, 224
The New Yorker (magazine), 229, 279
Newman, Randy, 153
Newport Jazz Festival, 137
Newsom, Joanna, 141
Newsweek (magazine), 68
Nice Nice, 117
Nicholson, Jack, 100
Nietzsche, Friedrich, 100, 176
Nieve, Steve, 94
Night Ride Home (album), 215
Nine Inch Nails, 159, 163–164, 165, 166
Nixon, Richard, 35
No Strings (musical), 30
Nolan, Frederick, 30
Nonesuch, 215
Norman, Philip, 202–203, 204–205
North (album), 90, 93–95
Note 'n Notes (album), 265
Novick, Julius, 281
Nuckel, Otto, 109
NWA, 8, 65

O Brother, Where Art Thou? (movie), 64
Oberlin, Karen (wife), 52, 54
Oberst, Conor, 117, 118, 271
O'Brien, Ed, 166
O'Connor, Flannery, 128, 129
O'Day, Anita, 40–44, 225
Odets, Clifford, 38
Oklahoma! (musical), 28, 29, 30, 31
Oliver, Joe "King," 196–197
Once in a Lifetime (album), 38
Onelinedrawing, 117
Ono, Yoko, 201, 202, 205, 210
Opus Collection, 152–154
Oral Fixation 2 (album), 160

and Satrapi, 298, 304
and Zorn, 284
Popular music
  and aging, 89, 104, 123
  and Beatles, 203, 204, 210
  and the blues, 61, 63, 67, 75
  and Branford Marsalis, 230
  and Brian Wilson, 97, 98
  and centennials, 59
  and Cohodas, 80
  and "concept albums" and "rock operas," 108
  and Costello, 91, 93, 94
  and country music, 131
  creative peak of jazz-oriented, 124
  and Darin, 45
  and EMP, 59
  and forms of recording, 22–23
  and gospel music, 76
  and Groban, 290, 291
  and homogeneity, 177
  and Joni Mitchell, 213, 214, 216
  and Leonard Cohen, 271
  and Lucinda Williams, 128–129, 132, 133
  and lulls, 105
  and Mercer, 137
  with nothing to say, 138–141
  and Opus Collection, 153
  overtly commercial phase of, 118
  and Presley, 124, 190
  and record producers, 156, 157
  and recording technology, 99, 163
  and Rodgers, 33
  and sex, 130, 291
  and Sobule, 142
  and social interaction, 145, 146
  and Starbucks, 154, 155
  and Sting, 105
  and Swift, 129–130, 131, 132
  and Tin Pan Alley, 67
Porgy and Bess (album), 85
Porter, Christopher, 92
Porter, Cole, 22, 23, 53, 67, 93, 124
Powell, Adam Clayton, Jr., 35
Power of Three (album), 268
Present Arms (musical), 29
Presley, Elvis, 31, 73, 121, 124, 153, 154, 156, 187–193, 204, 230
Presley, Gladys, 192
Presley, Priscilla, 189
Presley, Vernon, 192
Press to Play (album), 211
Pretenders, 118
Prince, 85, 213
Priore, Domenic, 101
ProTools, 117, 163
Pryor, Richard, 16
PS: The Preventive Maintenance Monthly (Eisner), 183
Ptolemy, 242, 245
Puccini, 102
Punk rock
  and Costello, 90, 91
  early, 98
  and improvisation, 284
  and MySpace, 147, 149
  and Ramones, 138
  and White Stripes, 119
Pussiau, Jean-Jacques, 265

Queen (Cohodas), 80
Queen of the Blues (Haskins), 75

Rachmaninoff, Sergei, 216
Radiohead, 163–165, 166, 167, 208, 293
Rage Against the Machine, 158
Raim, Walter, 49

emergence of, 23, 89, 124,
137–138, 176, 188
and EMP, 59
in garage, 98
and Glass, 270, 271
Hall of Fame, 124
and homogeneity, 177
and improvisation, 284
incompleteness of, 116
industrial, 165
and Lennon, 201
and Lucinda Williams, 129
and nostalgia, 103
and novelty songs, 80
and Presley, 124, 188, 204
re-shaping, 90
and record producers, 156, 159
and reinvention, 48
and Santelli, 60
and songwriting, 190, 211, 271
and Sting, 105, 107
and White Stripes, 116, 118
and youthful rituals, 138
Rocky Mountain Slim, 172
Rodgers, Jimmie, 131
Rodgers, Richard, 22, 23, 27–33, 52,
53, 94, 124
Rolling Stone (magazine), 48, 90, 132
Rolling Stones, 61–62, 68, 103, 105,
118, 154
Rollins, Sonny, 197, 231
*Roman Candle: The Life of Bobby
Darin* (Evanier), 45
Romano, Aldo, 264–265, 266
Romeo and Juliet (play), 130, 245
Rooney, Mickey, 251
Roosevelt, Franklin Delano, 173
Roperch, Marie-Laure, 268
Rorem, Ned, 257
Roselli, Jimmy, 45

Rosenfeld, Monroe, 59
Roshi, Kyozan Joshu Sasaki, 272
Rossini, Gioachino, 258
Rubin, Rick, 157–160, 161
Ruddock, Margot, 246
Rufus Jones for President (movie), 36
Run Devil Run (album), 208
Rundgren, Todd, 142
Rush, Otis, 63
Russell, Bob, 79
Russell, George, 222
Ruttenberg, Craig, 257

Sacco, Joe, 109–113, 114, 115
Saddle Pals, 173
Saddle Tramps, 173
Sade, 43
Safe Area Gorazde (Sacco), 110–112
Sahanaja, Darian, 100, 101
Sahl, Mort, 281
Sallie Martin Singers, 76
Sampson, Edgar, 196
Sanchez, Elvera, 35
Sandler, Kevin S., 254
Sandri, Andrea, 292
Santelli, Robert, 59–60
Satie, Eric, 286
Satrapi, Ebi, 299
Satrapi, Marjane, 295–304
Satrapi, Taji, 299
Scat, 43, 126, 197
Schaeffer, Pierre, 99
Schiff, Lisa, 234
Schoenberg, Loren, 225
Schruers, Fred, 91
Schubert, Franz, 293
Schuller, Gunther, 226, 286
Schultz, Charles, 184
Schultz, Howard, 152, 154
Schulz, Bruno, 97

The Unreleased Recordings (album),
131
U.S. Highball (hobo opera), 243

Valentine, Gerry, 8
Vallee, Rudy, 4, 11, 104
Van Gogh, 215
Van Heusen, Jimmy, 79
Van Kuijk, Andreas, 193
    See also Parker, Thomas A.
Van Ronk, Dave, 48, 49, 155
Variety (magazine), 9, 76–77
Vaughan, Sarah, 4, 7, 8, 9, 16, 124
Vega, Suzanne, 272
Vellenga, Dirk, 193
Veloso, Caetano, 213
Velvet Underground, 68
Verve Records, 23, 42, 122, 221
*Very Easy to Assemble But Hard to Take
    Apart* (album), 25
The Village Voice (newspaper), 157,
    276–282
Von Schmidt, Eric, 72

Wagner, Richard, 108
Wagner, Robert F., 31
Waller, Fats, 4, 11, 21, 85
Wallis, Hal, 190
Ward, Geoffrey C., 194, 196
Ward, Lynd, 303
Warhol, Andy, 180, 285
Warner Records, 221
Warner Bros., 186, 223, 250–254
Warner/Chappell Music, 166
Washington, Dinah, 74–80, 125
Washington Post, 35
Wasser, Harriet, 47
Water! Water! (musical), 249
Waters, Ethel, 51, 54
Waters, Muddy, 61, 64, 65, 67, 71

Wayne, John, 251
Wayne's World (movie), 254
*We Insist: Max Roach's Freedom Now
    Suite* (album), 125
Weavers, 72
Webb, Chick, 195, 199, 200
Webster, Ben, 7, 232, 235
Webster, Freddie, 8
Weill, Kurt, 32, 90, 125, 256, 257
Wein, George, 226
Weir, Frank, 80
Weirdo (comic book), 112
We'll Be Together Again (album), 123
Welles, Orson, 97, 181, 182
Wentz, Peter, 147
Wess, Frank, 4
West, Kanye, 5, 157, 160–161
West, Mae, 51, 54
West Side Story (play), 93
Westenra, Hayley, 293
Weston, Randy, 234, 262
*Whatever People Say I Am, That's What
    I'm Not* (album), 147
White, Jack, 116–121
White, Kristin, 33
White, Meg, 116–121
White Blood Cells (album), 118, 119
White Stripes, 116–121
White Teeth (album), 165
Whitman, Walt, 255–260, 277
Who, 123
Why Me? (Davis), 35
Wild Things Run Fast (album), 215
Wilde, Kim, 298
Will Eisner Reader, 186
William Schuman Award, 286
Williams, Andy, 15
Williams, Big Joe, 60
Williams, Cootie, 196, 198
Williams, Esther, 14